Communicative Language Teaching in Action

PUTTING PRINCIPLES TO WORK

Klaus Brandl
University of Washington
Seattle, Washington

PEARSON
Prentice
Hall

Upper Saddle River, New Jersey

Library of Congress Cataloging-in-Publication Data

Brandl, Klaus.
Communicative language teaching in action: putting principles to work/by Klaus Brandl.
    p. cm.
  Includes bibliographical references and index.
  ISBN 978-0-13-157906-4 (pbk. alk. paper)
    1. Language and languages—Study and teaching. 2. Communicative competence—
Study and teaching. I. Title.
  P53.255.B73 2008
  407—dc22

                                                                          2007027099

Senior Acquisitions Editor: *Rachel McCoy*
Director of Marketing: *Kristine Suarez*
Senior Marketing Manager: *Denise Miller*
Marketing Coordinator: *William J. Bliss*
Senior Managing Editor: *Mary Rottino*
Associate Managing Editor: *Janice Stangel*
Project Manager: *Manuel Echevarria*
Manufacturing Buyer: *Cathleen Petersen*
Editorial Assistant: *Alexei Soma*
Cover Design: *Jayne Conte*
Director, Image Resource Center: *Melinda Patelli*

Manager, Rights and Permissions: *Zina Arabia*
Manager: Visual Research: *Beth Brenzel*
Manager, Cover Visual Research & Permissions: *Karen Sanatar*
Image Permission Coordinator: *Vicki Menanteaux*
Manager, Print Production: *Brian Mackey*
Publisher: *Phil Miller*
Composition/Full-Service Project Management: *GGS Book Services*
Printer/Binder: *STP/RRD/Harrisonburg*
Typeface: 10/12 Sabon

Credits and acknowledgments borrowed from other sources and reproduced, with permission, in this textbook appear on appropriate page within text and starting on page 423.

Pearson Education LTD.
Pearson Education Singapore, Pte. Ltd
Pearson Education, Canada, Ltd
Pearson Education—Japan
Pearson Education, Upper Saddle
    River, New Jersey

Pearson Education Australia PTY, Limited
Pearson Education North Asia Ltd
Pearson Educación de Mexico, S.A. de C.V.
Pearson Education Malaysia, Pte. Ltd

10 9 8 7 6 5 4 3 2 1
ISBN 13: 978–0–13–157906–4
ISBN: 10: 0–13–157906–1

To Carmina

dream it
affirm it
realize it

and
in memory of my father

Klaus Brandl, Ph.D., is an applied linguist and specialist in foreign language pedagogy at the University of Washington, where he directs the language program in the Department of Scandinavian Studies and serves as the Language Pedagogue for the College of Arts and Sciences and College of Education. He is widely known for his research on language teacher training and language learning and technology. His articles have appeared in major journals such as *The Modern Language Journal*, *Foreign Language Annals*, and *Language Learning & Instruction*, and he has contributed chapters to many books. He is also the author of several computer programs. Currently he is writing a first-year language textbook for Bangla.

CONTENTS

Communicative Language Teaching in Action: Putting Principles to Work is designed as a basic text that intends to demonstrate principles and practices of communicative language teaching (CLT) and task-based instruction. Its primary purpose is to serve as a guide for second and foreign language teachers in training or for those who have embarked on a new career as language teachers. In particular, these include pre- and in-service teacher education majors, university teaching assistants, and English as a Second Language (ESL) majors and instructors. Furthermore, it is meant to be a resource for practicing teachers in continuing education programs.

Communicative Language Teaching in Action serves a dual goal: (1) It aims at providing a conceptual foundation on many issues related to language learning and teaching. A communicative approach to language teaching does not adhere to one particular theory of learning, but must be based on principles of learning. For this reason, the conceptual foundation in this book is based upon a plethora of theoretical and empirical findings drawn from second language acquisition (SLA) research, cognitive psychology, and brain research. (2) It puts forth those instructional practices that have been found to achieve the highest effects in communicative language learning. Emphasizing the pragmatic side of language teaching and also keeping the novice teacher in mind, it aims at demonstrating many theoretical concepts in context and how communicative language teaching CLT is put into action. Therefore, the book integrates a wide range of examples, taken from textbooks in different languages and from actual lessons, which were developed by experienced language teachers in the field. All chapters further include a set of practical guidelines that allow instructors to apply communicative teaching strategies to their own learning contexts.

Content

The content of this book is organized into ten chapters:. These include:

1. Principles of Communicative Language Teaching and Task-Based Instruction
2. Short-Term and Daily Lesson Planning
3. Getting Started: Introducing Vocabulary
4. Grammar and Language Learning
5. Feedback and Error Correction in Language Learning

6. Instructional Sequencing and Task Design
7. Developing Listening Skills
8. Developing Oral Communication Skills
9. Developing Reading Skills
10. Assessment and Language Learning

After many years of working as a teacher trainer, I have to come to believe that these topics are the most fundamental for any individual who intends to gain a conceptual foundation in the teaching and learning of second and foreign languages. This list of topics, however, is not meant to be comprehensive. Teacher trainers, depending on their own philosophy of teaching and the needs of their audience, may choose to complement this list with other topics.

Organization of Chapters

The first chapter of *Communicative Language Teaching in Action* defines communicative and task-based instruction and provides the theoretical foundation underlying the approach to language teaching as emphasized in this book. Chapter 2 deals with aspects of lesson planning in general. This chapter is best integrated during orientation or pre-service training. It also fits well into any teacher-training curriculum at a stage when students are ready to develop their own lesson plans or prior to any teaching assignment. Since any language curriculum for beginners typically begins by introducing vocabulary, which are also normally embedded in context and combined with grammatical structures, Chapters 3 and 4 have been placed early on in the book. The goals of these chapters are to introduce the most common techniques of presenting vocabulary and grammar efficiently and to discuss a range of issues that address the teaching of vocabulary and grammatical structures. Chapter 4 further elaborates on the complexity of grammar and language learning in more detail and addresses underlying processes of second language acquisition. Chapter 5, on feedback and error correction, has been placed after the grammar chapter. Feedback plays an important role in language learning affecting the learners' second language acquisition, SLA, process at all stages of instruction. Some practitioners may choose to deal with this topic at a different stage of their curriculum. Chapter 6 focuses on instructional sequencing and task design. This chapter discusses different types of pedagogical and communicative tasks and addresses issues related to sequencing and integrating learning tasks that require the use of multiple skills. As such, this chapter further serves as an introduction to Chapters 7, 8, and 9, which deal with the development of listening, speaking, and reading skills in more detail. While I have maintained the traditional way of referring to listening, speaking, and reading skills in my chapter titles, I would like to stress, however, that students do not develop listening, speaking, and reading skills in isolation.

Any communicative and task-based approach to language teaching involves the integration of multiple skills, whereas each skill must be considered as being equally conducive to a learner's language acquisition process. The book concludes with a chapter on performance-based assessment. By taking an assessment perspective, Chapter 10 readdresses many issues regarding task design and performance-based learning behavior. In addition, general issues on test design and assessment are discussed. Because many practicing teachers are often confronted with the task of formally evaluating their students' performance from day one on, teacher trainers may choose to integrate this chapter into the curriculum at an earlier stage.

Approach to Teacher Training and Development

My philosophical approach to teacher training is based on an approach to learning that is highly self-engaging, and task oriented. This approach is analogous to a well-developed communicative and performance-based language-teaching program. In this sense, I attempt to model in the teacher training approach, as much as this is possible, what I expect language teachers to apply in their own disciplines of teaching. As many of my students have repeatedly mentioned in my course evaluations, "He models what he preaches and walks the talk."

The organization in this training course book underlies the following methodological approach to teacher training. Each chapter includes three different kinds of tasks. These are categorized as "Reflections," "Explorations," and "Application."

Reflections

Each chapter starts with a set of reflective questions that ask the student teacher to think about his or her own learning experience of (a) foreign language(s) and their personal assumptions about language learning and teaching in general. Educational research provides ample evidence that teachers' perceptions of learning a second language are influenced by their own early and ongoing language-learning learning experiences. These experiences shape their beliefs about their role as language teachers, and about how languages should be taught, and they impact their approach to both respectively (Woods 1996). For this reason, I consider connecting with a teacher's belief system essential. Such a strategy provides a first step towards helping them understand their own views as much as possible allowing them to reflect how foreign language learning occurs. In this way, course participants also become firsthand hand consumers of the theory espoused in the text. The following questions, taken from Chapter 3, provide an example of the kind of reflective questions the trainees are asked to engage in throughout this book: "What kind of vocabulary instruction have you experienced as a learner of (a) foreign language(s)? What kind of strategies worked best for you? Please provide concrete examples.

Explorations

The "Explorations" section provides carefully scaffolded training tasks. These training activities are designed with different goals in mind. First, they are to promote the discussion and analysis of theoretical and empirical research findings on a metacognitive level. For this reason, some tasks are embedded within the text and can be used as a follow-up or reinforcement of a particular concept. Second, they are intended to engage the participants in exploratory or experiential learning tasks by placing them into the roles of learners. Giving teachers the opportunity to experience, explore, and analyze effective examples of learning materials, particularly through the eyes of learners, has been found to be an effective catalyst that leads to change. Most of the tasks with this purpose in mind are placed at the end of each chapter. Most of the "Explorations" tasks were designed so they can be integrated into the foreign language methods classroom, but many also lend themselves well to independent and self-instructional assignments. The following task, which can be found in Chapter 8, demonstrates this approach to teacher training:

> "To experience the design of a large group activity, form a group of six students. Your instructor will hand each group member a different cartoon from a picture story entitled "Story in Six Acts." Then, follow the instructions below.
>
> 1. Describe your cartoon to the rest of the group.
> 2. As a whole group, find the correct sequence of events of the story.
> 3. As a whole group, discuss what you think this story means.
> 4. Comment on the design of this group work activity. How are the first and second parts of this activity different from the third? Did you notice any difference in your group interaction?"

The goal of this teacher training task in particular to demonstrate different elements of group work design. It models a hands-on approach allowing the trainees to experience how group work can be effectively integrated in a foreign language classroom.

Task 11: Trying Out Input Strategies

> Spontaneously describe the picture story of the lion and the mouse (see Appendix 1.4) in the target language (TL) to your partner or the whole class. Make use of as many input strategies as possible to help your partner understand the story.

Application

Each chapter concludes with an "Application" section. The goal of the tasks in this section is for student teachers to apply and demonstrate what they have learned. In general, the tasks are designed to engage the trainees in observing and analyzing lessons taught by peers or experienced teachers in the field, doing problem-solving case studies, developing short lesson scripts, writing up whole lesson and unit plans, and demonstrating their skills through micro teaching. The following example, taken from Chapter 1, demonstrates such an application task. The goal of this task is to simulate a classroom situation that teachers often face when applying a whole language approach to teaching.

Note!

This activity works best if a true immersion experience can be created in the classroom. If possible, have the story be told in a language that is unknown to most class participants.

With the whole class, discuss how well you accomplished your goal. As the "input provider," were you capable of making yourself understood? What means did you make use of? As the listener, were you able to understand your partner's story? What challenges did you both encounter? How can you deal with such challenges in the language classroom?

ACKNOWLEDGMENTS

Writing this book was a journey of many years. I am thankful to many people who contributed during this process. These include my colleagues, many students, reviewers both known and anonymous, and the editors.

I am grateful to my colleague, Manfred Bansleben, who inspired me to take on this project. We had many discussions about teaching which influenced my understanding of teaching and learning languages in many ways.

My appreciation also likewise goes to Ali Moeller, Paloma Borreguero, Joan Fox, and Hedwige Meyer for providing me with valuable feedback and comments. Also special thanks to the many graduate students, who have given me the opportunity to try out the readings and training tasks during the last few years. Much of their feedback and reactions helped gradually shape this book.

I am also grateful to my editors, and to the production people and compositors at Pearson Prentice Hall who contributed their ideas and talents, time, and publishing experience to this project. I am particularly grateful to Rachel McCoy, acquisitions editor, for her energy, enthusiasm, and professional guidance. Thanks also to Alex Soma, editorial assistant, for his patience and diligent handling of many details.

I am also grateful to the numerous reviewers whose comments and suggestions allowed me to add the final touches.

Diane Fagin Adler—North Carolina State University

Heather Willis Allen—University of Miami

Stayc DuBravac—University of Kentucky

Jennifer Eddy—Queens College

Todd Hernández—Marquette University

Galina Kats—Siena College

Ji-hyun Philippa Kim—Syracuse University

Jeanette Kraemer—Marquette University

Jenifer Larson-Hall—University of North Texas

Michael J. Leeser—Florida State University

Mary E. O'Donnell—Purdue University

Nadine F. Olson—Oklahoma State University

Ruth S. Owens—Arkansas State University

Brigitte Rossbacher—The University of Georgia

Colleen Ryan-Scheutz—Indiana University, Bloomington
Carol McKenna Semonsky—Georgia State University
Gillian Lord Ward—University of Florida

Finally, I am most grateful to Jason Hendryx. Without his careful reading, comments, encouragements, and the many discussions we had, this book would not have turned out in the same way.

Klaus Brandl

CHAPTER 1

Principles of Communicative Language Teaching and Task-Based Instruction

Effective teaching is not about a method. It is about understanding and implementing principles of learning.

In this chapter you will learn about

- communicative language teaching.

- task-based instruction.

- characteristics of pedagogical and real-life tasks.

- principles underlying communicative language teaching methodologies.

- characteristics of good input.

- practical guidelines on how to maximize the use of the target language (TL) in the classroom.

- challenges in implementing communicative language teaching methodologies.

REFLECTION

What kind of methods or techniques have you experienced as a learner of (a) foreign language(s)? Which ones worked best for you, and which ones did not work at all? Why?

_____

_____

_____

_____

Introduction

The field of second or world language teaching has undergone many shifts and trends over the last few decades. Numerous methods have come and gone. We have seen the Audiolingual Method, cognitive-based approaches, the Total Physical Response (TPR), the Natural Approach, and many others (for a detailed description of these methods and approaches, see Richards and Rodgers 2001). In addition, the proficiency and standards-based[1] movements have shaped the field with their attempts to define proficiency goals and thus have provided a general sense of direction. Some believe that foreign language instruction has finally come of age (see Harper, Lively, and Williams 1998); others refer to it as the post-method area (Richards and Rodgers 2001). It is also generally believed that there is no one single best method that meets the goals and needs of all learners and programs. What has emerged from this time is a variety of communicative language teaching (CLT) methodologies. Such methodologies encompass eclectic ways of teaching that are borrowed from myriad methods. Furthermore, they are rooted not only in one but a range of theories and are motivated by research findings in second language acquisition (SLA) as well as cognitive and educational psychology. The purpose of this chapter is to provide an introduction to CLT and furthermore describe general methodological principles that function as theoretical and practical guidelines when implementing CLT methodologies.

The Shift Toward Communicative Language Teaching and Task-Based Instruction: A Historical Perspective

For many decades the predominant method of language instruction was the grammar-translation method. This method is rooted in the teaching of the nineteenth century and was widely used for the first half (in some parts of the world even longer) of the last century to teach modern foreign languages (Richards and Rodgers 2001). Textbooks primarily consisted of lists of vocabulary and rule explanations. By and large, students engaged in translation activities. Little oral proficiency would result from the Grammar-translation Method, and students often were expected to go abroad and immerse themselves to become a fluent speaker.

The Grammar-translation Method was not without its opponents, and the demand for oral proficiency led to several counter and parallel movements that laid the foundation for the development of new ways of teaching, as we still know them today (Richards and Rodgers 2001). One such method is the Direct Method, sometimes also referred to as the Berlitz Method as it was widely used in Berlitz schools. Some reformers of the nineteenth century (e.g., Gouin and Sauveur) believed that languages should be taught in a natural way, that is, how children learn language. As Richards and Rodgers (2001) point out, "Believers in the Natural Method argued that a foreign language could be taught without translation or the use of the learner's native language if meaning was conveyed directly through demonstration and action" (p. 11). For this reason, they also strongly promoted the spontaneous use of language.

Richards and Rodgers (2001, p. 12) describe principles of procedures underlying the Direct Method in the following way:

1. Classroom instruction was conducted exclusively in the target language.
2. Only everyday vocabulary and sentences were taught.
3. Oral communication skills were built up in carefully graded progression organized around question-answer exchanges between teachers and students in small, intensive classes.
4. Grammar was taught inductively.
5. New teaching points were introduced orally.
6. Concrete vocabulary was taught through demonstrating, objects, and pictures; abstract vocabulary was taught by association of ideas.

7. Both speech and listening comprehension were taught.
8. Correct pronunciation and grammar were emphasized.

Despite its success in private schools, the Direct Method was met with a great deal of criticism. Strict requirements to adhere to its principles and the need for native speakers or someone with native-like fluency prevented this method from becoming widely adopted by academic institutions (see Richards and Rodgers 2001).

Hailed in its day as revolutionary in foreign language teaching, the grammar-translation method was replaced by the Audiolingual Method in the 1950s and 60s. The belief in the effectiveness of this method was so strong that traces of audiolingual-based teaching theories can still be found in teaching materials. The audiolingual method was based on the school of behaviorism in psychology and structuralism in linguistics, for which reason it also become known as the "structural" or "behaviorist" method. Because of its primary emphasis on spoken language, it is also referred to as the "Aural-oral" Method. The underlying assumption of this philosophy was that, as Rivers (1964) put it, foreign language learning is basically a mechanical process of habit formation and automatization. In practice, this meant students were presented with language patterns and dialogues, which they had to mimic and memorize. Language practice by and large consisted of repetition of language patterns and drill exercises. Drill types included substitution drills, variation drills, translation drills, and response drills. The following Swedish example illustrates a combination of a substitution and translation drill.

ILLUSTRATION 1
Substitution/transformation drill

Han har alltid <u>HUNDEN</u> med sig. [He always has his <u>dog</u> with him].

the map—the fountain pen—the ink—the paper—the car

The teacher says, "Han har alltid hunden med sig." [He always has his <u>dog</u> with him].

Student chooses from a given list of English words, translates it into Swedish, and substitutes the underlined word of the example sentence.

A tenet of this method was that errors of any kind were to be avoided, so the learners were not to establish bad habits. For this reason, the native speaker teacher was considered the perfect model.

There were, however, many problems with audiolingual approaches. The teacher, who was often seen like the drillmaster, carried the responsibility of teaching and student learning like an atlas on his shoulder (Lee and VanPatten 2003). One of the most widely brought forward points of criticism toward this method is that the learners lacked engagement in meaningful language use and had only limited opportunities to use language creatively while interacting with their peers. As Willis (2004) points out, "This was because the emphasis was on eradication of errors and accurate production of the target forms, not on communication of meanings" (p. 4). Due to overcorrection of students' errors by the teacher, anxiety levels were often quite high among students. The Audiolingual Method failed to have the desired effect of helping learners become competent speakers in the TL.

Several factors and influences led to the demise of the Audiolingual Method and caused a shift in language teaching methodology. This brought forth communicative language approaches and a range of alternative methods.

1. The Audiolingual Method did not live up to its promise creating speakers who were able to communicate in the target language.
2. Theories of learning moved away from behaviorist views of learning. The most influential work was the one by Chomsky, which was published in his book *Syntactic Structures* (1957). He argued that language learning involves creative processes and perceived language as rule-governed creativity. As Willis (2004) describes it, "He believed that a basic rule system that underpins all languages is innate and that, given exposure to a specific language, children will naturally create the specific rules of that language for themselves. Learning is thus seen as a process of discovery determined by internal processes rather than external influences" (pp. 4–5).
3. Works by scholars and sociolinguists such as J. Firth, M. Halliday, D. Hymes, and J. Austin led to a change in the way language was viewed. As emphasized by many practitioners, the primary purpose of language is to communicate.
4. The development of a functional-notional syllabus in the 1970s in Europe by Van Ek (1973) and Wilkins (1976) initiated a new way of how teaching materials were organized. Traditionally, syllabi had been organized around grammatical structures and vocabulary units. The functional-notional syllabus attempted to show what learners need to do with language and what meanings they need to communicate, and organized the syllabus around functions and notions. Functions are communicative speech acts such as "asking," "requesting," "denying," "arguing," "describing," or "requesting." Notional categories include concepts such as "time" or "location." Notions and functions are different from topics and situations as they express more precise categories. For example, a topic may be "family," the situation "coming for a visit and having dinner." The function and the notion that is addressed in this unit may involve "inviting" and "time past" (e.g., past tenses, expressions like "last week," "a few days ago"). The functional-notional syllabus laid the groundwork that ultimately led textbook writers to organize their materials in terms of communicative situations, and some also in very concrete communicative tasks.

5. A growing number of research studies in applied linguistics have provided many new insights and a deeper understanding of second language learning and SLA processes. Some of these include

   - Learners move through different stages of development (Selinker 1972).
   - Learners develop an underlying language system that develops in a sequence that does not always reflect the sequence of what was taught in a curriculum (Dulay and Burt 1973). Work by Pienemann (1989) showed that learners develop language skills according to their own internal syllabus.

Alternative approaches and methods to language teaching

While communicative language teaching methodologies kept evolving and being more clearly defined, in the 1970s and 80s a set of alternative approaches and methods emerged. Some of these include comprehension-based methods such as the Total Physical Response (TPR), the Natural Approach, the Silent Way, or Suggestopedia (for a detailed description of these methods, see Richards and Rodgers 2001). Many of these methods never became widely adapted and had only a short shelf life. This is not to say that these methods did not contribute to the field of language teaching. On the contrary, some of these methods have helped shape and continue to have an influence on the field in many ways. For example, TPR, which James Asher (1969) originally developed as a method to teach language by combining action and speech, is still widely used. Many practitioners, however, promote and use TPR as a technique to introduce some vocabulary or grammatical structures. Some principles of learning that have been promoted through these methods are integrated in the discussion below.

What Is Communicative Language Teaching?

Communicative language teaching (CLT) is generally regarded as an approach to language teaching (Richards and Rodgers 2001). As such, CLT reflects a certain model or research paradigm, or a theory (Celce-Murcia 2001). It is based on the theory that the primary function of language use is communication. Its primary goal is for learners to develop communicative competence (Hymes 1971), or simply put, communicative ability. In other words, its goal is to make use of real-life situations that necessitate communication.

Defining communicative competence

Communicative competence is defined as the ability to interpret and enact appropriate social behaviors, and it requires the active involvement of the learner in the production of the target language (Canale and Swain

1980; Celce-Murcia et al. 1995; Hymes 1972). Such a notion encompasses a wide range of abilities: the knowledge of grammar and vocabulary (**linguistic competence**); the ability to say the appropriate thing in a certain social situation (**sociolinguistic competence**); the ability to start, enter, contribute to, and end a conversation, and the ability to do this in a consistent and coherent manner (**discourse competence**); the ability to communicate effectively and repair problems caused by communication breakdowns (**strategic competence**).

As frequently misunderstood, CLT is not a method per se. That is to say, it is not a method in the sense by which content, a syllabus, and teaching routines are clearly identified (see Richards and Rodgers 2001). CLT has left its doors wide open for a great variety of methods and techniques. There is no single text or authority on it, nor any single model that is universally accepted as authoritative (Richards and Rodgers 2001). By and large, it uses materials and utilizes methods that are appropriate to a given context of learning.

CLT has spawned various movements such as proficiency-based or standard-based instruction. While the early days of CLT were concerned with finding best designs and practices, the proficiency-based movement contributed to the field of language teaching by putting forward a set of proficiency guidelines (see American Council on the Teaching of Foreign Languages [ACTFL] guidelines in Chapter 8, Developing Oral Communication Skills). These guidelines describe language ability and are meant to be used to measure competence in a language (Omaggio-Hadley 2001). In this sense, the proficiency-based movement focused on measuring what learners can do in functional terms. By providing evaluative descriptions, that is, by specifying what students should know and how they should be able to use language within a variety of contexts and to various degrees of accuracy at different stages, it provided a set of broadly stated goals and thus a sense of direction for curriculum designers. The standard-based movement attempted to further streamline descriptions of what students should know and be able to do after completing a particular grade level or curriculum to meet national standards in foreign language education from kindergarten to university. In this way, both movements positively influenced and strengthened the development and implementation of communicative-oriented teaching practices.

As far as theories of learning and effective strategies in teaching are concerned, CLT does not adhere to one particular theory or method. It draws its theories about learning and teaching from a wide range of areas such as cognitive science, educational psychology, and second language acquisition (SLA). In this way, it embraces and reconciles many different approaches and points of view about language learning and teaching, which allows it to meet a wide range of proficiency-oriented goals and also accommodate different learner needs and preferences. Despite the lack of universally accepted models, from early on, there has been some degree of consensus regarding the qualities required to justify the label "CLT," which Wesche and Skehan (2002) describe as:

- Activities that require frequent interaction among learners or with other interlocutors to exchange information and solve problems.
- Use of authentic (non-pedagogic) texts and communication activities linked to "real-world" contexts, often emphasizing links across written and spoken modes and channels.
- Approaches that are learner centered in that they take into account learners' backgrounds, language needs, and goals and generally allow learners some creativity and role in instructional decisions (p. 208).

With no one particular method or theory that underlies their practical and theoretical foundation, CLT methodologies are best described as a set of macro-strategies (Kumaradivelu 1994) or methodological principles (Doughty and Long 2003). The following section describes such principles in more detail.

Methodological Principles of Communicative Language Teaching and Task-Based Instruction

Doughty and Long (2003) define methodological principles as a list of design features that can be generally regarded as being facilitative to second language acquisition. The following list, adapted from Doughty and Long (2003), serves as a guideline for implementing communicative language teaching (CLT) practices.

Principle 1: Use Tasks as an Organizational Principle

For decades traditional methods of language teaching have used grammar topics or texts (e.g., dialogues, short stories) as a basis for organizing a syllabus. With CLT methodologies this approach has changed; the development of communicative skills is placed at the forefront, while grammar is now introduced only as much as needed to support the development of these skills. This raises questions on how to organize a syllabus. Some proponents (see Breen 1987; Long 1985; Nunan 1989; Prabhu 1987) suggest using tasks as central units that form the basis of daily and long-term lesson plans. Such an approach to syllabus design has become known as **task-based instruction (TBI)**. The rationale for the employment of communicative tasks is based on contemporary theories of language learning and acquisition, which claim that language use is the driving force for language development (Long 1989; Prabhu 1987). For example, advocates of such theories (see Pica, Kanagy, and Falodun 1993) suggest that, as Norris et al. (1998) put it, "the best way to learn and teach a language is through social interactions. [. . . they] allow students to work toward a clear goal, share information and opinions, negotiate meaning, get the interlocutor's help in comprehending input, and receive feedback on their language production. In the process, learners not only use their interlanguage, but also modify it, which in turn promotes acquisition" (p. 31). In other words, it is not the text one reads or the grammar one studies but the tasks that are presented that provide learners a purpose to use the grammar in a meaningful context. This gives task design and its use a pivotal role in shaping the language learning process.

What are tasks?   Numerous competing definitions of tasks exist. Many of these definitions focus on different aspects of what constitutes a task. Below you will find three different interpretations of the word task, each of which highlights different nuances of the term.

One of the most widely quoted definitions for task is offered by Long (1985). He refers to a task as

> a piece of work undertaken for oneself or for others, freely or for some reward. Thus examples of tasks include [. . .] filling out a form, buying a pair of shoes, making an airline reservation, borrowing a library book, taking a driving test, typing a letter, [. . .], making a hotel reservation, writing a check, finding a street destination and helping someone across the road. In other words, by "task" is meant the hundred and one things people do in everyday life, at work, at play, and in between (p. 89).

Another well-known definition is provided by Nunan (1989). He considers a task as

> any classroom work which involves learners in comprehending, manipulating, producing, or interacting in the target language while their attention is principally focused on meaning rather than form (p. 10).

More recently, Skehan (1998) summarizes the parameters for a task activity in the following way:

> "(a) meaning is primary, (b) learners are not given other people's meanings to regurgitate, (c) there is some sort of relationship to comparable real-world activities, (d) task completion has a priority, and (e), the assessment of tasks are done in terms of outcome" (p. 147).

From these definitions, despite the various interpretations, several common design features can be identified. These features include: All three definitions emphasize the importance of focus on meaning. This criterion supports the notion that conveying an intended meaning is the essence of language use (see Principle 4 for further discussion). Long (1985) and Skehan's (1998) definitions emphasize the use of real-world tasks or activities that are comparable to authentic task behavior. Performing real-world tasks also necessitates the use of real language to accomplish these tasks. Skehan (1998) further suggests that task performance often involves achieving a goal or an objective, or arriving at an outcome or an end product. Meanwhile, Nunan's (1989) definition makes specific reference to the classroom environment and points out that task performance may entail employing a single skill or a combination of several skills. His description recognizes the pedagogical needs for focusing on skills in isolation in language learning.

One of the challenges of task-based learning and instruction is that engaging students in a variety of tasks is necessary to promote acquisition. Students have many pedagogical needs which often necessitate a different approach to teaching. For example, learners need to engage in psycholinguistic and metalinguistic processes such as repeating, noticing forms, hypothesizing and conceptualizing rules, which have been found by research as being conducive to the language acquisition process. For this reason, Nunan (1993) distinguishes between two kinds of tasks: Real-world tasks and pedagogical tasks. Real-world tasks are designed to emphasize those skills that learners need to have so they can function in the real world. Such tasks normally simulate authentic task behavior, and their primary focus is often the achievement of an end product. For such reasons, these kinds of tasks normally make up the final goal of a lesson or a unit.

In contrast to real-life tasks, pedagogical tasks are intended to act as a bridge between the classroom and the real world in that they serve to prepare students for real-life language usage (see Long, 1998). Such tasks are often referred to as "preparation" or "assimilation" tasks. They are designed to promote the language acquisition process by taking into account a teacher's pedagogical goal, the learner's developmental stage and skill level, and the social contexts of the second-language learning environment. They often have an enabling character, i.e., they aid the learners in their understanding of how language works and also in the development of learning skills and strategies in general. In addition, they focus on skills in isolation and within a narrow context. Pedagogical tasks do not necessarily reflect real-world tasks. For instance, the preparation task in Appendix 3 illustrates such an example. In this assimilation task, students complete descriptions with words that are missing. The rationale for this design is that students first need to learn some basic facts. Furthermore, their attention is directed to particular vocabulary and verb forms in isolation, which they need to apply in the subsequent task.

Sample task-based lessons. Illustrations 2 and 3 describe two different task-based lessons. The goal of the Lesson on organizing a welcome dinner (Illustration 2) is for learners to arrange a group of international students at dinner tables based on factors such as what the students' hobbies are, what languages they speak, or their age. The final goal of the lesson example in Illustration 3 is for students to set up and collect information for an address book. They are to find out the following information from three of their classmates: first name, last name, phone number or e-mail address, and why they are learning French. While both lesson models are organized by aiming at the achievement of a final task, they can be distinguished by what here is referred to as a "strong" or "dependent task" design. In the lesson on organizing a welcome dinner, which follows a "dependent" task design, all sub-steps are connected and situated within a contextualized framework. Students have to do something with the information they gather and also have to use this information in subsequent tasks, which lead up to a final task. The completion of all tasks involves multiple and different kinds of speech acts. For learners to achieve the final lesson goal, the successful completion of all tasks preceding the final tasks is required. Ultimately, performing the final target task is driven by gathering information in a communicative way during each subtask.

Illustration 3 follows a "task independent" design. The purpose of each task that leads up to the final task is to engage the learner in the development of skills that are needed to perform the final lesson task. While each task is contextualized and engages the learner in real-life speech application, they are not necessarily connected by one common theme. While communicative language use is still practiced during each task, the need for exchanging and gathering information in a communicative way to achieve the final lesson goal, however, is not the driving force.

ILLUSTRATION 2

Organizing a welcome dinner (see Appendix 3 for the entire lesson)

Step 1. Students organize the group of international students around three dinner tables. For example, a student might say: "On table 1, Andrew Smith and Sandra Mogambe sit next to each other, because they both speak Spanish and collect butterflies."

Step 2. Students listen to new information about the students given to them by their Spanish teachers and if necessary rearrange students at the tables.

Step 3. Students provide some personal information about themselves. Then they choose a student from their own group, who also wants to attend the welcome dinner, and select a table for this student.

Step 4. Now you are going to revise your distribution and write a brief report.

Step 5. A representative from each group presents their report and justifies the group decision.

Step 6. The groups and the teacher compare the results.

ILLUSTRATION 3

Setting up an address book

Step 1. You are in a language school and the instructor is taking attendance. Students read the names of students and check who is present.

Step 2. Students listen to their teacher pronounce French names and share with the class French names that they are familiar with.

Step 3. A. Students match (associate) numbers with twelve photos that represent cultural themes. The photos are marked with some letters from the alphabet.

B. Students count from 1-12.

Step 4. Students listen to the result of a song contest broadcasted on TV. They complete a chart and write down the points that each country was awarded.

Step 5. A. Students are asked to write down the names of seven European countries. (The article and the first letter of each country name are provided.) The teacher follows up with the question: How do you spell **L'Allemagne**?

B. Students locate the names of European countries on the map.

Step 6. Students express their opinions about where they believe a set of photos was taken. Students work in pairs. For example, one student would ask in French: **La photo numéro deux, c'est la France?** [Photo number 2, is this France?] Her partner might respond, **Non, ce n'est pas la France, je crois que c'est la Grande-Bretagne.** [No, it is not France, I believe it is Great Britain.]

Step 7. Students listen to a recording of first and last names, and compare the spelling. They look for letters that are pronounced the same way, and those that are pronounced differently.

Step 8. Students match names of famous French celebrities with a corresponding photo and caption. Students express who they believe these people are. For example, a student might say: **La photo numéro 1, c'est Marguerite Duras?** [Photo number 1, is this Marguerite Duras?] Her partner might respond, **Non, ce n'est pas Marguerite Duras, je crois que c'est Isabelle Adjani.** [No, it is not Marguerite Duras, I believe it is Isabelle Adjani.]

Step 9. A. Students listen to three different dialogues in which people explain why they are learning French. They have to number the sentences (reasons) to identify who says what.

B. Students share their reason for why they are studying French.

As seen from the examples above, task-based instruction as a model of syllabus design has an emphasis on performance. Achievement is measured based on whether or to what extent learners can successfully perform the pedagogic and real-life tasks. However, it needs to be pointed out that using tasks as organizational units of daily and long-term plans is not without challenges. These challenges have to do with task choice, task difficulty and sequencing. Furthermore, depending on the complexity of target language structures, task designs often require careful adaptations as to what linguistic structures learners can actually apply. Following a task-based approach also requires careful pedagogical consideration, especially in terms of task implementation. This includes knowledge of when and how to integrate pedagogical tasks as lead-up and follow-up to a real-life task. The topic of designing pedagogical and real life tasks is further discussed in different chapters throughout this book.

Principle 2: Promote Learning by Doing

A task-based approach to learning implies the notion of learning by doing. This concept is not new to communicative language teaching methodologies, but it has been recognized and promoted as a fundamental principle underlying learning throughout history by many educators (e.g., see Long and Doughty 2003 for a brief overview). It is based on the theory that a hands-on approach positively enhances a learner's cognitive engagement. In addition, as Doughty and Long (2003) remind us, "new knowledge is better integrated into long-term memory, and easier retrieved, if tied to real-world events and activities" (p. 58).

In research on SLA, the "learning by doing" principle is strongly supported by an active approach to using language early on. For example, Swain (1985, 1995) suggests that learners need to actively produce language. Only in this way can they try out new rules and modify them accordingly. According to Omaggio-Hadley (2001), learners should be encouraged to express their own meaning as early as possible after productive skills have been introduced. Such opportunities should also entail a wide range of contexts in which they can carry out numerous different speech acts. This, furthermore, needs to happen under real conditions of communication so the learner's linguistic knowledge becomes automatic (Ellis 1997).

Principle 3: Input Needs to Be Rich

Considering the rich input we each experience and are exposed to while developing our native tongue, growing up speaking in our native languages means that we are exposed to a plethora of language patterns, chunks, and phrases in numerous contexts and situations over many years. Such a rich exposure to language ultimately allows us to store language in our brains that we can retrieve and access as whole chunks.

Needless to say, there is no way we can replicate this rich input in the classroom alone in order to develop native-like language skills. Nevertheless, the input provided needs to be as rich as possible. As Doughty and Long (2003) put it, rich input entails "realistic samples of discourse use surrounding native speaker and non-native speaker accomplishments of targeted tasks" (p. 61). This makes one of the most obvious necessities in teaching a foreign language that the student get to hear the language, whether from the teacher, from multimedia resources (TV, DVDs, video and audio tapes, radio, online), from other students, or any other source, and furthermore be exposed to as rich a diet of authentic language discourse as possible. In the classroom environment, this can be achieved through the use of a wide range of materials, authentic and simplified, as well as the teacher's maximum use of the TL.

Corollary 1: Materials need to be authentic to reflect real-life situations and demands. One of the instructional practices promoted by communicative language teaching (CLT) is the extensive integration of authentic materials in the curriculum. **Authentic materials** refers to the use in teaching of texts, photographs, video selections, and other teaching resources that were not specially prepared for pedagogical purposes (Richards 2001). Examples of authentic audiovisual materials are announcements, conversations and discussions taken as extracts or as a whole from radio and television public broadcasting, real-life telephone conversations, messages left on answering machines, or voice mail. There are numerous justifications for the use of authentic materials. They contain authentic language and reflect real-world language use (Richards 2001). In other words, they expose students to real language in the kinds of contexts where it naturally occurs. Furthermore, they relate more closely to learners' needs and hence provide a link between the classroom and students' needs in the real world. The use of authentic materials also supports a more creative approach to teaching; that is, its use allows teachers to develop their full potential, designing activities and tasks that better match their teaching styles and the learning styles of their students. Last, the use of authentic materials requires the teachers to train their students in using learning strategies early on. These are essential skills that support the learning process at all levels of instruction.

Access to authentic data, such as text or audiovisual-based resources, is no longer a problem for most teachers. But in lower-level classrooms, the use of such materials faces numerous challenges. Authentic materials often contain difficult language. Usually, there is no particular text per se that ideally fits the learners' level of proficiency as a whole. For example, while one paragraph from a magazine article may be appropriate for beginning students, the next may be far too advanced and require special adaptation in task design to make it usable. In other words, to develop learning resources around authentic materials, teachers must be prepared to spend a considerable amount of time locating suitable sources for materials and developing learning tasks that accompany the materials and scaffold the learning process. Chapters 6 through 9 will address skill development and scaffolding the learning process in more detail.

As pointed out above, with the inception of CLT, language teachers have been turning to authentic materials for use in the classroom at increasingly lower levels of learner proficiency. At the same time, many published materials incorporate authentic texts and other real-world sources. Considering the advantages as well as limitations of using authentic materials, a mixture of both textbook-based and authentic materials, in particular at beginning levels, justifies practices that are pedagogically necessary and manageable.

Describe one of your former teachers' uses of the **target language (TL)** and the **native language (L1)** in the classroom. How much L1 versus the TL did your teacher use? How did the teacher help you understand the TL better?

_____

_____

_____

Corollary 2: The teacher needs to maximize the use of the target language. Another way to create rich input in the language classroom is by using the target language (TL) as a means of instruction. The exclusive or nearly exclusive use of the TL has been justified under what has come to be called a "maximum exposure" hypothesis—that is, learners need as much exposure as possible to the TL because the greater the amount of input, the greater the gains in the new language (Cummins and Swain 1986). The exclusive use of the TL by teachers in the foreign language has also become a strong principle advocated by teaching methodologies, notably in communicative approaches to language teaching (Rolin-Ianziti and Brownlie 2002).

There are a number of reasons you should use the target language (TL) in the classroom. Take the questionnaire in Appendix 1.1, Using the Target Language and L1. Which reasons do you agree or disagree with? Draw a conclusion on how to use the TL and English in the classroom.

Using the TL as the primary means of communication, however, has not been an issue without controversies. As teachers' practices reveal (see Rolin-Ianziti and Brownlie 2002), many teachers feel drawn in different directions regarding when and how much English should be used in the classroom. For example, Polio and Duff (1994) report that many teachers prefer to use English mainly to explain grammar, to manage the class, to indicate a stance of empathy or solidarity toward students, to translate unknown vocabulary items, and to help students when they have problems understanding.

Likewise, students' reactions to the teacher's use of the target language and English show a mixture of preferences. By and large, many students prefer the instructor to make extensive use of the TL. As Brandl and Bauer (2002) have shown, in particular, in those beginning language classrooms where teachers tend to use English more than the TL, students ask for an increase in the teacher's use of the TL. On the contrary, in those classes where teachers exclusively used the TL, many students expressed preference for some occasional use of English, in particular when providing directions or confirming the students' understanding.

There are numerous benefits to the extensive use of the TL. Nevertheless, the input that is provided—such as information or concepts teachers present in the TL—must be comprehensible to the students, otherwise no learning can occur (see Principle 4 on comprehensible input). A teacher's goal needs to be to find the right balance between the use of the TL and English, which makes sure students understand and at the same time maximizes the use of the TL.

To deal with resistance and some potential frustrations by students to this instructional practice of an extensive use of the TL, the following guidelines provide some strategies.

1. *Do not constantly switch back and forth between the TL and the students' L1*. Use the TL in longer chunks as much as possible. Although some purists suggest that the use of the TL and students' native language must be kept distinctively separated, switching between different languages is a common language phenomenon that occurs in any normal social interaction between speakers who share knowledge of the same languages. This language behavior is known as **code switching**. As such, code switching must be seen as a vital communication strategy. Students should not be discouraged from using code switching if they do not know how to say something in the TL and if it keeps the communication afloat. Nevertheless, code switching is different from language behavior where a teacher begins a sentence in one language and ends it in another—or constantly switches back and forth between languages due to either lack of proficiency skills or laziness.

2. *Set a good example for the students*. Do not expect students to use the TL if you cannot use it consistently yourself.

ANALYSIS AND DISCUSSION

What challenges might you encounter when making extensive use of the target language (TL) in the classroom? What will your students' reactions be? Can you think of any other suggestions for helping your students deal with the teacher's extensive use of the TL?

3. *Provide clear guidelines*. You need to let your students know when it is appropriate to use English in the classroom and for what purposes. Set aside specific times during each class for the use of English. For example, students most frequently request English for task instructions, brief explanations of grammar, or confirmation checks. Adhere to these guidelines as much as possible.

4. *Discuss the rationale for using the TL in the classroom early in the term.* Let students know why it is important to use the TL extensively in the classroom. For communicative purposes, it is critical for students to realize they do not need to understand every single word at all times.

Principle 4: Input Needs to Be Meaningful, Comprehensible, and Elaborated

A fundamental prerequisite for learning to occur is that the information we process must be meaningful. This means the information being presented must be clearly relatable to existing knowledge that the learner already possesses. This existing knowledge must be organized in such a way that the new information is easily assimilated, or "attached," to the learner's cognitive structure (Ausubel 1968). The necessity of meaningfulness is not in particular new to CLT. Throughout the history of language teaching, there have always been advocates of a focus on meaning as opposed to form alone, and of developing learner ability to actually use language for communication. Meaningfulness, however, has emerged as a primary principle of CLT—and as a counter-reaction to audiolingual teaching, which was criticized for repetitive drills that did not require the processing of language so the content made sense or was meaningful to learner.

In addition to being meaningful, input should adhere to several general characteristics that make it potentially useful to the learner. As Lee and VanPatten (1995a) suggest, "the language that the learner is listening to (or reading, if we are talking about written language) must contain some message to which the learner is supposed to attend" (p. 38).

In language learning, input cannot be meaningful unless it is comprehensible. This means, as Lee and VanPatten (1995a) put it, "The learner must be able to understand most of what the speaker (or writer) is saying if acquisition is to happen. [. . .], the learner must be able to figure out what the speaker is saying if he is to attach meaning to the speech stream coming at him" (p. 38). The authors further describe the importance of this hypothesis in the following way:

> Acquisition consists in large part of the building up of form-meaning connections in the learner's head. For example, the learner of French hears the word *chien* in various contexts and eventually attaches it to a particular meaning: a four-legged canine. As another example, a learner of Italian might hear *–ato* in various contexts and eventually attach it to a particular meaning: a past-time reference. Features of language, be they grammar, vocabulary, pronunciation, or something else, can only make their way into the learner's mental representation of the language system if they have been linked to some kind of real-world meaning. If the input is incomprehensible or if it is not meaning-bearing, then these form-meaning connections just don't happen. (p. 38)

As pointed out previously, ways of creating rich input in the classroom environment are either through extensive use of the TL or through a wide range of authentic or linguistically rich resources. On the downside, creating this environment involves numerous pedagogical challenges, particularly in regard to making such input accessible—that is, meaningful and comprehensible to the learners. These challenges can be met by means of numerous input strategies, or by what Doughty and Long (2003) refer to as **elaborating input**. Elaboration in this context has several meanings. On the one hand, it is the myriad ways native speakers modify discourse, that is, the way they use language to make it comprehensible to the non-native speaker (Doughty and Long 2003). Such strategies include

- confirmation checks (e.g., "You mean . . . ; What you are saying is . . .")
- comprehension checks, (e.g., "Is this correct? What you are saying is . . .")
- the teacher's accessibility to students' questions
- providing nonlinguistic input through body language (e.g., modeling, gestures, visuals)
- modified language use through
  a. repetition
  b. slower speech rate
  c. enhanced enunciation
  d. simplifying language (e.g., high-frequency vocabulary, less slang, fewer idioms, shorter sentences)
  e. use of cognates
  f. limited use of English

Research supports such strategies and has pointed out numerous benefits. For example, Hatch (1983) examined simplified input in terms of five general categories: (1) rate of speech, (2) vocabulary, (3) syntax, (4) discourse, and (5) speech setting. As a result, she suggests that such speech modifications potentially aid with the comprehension process. This is presumably the case because clear enunciation, repetition, and slower speech rate make language acoustically more salient and provide a greater chance for the learners to perceive language structures and process form-meaning connections. Likewise, simplified syntax or modifications of input further reduce the burden on process and increase the chance that the learner will hear certain forms and structures (Lee and VanPatten 1995a). In another study, Brandl and Bauer (2002) investigated beginning language students' preferences of teacher's use of input strategies. They report that students in particular find confirmation checks, use of body language, visual representations, repetitions, slower speech rate, and occasional use of English helpful with their comprehension of the input.

On the other hand, elaborating input can be further enhanced through a thoughtful plan of how input is presented. This requires mindful attention to task design by taking into account task choice and difficulty, learner processing skills, and scaffolding strategies. This topic will be discussed in more detail in Chapter 6.

Principle 5: Promote Cooperative and Collaborative Learning

In general education, **cooperative** or **collaborative learning** has long been recognized as a strong facilitator of learning (e.g., see Kagan 1989). In such an approach, classrooms are organized so that students work together in small cooperative teams, such as groups or pairs, to complete activities. In second language learning environments, students work cooperatively on a language-learning task or collaboratively by achieving the goal through communicative use of the target language. Particularly in the latter case, if the learning tasks are designed to require active and true communicative interaction among students in the target language, they have numerous benefits on attainment (for a detailed list and discussion, see Chapter 8, Developing Oral Communication Skills). Key to learning in these situations is what takes place during the interaction between the learners and the teacher, and among the learners.

While interaction normally involves both input and learner production, learners cannot simply listen to input. Rather, they must be active conversational participants who interact and negotiate the type of input they receive. Speakers also make changes in their language as they interact or "negotiate meaning" with each other. They do so to avoid conversational trouble or when trouble occurs. In this way, the interaction functions like a catalyst that promotes language acquisition. This claim has become widely known as Long's "Interaction Hypothesis" (1983).

A large body of research supports this hypothesis. A recent **meta-analysis**[2] that investigated the empirical link between task-based interaction and acquisition showed positive evidence for those tasks in particular that push learner output, that is, tasks that require communicative exchange of information and the production of the target language features during learner-to-learner interaction.

While the ability to develop a new language is fostered between and among learners, the social interaction between the teacher, as the expert, and the student, as the novice, which has been the focus of traditional instruction, is of equal importance and should not be ignored. The importance of this kind of social interaction is well described by the works of social psychologist Vygotsky (1978). Through the assistance of the teacher and the social interaction, the learner is led to reach a potential that exceeds his current level of development. In communicative language classrooms, however, as soon as students are able to perform speech acts or language tasks on their own—that is, without a teacher's assistance—the focus shifts from teacher-led to student-centered language application.

Principle 6: Focus on Form

One of the debates about grammar teaching centered on the issue of whether to make grammar explicit or whether to have the learners figure out the rules themselves. In this context, *explicit* means that the rules become salient or are laid out to the learner at one point during the course of instruction. Although not everybody agrees (see Krashen 1981), research provides ample evidence for the benefits of making grammar rules explicit to adult language learners (for a review of studies, see Norris and Ortega 2000). Within explicit ways of teaching grammar, Long (1991) conceived a further distinction between what he calls "focus on form" and "focus on formS." A **focus on formS** approach represents a fairly traditional approach to teaching grammar where "students spend much of their time in isolated linguistic structures in a sequence predetermined externally and imposed on them by a syllabus designer or textbook writer . . .," while meaning is often ignored (Doughty and Long 2003, p. 64). In contrast, a **focus on form** approach to explicit grammar teaching emphasizes a form-meaning connection and teaches grammar within contexts and through communicative tasks (see communicative language teaching principles above).[3] Doughty and Long (2003) point out that overwhelming empirical evidence exists in favor of a focus-on-form approach, hence they proclaim it a fundamental methodological principle in support of CLT and task-based language instruction. (For a statistical meta-analysis of some 60 studies comparing focus on form with other types of instruction, see Norris and Ortega 2000).

Chapter 4, Grammar and Language Learning, discusses some of the controversies on grammar teaching in more detail. It also provides an overview of techniques ranging from self-instructional, discovery, teacher-guided, or teacher-student co-constructed approaches to making rules explicit.

Principle 7: Provide Error Corrective Feedback

In a general sense, feedback can be categorized in two different ways: **positive feedback** that confirms the correctness of a student's response. Teachers demonstrate this behavior by agreeing, praising, or showing understanding. Or, **negative feedback**, generally known as error correction (see Chaudron 1988), which has a corrective function on a student's faulty language behavior. As learners produce language, such evaluative feedback can be useful in facilitating the progression of their skills toward more precise and coherent language use. Both types are vital during a learner's interlanguage development since they allow the learner to either accept, reject, or modify a hypothesis about correct language use.

The study of feedback in learning situations has a long history. In language learning, many research studies have documented that teachers believe in the effectiveness of feedback and that students ask for it, believe in the benefits of receiving it, and learn from it. Yet the degree to which information provided through feedback aids a learner's progress is not always clear. Such a claim can be illustrated by what teachers frequently experience; namely, that their students, after receiving feedback, often keep making the same mistakes—or even when they get it right initially, many still fall back into their previous and faulty language behavior. "Acquisition is a process that is not usually instantaneous" (Doughty and Williams 1998, p. 208). Achieving positive effects with error corrective feedback involves a long-term process that depends on corrective strategies and most of all on individual learner factors.

For example, in a classroom study of the effectiveness of various feedback techniques, Lyster and Ranta (1997) found that **recasts**—that is, when a teacher repeats a student's faulty language production, but in a correct way—were the most widespread response to learner error. Yet recasts were in fact the least effective in eliciting learners to immediately revise their output. Instead, direct error corrective strategies that involved the teacher's help—such as providing metalinguistic clues or clarification requests—were the most effective in stimulating learner-generated repairs (for a more detailed discussion, see Chapter 5, Feedback and Error Correction in Language Learning).

As suggested by Lyster and Ranta's study, the value of negative feedback lies in drawing learner attention to some problematic aspect of their interlanguage. In other words, many learners may require help in "noticing" (Schmidt 1990, 2001) their mistakes. Another factor that may also play a crucial role concerns the timing of that feedback. "Where corrective recasts are concerned, the information must be provided as-yet-little-understood cognitive processing window [. . .] such that learners can make some sort of comparison between the information provided in the feedback and their own preceding utterance" (Doughty and Long 2003, p. 14).

While the type of error corrective strategy may make a difference, **learner readiness** may be the most decisive factor in predicting success in the acquisition process. Readiness implies that the learners are able to make a "comparison between their internal representation of a rule and the information about the rule in the input [i.e., feedback] they encounter" (Chaudron 1988, p. 134). Simply put, if a learner makes a mistake and has no clue that he made a mistake, nor does he know what he did wrong, in other words there was no hypothesis that he was testing either, then any kind of error corrective feedback may simply be ineffective as the learner is not ready yet (see Brandl 1995).

In general, there is little doubt about the role of feedback as a facilitator to learning, despite many challenges in delivering it effectively. The provision of "error corrective" and "positive" feedback as a fundamental principle permeates all areas of instruction and constitutes a necessity in support of the learning process.

Principle 8: Recognize and Respect Affective Factors of Learning

Over the years, consistent relationships have been demonstrated between language attitudes, motivation, performance anxiety, and achievement in second language learning (Gardner 1985; Gardner and McIntyre 1993; Horwitz and Young 1991). Needless to say, all teachers eventually experience how learners feel about the target language or how their attitudes toward it impact their motivation and subsequently their success. As Gardner and McIntyre (1993) put it, a learner who is motivated "wants to achieve a particular goal, devotes considerable effort to achieve this goal, and experiences in the activities associated with achieving this goal" (p. 2).

One characteristic of language learning that has received a great deal of attention over the past years is the role of anxiety during the learning process. In particular, with active language performance as a major goal of CLT, anxiety has been noticed as a trait with many individual learners. Anxiety manifests itself in many ways such as self-belittling, feelings of apprehension, stress, nervousness, and even bodily responses such as faster heartbeat. Numerous studies have corroborated what Krashen contended in his Affective Filter hypothesis, which states: "Language learning must take place in an environment where learners are 'off the defensive' and the affective filter (anxiety) is low in order for the input to be noticed and gain access to the learners' thinking" (Krashen 1982, p. 127).

There is a clear negative relationship between anxiety and learning success. Anxiety as a personal trait must be recognized and kept at a minimal level for learning to be maximized. Anxiety and its impact on learner performance are discussed in more detail in later chapters.

Challenges in Communicative Language Teaching

CLT or a task-based approach is not a panacea to language teaching. There are numerous challenges to making communicative language teaching happen. These issues have to do with the choice of content, context, specific skill areas (e.g., vocabulary, grammar, etc.), and particular learning tasks that determine a curriculum.

These choices are tightly linked to questions about what it means to "know" a language, to be proficient in a language, and what communicative abilities entail. While the literature on language teaching has attempted to provide answers to such questions, there are no universally accepted standards. The proficiency and standards movements have attempted to provide some guidelines, but they often remain broad in learner performance descriptions (see Appendix 8.3, ACTFL Proficiency Guidelines). This ultimately makes assessment of individual learners' communicative ability challenging, and it essentially leaves judgment of learner progress up to the teachers.

Communicative abilities cannot be simply categorized as speaking, listening, reading, or writing skills, as it was done in a traditional four-skills approach. For example, when two people talk to each other, the process normally involves speaking and listening skills as well as active communicative strategies such as asking for clarification and adjusting language to make each other understood. The endeavor to teach languages in a way that encompasses all skills, based on an interactive view of language behavior, has posed many challenges on how to go about integrating the four skills effectively in a daily and long-term curriculum.

The teaching of proficiency and communicative-based skills raises the question not only about content but also about the choice of learning tasks or best teaching practices. CLT does not promote one standardized method or curriculum, but is eclectic in its approach. Being eclectic means it promotes the best or most effective techniques or methodologies. At the same time, the choice of techniques and learning tasks is not an arbitrary decision, but is firmly grounded in principles of learning as they are motivated by research in second language acquisition (SLA) and educational psychology. Learning what constitutes effective ways of learning and teaching initially requires intensive training and in the long run staying in touch with current SLA research findings.

As a last point, the quality of CLT also often depends on the quality of teaching materials. Unfortunately, only in the most commonly taught languages—such as English, Spanish, French, and German—does an abundance of materials exist to support the development of communicative language abilities over a wide range of skills.

Conclusion

The purpose of this chapter was to provide an introduction to communicative language teaching (CLT) and to describe methodological principles that facilitate the language learning process. CLT furthermore takes a pragmatic or performance-based approach to learning. Its goal is to promote the development of real-life language skills by engaging the learner in contextualized, meaningful, and communicative-oriented learning tasks. CLT methodologies embrace an eclectic approach to teaching, which means they borrow teaching practices from a wide array of methods that have been found effective and that are in accordance with principles of learning as suggested by research findings in research in SLA and cognitive psychology. Its open-ended or principle-based approach allows for a great deal of flexibility, which makes it adaptable to many individual programmatic and learner needs and goals. Such an approach further supports the notion that no second language teaching method can be the single best one. It recognizes the wide range of factors—such as learner ability and motivation, teacher effectiveness and methodology—that contribute to success in foreign language learning. Last, it leaves the door open to redefine and adapt new teaching practices, as research findings evolve in the future.

Checking chapter objectives

Do I know how to . . .

- ❑ define communicative and task-based language teaching?
- ❑ describe different characteristics of pedagogical and real-life tasks?
- ❑ describe principles underlying communicative language teaching methodologies?
- ❑ identify characteristics of good input?
- ❑ maximize the use of the TL in the classroom?
- ❑ deal with challenges in implementing communicative language teaching methodologies?

Explorations

TASK 1: DISCUSSION

Discuss the following questions. In a communicative-based language class,

how is a lesson structured?

what promotes learning?

what is the role of input and resources?

what is the role of grammar?

what is the role of feedback?

what is the atmosphere like?

TASK 2: LESSON ANALYSIS

All of the following lessons have been claimed to follow communicative language teaching methodologies. Read through the different lesson descriptions and identify principles of CLT in action in each of these lessons. Which lessons are most in alignment with CLT?

Lesson 1

What's her name?

1. Listen and read: Students listen to a taped recording and read a dialogue between two men talking about finding a suitable milkman to deliver milk. They talk about two possible assistants, a boy and a girl. The dialogue is tightly structured around giving personal information

in reply to *Wh–* questions: What's her name? Where does she live? The listening activity lasts around three minutes.

2. Answer: Students listen to the conversation again and complete a chart about the girl and the boy. They listen for name, age, address, hobbies, and description.

3. Listen and repeat: Students listen to the question format on the tape and repeat what they hear: What's her name? What's his name?

4. Write and speak: Students are directed to look at the dialogue in Activity 1 and find all the questions. They need to write the questions in their notebooks. Then they practice asking each other the questions and giving the appropriate reply for the boy and the girl in the textbook.

5. Write and speak: Students copy a chart similar to that in Activity 2. They fill in the chart with information about themselves first; then they interview a partner and fill in his/her information.

6. Listen: Students listen to a new conversation about a film producer looking for a boy and a girl to act in a new movie. The producer has a conversation (similar to that in Activity 1) to find out information about two possible candidates. Students listen only and complete a personal information form.

7. Write: Students are given a cloze passage about the girl the producer in Activity 6 above was enquiring about. Then they write a similar paragraph about the boy.

Source: Flowerdew and Miller (2005), 103–104.

Lesson 2

Who has the coolest room?

1. Warm up. The instructor points at object(s) in the classroom and students name it or them.

2. Writing: Doing an inventory. Students individually make a list of the objects that they have in their room. They compare their list with another student asking their partner whether they have the same things in their rooms. Students mark off those items they have in common, and they write down those they do not have in common.

3. Guided control: Finding misplaced objects. Students switch partners and do an information gap activity in pairs. Each student has a different picture of a room containing many objects. They ask each other about the location of a variety of objects they are looking for and then mark them on their picture.

4. Communicative exchange: Describing and finding out what each other's room looks like. Students describe their rooms to each other. They draw a picture of each other's rooms.

5. Extension and task: Students identify who has the coolest room. Students report to the class on what their partner's room looks like.

The instructor asks the rest of the class which room they like best. Students in addition have to provide the rationale for their decision.

Lesson 3

The topic of this Indonesian class was to introduce colors and learn expressions such as "How much does it cost?" and "It costs. . . ." While showing the students the colors in Indonesian, the instructor took the opportunity to introduce expressions of preference, such as "What is your favorite color?" She had a stack of cards made of different-colored paper, with the Indonesian word written on the back of each one. There were two cards of each color. Each student had to pick his or her favorite color from the stack. Then the students had to ask each other what their favorite colors were. This activity involved listening, reading, and speaking, since the students first had to listen to the instructor for cues on how to ask and answer the question, then had to read their color from their card, and finally had a short conversation about their favorite color.

The instructor then moved to the main part of her lesson, which centered on buying things at a store. She introduced the basic vocabulary by first posing the question, "How much is the . . .," and then answering it. She handed out copies of a real-world Indonesian advertisement for sunglasses, contact lenses, and hearing aids. These products enabled the students to use the expressions with vocabulary that consisted entirely of words borrowed from English (sunglass, *lensa kontak*). The purpose of the pairs of colored cards from the first activity now became clear, because the students had to pair up according to their favorite color and then practice asking each other how much each of the products from the advertisement cost.

For the last part of the class, the instructor introduced a guest as the "mystery celebrity" and told the students to imagine that they were journalists who wanted to find out personal information about him. They had to ask the guest speaker questions in English, but could use only the questions they would also be able to ask in Indonesian. The guest speaker answered in English, and the journalists took notes on his answers. When they were done, each student had to volunteer at least one piece of information about the guest speaker—in Indonesian.

Lesson 4

In this elementary-level Czech language class, the topic revolved around a long list of vocabulary, most of it related to basic concepts such as people and places and a few adjectives and verbs. The class period began with a small quiz over the previous week's vocabulary, and then the instructor began the new lesson. She went down a list of new vocabulary terms in the book, saying each word. The students would then repeat the word after her. After a page of this vocabulary, the teacher had her students go on to a text in the book. They went around the room, each student reading a sentence of the text aloud, with the teacher correcting any errors. Then they went around the room again, each student translating one sentence into English.

TASK 3: TEXTBOOK ANALYSIS

Analyze the chapter of a textbook. Make a list of all the learning tasks, identifying the kinds of skills in which the learners get engaged. Categorize the tasks as non-communicative learning, pre-communicative language practice, communicative language practice, structured communication, and authentic communication. In which skills do most of the learners get engaged? Draw a conclusion about the communicative nature and focus of the textbook.

TASK 4: DISCUSSION

Figure 1-1 contains a list of useful strategies that help you to create comprehensible input in the language classroom. Which of these strategies do you believe are more important for beginning-level learners than for learners who had two to three years of classroom exposure?

TASK 5: PART A. VIDEO ANALYSIS OF INPUT STRATEGIES

In the following microteaching performance (see video), the instructor introduces the Spanish past-tense form *imperfecto*. Which of the strategies listed in Figure 1-2 does the instructor use in her presentation?

Interactive strategies

1. confirmation checks/pauses
2. accessible for questions

Use of the target language

1. modeling/body language
2. examples
3. visual representation
4. repetition
5. clear enunciation
6. lower speech rate
7. rephrasing
8. use of simplified language

Use of English

1. use of English for directions
2. use of English for explanations
3. use of English for confirmations

FIGURE 1-1 List of input strategies (Source: Brandl and Bauer (2002); original materials.)

Use of language	Visual input (linguistic)	Visual input (nonlinguistic)	Interactive strategies
• speaks slowly • pauses frequently • enunciates clearly • uses repetitions • uses simplified syntax (S-V-O) • uses short sentences • uses examples • uses high frequency vocabulary	• writes words on the board or overhead	• models actions • uses gestures • uses pictures/props	• checks students' comprehension directly (e.g., Do you understand *x*?) • clarifies student's comprehension indirectly (e.g., What did he want? . . . a book? . . . a pen? . . . a pencil?)

FIGURE 1-2 List of strategies

Using the list in Figure 1-2, check off all the strategies that you can identify.

NOTE!
If you do not have the video available, work with the transcript in Figure 1-3.

If you are not familiar with Spanish, it may be more difficult to identify all the strategies used in Figure 1-3. In that case, make use of the translation of the teacher's script. Furthermore, place yourself in a student's position and focus on those strategies that helped you understand the instructor's presentation.

Ok clase, buenos días clase. Ustedes ya saben que estudiamos el verbo de pasado que se llama "pretérito." Hoy, vamos a estudiar el verbo pasado que se llama "imperfecto." Y se llama . . . El verbo pretérito ocurrió sola una vez. Como cuando yo dejo caer muñeco, no más. *[drops the doll on the table]* No se mueve más. Una sola vez al pasado. Cuando yo hablo del imperfecto, el imperfecto es un verbo que ocurre repetidamente, como un yo-yo. Arriba, abajo, arriba, abajo. *[plays with the yo-yo]* Es un verbo que tiene movimiento, que no parada existir.

OK class, good morning class. You already know that we studied the past-tense verb form that is called the preterite. *Today, we are going to study the past-tense verb form called "imperfective." The preterite verb occurs only once. Like when I let the doll fall . . . no more.* [drops the doll on the table] *It doesn't move any more. It only happens once. When I speak of the imperfective, it's a verb that occurs repetitively, like a yo-yo. Up, down, up, down.* [plays with the yo-yo] *It's a verb that has movement, that doesn't cease to exist.*

FIGURE 1-3 Transcript of a Spanish Microteaching Presentation

TASK 6: PART B. VIDEO ANALYSIS OF INPUT STRATEGIES

How would you continue this lesson? What input strategies would you make use of next? Briefly outline how you would continue this lesson.

_____

_____

When you are finished, watch the second part of the video excerpt to see how the teacher continues her mini-lesson. What strategies did she further use to make herself understood? Compare the teacher's script with your own and discuss the results with your class.

_____

_____

NOTE!

If you do not have the video available, see the transcript in Appendix 1.2.

TASK 7: ANALYSIS

Evaluate how comprehensible the language in each of the following contexts would be to first-year learners of the language you (will) teach. Why does the language differ so much from one context to the next?

a. a TV commercial for laundry detergent
b. a comic strip
c. a cooking demonstration
d. a diary entry
e. the beginning of a fairy tale
f. an interview about your life on campus

Source: Lee and VanPatten (1995b), p. 24.

TASK 8: EXPLORING YOUR BELIEFS

Find out whether your classmates agree or disagree with the statements below. Choose three to four issues and discuss them with at least three to four different students in class. Make sure to provide a rationale for your answers.

STATEMENT	I agree	I disagree	I agree with reservations.
1. People have learned languages for centuries, so the methods we use do not really matter.			
2. The most important thing is to let students experiment with the language (spoken and written). They learn the language by using it and need to be given many opportunities to do so.			
3. Students learn best when they are first presented with a clear explanation of grammar rules. Then, they can apply the rules and use them freely.			
3. Class time should mostly be spent focusing on language structures. Meaning can be added later on, once students can express themselves.			
4. Drilling language patterns does not guarantee that the students will internalize them and produce them on their own outside the framework of the exercise.			
5. Accuracy develops naturally. We should not worry too much about students producing perfect structures right away. It is best for teachers not to overcorrect.			
6. Teacher input needs to be rich but comprehensible if learning is to take place.			
7. Language is best learned interactively, in a social environment. In an ideal class, students work together a lot.			
8. Student motivation does not matter. They will learn regardless of their motivation.			

Source: Hedwige Meyer, University of Washington

Application

TASK 9: MAXIMIZING STUDENT INTERACTION

The goal of this foreign language lesson is for students to talk about and compare the lifestyles of male and female adolescents. The setting is an American classroom. In a traditional classroom, the teacher might ask questions such as: What do young American women and men like to do in their free time? What are their hobbies? What are common activities? Which ones are less common? In communicative language teaching, the teacher would maximize the communicative use of language by creating multiple opportunities for students to interact with each other.

Design a lesson outline that consists of different steps. Project yourself into the classroom, and demonstrate how you would enact each step to create maximum interactions among students.

NOTE!
Step 1 below is a possible way of getting started, but feel free to change it.

Steps	Task description and teaching routine
1	In pairs (preferably pairs consist of male and female students only), students make a list of activities that describe the lifestyles of young men or women.
2	
3	
4	
5	

TASK 10: ELABORATING A TEXT

Review the following conversation between two adults. Then modify the second person's (the friend's) speech, so that a beginning learner could more easily understand it.

PARENT: I'm pretty fed up with my job these days. I mean, I can't believe that the company thinks we will take a cut in pay and not say anything. I mean, it's just—I don't know.

FRIEND: But it's like that everywhere! Last week I read in *Newsweek*—at least I think it was *Newsweek*. We get both *Newsweek* and *Time*—but anyway I read where IBM is cutting another 500 jobs this next week. I bet those people wouldn't mind a cut in pay just to keep food on the table.

PARENT: Come on! It's not that easy and you know it . . .

_____

_____

_____

Source: Lee and VanPatten (1995b), p. 24.

TASK 11: TRYING OUT INPUT STRATEGIES

Spontaneously describe the picture story of the lion and the mouse (see Appendix 1.4) in the target language (TL) to your partner or the whole class. Make use of as many input strategies as possible to help your partner understand the story.

NOTE!

This activity works best if a true immersion experience can be created in the classroom. If possible, have the story told in a language that is unknown to most class participants.

With the whole class, discuss how well you accomplished your goal. As the "input provider," were you capable of making yourself understood? What means did you make use of? As the listener, were you able to understand your partner's story? What challenges did you both encounter? How can you deal with such challenges in the language classroom?

APPENDIX 1.1

Using the Target Language and Native Language

There are a number of reasons you should use the target language in the classroom. Test yourself! Check off those items that you consider most appropriate:

❑ I don't speak my students' native language, or I don't feel confident speaking my students' native language because I make many mistakes.
❑ I teach multinational students.
❑ The students should be prepared for real communicative situations in the target language.
❑ Students should learn to make themselves understood by making use of the limited vocabulary and grammatical structures they know.
❑ Students should learn to work with monolingual dictionaries.
❑ In the foreign language classroom, the primary mode of articulation [i.e., the target language] should not be changed to improve the students' pronunciation.
❑ I want to create an environment in which students pay attention when I speak the target language. They should not be waiting for a translation.

❏ The students should learn how to comprehend texts globally and not always translate word by word.

❏ The students should learn how to think and speak in the target language as much as possible.

❏ It is difficult to find the correct answer from all the entries listed in a bilingual dictionary.

If you checked off most of the items above, you principally are in favor of using the target language as much as possible in the classroom.

Reasons for occasional use of the students' native language are:

❏ when there is the risk of miscomprehension.

❏ when the expenditure of time required to give an explanation in the target language cannot be justified by the results.

❏ when the exclusive use of the target language interferes with interpersonal communication.

❏ to explain difficult cultural concepts.[4]

Source: Weigmann (1992), 22–23. Translated here by Klaus Brandl.

APPENDIX 1.2

Transcript of the Microteaching Lesson Introducing the *Preterito* (second half)

Entonces, gustar es un verbo que habla. Gustar. Es el infinitivo del verbo "me gusta." En el pasado, en el imperfecto, el verbo "gustar" era "gustaba." Cuando todo me gustaba siempre, repetidamente, siempre gustaba—gustaba. Es el imperfecto del verbo gustar. Gustaba.

[referring to the items on the overhead screen]

Por ejemplo, aquí. Cuando yo era niña, cuando yo era pequeña, me gustaba trepar los árboles, subir bien alto. Trepar los árboles. Digan por favor—trepar los árboles. Cuando yo era niña, me gustaba tirar piedras. Tirar piedras. Tirar. Me gustaba. Siempre. Yo era así siempre, un verbo repetido. . . . Me gustaba romper vítreos. Romper. Romper vítreos. Me gustaba.

Then, *gustar* (to be pleasing; to like) is a verb that we say. It is the infinitive form of the verb *me gusta* (it is pleasing to me; I like). In the past tense, in the imperfective, the verb *gustar* is *gustaba*. When I liked everything all the time, repeatedly, always, "gustaba"–it's the imperfective of the verb *gustar*. *Gustaba* (I liked).

[referring to the items on the overhead screen]

For example, here. When I was a little girl, when I was small, I liked to climb trees, to get up to a good height. To climb trees. Say it, please: *trepar los árboles*. When I was a little girl, I liked to throw stones. . . . throw. Liked. Always. I did it always, a repetitive verb. . . .

APPENDIX 1.3

The Dinner Game

32 **TAREA**

Gente con gente ♦ 2

♦ Conocer (*meet*) a un grupo de estudiantes internacionales y organizarlos para una cena de bienvenida (*welcome dinner*).

NOTAS
TN02-17

♦ **PREPARACIÓN** ♦

La clase se divide en grupos. Ustedes están (*you are*) en un curso de verano (*summer*) en la "Escuela de Español Golfo de México". Estos estudiantes también están en la escuela. Son estudiantes de todo el mundo. ¿Conocen a sus compañeros/as de escuela? Completen estas descripciones con las palabras que faltan (*are missing*).

TASK

Meet a group of international students and organize them for a welcome dinner party.

Preparation

The class is to divide into groups. You are participating in a summer course in a Spanish language school, "Golfo de México." These students are also in the school. They are students from around the whole world. Have you met your classmates? Complete the descriptions with the words that are missing.

---

1. SANDRA MOGAMBE
ES _____ DE BIOLOGÍA.
TIENE 17 _____.
HABLA ESPAÑOL.
ES _____ GUINEA ECUATORIAL.
COLECCIONA MARIPOSAS.

2. MARK SELLIGSON
ES _____ DE ARTE.
_____ 45 AÑOS.
_____ ESPAÑOL Y ALEMÁN.
MUY _____ AL FÚTBOL.

3. SILVIA OLIVEIRA
_____ 23 AÑOS.
_____ PROFESORA DE PORTUGUÉS.
_____ PORTUGUÉS E INGLÉS.
ES SOLTERA.

4. ANDREW SMITH
PROFESOR _____ GIMNASIA.
_____ 50 AÑOS.
_____ SEPARADO.
HABLA ESPAÑOL E INGLÉS.
_____ MARIPOSAS.

5. KEIKO TANAKA
_____ 20 AÑOS.
_____ JAPONÉS Y UN POCO DE ESPAÑOL.
_____ CASADA.

6. AKIRA TANAKA
_____ PINTOR.
TIENE 22 _____.
HABLA JAPONÉS Y UN _____ DE ESPAÑOL.

7. SAMUEL SOHAMY
_____ ISRAELÍ.
_____ ESTUDIANTE.
TIENE 18 AÑOS.
_____ HEBREO Y UN _____ DE INGLÉS.

8. LANA SOHAMY
_____ ISRAELÍ.
_____ ESTUDIANTE.
TIENE 20 AÑOS.
_____ HEBREO, INGLÉS Y UN POCO DE JAPONÉS.
MUY _____ AL FÚTBOL.

9. JENNY DONALDSON
ES _____ ESTADOS UNIDOS.
_____ PIANISTA.
TIENE 20 AÑOS.
_____ SOLTERA.
_____ INGLÉS.

10. NICOLE TOMBA
_____ ESTADOUNIDENSE.
_____ INFORMÁTICA.
TIENE 26 _____.
_____ SOLTERA.
HABLA INGLÉS Y ESPAÑOL.

11. MISHA GÁLVEZ
_____ FUNCIONARIA.
_____ 33 AÑOS.
_____ CASADA.
SÓLO _____ TAGALO Y UN POCO DE ESPAÑOL.
MUY AFICIONADA AL FÚTBOL.

12. ALI AL-HALEB
EXPERTO EN COMPUTADORAS.
_____ SOLTERO.
TIENE 30 AÑOS.
_____ ÁRABE, INGLÉS Y ESPAÑOL.

13. MARK DORFMAN
_____ ARQUITECTO.
_____ SOLTERO.
TIENE 47 AÑOS.
_____ ALEMÁN E INGLÉS.
_____ AFICIONADO A LA _____ CLÁSICA Y AL PIANO.

---

1. SANDRA MOGAMBE
She is a biology student.
She is 17 years old.
She is from Equatorial Guinea.
She collects butterflies.

2. MARK SELLIGSON
He is an art student.
He is 45 years old.
He studies Spanish and German.
He is very good at soccer.

3. SILVIA OLIVERA
She is 23 years old.
She is a Portuguese teacher.
She speaks Portuguese and English.
She is single.

Paso 1: La distribución de los estudiantes en la cena de bienvenida.
Organicen a los estudiantes en las tres mesas para cenar. Es importante tener en cuenta (*keep in mind*) la información que ustedes saben (*you know*) sobre estas personas.

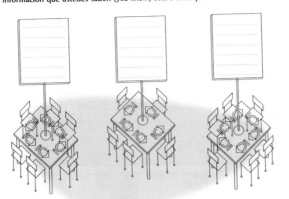

Step 1: The distribution of the students at the welcome dinner.
Organize the students around three tables for the dinner. It is important to keep in mind the information you know about these people.

Step 2: Now listen to the following Spanish teachers. They talk about the new students and offer a great deal of new information. Do you need to change the tables?

LES SERÁ ÚTIL

En la mesa 1: Manuel, Celia...

Manuel **al lado de** Celia porque...

Manuel y
Celia tienen { la misma edad.
el mismo hobby.
los mismos intereses.

Los dos estudian español.

Manuel habla francés y Celia **también**.

Paso 2: Escuchen (*listen to*) ahora a estos profesores de español. Hablan de los nuevos estudiantes y ofrecen mucha información nueva. ¿Necesitan cambiar (*do you need to change*) las mesas?

EDAD:
Tengo _____ años.

ESTADO CIVIL:
Soy ☐ soltero/a.
☐ casado/a.
☐ viudo/a.
☐ divorciado/a.

CARÁCTER:
Soy muy _____
Soy bastante _____
Soy un poco _____
No soy nada _____

IDIOMAS:
Hablo _____

AFICIONES: _____

Paso 3: Un/a estudiante de su grupo también asiste (*attends*) a la cena de bienvenida. ¿Dónde va a sentarse? Elijan (*choose*) al/a la estudiante, completen la ficha con sus datos y seleccionen la mesa.

Ⓦ **Paso 4:** Ahora van a revisar su distribución y escribir un pequeño informe (*report*).

Paso 5: Un/a representante del grupo presenta a la clase el informe y justifica las decisiones del grupo.

Paso 6: Los grupos y el/la profesor/a comparan sus resultados.

AGE	CHARACTER
I am... years old	I am very... I am fairly... I am a little... I am not all...
CIVIL STATUS	LANGUAGES
I am single I am married I am widowed I am divorced	I speak____ WHAT I LIKE. _____

Step 3: A student from your group also attends the welcome dinner. Where is s/he going to sit down? Choose the student, complete the card with their information and select the table.

Step 4: Now you are going to revise your distribution and write a brief report.

Step 5: A representative from your group presents your report and justifies your group decision.

Step 6: The groups and the teacher compare the results.

Source: De la Fuente, Martín, and Sans (2007a), 32–33.

APPENDIX 1.4

The lion and the mouse

Endnotes

1 *Standards* is a discipline-specific document that was triggered by the national reform effort initiated at the 1989 Education Summit in Charlottesville, Virginia. Essentially, this document constitutes content standards that define what students should know and be able to do in foreign language instruction in a K–12 sequence. Given that states and school districts have their own specific goals and define their own curricula, the *Standards* provide a description of a set of common goals. In this sense, the standards document is a political document, delineating the goals of the profession and setting a direction for the field of foreign language learning in the United States.

The standards are not a curriculum guide. As LeLoup and Ponterio (1998) emphasize, "They are not meant to dictate local curricula or even assessment . . . . Nor are the standards tied to any particular instructional method." The standards articulate in a fairly generic way essential skills and knowledge students need in order to achieve language proficiency as lifelong learners.

The standards are organized around five main goals. These are as follows:

COMMUNICATION

Communicate in Languages Other than English

> Standard 1.1: Students engage in conversations, provide and obtain information, express feelings and emotions, and exchange opinions.

> Standard 1.2: Students understand and interpret written and spoken language on a variety of topics.

Standard 1.3: Students present information, concepts, and ideas to an audience of listeners or readers on a variety of topics.

CULTURES

Gain Knowledge and Understanding of Other Cultures

Standard 2.1: Students demonstrate an understanding of the relationship between the practices and perspectives of the culture studied.

Standard 2.2: Students demonstrate an understanding of the relationship between the products and perspectives of the culture studied.

CONNECTIONS

Connect with Other Disciplines and Acquire Information

Standard 3.1: Students reinforce and further their knowledge of other disciplines through the foreign language.

Standard 3.2: Students acquire information and recognize the distinctive viewpoints that are available only through the foreign language and its cultures.

COMPARISONS

Develop Insight into the Nature of Language and Culture

Standard 4.1: Students demonstrate understanding of the nature of language through comparisons of the language studied and their own.

Standard 4.2: Students demonstrate understanding of the concept of culture through comparisons of the cultures studied and their own.

COMMUNITIES

Participate in Multilingual Communities at Home and Around the World

Standard 5.1: Students use the language both within and beyond the school setting.

Standard Students show evidence of becoming lifelong learners by using the language for personal enjoyment and enrichment.

The standards document is promoted at the K–12 level. As such, any teacher or trainer of secondary school teachers needs to be informed about this document and understand its benefit and value. To this author's knowledge, the document is not used at the higher educational level. More information about the standards can be found at the American Council on the Teaching of Foreign Languages (ACTFL) website at http://www.actfl.org/ or the Center for Applied Linguistics at http://www.cal.org/.

2 A meta-analytic study synthesizes the findings of a body of experimental research studies based on the effect size of each study, and consequently draws a conclusion of the research question in focus. Keck et al.'s study (2006) includes 14 studies on task-based interaction that were published between 1980 and 2003.

3 For a detailed discussion of other psycholinguistic characteristics that distinguish a *focus-on-formS* versus a *focus-on-form* approach, see Doughty and Williams 1998.

4 This item is not part of the original source as listed in Weigmann's text.

CHAPTER 2

Short-Term and Daily Lesson Planning

Get to know the road, so you know where you are going.

In this chapter you will learn about

- the importance of lesson planning.

- the structure of a language lesson.

- different phases of a language lesson.

- the different aspects that need to be considered when planning lessons.

- lesson goals and objectives.

- how to go about planning lessons.

REFLECTION

What do you associate with the term *lesson plan*? Write down what comes to your mind.

_____

_____

_____

_____

Introduction: What Is a Lesson Plan?

Excellent teachers are always prepared and have a plan. A lesson plan can mean different things to different teachers based on their experience and planning style or preferences. While some novice teachers refer to their plan as the "rock to stand on," spelling out a great many details, more experienced teachers may list only an outline or list of activities, like a road map, determining the direction they want to go. Teachers also go about the planning process in different ways. Some teachers write down elaborate daily plans; others do the planning inside their heads. In essence, one characteristic all lesson plans have in common is that they are a way of organizing and thinking about lesson components. A **lesson plan** is a systematic record of a teacher's thoughts about what will be covered during a lesson. Or, from a learning perspective, it describes or outlines the pedagogical procedures that will result in students learning or attaining specific objectives. It is an "extremely useful tool that serves as a combination guide, resource, and historical document reflecting our teaching philosophy, student population, textbooks, and most importantly, the goals for our students" (Jensen 2001, p. 403). A lesson plan is essential for novice and experienced teachers.

The focus of this chapter is to provide an introduction to lesson planning and writing. In particular, we will look at different lesson phases, how to structure lessons, and discuss numerous aspects that need to be considered during the planning process. By and large, this chapter will serve as a guide and checklist for creating formalized lessons.

Why Do We Plan?

Richards (1998) stresses the importance of lesson planning for language teachers: "The success with which a teacher conducts a lesson is often thought to depend on the effectiveness with which the lesson was planned" (p. 103). There are numerous internal and external reasons for planning lessons (McCutcheon 1980).

Daily lesson planning can benefit teachers in the following ways:

- A lesson plan helps the teacher think about the lesson in advance to "resolve problems and difficulties, to provide a structure for a lesson, to provide a 'map' for the teacher to follow, and to provide a record of what has been taught" (Richards 1998, p. 103). Daily planning of lessons also benefits students because ideally it takes into account the different backgrounds, interests, learning styles, and abilities of the students in one class.
- A plan provides security (in the form of a map) in the sometimes unpredictable atmosphere of a classroom. Lesson planning is especially important for novice teachers because they may feel more of a need to be in control before the lesson begins.
- A plan is a record of what has been taught. This record helps as a valuable resource when planning assessment measures such as quizzes and exams (Jensen 2001).
- Having a record is also useful when we teach the same course again. This saves time not only in the planning process but also when refining and improving the plans.
- A plan can help a substitute to smoothly take over a class when the teacher cannot teach (Purgason 1991).
- A plan may help with classroom management problems. A well-planned lesson is a way of keeping students focused and on track.
- When a teacher comes prepared, it creates respect with the students. It signals to the students that the teacher is caring and interested in the students' learning.
- A lesson plan is an action plan. Having a lesson plan is imperative for novice teachers. It allows supervisors to discuss this plan with beginning teachers and provide feedback before and/or after class.

Short-Term and Daily Lesson Planning

Language lessons do not take place as isolated events, but as part of a whole unit or program. Thus, when planning daily lessons, teachers need to keep in mind a broader perspective or a particular communicative-based goal. For example, so that students develop all the necessary skills components to perform a simple communicative task—such as introducing themselves or others—even in a fairly narrow context, requires several periods of instruction. While daily lesson planning concentrates on one individual class period at a time, short-term planning takes the perspective of a sequence of several lessons. Such a perspective is necessary, as it allows the teacher to design individual lessons that focus on different skill-building phases that in turn build on each other, while progressing toward a broader range of communicative skills.

The following section describes different lesson segments as they make up the structure of sequences of lessons and individual class periods.

Structure and segments of language lessons

Unlike traditional language teaching, which uses grammar structures as the primary organizational principle, the primary goal of communicative language teaching (CLT) is to get students to use language in communicative ways—that is, in practical terms—to perform communicative language acts or real-world tasks. Thus, most communicative lessons are organized by different lesson segments, or skill development phases, so that learners can build the skills that allow them to perform the communicative lesson goal. T. Ballman (1997) refers to these segments as "Setting the stage, Providing input, Guided participation, and Extension." Each of these segments has a particular pedagogical purpose and can be divided into a sequence of subtasks.

The following paragraphs briefly describe each lesson segment.

Setting the stage. Most lessons begin with some kind of introduction to the topic. The purpose of this lesson segment is to set the stage or establish the topic of the lesson. General ways to do this include announcing the topic, providing objectives for part or the whole lesson, describing the outcome of a learning task, or engaging the learners in a specific activity such as brainstorming or a discussion.

Providing input. The second phase involves presenting the new materials, such as functional skills (asking, answering questions, introducing, describing), the target language (TL) vocabulary, grammar or content (e.g., cultural information). The new forms are normally embedded in a context and presented through stories, written or audio- or video-based dialogues, acted-out scenes, or specially designed learning activities. The primary goal of this lesson segment is to help the learners understand the meaning and the contents. This is done with visual support in the form of pictures, gestures, and other input strategies.

Guided participation/controlled practice. This phase is also often referred to as the "assimilation," "skill getting," or "controlled/ guided" phase. During this phase, students engage in a variety of specific learning activities by zooming in on isolated skills in narrow contexts. The goal of this lesson segment is for students, with the teacher's help, to incrementally build vocabulary, grammar, and functional skills that involve listening, speaking, reading, and writing. The tasks are designed in meaningful and/or communicative ways.

Extension. This phase is also often referred to as the "assimilation," "skill getting," or "controlled practice" phase. The extension phase constitutes the ultimate goal of communicative-based language teaching. In this lesson segment, the learners are given the opportunity to apply and perform the lesson goals and to demonstrate what they have learned.

While each segment plays an important role contributing to the learners' skill progression, each lesson phase has a pedagogical purpose that determines the kind and design of learning activities. As research points out (see Rosenshine and Stevens 1986; Lee and VanPatten 2003), new materials need to be introduced in small parts, or broken down into subskills; then, to be effective, each part must be followed up by guided practice activities. Although extension or communicative application activities are usually found toward the mid or end point of a lesson, input and guided practice phases do not necessarily take place in a linear progression.

Effective lesson designs follow a spiral approach; that is, they cycle through input and guided participation phases several times, until the students have developed all the individual skill components that allow them to apply these skills in more open-ended extension activities. Programs and teachers vary in their design and choice of instructional practices and in the number of class periods they spend in any of these instructional phases. For example, secondary schoolteachers and teachers of younger learners tend to spend increased periods of time in the input phase. The decisions on how to optimize their students' learning experience are guided by the teachers' own beliefs and understanding of how languages are learned. Primarily, however, they are influenced by the level of difficulty of the subject matter, the scope of skills, the learner aptitude, and the age group.

Daily lesson structure

The way language teachers structure and organize their daily lessons contributes to the success of a language class. Effectively organized language lessons constitute a conceivable structure. They have a clear beginning, a main lesson phase, and an end. Individual phases consist of a single activity or a sequence of activities (see Figure 2-1).

```
Warm-up/first activity

Review
• guided participation/controlled practice
• communicative application/extension

Introduction of new materials
• providing input
• guided participation/controlled practice
• communicative application/extension

Closure/wind-down
```

FIGURE 2-1 Possible segments of a daily lesson structure

Warm-up or the first activity. The first activity of a language lesson is typically referred to as the "warm-up" or "opening" activity. The primary goal of this initial phase is to announce that class has begun and to catch the students' attention. Research on teaching suggests that the beginning activity of a lesson generally occupies up to five minutes and can have an important impact on the outcome of a lesson (Kindsvatter, Wilen, and Ishler 1988). McGrath, Davies, and Mulphin (1992) also found that students often react sensitively to teachers' lesson beginnings, which primarily influence the students' affective response to learning. The activity a teacher chooses may vary and can serve many purposes. Some practitioners suggest that "A warm-up should relate the new lesson to the previous one. It should recycle known material through personalized practice (Bansleben 1998). Others believe that warm-ups can encompass a wide variety of activities but should primarily focus on getting students' interest. The following examples provide some general strategies (modified, based on Richards and Lockhart 1994, pp. 115–116):

- Do something to capture the students' interest and motivation (play a short game, tell a joke or an anecdote, briefly discuss a current news topic or event, read a short poem, etc.).
- Review content from a previous lesson; for example, ask questions about concepts or skills taught in the previous lesson (alternatively, this could be done as an individual writing activity or in pairs).
- Have students prepare questions about previous lessons or homework (individually, in writing, or in groups).
- Have students meet in pairs to review homework.

Main lesson segments

Opening statements. Many teachers like to set the stage by beginning with some kind of general opening statement. One of the most common strategies is to give students a sense of direction about what will be accomplished in the lesson. This further implies that a teacher has thought about a lesson and is prepared. Here are some general strategies:

- Describe the goal of a lesson.
- State the skills the students will learn.
- Preview the lesson.
- Describe the relationship between the lesson/activities and a real-world need.
- Describe what students are expected to do in a lesson.
- Describe the relationship between the lesson/activities and a forthcoming test or exam.
- Point out links between the lesson and previous lessons.
- State that an activity the students will do is something they will enjoy.

Review. The first activity of the main lesson segment normally involves the review of previously introduced materials. The review activity makes a direct link to the previous lesson, and provides an indirect assessment of how well the students have retained or learned these materials. It may furthermore function as a springboard to introducing new lesson materials of the day. Some lessons may entirely consist of activities with the purpose of reinforcing and broadening different aspects of the learners' communicative skills. Review activities are usually guided and involve the communicative application of language in different degrees.

Introduction of new materials. Lessons whose purpose it is to introduce new subject materials—such as vocabulary, grammar, or functional skills—make up the large part of a lesson. Skills are introduced in context, one at a time, through meaningful and/or communicative activities. These by and large involve input-based activities interwoven by comprehension checks or guided and controlled communicative learning tasks (see Appendixes 2.2 and 2.3 for sample lessons). Normally, it takes several class periods of skill-building learning activities to give students the foundation to apply a combination of skills in more extended communicative tasks.

Closure/wind-down. The last phase of a class period is generally referred to as the closure or wind-down. Similar to the opener, the wind-down lets students know the class is coming to an end. There are many different ways of concluding a lesson:

- reviewing or summarizing key points of the lesson
- relating the lesson to the course of lesson goals
- making a link to the forthcoming lesson
- encouraging students so they leave positively
- praising students for what they have accomplished during the lesson
- announcing homework assignments
- telling a cultural tidbit or anecdote

Another common and valuable pedagogical practice during wind-down is inviting students to ask questions about the lesson of the day. As an alternative, some teachers encourage their students to write down their concerns and questions and turn them in at the end of class.

Aspects of Planning: Decisions and Considerations

There are many different formats of a lesson plan. Some teachers have daily and weekly outlines listing only types of activities, others write down detailed notes of how and what they teach every day. While the actual form of a lesson plan is in fact less important, what matters most is the thought that has gone into it (Harmer 1991). This involves numerous pre-decisions regarding not only what the lesson will contain but also how to go about attaining goals and implementing pedagogical procedures.

   The following section describes general issues and aspects that need to be considered while designing and planning a language lesson.

REFLECTION

1. Make a list of questions that you need to ask yourself when preparing a lesson. For example, "What activities will I do?"

   _____

   _____

   _____

2. Now read over the list of sample questions in Appendix 2.1 and compare it with your own. Which aspects have you not considered yet?

   _____

   _____

   _____

Learners

Being learner-centered is a vital principle that defines the communicative language classroom. With regard to lesson planning, this requires the teacher to take into account numerous aspects about the learners. Initially, such aspects may include general background knowledge (e.g., age, gender, general learner profile of a particular learning environment), language proficiency skills, other language skills, or their reasons and goals for taking a language course. In the long run, once a teacher gets to know her students and her learner types, she can tailor her lesson plans to her learner needs. Needless to say, because many of these factors may affect the class dynamics and learning outcome, they need to be considered during the planning process.

Contents

When preparing a class, a teacher informally might ask herself, "What am I going to do in class? or "What do I want my students to learn and be able to do?" As these types of questions indicate, the initial decisions teachers have to make deal with the contents of a communicative lesson.

In particular, decisions on content may involve choosing the topic or theme (e.g., shopping, family, traveling), the context (e.g., classroom environment, in the shopping center, informal gathering of friends at home), and some specific linguistic skills. The latter includes functional skills (e.g., asking and answering questions, giving directions, making suggestions, describing, narrating,) and knowledge of vocabulary and grammar skills, which enable the learners to use language in a communicative way. Furthermore, the teacher needs to consider the choice of the materials (e.g., reading texts, video or audiotape materials, textbook-based materials) and, most of all, the activities or learning tasks that engage the learners in the learning process.

Activities/Tasks

Activities are generally considered the building blocks of a lesson. Many teachers organize their lessons around the completion of activities. Some teachers also use activities as an outline for their lesson plans. Traditionally the term **activity** has been used as a general description of what happens in the classroom (Harmer 1991, p. 266). For example, when asked what they do, teachers usually refer to a textbook activity, a group work activity, a fill-in-the blank activity, a listening activity, a vocabulary activity, a TPR (Total Physical Response) activity, a video activity, or a grammar activity. (See "Principle 1: Use Tasks as an Organizational Principle" in the previous chapter.)

The implementation of an activity—that is, the enactment of pedagogical procedures during an activity—involves numerous planning decisions. Thus, a better way of describing activities is in terms of students' engagements (i.e., what students actually do such as listen, fill-in, read, draw, respond, etc.) and teaching routines (i.e., how teachers present an activity/task and manage instructions). Such a distinction takes into account the different roles teachers and students perform, as well as the different ways of mental and physical engagements during the learning tasks. For example, the successful implementation of a pair-work activity in which students ask each other a list of different questions about their daily routines asks for some kind of teaching routine or strategy that tells students what to do and what they need to accomplish. This usually involves the modeling of examples and/or asks for written or oral instructions. Performance of the learning task requires the students to ask each other questions and then record each other's answers. The skills involved include interpersonal skills (listening and creative speaking) and some writing skills, in particular note-taking. When the students have performed the learning task, the teacher needs to follow up or conclude the activity with another teaching strategy to check on students' learning and accomplishment.

Many textbooks often provide only general ideas on how to implement an activity, thus leaving the pedagogical procedure up to the instructor's knowledge and creativity. The successful implementation of a learning activity requires clear understanding of the teaching routines (teacher's tasks) and the students' learning task. In general, one strategy that works well during the planning process is for you, the teacher, to project yourself into the classroom by looking at a learning activity from the teacher's perspective and then from a student's point of view. Placing yourself in the role of a student, you might ask yourself, "Do I clearly know what I am supposed to do?" As a teacher, you may ask, "How does this activity work? How do I need to instruct the students on what to do?"

Many activities follow similar instructional patterns and routines. Some you may recognize from your own experience as a language learner; others you may have to familiarize yourself with and learn about the exact procedures. When in doubt about how a learning task works, try out the activity yourself.

The following list of general questions supports the planning process for communicative-based language activities:

- What is the pedagogical procedure of each activity? How does each activity work? How are students engaging? What is the learner's performance task?
- Do I have a variety of activities?
- How are the activities sequenced?
- Do the activities follow a sequence from input (comprehension-based) to output (production-based) activities (see Chapter 6, Instructional Sequencing and Task Design).
- Do I have a balance between teacher- and student-centered activities?
- How will I introduce the students' learning task? Will I model an example or give instructions in English? (See "Use of Language," later in this chapter.)
- How much time will I need for each activity? (See "Pacing and Timing," later in this chapter.)

Regarding group work activities (see Chapter 8, Developing Oral Communication Skills):

- How will students interact during group work?
- Does the design of the learning task allow for equal engagement of all students?

- Are the students sufficiently prepared to perform the learning task?
- Can students perform the tasks only using the target language?
- How do I introduce the learning task? Do I model or explain the task?
- What instructions will I give?
- How long will the students interact in groups?
- How will I follow up?

Pacing and timing

Pacing is defined as "the extent to which a lesson maintains its momentum and communicates a sense of development" (Richards 1994, p. 122). In this sense, decisions related to pacing and timing constitute important aspects of planning a lesson, and they may influence the effectiveness of a lesson. In particular, here are some questions a teacher may ask herself: How many activities should a lesson contain? How much time will I need for each activity? How much time should I spend on an activity? Should I complete each activity that I have started?

There is no prescribed rule on the length of one activity. While some may last as little as 1 minute, others may range up to 10–15 min or even longer. In general, several factors determine a teacher's decision on how much time to spend on an activity. These are based on the goal and the design of a learning task, the learner's skill performance, the learners' proficiency level, and the class dynamics. As Richards (1994) points out, "teaching involves monitoring students' engagement in learning tasks and deciding when it is time to bring a task to completion and move on to another activity before students' attention begins to fade" (122).

In a beginning language class, activities are normally kept shorter. For example, process-oriented activities that are somewhat repetitive in tasks, or narrow in skill application, should be kept short. There is no need to go through 20 examples just because an exercise contains 20 examples. Students may lose interest or get easily de-motivated. On the other hand, product-oriented or real-life tasks in which students need to apply multiple skills and show creativity, such as writing up role-play or developing interviewing questions, usually require much more time. As a general guideline, aiming at an average length of 8–10 min per activity in a beginning language classroom helps keep the momentum at a steady pace considering the attention span of many learners within a classroom environment.

When determining the pacing and timing for lesson activities, it is also important for teachers to consider the length of the lesson period itself as well as the time of the day when a lesson is taught. In general, the average lesson period is 45–50 minutes long in most college and secondary school environments. Recently, some high schools have adopted block schedules, with periods lasting up to 90 minutes and longer. In particular, in longer class periods, the timing and pacing of activities is momentous. Students are usually most alert during the beginning phases of a lesson, go through a down time, and then pick up steam again toward the end of class. This is contrary to traditional thinking for lesson designs, in which structured activities are done at the beginning; group work, which is usually more skill demanding, occurs in the middle; and controlled activities are at the end. Another factor to be considered is the time of the day. Early morning or late afternoon classes may also affect the lesson and class dynamics.

In conclusion, time management is one of the hardest skills to learn; considering the many factors that play a role, even experienced teachers cannot always accurately predict how long a certain activity will take. The following list of suggestions may help achieve suitable pacing within a lesson (Richards 1994, p. 123):

- Avoid needless or over-lengthy explanations or instructions, and let students get on with the job of learning.
- Use a variety of activity within a lesson, rather than spending the whole lesson on one activity.
- Avoid predictable and repetitive activities, where possible.
- Select activities of an appropriate level of difficulty.
- Set a goal and time limit for activities: activities that have no obvious conclusions or in which no time frame is set tend to have little momentum.
- Monitor students' performance on activities to ensure that students have had sufficient but not too much time.
- Decide ahead of time what activities could be shortened, in case some learning tasks take longer than expected (Jensen 2001—this item only).

ANALYSIS AND DISCUSSION

Comment on the following statements made by two different teachers in their approaches to dealing with pacing. How might their decisions affect their lessons?

Teacher A: "If I see students having a lot of fun and being really engaged, I always let the activity run longer."

Teacher B: "I always time each activity to the minute. I never spend any more time on an activity than planned, and stop and interrupt the activity when the time is up."

Transitions

In breaking down a lesson into sub-activities, teachers need to consider the transitions between activities within a lesson. **Transitions** are boundary markers that signal either the end or the beginning of a new activity or sub-activity. Their purpose is to provide a smooth flow from one segment to another, creating a link between one activity and the next. In this way, the momentum of a lesson can be maintained and students' attention can be held (Richards 1998). Here are some general strategies that allow for smooth transitions between activities:

- allowing for questions
- providing a summary statement
- encouraging and praising students for what they did
- providing an overview of the next activity
- providing a rationale for the previous or next activity
- stating the objective of the next instructional phase

Comprehension checks and assessment of student learning

The ability to monitor and assess students' learning, and their response to teaching, is an essential aspect of teaching. Successful teachers do so continuously—before the lesson, as part of the planning process; during the lesson; and after the lesson. Awareness of students' learning enables teachers to make decisions, modify their instruction, and tailor the lesson to the learners' needs.

When planning lessons, teachers need to consider the following questions on how to monitor students:

- How do I monitor the success of my own instruction?
- How do I know that students understand?
- How will I check on student understanding?
- How do I know that the learning tasks are effective?
- How do I assess that students are learning?

An array of direct and indirect instructional strategies can be applied to monitor and assess student learning. The most common are indirect approaches that simply involve assessing whether and how well students perform the learning tasks. In addition, direct approaches often play an important role as an alternative or as a follow-up strategy. These constitute comprehension and confirmation checks such as asking, "Do you understand? Do you want me to repeat what I just said? Do you want me to give you more examples? Do you want me to explain this one more time? Is this what you mean? So, you are saying . . .?" Alternative strategies are asking students to provide answers themselves, such as giving English word translations, explaining grammatical concepts, or commenting on their cultural understanding.

Use of language

Most practitioners of CLT promote instructional strategies that maximize the use of the target language (TL) in the classroom. While some go as far as using the TL exclusively, others believe that using English is a necessary pedagogical practice to make oneself understood in the classroom. Planning ahead and thinking about strategies (e.g., how to model and explain new vocabulary; how to simplify the use of the TL; how to use gestures, repetitions, and comprehension checks) allows teachers to maximize the use of the TL. Furthermore, careful planning results in fewer attempts to use English in the classroom.

Recent work and review

A vital aspect of daily lesson planning involves integrating the work that students have done in previous lessons. Because learners' skills do not necessarily evolve in a linear fashion or in the order they were introduced, most materials need to be reintroduced, often also re-explained, and they usually require a great deal of additional targeted practice. **The decision on when and how to review previously introduced content is determined by the teacher.** This decision needs to be based on learner needs, on their performance—for example, on in-class or homework assignments—and/or on the difficulty of the learning tasks and learner developmental issues (see Chapter 4, Grammar and Language Learning). As commonly practiced by many teachers, the review of previously introduced materials is best integrated at the beginning of a lesson period.

Instructional aids and materials

The use of instructional aids and materials is part of every lesson. It is imperative that teachers know how to use an overhead, CD player, and television or DVD player, including the remote control, LCD panels, or other projection devices. Problems with instructional aids may interrupt the flow of a lesson, and some lessons may render themselves ineffective, particularly if your lesson depends on the use of these instructional tools. Needless to say, having the right handouts, overheads, pens, or whatever aids needed helps the teacher to function smoothly in the classroom.

Possible problems

It is important to anticipate where lessons may break down. Teachers need to think about what might go wrong, especially when teaching a grammar point or activity for the first time. Ask yourself questions such as, "What parts of the lesson may be difficult for the students? What kinds of questions can the instructor expect? Will there be problems with student-to-student interactions? At the same time, be aware it is impossible to anticipate all the problems that may occur, especially if you are teaching a topic for the first time. Despite potential problems, have the courage to let the students know when you do not have an answer to a question, and deal with the issue later.

Rationales

A rationale is a teacher's underlying reason for why and how he teaches in a particular way. Rationales reflect a teacher's belief and philosophy as well as an understanding of learning processes, language acquisition, and effective teaching procedures. Usually, teachers do not spell out these thoughts, but when asked they can justify their pedagogical procedures. This means effective teachers consciously think about the design of a lesson and how to implement it. For example, this includes questions such as: How do I pair up students? What is my reason for asking students to work in groups of three or two? Do I pair up quiet with talkative, or strong with weak students (for more detail, see Chapter 8, Developing Oral Communication Skills)? What is the learning outcome of this task? In which skills do students engage? For students it can be very helpful to learn about a teacher's rationale as well. It lets them know that a teacher is prepared, has thought about his teaching, and has a reason for why he teaches in a certain way. Students who are informed about a teacher's rationale are normally more willing to go along when a teacher tries out something new.

Homework

Final considerations of lesson planning should be given to homework assignments. There are several common practices for assigning homework to students. One way is to write the homework on the board at the beginning of the class. Jensen (2001) suggests posting the homework consistently in the same place, so students know where to check for it. The advantage of this practice is that students can write it down before the final hectic minutes of the class when they are packing up and running out the door. It is also less stressful for most teachers, since it is often easy to forget to write down the homework at the end of the class. Providing homework at the end, however, has the advantage that the teacher can tailor the assignment better as a follow-up to what has been accomplished in class.

What kind of homework should you assign? What kind of learning tasks should the students get engaged in? It would seem obvious that work done outside of class should somehow be tied to the objectives or learning tasks of a lesson. It is this author's position that the goal of homework has a multiple function. On the one hand, it should be an extension of class. As Lee and VanPatten (2003) emphasize, it "should not necessarily [be] something different or unenjoyable" (p. 92). It is imperative for students to use their time outside of class to explicitly review and reinforce grammatical structures and vocabulary. In-class exposure alone does not give students enough time to learn these linguistic tools. Priority of classroom time should be allotted to communicative interaction between students, and between teachers and students. However, this does not suggest that learners should be assigned pages of drill-type activities as they are often found in lab and workbooks. Learning tasks assigned as homework should also adhere to design principles of being meaningful and communicative. This means, for students to be able do the learning tasks, a form-meaning connection should be a prerequisite. Furthermore, students should engage in activities that use up a great deal of class time and that are frequently best done at the learners' own pace, as is the case with reading and extensive writing activities.

Homework assignments should also encourage autonomous thinking and help students develop learning strategies that do not require the intervention of a teacher (e.g., self-checking and correction of errors, working with dictionaries, etc.).

The following questions may help with this decision:

- What kind of lab work or computer software is available to the students?
- Are learners encouraged to try out the language in a creative way?
- Are the learners engaged affectively—that is, are they encouraged to bring in their own experiences?
- Are the activities as varied as in-class activities?

Backup/contingency plan

Lessons rarely take place exactly as they are planned. There are always times when activities go faster than expected. Even experienced teachers cannot always predict the length of an activity. That is why it is a safer strategy to be over-prepared and plan out every minute in a lesson, especially as a novice teacher. One should always have a backup plan or a repertoire of activities ready at any time. For example, general review activities, generic game activities, or even a discussion about how students are learning are some instructional strategies that lend themselves well as backup activities at any time.

In the previous sections, I have discussed numerous aspects and issues that teachers need to consider when planning a lesson. The planning process involves many decisions that need to demonstrate a clear understanding of the composition of a whole lesson, its subcomponents, and how to go about implementing the pedagogical procedures for each segment. Furthermore, a teacher should be able to support his choice and implementation of each activity with a clear rationale. Appendix 2.3 provides an example of a lesson plan that describes in detail the student learning tasks, (i.e., how students engage) the pedagogical procedures (teacher tasks), the teacher's rationale, and the skills that are addressed in each lesson phase. Nevertheless, it needs to be kept in mind that decisions and strategies on how to implement specific pedagogical procedures (e.g., whether or not, and when and how, to group students in different ways) are based on different instructional philosophies as well as theoretical and empirical-based research findings in second language learning and teaching. Examples of various communicative-based teaching practices will be discussed in more detail throughout this book in the context of teaching different language skills.

How Does a Teacher Go About Planning?

There are different ways to go about daily lesson planning. The most dominant and widely promoted model of lesson planning is based on Tyler's (1949) **rational-linear framework**, which involves four steps that run sequentially. The teacher

1. specifies objectives;
2. selects learning activities;
3. organizes learning activities; and
4. specifies methods of evaluation.

This model follows a **macro** or a **top-down approach** to curricular planning, which means the teacher determines lesson objectives first and then proceeds to the selection or development of learning activities. However, as research has shown, teachers rarely apply such an "end-product" approach to planning lessons in their daily practices. Teachers do not state their goals in terms of students' behavioral objectives (Richards and Lockhart 1994; Bailey 1996). They rather tend to state what they do in terms of instructional objectives; that is, they refer to the contents (e.g., a grammar topic or vocabulary) or activities they do, such as read a text, listen to a CD, or do activities in the textbook (Brindley 1984). Most teachers apply an activity-based approach to daily planning. In other words, rather than meeting particular objectives, they blend content with activity and generally focus on their particular students (Clark and Peterson 1986). Furthermore, they tend to visualize, plan, and organize their lessons as sequences of activities (Freeman 1996).

Although commonly practiced by many teachers, an exclusively activity-based approach to daily planning has some pitfalls. For it to be effective, the planning process needs to involve critical questioning of the pedagogical value of the learning tasks, if an actual performance-based learning outcome is to be achieved. This requires a conscious reflection and an understanding of the nature of the learning tasks, in particular the kind of cognitive learning behavior in which the learners engage. Thus, a conscious reflection focusing on actual performance-based learning outcome or objectives can serve as a vital strategy that is conducive to successful lesson development. It sets the direction regarding what skills students are to develop. And furthermore, it functions as a measurement device and control check for attaining students' performance-based skills.

Understanding Goals and Objectives

Clear lesson objectives are generally regarded as an important part of developing effective lesson plans (Farrell 2002). Expressing goals and lesson objectives in terms of actual student performance is essential, particularly with regard to achieving proficiency-based language skills. The following subsections point out the difference between goals and objectives and further demonstrate how to formulate clear lesson objectives.

Goals (aims)

In curriculum discussions, **goals** or **aims** are general statements that describe the focus and general purposes of a curriculum. In general, the purposes of goal statements are (Richards 2001, p. 120) as follows:

- to provide a clear definition of the purposes of a program
- to provide guidelines for teachers, learners, and materials writer
- to help provide a focus of instruction
- to describe important and realizable changes in learning

It is common practice for teachers to provide a brief goal statement on their course syllabi. General goal statements, describing the focus and ideology of an author's approach, are also usually found in the preface of commercial language teaching textbooks. Most current language textbooks also provide an overview of the contents, listing more detailed goal statements for each chapter. Typical examples are statements like these: In this chapter, you will learn how to . . .

- identify people and things in the classroom.
- describe everyday activities.
- indicate likes and dislikes.
- form the singular forms of present-tense verbs.

As seen from these examples, detailed goal statements are generally introduced by a phrase such as "You will learn (how) to . . ." Rather than simply naming a subject matter or contents, describing goal statements in this way emphasizes the changes in learners that will result (Richards 2001).

Behavioral or performance-based objectives

While goal statements are generally very broad, **objectives** are specific descriptions of what learners are expected to be able to do at the end of the period of instruction (Richards, Platt, and Platt 1985). Shrum and Glisan (2000) consider well-written objectives to be those describing a learner's performance or having an observable outcome (e.g., a product).

Performance-based objectives and outcomes

Students will be able to:

- give directions to various destinations using a map
- follow directions given, using a map
- use basic courtesies when asking for directions
- recognize the differences between American and German city maps

Linguistic skills/content knowledge

Students will be able to apply these terms and concepts:

- links, rechts, geradeaus [left, right, straight ahead]
- Strasse, Ampel, Platz [street, traffic light, square]
- names of buildings (review)
- prepositions: vorbei, entlang, hinunter [passed, along, down]
- command forms (review)
- basic questions (review)
- polite questions

FIGURE 2-2 Sample statement of objectives

The outcome or product should also be measurable or assessable. Figure 2-2 demonstrates an example of performance-based objectives of a teacher's three-day lesson plan. It also lists the essential skills and content knowledge required to achieve the objectives.

When planning lessons, having clear objectives that precisely state what the teacher wants students to learn in terms of expected performance has numerous advantages. It provides an overall lesson focus and direction (Farrell 2002). The teachers as well as the students come to have a more realistic idea of what can be achieved in a given course or lesson. The lesson plan helps guide the selection of appropriate learning tasks that are centered on the learners and that support the development of real-life and proficiency-based language skills. Furthermore, when learners can demonstrate what they can do with the language, the teacher can more easily assess the success of a lesson. In addition, having clear goals also increases teacher and learner accountability.

In writing performance-based objectives, the language a teacher uses is important. Expressions such as "will study," "will learn about," and "will prepare" are avoided because they do not describe the result of learning but rather what students will do during a course. Objectives are best described with phrases like "will learn how to" and "will be able to" (Richards 2001). Similarly, some practitioners suggest that teachers avoid using verbs that cannot be observed or measured, such as *know* or *understand*. Instead the plan should contain specific action verbs such as *present, identify, list, explain, name, compare, contrast*, and *debate* (Kowalski, Weaver, and Henson 1990). Using such verbs makes it easier for teachers to design performance-based lesson activities. At the same time, they make it easier for students to understand what will be expected from them (Farrell 2002).

The following lists are examples of performance-based objectives for different skill areas as commonly found in beginning language programs.

Speaking (presentational mode of communication)

- Using different cues, students will be able to exchange personal information (e.g., by performing a communication gap[1] activity).
- The students will be able to introduce themselves, saying what their names are and where they are from.
- Students will be able to spell their names orally.
- Students will be able to describe their families by identifying their family members, saying where they live, what they do, how old they are, and what they are like.

Listening (interpretive mode of communication)

- Students will be able to understand and carry out instructions given orally (Richards 2001, p. 126).
- Students will be able to answer questions of differing levels based on what they have heard on an audiotape.

Reading (interpretive mode of communication)

- Students will be able to identify the main topic (theme) of a given text form.
- Students will be able to scan a text locating specifically required information.
- Students will be able to identify the main ideas of a text.

Process-oriented objectives

One disadvantage of stating objectives in terms of student performance is that they do not capture a learner's whole learning experience. Performance-based objectives are unsuited for describing many other important aspects of language use or learning (Richards 2001, p. 128). Many nonlanguage outcomes go beyond the content of a linguistically oriented or task-based syllabus and so cannot be easily measured. Such outcomes include understanding of culture, critical thinking, or literary appreciation.

Richards (2001) suggests that objectives need not be limited to observable outcomes. They can also describe processes and experiences that seem to be an important focus of a lesson or curriculum. Objectives describing such processes are known as **process objectives** (Richards 2001). For example, the American Council on the Teaching

---

[1] A communication or information gap activity involves the exchange of information that is known by only one or some of those who are participating.

of Foreign Languages (ACTFL), in its National Standards for Foreign Language Learning (1996), identifies a number of objectives for language programs that relate to the philosophy of cultural pluralism. Cultural pluralism refers to "a situation in which an individual has more than one set of cultural beliefs, values, and attitudes" (Richards, Platt, and Platt 1985, p. 93). For example, the United States has many minority or ethnic groups that coexist side by side, sharing the values of a larger society while maintaining their own cultural identities. Here are some examples of describing nonlanguage outcomes or process objectives:

- Students demonstrate their understanding of the concept of culture through comparisons of the cultures studied and their own.
- Students acquire information and recognize the distinctive viewpoints that are available only through the foreign languages and the curriculum.

Guidelines for Lesson Planning

The following guidelines describe different stages of the lesson planning process. Although the planning steps are presented here in a linear way, it has to be noted that lesson planning is not a linear process, but rather is done recursively—meaning that while planning lessons, most teachers progress through these stages in a circular fashion, constantly evaluating the learning tasks and readjusting their plan based on their learners' needs and goals.

Identify the main teaching points and learning activities

Identify the contents, the main goal, the topic, and the materials of your lesson. Select concrete functional skills and learning activities that integrate these skills (e.g., asking and answering questions, making declarative statements, listing items, describing, naming objects, talking about everyday events and actions, performing, communication gap activities, and role plays). Identify vocabulary and grammar skills that are needed to perform the communicative tasks. Also think about the contexts in which the learners would perform these tasks. If you use a textbook, look at the beginning or the end of a chapter of your textbook, where you will normally find general goal statements of what the textbook tries to accomplish.

The following questions suggested by Lee and VanPatten (2003, p. 77) may assist you with the planning process:

- What vocabulary do learners need to have under control to complete this task?
- What grammar or pieces of grammar do the learners need to be able to comprehend or produce to complete this task?

- What functions of language will they need to perform (e.g., asking questions, making declarative statements, listing items, narrating with connective devices)?
- What content (e.g., cultural information on a given topic) needs to be included?

When you select learning activities, identify the actual skills in which the learners engage when performing these activities. This allows you to see if the skills that are required to perform an activity are in alignment with the pedagogical purpose of your lesson. With traditional exercises, it is normally fairly obvious what these skills are, because they primarily require the manipulation of grammar forms. This is not the case with communicative tasks that involve multiple skills such as applying targeted vocabulary, grammar, and language functions in single or combined modes of communication. Furthermore, a task analysis is vital for several other reasons. It helps you: 1) arrange activities along appropriate lesson segments—from input to structured/guided to open-ended application; 2) plan lesson steps in a sequence that support cognitive processing that is manageable to students; 3) modify the contents of activities; and 4) vary pedagogical procedures in implementing activities. For example, some learning activities lend themselves best for individual work, others for social interactions. Most communicative activities also require introductions and follow-ups.

Here are some general questions that help with the planning process:

- Which stage of practice is to be attempted?
- What are your learners' needs?
- In what kinds of skill practice do the learning tasks engage the learners?
- Do the learning activities/tasks provide a variety of skill practice (input, controlled/structured, open ended)?
- Are the learning activities/tasks contextualized?
- Do the learning activities/tasks integrate different modes of communication? Which kind?
- Do the learning activities/tasks allow for different interactions?
- Do the learning activities/tasks engage the learners in communicative language skills (e.g., asking somebody a question versus doing a grammatical drill)?
- Do the learning activities/tasks emphasize a performance-based learning behavior (e.g., real-life language use versus manipulating grammar forms)? What is the pedagogical procedure for each lesson step; that is, how will you enact each step?

Prepare a rough outline of lesson activities

Determine a feasible communicative or performance-based learning task as a lesson goal or objective. Until students are ready to perform communicative language skills in an open-ended forum, they usually require several language lessons of guided instruction. While the initial focus of lessons usually involves skill-building tasks, a controlled or open-ended learning task or activity, with a focus on a communicative language act, can serve as a final lesson objective. For example, Lee and VanPatten (2003) suggest that instructors could adopt an information-exchange task as a lesson objective. In other words, the end-of-lesson objective could be an activity involving a communicative exchange that is unknown to the participants, such as finding out information from classmates. The information to be found out could be authentic or predetermined—and thus controlled, if provided by the teacher and given only to some students. Even if a task involves only a narrow range of skills and is applied within a narrow range of context, a task can be given a communicative goal. Ask yourself the question, "What makes (a) feasible lesson objective(s) that engages the learners in a communicative language act and that is also conducive to the development of open-ended communicative language application?"

Organize and sequence the activities. Well-planned and structured lessons consist of lesson tasks (see Principle 1 in the previous chapter on the description of lessons with task dependent and task independent designs) that are **scaffolded**, progressing step by step so that one activity becomes the basis for the subsequent one. This means the learning tasks are not only contextualized but also centered on one theme. In reality, however, it is often difficult to maintain one single theme that connects all lesson tasks. Often there is unfinished business from previous classes, or particular student needs to be addressed. Nevertheless, lesson activities should be arranged and presented in thematic, coherent blocks as much as possible.

- Sequence the learning tasks from input to output, from teacher- to student-centered activities, from written to oral application, from yes/no and either/or questions to one-word or short phrase answers.
- Break down the activities into subtasks.
- Check for flow and a logical sequence of all tasks.
- Create additional tasks and materials, or modify tasks if the skill progression from one task to the next is too demanding.
- Arrange lesson tasks in coherent blocks that are contextualized and pertain to one theme.
- Write down the estimated length of time.

Reevaluate and reorganize.
- Check for flow and transitions.
- Check for variety of skills and modes (e.g., presentational skills (listening or speaking); interpersonal skills; controlled versus open-ended communicative application).
- Check for variety in teacher-to-student and student-to-student interactions.

I. Lesson preparation
   ❏ I had a clearly developed lesson plan.
   ❏ I was clear on each segment of the lesson, and knew what I was doing and what my students were supposed to do.
   ❏ I successfully achieved the objective(s) of my lesson.

II. Methods/Instructional strategies
   ❏ I had a variety of activities.
   ❏ There was an appropriate balance of structured and open-ended/communicative activities.
   ❏ My activities focused on different skills (e.g., speaking, writing, reading, listening, or grammar).
   ❏ All the learning activities were contextualized.
   ❏ The activities were appropriate for my students' skill level.
   ❏ I integrated a variety of small-group interactions.
   ❏ I integrated cultural instruction and information in my lesson.
   ❏ I made use of smooth transitions between activities.
   ❏ I used the class time efficiently.
   ❏ My lesson was appropriately paced for the level and needs of my students.
   ❏ My students had a clear idea of what was expected of them; that is, my instructions, modeling, and/or examples were clear.
   ❏ I facilitated students' responses and gave corrective feedback.
   ❏ My explanations were clear, brief, and accurate.
   ❏ I made effective use of appropriate teaching materials (e.g., board, visuals, audiovisual aids).
   ❏ I equally integrated all my students.

III. Language use
   ❏ I maximized the use of the target language.
   ❏ My use of language, pronunciation, intonation, and fluency was appropriate and acceptable.
   ❏ My use of English was appropriate to my students' needs.

IV. Affective aspects
   ❏ There was active and lively participation in the classroom.
   ❏ There was a warm, open, and accepting atmosphere in my class.
   ❏ My students felt comfortable and relaxed, free to participate and ask questions.
   ❏ I treated my students fairly, impartially, and respectfully.
   ❏ I encouraged my students to do their best.

V. Classroom management
   ❏ I was able to control and direct the class.
   ❏ I dealt appropriately with unexpected problems both during and outside the lesson period.

VI. Assessment of student learning
   ❏ My students had ample opportunities to use the target language.
   ❏ My students were actively engaged throughout the whole class.

FIGURE 2-3 Self-evaluation checklist

❏ I knew when my students had trouble understanding.
❏ I was aware of individual student needs.
❏ I feel my students were learning what I intended them to learn.
❏ I need to focus on the following issues:

_____

_____

_____

FIGURE 2-3 (*Continued*)

- Check for timing and pacing.
- Check your instructional aids.
- Check your pedagogical procedures; that is, is it clear to you how to implement each lesson phase and activity?

Make a final plan

Depending on your comfort zone and experience, write down as many detailed notes as you need. Some teachers prefer to use index cards; others have a summary of their lesson plan on a single piece of paper. Use the method that works best for you, one that allows you to unobtrusively consult your plan, if necessary.

- List the final sequence of learning tasks that you plan to implement.
- Make any additional notes that serve as quick reminders when implementing the lesson.

Evaluating Lesson Effectiveness

It is important to stop and think after giving a lesson whether it was a good one or not, and why. As many novice teachers have reported (personal communication to author, 2002), initially it is difficult not to think about a class that you have just finished teaching. Even if you feel your class went just the way you planned, the success of your lesson may depend on many different factors. Sometimes the factor is the dynamics of a group, or the way you feel on a particular day. In most cases, however, the factor is an evolving understanding of how students learn and how we teach, which are the primary reasons we would approach the same class in a different way the second time around. Reflecting about your classes is important because it may guide your planning for consecutive classes. The best time to mark down your impressions or changes is right after the class, or when preparing for the following class. Figure 2-3 provides a list of general questions that may aid you during your reflection.

ANALYSIS AND DISCUSSION

Imagine you have just come out of a lesson—whether your own, or one that you have observed—and wish to assess how effective it was. By what criteria will you evaluate it? In this box, you will find a list of criteria that have been suggested by teachers; you may wish to add more. Rank them in order of priority, in your opinion: from the most important to the least important. You may, of course, put two or more criteria at the same level if you think they are of the same importance.

a) The learners were active all the time. _____

b) The learners were attentive all the time. _____

c) The learners enjoyed the lesson, were motivated. _____

d) The class seemed to be learning the material well. _____

e) The lesson went according to plan. _____

f) The language was used communicatively throughout. _____

g) The learners were engaging with the foreign language throughout. _____

h) _____

i) _____

Source: P. Ur, *A course in language teaching: Practice and theory* (Cambridge: Cambridge University Press, 1996), 219.

Conclusion

Lesson planning is a dynamic process involving teachers making choices before, during, and after each lesson. As pointed out in this chapter, thinking about the many decisions and issues ahead of time has numerous benefits. In light of many unpredictable situations that an instructor may face in the classroom, planning will make the teaching process go more smoothly, alleviating the pressure of having to make quick decisions at any moment. The practice of thorough lesson planning is an essential part of teaching. It is particularly important for novice teachers who do not yet have an experienced repertoire of routines that they can fall back on in case of unexpected situations.

Despite the many benefits of planning, a lesson plan is not written in stone. However carefully prepared, few lessons work out exactly as planned. Furthermore, a lesson plan is not meant to keep a teacher from making changes, if the situation warrants. Flexibility in carrying out a plan is one sign of a good teacher. To same extent, teachers must rely on their experience and instincts to do the right thing when the unexpected occurs. For example, sometimes it may be necessary to deviate from the original lesson plan because one student raised an issue that the teacher perceives to be relevant for the other students. At other times, it may be appropriate to make a procedural change as a means of promoting the progress of the lesson, to eliminate some steps, or to accommodate the students' learning styles if the original plan has not accounted for them. Nevertheless, it is always safer to have an original lesson plan that you have thoroughly thought through and that you can return to when needed.

Checking chapter objectives

Do I know how to . . .

- ❏ state reasons for why lesson planning is important
- ❏ structure a language lesson
- ❏ describe and define different phases of a language lesson
- ❏ identify aspects that need to be considered when planning lessons
- ❏ define lesson goals and objectives
- ❏ go about planning lessons

Explorations

TASK 1: LESSON PREPARATION

Following are seven questions about lesson preparation. Start by answering them yourself, in writing. (If you are a beginning teacher with limited experience, then note how you hope to prepare lessons yourself, or how you have done so in teaching practice.)

Questions on lesson preparation

1. How long before a specific lesson do you prepare it?
2. Do you write down lesson notes to guide you? Or do you rely on a lesson format provided by another teacher, the course book, or a Teacher's Book?
3. If so, are these notes brief (a single page or less) or long (more than one page)?
4. What do they consist of?
5. Do you note down your objectives?
6. Do you actually look at your notes during the lesson? If so, rarely? Occasionally? Frequently?
7. What do you do with your lesson notes after the lesson?

Source: P. Ur, *A course in language teaching: Practice and theory*. (Cambridge: Cambridge University Press, 1996), 215.

TASK 2: INQUIRY ON LESSON PREPARATION

Interview at least two language teachers who are experienced and (as far as you can tell) conscientious and competent professionals. Ask them the same questions, stressing that you want to know what they actually do in daily practice, not what they think they ought to do!

_____

_____

_____

TASK 3: OBSERVATIONS

Observe a typical beginning or advanced language lesson. How is the lesson structured; that is, what sequence of activities or segments make up the lesson?

Application

TASK 4: WRITING LESSON OBJECTIVES

The following is a list of objectives. Which of these statements are measurable? Provide a rationale for your answers, and if necessary, rewrite the objective that can be measured.

Objective	Rationale/Revision
1. Students will understand the difference between the two different forms of past tense: **preterito** and **imperfecto**	
2. Students will understand the difference between the two forms of *to be*, **ser** and **estar**, and use these two forms when they describe themselves.	
3. In this lesson, I will teach the students to pronounce the German *–ch* (e.g., as in words such as **ich, frech, doch**).	
4. The learners will be able to spell their names.	
5. Students will perform an information-exchange task.	
6. Through this lesson, students will improve their understanding of Swedish culture.	
7. By the end of this class, students will be able to introduce themselves, saying who they are and where they come from.	
8. Students will know the numbers.	
9. Students will be able to describe their family.	
10. Students will write down two-paragraph weather reports focusing on conveying meaning while using appropriate second-year grammar.	
11. Students will demonstrate their ability to read imperfect tense by reading a short paragraph and by formulating questions about the reading.	
12. Students will listen to weather reports and deduce meaning by listening to the main points.	

TASK 5: PLANNING A MINI-LESSON

The content of your lesson is the alphabet. Develop an outline of a sequence of activities in which you introduce either parts of or the whole alphabet. When planning your lesson, consider the following questions: In what communicative contexts do we need to know the alphabet? How do we use it? What particular language skills are involved?

TASK 6: ASPECTS OF LESSON PLANNING

You have been asked to substitute in a beginning language class. Your colleague hands you the following lesson plan (see Figure 2-4). What aspects of this lesson plan are clear to you? What questions would you ask your colleague teacher?

_____

_____

_____

_____

_____

_____

10:30	Take attendance.
10:30–10:40	Administer quiz.
10:40–10:45	Warm-up: review time and expressions. I talk about my schedule—when I get up, when I go to school, etc. Call on students and ask when they get up, go to school, etc.
10:45–10:55	**Du hör/ du sager** [you hear it/you say it] exercise: Practice saying/understanding time. Students in groups of four take turns reading aloud times and finding them on their sheets.
10:55–11:10	**Vem i klassen exercise** [who in the class?] (bingo): Review of new verbs and word order for questions and answers. Working from the sheets, students form and reply to questions, trying to get a whole row completed.
11:10–11:20	Ask if there are any questions, review concepts, return journals, and assign this week's topics.

FIGURE 2-4 Lesson plan of a novice teacher of a beginning Swedish class

APPENDIX 2.1

Sample questions when preparing a lesson

What do I want my students to learn from this lesson?

What are my objectives?

What is the topic or theme of this lesson?

What resources (textbook, workbook, other sources) are available?

What instructional materials do I need?

How will the lesson connect to what students already know?

How will I begin and conclude the lesson?

How do I know that my students are learning?

How will I arrange student groupings?

When and how do I use the target language?

What activities will I use?

Why should I teach this lesson?

How well do I understand the content of the lesson?

What activities will be included in the lesson?

Do I exactly know what the students have to do during each activity?

Do I exactly know how to set up an activity?

How much time will I need for each activity?

How will I organize the lesson into stages or sections?

What will I do if I have too little or too much time?

APPENDIX 2.2

Finnish Lesson Script

Step 1: Teacher introduces herself by saying the following phrase. She repeats this phrase at least three to four times.

> Minä olen Heljä.
>
> Hauska tutustua.

Step 2: The instructor writes this phrase on the board:

> Minä olen Heljä.
>
> Hauska tutustua.

Step 3: The instructor plays a DVD showing several different situations where two Finnish people (P1 and P2) introduce each other. Finnish people tend to be rather informal; that is why they often introduce themselves by using their first name.

Scene 1:   P1:   Hei.
                       Minä olen Otto.
                       Hauska tutustua.
              P2:   Hei.
                       Minä olen Matti.
                       Hauska tutustua.

Scene 2:   P1:   Hei.
                       Minä olen Tiina.
                       Hauska tutustua.
              P2:   Hei.
                       Minä olen Saana.
                       Hauska tutustua.

The instructor briefly mentions what the phrase "Hauska tutustua" means, writing its English equivalent, "Nice to meet you," on the board.

Step 4: The instructor (T) points at the phrase Minä olen _____, gesturing to the whole class as a group to repeat this phrase several times.

Step 5: The instructor (T) walks up to at least three different students (S), introduces herself in Finnish, and gestures for the student to do the same.

T: Minä olen Heljä.
         Hauska tutustua.
S: Minä olen Pete.
         Hauska tutustua.

Step 6: The instructor gestures for the students to get up and introduce themselves to at least four other students.

Step 7: The instructor plays a DVD showing several different situations where children (C) introduce themselves.

Scene 1:   C1:   Hei.
                       Kuka sinä olet?
              C2:   Minä olen Liisa.
Scene 2:   C1:   Hei.
                       Kuka sinä olet?
              C2:   Minä olen Timo.

Step 8: The instructor writes the following two phrases on the board:

Kuka sinä olet?
Minä olen Heljä.

Step 9: The instructor models the following dialogue with at least three different students:

Minä olen Heljä.

Kuka sinä olet?

Step 10: The instructor gestures for at least three different students to ask a fellow student:

Minä olen _____.

Kuka sinä olet?

Step 11: The instructor gestures for the students to get up and introduce themselves to at least four other students.

APPENDIX 2.3
Sample Lesson

Proficiency Level/Class: 3rd year high school/1st year college

Estimated Time of Lesson: 50 min

Theme/context:

Performance outcomes/objectives:

Content knowledge/skills:

Resources/materials needed:

Outline/Description of learning/teaching activities

Segment	Time	Teacher Tasks	Student Learning Tasks	Rationale	Skills
Warm-up	11:30	1. The instructor starts the class by announcing that they have won the lottery. She hands each student an envelope containing the paper money that the student has won. 2. The instructor provides an example by saying how much money she has won. 3. The instructor asks several students about their winnings.	Students respond to teacher's questions stating how much money they have won.	The activity is to get students' attention.	interpersonal skills (listening/speaking); short answers (phrases)

(Continued)

Segment	Time	Teacher Tasks	Student Learning Tasks	Rationale	Skills
	11:35	1. The instructor poses the following question in present indicative: "Was machst du mit dem Geld?" [What do you do with the money?] 2. The instructor provides several examples describing how she will spend the money and guesses what some of her students may do. Example: "Ich glaube, Gerd kauft sich ein Auto. Gerd, ist das richtig?" [I believe, Gerd buys himself a car. Gerd, is this correct?]	The students listen.	The new phrases are modeled.	
Input Phase (written)	11:40	1. The instructor mentions that unfortunately, the money is only fake money. The instructor mentions that she would like to find out what everybody would do if this were real money. Before that, however, she wants to know what some of the Germans would do. 2. The instructor announces that they will do a matching exercise from the book entitled: *Was würden Sie machen, wenn Sie 10 Millionen Euros gewinnen?* [What would you do if you won 10 million Euros?] 3. The instructor explains the task, asking students to match a list of questions with personal statements. She provides the following example: Statement: "Ich weiß noch nicht, was ich mache." [I am not sure yet, what I am going to do.] Question: "Wer ist sich noch nicht sicher?" [Who is not sure yet?]	The students carry out the task individually and silently, matching a question with a personal statement.	• Doing this task individually allows all learners to get engaged. • Doing this reading task silently allows for more processing time. • It provides written exposure to numerous examples that use the new forms. • The learning task is meaningful; that is, students have to comprehend the language to successfully complete the task.	interpretive (reading)

Segment	Time	Teacher Tasks	Student Learning Tasks	Rationale	Skills
		The instructor asks follow-up questions using the new grammatical form, for example: "Wer würde sich eine Eigentumswohnung kaufen?" [Who would buy a condominium?]	The students orally respond to the teacher's questions, using the new grammatical structure.	By following up on the matching task, the teacher provides feedback. The activity involves a meaningful and guided application of the new grammatical structure.	interpersonal skills with a focus on listening; one-word answers
Input phase (aural)	11:50	1. The teacher introduces a listening activity from the textbook. Different people describe what money means to them and what they would do with it. 2. The instructor asks her students to read the instructions and the eight statements in the textbook, for example: 1. "_____ lange Urlaub machen and dann wieder arbeiten" [1. _____ taking a long vacation and then back to work]. 3. The instructor plays the tape twice and briefly pauses the tape after each speaker.	The students match eight statements with three different German speakers (Jens, Lucia, and Elke) and write down each speaker's name next to the statement.	The activity provides additional exposure to the new forms, this time with a focus on the aural mode.	interpretive (listening)
Controlled and guided practice	11:58	The instructor asks follow-up questions, for example: "Was würde Jens tun?" [What would Jens do?]	The students orally respond to the teacher's questions. They rephrase the speakers' statements using the new grammatical structure.	• The activity follows up on students' comprehension. • Students apply new forms in a meaningful context. • More comprehension-based practice and exposure to the new forms is provided.	interpersonal mode

(Continued)

Segment	Time	Teacher Tasks	Student Learning Tasks	Rationale	Skills
Guided/ controlled application	12:00	1. The instructor mentions that she is curious to find out what everybody in the class would do if they had real money. 2. She poses questions: "Was würdest du mit dem Geld machen?" [What would you do with the money?] What would you do if you had won that much money in the lottery? 3. The instructor passes out a handout with several statements: "Ich würde anderen helfen. Ich würde ein Auto kaufen. Ich würde eine Reise machen." [I would help others. I would buy myself a car. I would go on a trip.] 4. The instructor asks students to write down their name underneath each statement describing how they would spend the money, and to list their classmates' names, based on how they believe they would spend their money.	Students write down their answers, describing how they would spend the money.	• This teacher's comment provides a transition for the next activity. • This activity introduces and models conditional phrases in writing. • The design of this activity allows for a communicative follow-up. • Students apply new form in writing first, which allows for more processing time. • This activity also provides controlled practice.	
Extended practice	12:10	The instructor asks several students about what Rolf (a student in class) would do with his money. She elicits answers from several students to see if they agree. She concludes the activity by asking Rolf if his classmates' guesses are correct.	Students provide answers describing how they would spend the money and guess what their classmates would do.	• The activity allows for the communicative application of new structures asking students to guess how others spend the money. • It further provides enhanced interaction among students. • Students apply prepared and spontaneous speech.	interpersonal skills (listening and speaking); short phrases

Segment	Time	Teacher Tasks	Student Learning Tasks	Rationale	Skills
Grammar review	12:15	The instructor writes the following two sentences on the board: "Ich werde ein Auto kaufen." [I will buy a car.] "Ich würde ein Auto kaufen." [I would buy a car.] In English, she elicits students' comments about the difference between **werden** and **würden.**	In English, the students explain the difference between **werden** and **würden**.	This non-communicative activity allows the teacher to see if the students understood the concept of the new grammar rules.	
	12:18	The instructor writes the whole paradigm on the board: "Ich würde . . . du würdest . . ." [I would, you would, etc.] She briefly summarizes the new grammatical topic.		An explicit summary of the newly introduced grammar concept is provided.	
Wind-down	12:20	The teacher asks the students to take out their vocabulary notebooks. On the board, the instructor lists vocabulary from the textbook. She writes the German word as well as its English equivalent. The vocabulary deals with student finances. She models the use of the words, provides examples from her own life, and asks students questions about their own expenses. For example: T: "Wieviel Geld gibst du für Benzin aus?" [How much money do you spend on gas?] S1: "$50 in der Woche" [$50 per week] T: "Wer bezahlt deine Versicherung?" [Who pays for your insurance?] S2: "Meine Eltern" [My parents]	The students orally respond to the teacher's questions.		
	12:25	The teacher announces that there will be a quiz on Friday. Class ends.		The teacher foreshadows what is going to happen later on during the week.	

APPENDIX 2.4

Lesson plan form

Proficiency Level/Class: _____

Estimated Time of Lesson: _____

Theme/context:

Identify the theme and context in which the students perform the learning objectives, e.g., school, classroom environment.

Performance outcomes/objectives:

List the performance-based learning outcomes. For example, "Students will be able to list personal objects."

Content knowledge/skills.

If applicable, list the content skills such as vocabulary or grammar skills (e.g., personal objects such as pencils, books, calculator; first and second person in present tense of the verb to *have*.

Resources/materials needed.

List the primary resources used for this lesson, for example, realias, textbook "Title."

Outline/Description of learning/teaching activities.

In the following, provide a clear description for each learning task or segment of your class.

Student Learning Tasks	Teacher's Task (teaching routine)	Rationale
Instructions:	*Instructions:*	*Instructions:*
Describe or provide an example of the student's learning task.	*Clearly describe how you go about teaching this activity. Also provide an estimated amount of time.*	*Provide a brief pedagogical rationale that explains why you have chosen this instructional strategy, how learning is taking place and how your approach or technique is supporting the learner's learning process.*
Example	**Example (8-10 min)**	
Communication Gap Activity	1. I assign students in pairs asking students to work with the person who sits next to them.	**Example**
In pairs, students perform a communication gap activity, asking and answering questions about personal possessions. Example: Student A: "Do you have a computer?" Student B: "Yes, I do. Do you have a TV?"	2. I hand out the instructions, explain the activity, and ask one pair to model it.	Students practice listening and speaking asking personal questions in a communicative way. The activity is controlled and guided.
See handout X or activity X, on p. XX.	3. While students work on the activity, I circulate around class.	
	4. After the activity, I call on several students to report what they have found out.	

CHAPTER 3

Getting Started: Introducing Vocabulary

Smell it, touch it, hear it, say it, see it, write it, feel it.

In this chapter you will learn about

- cognitive processes relevant to the learning of vocabulary.
- methodological principles that support the presentation of vocabulary input.
- different techniques for presenting new vocabulary.
- multimedia-based input.

REFLECTION

What kinds of vocabulary instruction have you experienced as a learner of (a) foreign language(s)? Which strategies worked best for you? Please provide concrete examples.

_____

_____

_____

What does it mean to know a word? Do you just know the meaning(s) of a word, or is there other knowledge associated with being able to say you know a word?

_____

_____

_____

Introduction

As the goal of communicative language teaching (CLT) is for learners to develop communicative skills, the learning and acquisition of vocabulary plays one of the most vital roles in becoming proficient in the target language (TL). Having knowledge of vocabulary involves a variety of other subskills. For example, for speakers to communicate effectively through different modes of communication (e.g., orally or in writing), they need to know how to spell and pronounce a word as well as understand its grammatical behavior. Words also have multiple meanings, and how the meaning of a word is interpreted depends greatly on the context in which it is used. As some scholars claim, there is no doubt that when learning another language, the acquisition of new vocabulary is a long-term process.

Learning vocabulary might even be considered the most challenging component of learning a language.

The focus of this chapter is first to discuss cognitive processes that support the learning of new vocabulary, and second to consider a variety of approaches to introducing vocabulary that are commonly used in beginning second language classroom environments. These include teacher-led or direct strategies, and implicit approaches that encourage learners to decipher words from contexts.

Guiding Principles

For decades, teachers have been using the board or an overhead projector to present drawings and photos as instructional resources. Today televisions with video or DVD players, or even computers with access to the Internet, have now become part of the standard equipment one would expect to find in foreign language classrooms. With the rise in computer use, multimedia presentational tools, such as Microsoft PowerPoint or Apple Keynote, have increasingly gained in popularity.

While numerous instructional resources are at an instructor's disposal, the question that often arises is how to most effectively employ these resources to introduce vocabulary in the classroom.

Introduce vocabulary through multisensory and multimedia input

While the term *multimedia* is commonly associated with technology, in cognitive psychology **multimedia** is defined in a more general sense. As Mayer (2001) puts it, "Multimedia refers to the presentation of material using both words and pictures" (p. 1). By *words*, he refers to materials presented in verbal form, such as those using printed or spoken text. By *pictures*, he refers to materials presented in pictorial form, such as those using still graphics—including illustrations, graphs, photos, or maps—or those using dynamic graphics, including animation or video. In a foreign-language-learning context, printed text also includes text in the TL and the learners' native language (L1).

In foreign language learning, creating multimedia input serves several pedagogical purposes: First, multimedia input can support the comprehension process, allowing the learner to make a meaningful connection between the TL input—that is, the written (symbolic) and verbal (phonological) representation—and the visuals. That is to say, multimedia input can help with the learning process by giving learners the opportunity to tag a new or existing semantic concept with a phonological and written representation. Second, this type of input can support the retention process, helping embed this information in the learner's long-term memory.

Considering the multiple skill components that are involved, a multimedia approach to presenting vocabulary raises many questions. In particular, these include the following: Do students learn better from words and pictures than using words alone? Would it be simply sufficient to present new vocabulary in word lists matched with TL equivalents? What effect does a simultaneous presentation of two types of input (e.g., aural plus written words, or aural plus images) have on learners' comprehension and retention process? Why is multisensory input important?

Drawing on research in cognitive psychology as well as what is known about how the brain stores information, numerous arguments can made in support of presenting input in different modalities. Let us take a look at brain research first.

For a long time, neuropsychologists believed in a clear division of brain functions. They associated motor behavior, creativity, emotions, and images with the right brain hemisphere, and analytical and language activities with the left brain hemisphere. As Linke (1996) contends, such a view is no longer supported; now it is believed that during most activities, multiple parts of the brain are activated. This is also the case for language learning and acquisition.

"We have observed cases with right-handed people whose language centers are located in the right brain hemisphere—in other words, in the opposite hemisphere. These cases provide evidence counter to previously held beliefs, which promoted one dominating brain hemisphere in control of language skills. We have also observed cases where language was distributed across both brain hemispheres while it required activation of both hemispheres to perform language acts" (Linke 1996, p. 28; trans. K. Brandl).

According to the most recent findings on brain research, the human brain is viewed as a system of neural networks that keep organizing themselves. During a learning activity this means the activation of not only one connection, but a network of connections (see Bohn 1999, 82).

"As connections are formed among adjacent neurons to form circuits, connections also begin to form with neurons in other regions of the brain that are associated with visual, tactile, and even olfactory information related to the sounds of words. These connections give meaning to the sounds of words. Some of the brain sites for these other neurons are far from the neural circuits that correspond to the component sounds of the words; they include sites in other areas of the left brain hemisphere and even sites in the right hemisphere. The whole complex of interconnected neurons that are activated by words is called a **neural network**" (Genesee 2001, p. 2).

How and what causes these connections to form can be further explained by research in cognitive psychology and second language acquisition (SLA). Underwood (1989a) suggests, "A commonplace principle of human learning [is] visual memory. We remember images better than words; hence we remember words better if they are strongly associated with images" (p. 19). This rationale is based on the **dual coding**

theory, which postulates that the mind contains a network of verbal and imaginal—that is, nonverbal—representations of words (Paivio 1986). "Information in a symbolic representation [e.g., written words] is stored in the verbal system, and information in a nonverbal, analog representation [e.g., images] is stored in the nonverbal system" (Chun and Plass 1997, p. 66). In other words, the mind has the capacity not only to process but also to encode information in multiple ways, which ultimately also enhances the learner's ability to recall information.

Ample research supports the use of visual input in language learning. For example, Kellogg and Howe (1971) showed that students learned foreign words associated with actual objects or imagery techniques more easily than words without these associations. What happens during this process? As learners are trying to build connections between words and pictures, they are able to create a deeper understanding of these vocabulary items than they can from words or pictures alone (Mayer 2001). Another study by Chun and Plass (1996) that investigated the effectiveness of multimedia annotations—text, pictures, and motion video—on vocabulary acquisition also showed that recall of vocabulary words with visual annotations (text + picture and text + video) was better than words with text-only annotations.

In a more recent study, Jones (2003) analyzed what kinds of annotation are most beneficial to students in creating comprehensible input, as well as in their impact on retention, when presented in the auditory mode. Furthermore, she investigated the impact of annotations on retention. The students could look up a word and retrieve its textual translation, or a visual image, or a textual translation and an image. They also could listen to an audio rendering of the word. Results show that students with access to visual images outperformed all other groups on a delayed posttest, while there was no difference between the visual group and the visual-textual group. This finding strongly suggests that the images helped the learners retain the new words better than the representation of a written translation did.

One study also investigated the impact of simultaneously presented aural and written input, that is, whether hearing the words as they were seen improved retention levels (Greifnieder 1995). Results indicated that audio support had no positive effect on the retention of words, suggesting to the researcher that visual perceptions dominated audio input in processing and retaining information.

A few studies also investigated the effect of multimedia on different learner types and abilities. For example, several studies have shown that multimedia effects are stronger for students who have a high ability to generate, maintain and manipulate mental images, that is, who have high spatial ability than for those who have low spatial ability (Mayer and Gallini 1990; Mayer and Sims 1994; Mayer et al. 1995). Some studies on illustration effects also attribute advantages of providing visual aids to learners with low verbal ability (Peek 1993).

The combination of written and aural input may also have a redundancy effect. For example, research on how children learn new vocabulary in their native language (L1) has shown that children's intact storage capacity of the visual short-term memory can compensate for weak verbal storage and processing capacities (Pickering and Gathercole 2004).

Proceed from input to output, dealing with visual and auditory input in separate tasks

Proceder del input al output, separando el input visual del output auditivo

The review of research just presented clearly suggests the power of images on creating input and their long-term effect on retention. The visual memory seems to be dominant with many learners, which also explains why many of them, in particular beginning language learners, prefer this kind of input (Brandl and Bauer 2002). Drawing on the theory of information processing, the exposure to written information allows for more processing time than does aural input. When learners are encountering new verbal information for the first time, it takes time to anchor this information in the brain. Visual input has the advantage that it remains longer in learners' short-term memory, while the memory span of auditory input lasts only a split second. In addition, the processing of spoken and written text involves similar cognitive processes because they are symbolic representations of information (Chun and Plass 1997).

Despite the advantage of visual input, the fact that most learners direct their attention to the visual channel warrants a pedagogical approach that gives equal attention to the development of auditory skills and the need for additional practice. This means, to create binding between the image and the aural input, the written input needs to be gradually removed during the sequence of instruction. A prolonged input phase consisting of several comprehension-based activities (e.g., pointing, T/F, yes/no, matching activities, using gestures) that lead up to output tasks (written and oral) must therefore be considered beneficial to the learning and retention process of the targeted words.

Use culturally authentic visuals and illustrations

usar ilustraciones visuales culturalmente auténticas

As mentioned earlier, a word can have multiple meanings. These meanings can be **connotative**, words that have secondary meanings and are defined within a cultural context. For example, with some words we associate images that are generic and universal, such as *airplane*. Others have culture-specific connotations attached that imply a whole range of other notions. Food items, breakfast, family, house, and so on are good examples that illustrate this point well. Let us look at the word *bread*. Depending on the culture, bread tastes different, consists of different ingredients, looks different, comes in different shapes and sizes, is packaged differently, is bought several times a day, is eaten in different ways, and so forth. Showing a picture of bread that is not culturally authentic would portray only a simplistic view of the culturally loaded notion of bread.

When teachers introduce new words in the beginning classroom, initially it may not be critical to convey the full range of meaning, for example, all the **denotative** (core) and connotative (secondary) meanings of a word, but an authentic depiction enhances cultural literacy without the need to resort to words.

Introduce vocabulary in context using real and authentic language

As research has repeatedly pointed out, context plays a major role in language learning. It enables language learners to process and produce a foreign or second language (Swaffar, Arens, and Byrnes 1991). According to the *American Heritage Dictionary* (2000), the word **context** is defined in two ways: (1) "The part of a text or statement that surrounds a particular word or passage and determines its meaning" and (2) "The circumstances in which an event occurs; a setting." In other words, context demonstrates the actual use of language. One might even go so far as to concede that the actual meaning of a word is established only through its context. Furthermore, context assists in language comprehension. Simply put, the more familiar learners are with the context of a text or situation, the easier it is to understand the contents of a text or function within a situation (see Chapter 7, Developing Listening Skills and Chapter 9, Developing Reading Skills).

The emergence of teaching language in order to achieve proficiency-based outcomes has also underscored the importance of meaning and context in comprehension and production. As pointed out before, one of the assessment criteria underlying the proficiency description refers to context. Examples of contexts that are likely to be included at the beginning and intermediate level are basic travel and survival needs (food, clothing, hotel accommodations, transportation, and the like), handling daily social encounters appropriately, and coping with school- or work-related situations (Omaggio-Hadley 2001). Other settings and topics that provide us with rich contexts are students' backgrounds, family, and interests.

The context for language practice should be derived from culturally authentic sources (Omaggio-Hadley 2001). These include real or simulated texts such as travel documents, hotel registration forms, biographical data sheets, train and plane schedules, restaurant menus, newspapers, magazines, personal letters, e-mail, literary texts, and others. Other sources constitute video/DVD and audio materials, radio, TV, and the Internet.

While the use of authentic materials is not without its challenges (see Ch. 7 and 9 for further discussion on task adaptation), such materials have developed a reputation of being more difficult to integrate than edited materials are (Chaves 1998). This situation has led some teachers to create their own contexts, materials, or stories in trying to reduce the complexity of language as it appears in authentic documents. There is no doubt, because of many reasons, language teaching warrants the use of scripted or semiscripted materials. In case a teacher or curriculum designer decides to do so, here are some questions to consider when creating such inauthentic materials: Is the story motivating? Is language used in a culturally authentic and meaningful way? Does the context simulate or represent an authentic version of the situation?

Introduce vocabulary thematically or through thematic units

Introducir el vocabulario en unidades temáticas coherentes.

The previous section has provided several arguments illustrating the importance of introducing vocabulary in context. A closer look at a specific context illustrates that it consists of a set of themes or units that are more closely connected. For example, within the context of the classroom there are topics such as objects in the classroom, things you do in the classroom, sounds that you hear in the classroom, and typical phrases used in the classroom. Introducing vocabulary in chunks or units has implications for comprehension and the learning process. Research has shown that the two mental processes that play a major role helping us anchor words into our existing networks are creating associations and sorting (Rohrer 1993). This means that information is not stored randomly in our brains, but in association and connection with existing information.

Through **word associations**, we understand "ways in which words come to be associated with each other and which influence the learning and remembering of words" (Richards, Platt, and Platt 1992, p. 406). Bohn (1999) describes this process with the following analogy: Words are like knots in our brain, which are connected through many threads. There is not only one, but many different and separate networks that are also connected with each other. Thus one can say that words are simultaneously part of different networks, for example the semantic, the morphologic, the affective, and the phonetic network. The wider and deeper a word is anchored in all the networks, the more securely it is stored in the memory, therefore making it easier to access.

Sorting is another important process that enhances our thinking. While existing vocabulary is already stored in an organized way in our brain, learning new words means anchoring them into already existent networks. The brain does so by sorting the information and associates it with existing information. It is like putting the word "banana" into the fruit basket, another basket that has yellow objects, and a basket that has sweet and eatable things. This strategy, furthermore, allows the brain to access the information, and once again retrieve it.

Presentar el vocabulario en forma interactiva (estudiante-estudiante/ estudiantes-profesora)

Present input in an interactive way

While vocabulary presentations such as the use of pictures, objects, or multimedia often result in a teacher-centered position, there is a need to make the presentation interactive. From a cognitive and pedagogical point of view, interaction between the teacher and the students and between students has many benefits. An interactive presentation implies that the learners cognitively engage with the input; that is, they do something with the input. For example, students mark off words they recognize, answer questions, sequence, or write a summary in L1 or the TL. As the learners became engaged, the pacing is slowed down; this avoids overloading the memory, and a better transfer of information can occur. The quality of the task in which the learners engage, also plays an important role. As Mayer (2001) reminds us, it is not as much what the learner does (his behavior) but the depth of the cognition that a learner engages in that determines a meaningful outcome. For example, asking the learners to repeat words engages the learners in doing something. That is not to say that repetition is not important. On the contrary, it helps students with the pronunciation and with building a phonological memory initially. However, repetition is a cognitively low engaging activity, which does not require much thinking. On the other hand, naming a word, or providing its opposite (antonym), or using it in context are cognitively more engaging.

Realizar el Significado y uso del vocabulario usando aplicaciones multimedia

Enhance vocabulary input through the use of multimedia applications

Several arguments can be made in support of multimedia input and the use of multimedia presentations in the classroom. First, compared to traditional media (e.g., the board or overhead projector), multimedia presentation tools allow us not only to convey information in a wider variety of modalities (e.g., oral, textual, pictorial, animated) that can be combined in different ways but also to do so more efficiently. For example, images, pictures, or animations can be presented orally alone or in combination with textual representations, which can be presented simultaneously or in sequence.

Second, the use of technology-based applications to present multimedia input has additional advantages. The vast amount of culturally authentic materials and images that are available on the Internet can be brought into the classroom and integrated into the curriculum. Such integration can be achieved in only limited ways through traditional means such as objects or props.

The question that arises is how can teachers present and design multimedia materials? Mayer (2001) has proposed the following research-based principles for the design of multimedia messages such as PowerPoint slides: He claims that students learn better when corresponding words and pictures are near rather than far from each other. Mayer refers to this concept as the principle of **spatial contiguity**. As he further points out, cognitive theory explains this effect: "when words and pictures are presented next to one another on the page, the learner is more likely to be able to hold corresponding verbal and visual representation in working memory at this same time" (p. 189). The same principle applies to what is called **temporal contiguity**. In other words, students learn better when corresponding words and pictures are presented simultaneously rather than successively.

Mayer (2001) further suggests that students learn better when extraneous words, pictures, and sounds are excluded rather than included. "When extraneous material is presented, working memory may become cluttered with irrelevant words and/or irrelevant images, making it more difficult to hold corresponding relevant words and images in working memory at the same time." He calls this the **coherence** principle. In the context of multimedia-based vocabulary presentation, the playing of background music, as some teachers like to do, may thus have a more distracting than enhancing effect and may be better used before or after the actual presentation.

Another advantage of using multimedia presentations is its animation capability, which has become a standard feature in multimedia applications. The question that arises is whether animations further enhance the learning process. A study by Chun and Plass (1996) investigated this issue by comparing the effects of annotations illustrated with static pictures to annotations using motion video sequences. They found that static pictures proved more effective than animated annotations. Such results could be explained by the generally unfixed, transient nature of motion sequences, which may lead to a lower amount of invested mental effort—that is, a more superficial processing than the use of static pictures (Chun and Plass 1996; Salomon 1983; Schnotz and Grzondziel 1996). When too many visual images are presented at once, the memory seems to more easily experience overload and the learners may have to split their attention. In some instances, however, animations may be superior to a static picture because they allow for a better demonstration and transfer of the actual meaning of a word such as an action verb or a semantic concept.

In conclusion, the use of multimedia presentation tools allows for a wide range of vocabulary introductions that can make for a great extension of traditional means such as props or textbook pictures. Of course, while such presentation tools tend to put the teacher into a teacher-centered role, principles such as providing vocabulary input in a step-by-step mode and making the learning interactive need to be equally applied.

Promote a deeper level of processing

Better learning will occur when a deeper level of semantic processing is required by the learner. That is, according to Baddeley (1990), elaborative rehearsals and richer levels of encoding positively impact the learning process. Rich levels of encoding can be achieved by asking students to manipulate words, relate them to other words and to their own experiences, and to deduce the meaning of new words by immersing them in contexts that are familiar to them. An example demonstrating such a strategy is giving students a calendar and asking them to figure out the days of the week from the calendar alone (see examples in Appendix and in the following section). Such instructional strategies are generally referred to as **discovery learning**, which has many pedagogical advantages. It provides a learning situation similar to what students encounter in a true immersion environment. It promotes higher-level thinking skills by asking students to apply their background knowledge and encourages them to use their decoding skills to extract new information from context.

Traditionally, this technique has been reserved for intermediate and advanced language learners. Although the implementation of discovery learning activities is more challenging with beginning-level language learners due to students' small range of vocabulary, it is not impossible. The implementation of discovery activities requires two preconditions: First, the words whose meanings are to be deciphered need to be embedded in contexts that provide ample clues to make this possible. This presupposes the careful selection of texts. Second, discovery activities require students to activate their background (preexisting) knowledge. Commonly observed student practices have demonstrated that they prefer to look up the meaning of unknown words in dictionaries, based on a rationale that the meanings of the words that they receive are more precise and less ambiguous in this way. Consequently, sufficient and systematic strategy training and/or a combination with the use of other techniques are often asked for to make the presentation of new vocabulary in this way successful (see Chapter 9, Developing Reading Skills, for further discussion). Classroom activities, which demand deeper processing, can also be time-consuming and hard work for students and teachers. However, the critical thinking and problem-solving skills are greatly enhanced by such a learning process (Sökmen 1997).

Vocabulary Presentation Techniques

Building up a repertoire of many different techniques and knowing how to use them should be every language teacher's goal. In this way the instructor can design and present classroom instruction in a variety of ways, reaching out to as many different learning styles as possible. Furthermore, the instructor can identify which technique prevails as the most adequate and effective for a particular teaching situation. Last, having mastered these techniques allows the instructor to better focus on the learner, and to monitor whether and how learning is taking place.

Making use of realia (cultural objects, pictures, photographs, drawings)

Realia (cultural objects). Using this technique to present vocabulary, the instructor integrates authentic cultural objects into the lesson. Realia include items such as clothing, classroom objects, kitchen objects, real fruit, and so forth.

ANALYSIS AND DISCUSSION

Before you continue to read, record some strategies that you can employ to anchor meaning in different ways when you introduce vocabulary to your students.

_____

_____

_____

_____

ILLUSTRATION 1

The following lesson outline illustrates a range of steps on how a teacher introduces fruit items:

Steps	Teaching routines
1	Mr. Santana, the teacher, introduces three to four pieces of fruit to his class a. by showing a piece of fruit b. by writing the word for that fruit on the board c. by having students pronounce the new word
2	Teacher has students pick up a piece of fruit from a basket. For example, he tells a student to give him—or simply to pick up—the banana.
3	Teacher has students draw each piece of fruit being introduced on separate pieces of paper.
4	Teacher has students hold up the piece of fruit, that is, the piece of paper with the drawing of the fruit that he asks for in the TL.
5	Teacher sends a student on a shopping spree. He spreads the fruit around the classroom and hands students a shopping list he made up earlier. The student is to pick up each item as it appears on the list. The teacher posts the shopping list on the board for all the students to see.
6	Teacher asks students either/or questions. Example: Would you like to have an apple or a pear?
7	Teacher asks students to name the fruit in chorus.
8	In pairs, one student names the fruit item, and the other holds up the corresponding drawing.
9	Teacher asks individual volunteers to name all the fruit items being learned. If they name each fruit correctly, he offers them a piece of the fruit and invites them to eat it.

The lesson in Illustration 1 shows a sequence of sample steps that lead students from input or comprehension-based activities toward oral output.

1. List all the different ways the activity above engages the learner. What different senses and modalities does the teacher make use of?
2. Provide a brief pedagogical rationale for each separate step. Use the chart in Appendix 3.3.

Pictures, photographs, and drawings. Not all objects can be brought into the classroom. Making use of pictures, photos, and still shots taken from videos allows the teacher to illustrate the meaning of vocabulary items. Visuals can also be used to demonstrate the meaning of concepts such as these: locations (in front of, behind, etc.), emotions (laughing, angry, etc.), time (morning, evening, early, late), and so on. Recently published textbooks contain numerous pictures, photos, and drawings. Other sources for visual materials include magazines, newspapers, and the Internet.

The value of pictures as a means to demonstrate meaning hardly needs to be justified. One word of caution, however, needs to be expressed. Since pictures can "express a thousand words," they need to be carefully selected to make sure the visual element contributes to the comprehension of the new concept, object, or word.

Textbook pictures. A picture or a drawing is used to illustrate the meaning of new words or vocabulary. The drawings are presented with a short caption in order to anchor the new vocabulary in the learner's memory.

ILLUSTRATION 2

Students are instructed to read the captions of the drawings silently before engaging in an activity such as filling out a questionnaire. That allows them to demonstrate that they understand the meaning of the targeted words. An alternative strategy is to have the teacher ask the students to focus on one picture at a time while reading the descriptions for each picture out loud. In the latter version, the students are also introduced to the pronunciation of the words; for example, they establish the meaning of the new word through the picture and connect the word to the written and aural form (Figure 3-1).

Using multimedia presentation tools

An alternative option to introducing vocabulary is the use of multimedia presentation tools such as Microsoft PowerPoint or the Apple Keynote program. The universal access to the Internet allows for an easy integration and demonstration of multiple authentic images. The following illustration demonstrates how PowerPoint can be used to introduce

Usar formas de presentación multimedia.

VÍNCULOS

To practice present tense of *hacer, poner, salir, traer,* and *oír*
- SAM-OneKey: WB: 4-12, 4-13, 4-14 / LM: 4-36, 4-37
- Companion Website: AP 4-4
- IRCD: Chapter 4; pp. 140–141.

3. Present tense of *hacer, poner, salir, traer,* and *oír*

El padre pone la mesa.

La madre oye música y también las noticias.

La hija trae las tostadas a la mesa.

El hijo hace la cama.

El abuelo pone la televisión.

La familia desayuna y sale.

Note. Some of the house chores shown in the illustration serve as a preview for those that will be presented in the next lesson, where students will be talking about their home/apartment and the house chores they do.

You may wish to present the expression *tender la cama*. Point out that *tender* is a stem-changing verb.

Picture 1: The father sets the table.

Picture 2: The mother listens to music and the news.

Picture 3: The daughter brings the toast to the table.

Picture 4: The son makes the bed.

Picture 5: The grandfather turns on the television.

Picture 6: The family has breakfast and leaves the house.

FIGURE 3-1 Doing things at home
(Source: De Castells et al. (2006), p. 140.)

vocabulary describing materials and designs. In this lesson, the names of the clothes have already been introduced. Figure 3-2 shows four slides excerpted from a multimedia PowerPoint presentation.

ILLUSTRATION 3

1. Slides 1 and 2 show two examples of how the instructor introduces the words *polka-dotted* and *woolen* in a beginning French class. The teacher shows several slides, pronounces the words, and has the students repeat them. For example, she would say in French: "This is a polka-dotted dress."
2. Slides 3 and 4 are used for follow-up practice. Regarding slide 3, the instructor asks in French: "Which of these items are made of wool?"

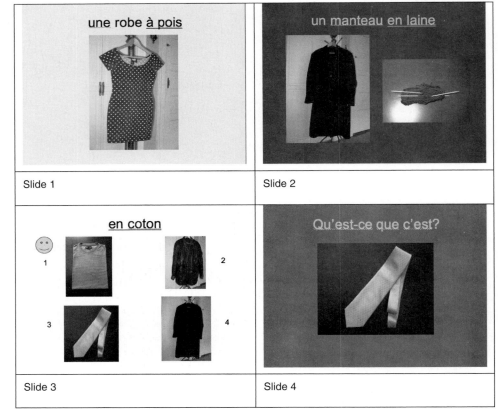

FIGURE 3-2 Sample PowerPoint Slides

The word *en laine* [woolen] can be hidden, if the instructor decides only to focus on aural comprehension.

3. In slide 4, the instructor shows single clothes items and asks questions such as: "What is this?" and "What is it made of?" The instructor has the option to show the correct answer in writing or only orally.

Making use of the learners   Aprovechar el conocimiento de los estudiantes.

The classroom is a rich resource for teaching daily vocabulary. Initially, instructors can make use of objects that they can find in the classroom, and they can also make use of the learners, their features, and their belongings to teach vocabulary. Lee and VanPatten (2003) point out that "involving learners heightens attention and adds a personal element to the class as learners become active participants in the teaching process" (p. 51).

ILLUSTRATION 4

The following example demonstrates a 2- to 3-minute-long lesson script of an instructor using learners in the classroom to teach the vocabulary associated with clothing.

Schauen wir uns einmal im Klassenzimmer um. Schaut mal… was trägt jeder… was hat jeder einzelne an. *[Instructor points at John, gesturing for him to get up and come to the front of the classroom.]* John, komm mal hierher. Komm mal nach vorne. *[Instructor points at John's jeans.]* John trägt heute Jeans. Das sind Jeans oder man sagt auch Bluejeans. *[Instructor looks around in the classroom, pointing at different students.]* Wer trägt noch Jeans. Tom trägt Jeans. Judith hat auch Jeans an. Camille trägt Jeans.

[Instructor goes to the board and writes down "die Jeans."]

[Instructor has the whole class say in chorus, "die Jeans."]

[Instructor points at John's shirt.] Was hat John noch an? Er trägt auch ein Hemd. *[Instructor points at John's shirt.]* Das ist ein Hemd. Wer hat noch ein Hemd an? Oh, ja. *[Looking around in the classroom.]* Pete trägt ein Hemd. Tom hat ein Hemd an. *[Instructor points at his own shirt and says:]* Ich trage ein Hemd.

[Instructor goes to the board and writes down "das Hemd."]

[Instructor has the whole class say in chorus, "das Hemd."] [Instructor points at John again and asks.] Was trägt John noch? *[Instructor says: He is wearing sneakers.]* Oh, ja. Er trägt Turnschuhe. Er hat Turnschuhe an. *[Instructor is looking around again and asks:]* Wer trägt auch Turnschuhe? Dann stehen Sie bitte auf! Danke, setzen Sie sich. *[Instructor asks the students to stand up and then sit down again if they are wearing sneakers.]* Haben Sie ein Hemd an? Dann stehen Sie bitte auf! *[Instructor asks the students to stand up and then sit down again if they are wearing a shirt.]* Tragen Sie ein Hemd oder ein T-Shirt? [Pointing at a student, instructor asks a student whether he is wearing a shirt or a T-Shirt.]

> Let's take a look around at what everybody is wearing. Take a look... what is everybody wearing... what is each of us wearing. *[Instructor points at John, gesturing for him to get up and come to the front of the classroom.]* John, come here. Come to the front. *[Instructor points at John's jeans.]* John is wearing jeans today. These are jeans, or you can also say blue jeans. *[Instructor looks around in the classroom, pointing at different students.]* Who else is wearing jeans? Tom is wearing jeans. Judith is also wearing jeans. Camille is also wearing jeans. *[Instructor points at John's shirt.]*
>
> *[Instructor goes to the board and writes down "die Jeans."]*
>
> *[Instructor has the whole class say in chorus "die Jeans."]*
>
> What else is John wearing? He is also wearing a shirt. *[Instructor points at John's shirt.]* This is a shirt. Who else is wearing a shirt? Oh, yes. *[looking around in the classroom]* Pete is wearing a shirt. Tom is wearing a shirt. *[Instructor points at his own shirt and says:]* I am wearing a shirt. *[Instructor points at John again.]*
>
> *[Instructor goes to the board and writes down "das Hemd."]*
>
> *[Instructor has the whole class say in chorus, "das Hemd."][Instructor points at John again and asks:]* What else is John wearing? *[Instructor says: He is wearing sneakers.]* Oh, yes. *[Instructor is looking around again and asks]* Who else is wearing sneakers? Please, stand up! Thanks, sit down. *[Instructor asks the students to stand up and then sit down again if they are wearing sneakers.]* Are you wearing a shirt? Then please stand up! *[Instructor asks the students to stand up and then sit down again if they are wearing a shirt.]* Are you wearing a shirt or a T-shirt? [Pointing at a student, instructor asks a student whether he is wearing a shirt or a T-Shirt.]

ANALYSIS AND DISCUSSION

List as many vocabulary items as you can think of that can be introduced in this way. Here is one example: colors.

_____

_____

Making use of body language

Some meaning of words can easily be illustrated through mime, gestures, physical actions, and modeling. For example, some meanings of words can be identified by their sound, such as whistling, coughing, knocking, clapping, and so on. Other word meanings, such as those of action words, can be demonstrated by acting them out. For example, concepts like running, walking, 'open your books,' and so forth are easy to introduce in this way. Actions can be performed by the instructor, or as in Illustration 4, he can make use of the students, or by both, as we will see in the following description of Total Physical Response. Other rich resources are videos and films to demonstrate action.

A technique for teaching vocabulary that has actually been formalized as a method is the **Total Physical Response**, generally referred to by practitioners as TPR (see Asher 1969). Developed by James Asher of San Jose State University in the early '70s, TPR in its simplest terms refers to learners carrying out the actions commanded by the instructor. Combining words and phrases with related gestures, TPR works well for introducing many different vocabulary items (e.g., action verbs, colors, prepositions, physical objects) and also grammatical structures (e.g., command forms, prepositions, direct and indirect objects, pronouns (see Chapter 4, Grammar and Language Learning) in meaningful and comprehensible ways.

ILLUSTRATION 5

The following lesson script from a Spanish TPRS[1] lesson outlines three different steps the instructor would follow to introduce new vocabulary by using gestures or actions.

Step 1

As you say each word, demonstrate the associated gesture. Present the vocabulary in groups of three words or phrases at a time. This will allow students to focus on the new terms and will facilitate retention. Have students practice the gestures as you say the words.

Instructor	Students
says un **gato** [a cat] and performs a gesture repeats the word and gesture several times	imitate the gesture
says **triste** [sad] and performs a gesture repeats the word and gesture several times	imitate the gesture
says **agarra** [grab] and performs a gesture repeats the word and gesture several times	imitate the gesture

Step 2

After presenting a group of words, rearrange the order in which you say the three words to check comprehension.

Instructor	Students
says **un gato** [a cat] **agarra** [grab] **triste, agarra, un gato, triste, un gato, un gato, agarro, triste, un gato**	perform the gesture based on the word they hear

Step 3

After students have practiced the gestures a few times, have them close their eyes and perform the gesture for each word as they hear you say it. Practice the gestures and words extensively, and assess comprehension by saying the words and having students demonstrate the gestures.

Keep the pace lively so that students are challenged and focused on the activity at all times. Monitor one or more of your students who tend to acquire language slowly.

Making use of preexisting knowledge and contexts

A common technique for introducing new vocabulary is to present unfamiliar words in a context that is familiar to a student. This technique asks the students to infer the meaning of a word by making use of their pre-existing knowledge. Many documents such as forms, charts, ads, cartoons provide many contextual clues that support the comprehension process. Some of these clues can often be found within the text; other clues students may be able to use based on knowledge they have about the type of document, information they expect to find in a particular type of text, or accompanying pictures, photos, or drawings. The teaching of such strategies is important, as it is ultimately impossible to teach and explain every single word that is introduced in a text. This section examines some of these techniques in more detail (also see Chapter 9 on Developing Reading Skills).

Students come to class with a great deal of preexisting knowledge or background, which is often referred to as knowledge of the world (Omaggio-Hadley 2001). This knowledge means they know how life functions in their own environment. To illustrate this point within the context of traveling, students have filled out forms, dealt with authentic documents, made plans, arranged schedules, and studied calendars. Students are most likely familiar with the general contents of such documents and their layouts. Tapping into the students' preexisting knowledge is one strategy that allows instructors to exemplify the meaning of new vocabulary in the TL. Furthermore, the students have acquired a complete language system. This means, depending on the TL, that students may detect some similarities between the TL and their own mother tongue. An example of this phenomenon is the cognate. **Cognates** are defined as words that are similar in form and meaning to words in another language (Richards, Platt, and Platt 1992). Another example is an internationalism. These are words that have been adopted in the same or in a similar form (pronunciation, spelling) by many different languages and share the same meaning. For example, the word *music = musik = musique = musika = muzika = müzik*. Students may also make use of contextual information to decipher the meaning of new words. They may recognize personal names or place names, or extract meaning from examples that are repeated in different ways.

ILLUSTRATION 6

The following example from a beginning German textbook (see Figure 3-3) demonstrates the instructional strategy of introducing new words through context. In this example, it is assumed that the context is familiar to the students. The teacher does not introduce any of the words, such as *Nachname, Vorname, Geburtsdatum*, and so forth [family name, first name, birth date], nor are any translations provided. Students are instructed to read or scan[2] the text before engaging in an activity that tests their comprehension of some of the newly introduced words. Why does this example work well

Thema 1

Persönliche Angaben°

information

Wer sind diese Leute? These people come from three different German-speaking countries. Scan the information, then read the summary about each person. Mark what is correct (**das stimmt**) and what is incorrect (**das stimmt nicht**) in each summary.

Vorname: Harald
Nachname: Rohmann
Geburtsdatum: 23.5.56
Geburtsort: Dessau
Beruf: Hochschullehrer
Wohnort: Magdeburg
Straße und Hausnummer: Bahnhofstraße 20
Land: Deutschland

Vorname: Daniela
Nachname: Lercher
Geburtsdatum: 7.1.1974
Geburtsort: Graz
Beruf: Studentin
Wohnort: Wien
Straße und Hausnummer: Mozartstraße 36
Land: Österreich

Vorname: Anton
Nachname: Rüthi
Geburtsdatum: 14.10.53
Geburtsort: Luzern
Beruf: Architekt
Wohnort: Luzern
Straße und Hausnummer: Schulstrasse 8
Land: Schweiz

FIGURE 3-3 Personal information
(Source: R. Di Donato, M. Clyde, and J. Van Sant, J. *Na klar! An introductory German course*, 2nd ed. (New York: McGraw-Hill, 1995), p. 24.)

with most Indo-European languages? Why are students perfectly capable of answering the T/F questions? The title of this exercise, "Persönliche Angaben" [Personal Information], indicates the theme foreshadowing what information students will find in the text. Furthermore, the three different examples contain cognates (e.g., Architekt, Studentin, Name), place names, numbers, and addresses, all of which allow the students fairly accurately to predict the meaning of words such as *Vorname, Beruf, Wohnort, Geburtsdatum, Geburtsort* [first name, occupation/profession, etc.].

Another technique for introducing new vocabulary is to use the students' exclusive knowledge of the TL itself. This obviously presupposes some knowledge of the TL. Here is the idea: students are given reading texts, preferably authentic documents, or listening texts (intermediate and advanced levels), with the task of deciphering the meanings of the particular words and/or how they are used in context.

ILLUSTRATION 7

As pointed out before, only the presentation of vocabulary in context allows us to extract its most precise meaning. The immediate environment (syntactic position)—where a word occurs within a sentence—often provides some further important clues about the word's meaning. Often, the context allows us to infer a general meaning of the word. The following example, in which we use a made-up word, *snubble*, illustrates this strategy (Bohn 1999).

He snubbled.
He snubbled the book back.
He snubbled the book back on the shelf.
Based on the context, we can guess the general meaning of the word *snubble*, which must mean something like *put*.

ILLUSTRATION 8

The instructor asks the students to read the following question: Welche Wörter erklären das neue Wort "Zirkel"? [Which words explain the new word, "a pair of compasses"?] The students silently read a text (see below) and then answer the question orally.]

Peter will jetzt Hausaufgaben machen. Er soll eine Gerade und einen Kreis zeichnen. Dazu braucht er einen Bleistift, ein Lineal und einen Zirkel. Die Gerade zeichnet er mit dem Lineal. Den Kreis zeichnet er mit dem Zirkel.

[Peter wants to do his homework now. He is supposed to draw a straight line and a circle. To do so, he needs a pencil, a ruler, and a compass. He draws the straight line with the ruler. The circle he draws with a compass.]

Source: Röhr (1993); cited in Bohn (1999), p. 50.

On Using the Techniques: Which and When

The previous section introduced a variety of techniques and ideas on how to present the meaning of new vocabulary to beginning language learners. Techniques that make exclusive use of the TL—such as examples, synonyms, definitions, and so on—have not been included, because many of them are self-explanatory. This still leaves us with questions regarding when to use a particular technique, and which one is best in a particular situation or for a set of vocabulary. Unfortunately, there are no simple answers to these questions. Neither is there only one correct way to present vocabulary.

The choice of techniques depends on several factors: the objective and purpose of the vocabulary lesson—that is, will the students be required to use the vocabulary productively or only recognize it at a receptive level?—the target language, available materials (pictures, realia, etc.), the level and knowledge of the students, the teacher's and students' personality, the teaching approach, and above all the nature and content of the vocabulary itself.

Comprehension Checks *Realizar frecuentes chequeos de comprensión*

Presenting new vocabulary is often the first activity of a new language lesson. When introducing new words with more than one modality (e.g., through gestures, physical actions, pictures, sounds, etc.), mismatches may occur. For students to avoid making false connections between the meaning of a word, label, or object, and for students to retain, recognize, and/or apply the new vocabulary, it is imperative to check the students' comprehension of the new words. Comprehension checks can be used in many different ways; usually they immediately follow the introduction or explanation, before the new vocabulary is further practiced or applied. Comprehension checks must not be omitted, since they otherwise may impede the learning process.

Conclusion

This chapter has argued, based on ample evidence from research, that multimedia-based input is powerful. It has many positive effects not only during the input process but also on the learner's retention of vocabulary items.

SUMMARY OF TECHNIQUES

- The use of
  - realia, pictures, photographs, drawings, the learners, multimedia presentation tools
  - mime, gestures, physical actions, and modeling
  - contexts
- Verbal explanations in the TL such as word derivations, synonyms, antonyms (opposites), paraphrasing, definitions, and associated ideas (e.g., "Apples and oranges are fruit."), descriptions, examples
- Word glosses

Considering that the visual mode is dominant for many learners, the auditory mode requires additional attention and practice. Note also that language learning must be considered an individual process. Any kind of methodologically restricted and narrow approach to language teaching must therefore be discarded. As far as the teaching of vocabulary is concerned, it must be presented and practiced so it appeals to multiple senses and to the learners' creativity. Sökmen (1997) points out that an eclectic approach is particularly appealing to students because it promotes variety and optimizes word associations. It also embraces various verbal and nonverbal learning styles. Familiarity with a variety of techniques and knowing how to use them necessitates the effective implementation of an eclectic approach, so that a wide range of learners can be reached.

Checking chapter objectives

Do I know how to…

❏ identify cognitive processes relevant to the learning of vocabulary
❏ adopt a particular technique to meet a particular learning goal
❏ introduce vocabulary in different ways
❏ describe pros and cons of multimedia-based input

Explorations

TASK 1: ANALYSIS AND DISCUSSION

Read the list of research findings in Appendix 3.2 describing how language is learned and stored in the brain. What pedagogical implications can you draw from these findings?

TASK 2: DISCOVERY LEARNING ACTIVITY

Part 1

To experience a discovery learning activity from a student's perspective, look at the excerpt from a Spanish magazine in Appendix 3.1. See if you can figure out the names of the days of the week in Spanish. Note! October 1 is a Wednesday.

Which strategies did you use to fulfill this task?

Did this activity encourage higher-level cognitive thinking skills? If so, how?

Part 2

An alternative way for students to decipher the days of the week in pairs is a technique called guided participation. Using this technique, the teacher directs the students' attention toward particular words or sections in the handout, and guides them through the activity by asking specific questions.

What questions would you ask to scaffold the deciphering process in the Spanish Calendar activity in Appendix 3.1?

_____

_____

What is the pedagogical advantage of this technique compared to having students engage in this activity in pairs?

_____

_____

TASK 3: REVIEW AND ANALYSIS

Review all the strategies and techniques mentioned in this chapter. Select at least two techniques, and describe when and how you would use them in your classroom. Analyze why these techniques are appropriate with regard to proficiency and age factors.

TASK 4: TEXTBOOK ANALYSIS

In a textbook of your choice (instructor's edition), review the beginning of at least three different chapters and describe how new vocabulary is presented (e.g., through texts, drawings, photos, charts, tables, etc.).

What suggestions do the textbook authors provide on how to present the new vocabulary? Do you find any of the authors' suggestions helpful? How would you further enhance their strategies? Focus on one example and demonstrate or explain what you would do.

_____

_____

TASK 5: CLASSROOM OBSERVATION

Observe an experienced language instructor and describe how she or he introduces new vocabulary to the class. Preferably, choose a beginning class in a language other than the one you teach, if you have access to such a class. Comment on the teacher's use of instructional strategies. Would you have introduced the vocabulary in the same way?

Application

TASK 6: DEVELOPING A LESSON SCRIPT

The following dialogue, entitled "Information erfragen" (see Fig. 3-4) [Requesting information], represents an example from a first-year German textbook. The purpose of this dialogue is to introduce new vocabulary, which is printed in bold type. The following instructions were provided to instructors in the margin:

> *Thema 2: Note: To introduce the new vocabulary, play or read the dialogue to the class.* Remind your students that they do not need to understand every word at first, rather they should use the context to arrive at the meaning of words they do not know. [. . .]

1. Assuming you would teach this dialogue, predict which words students will be able to derive from context. How? Which words will you have to introduce in an alternative way to aid students with comprehension?

2. If you were carrying out this activity as an instructor, how would you be introducing this dialogue? Project yourself into the classroom.

TASK 7: DEVELOPING A LESSON SCRIPT

Choose one of the following two activities.

Version A

Figures 3-5 and 3-6 demonstrate visuals that present examples similar to what you typically find in first-year textbooks. Develop a lesson script that demonstrates how you would present the new vocabulary introduced in these visuals. Be specific, and write down students' potential responses. Be mindful of the students' current level of proficiency and what they currently can produce.

Version B

Select several items from the vocabulary section of a foreign language textbook of your choice. Brainstorm how the meaning of these items would best be presented to learners who are encountering them for the first time.

TASK 8: TRYING IT OUT

Choosing from the versions presented above, prepare a mini-lesson (5–8 minutes long) demonstrating how you'd introduce a set of new vocabulary items to the class. Make sure to include some strategies that check the learners' comprehension of vocabulary.

Thema 2

Information erfragen°
„*Glücksrad Fortuna*"

QUIZMASTER: Guten Abend, meine Damen und Herren. Mein Name ist Dieter Sielinsky, und ich bin Ihr Quizmaster für die Show Glücksrad Fortuna. Wer **gewinnt heute abend**—und was? Das ist die große Frage! Und **nun** zu **Gast** Nummer 1: Wie ist Ihr Name, bitte?

GAST: Lentz, Gertraud Lentz.

QUIZMASTER: Woher kommen Sie, Frau Lentz?

GAST: Aus Augsburg.

QUIZMASTER: Frau Lentz, was sind Sie von Beruf?

GAST: Ich bin Architektin.

QUIZMASTER: Haben Sie **Hobbys**, Frau Lentz?

GAST: Ja, **viele**! **Lesen, Reisen, Tanzen, Wandern** und **Kreuzworträtsel.**

QUIZMASTER: Wie **finden** Sie Berlin?

GAST: **Sehr** interessant, **wirklich** faszinierend.

QUIZMASTER: Danke sehr, Frau Lentz.

GAST: Bitte schön.

QUIZMASTER: Ich wünsche Ihnen **viel Spaß** und **viel Glück.**

requesting

FIGURE 3-4 Requesting information
(Source: R. Di Donato, M. Clyde, and J. Van Sant, *Na klar!* 2nd ed. New York: McGraw-Hill, 1995), p. 27.)

Requesting Information
"Fortune Wheel Fortuna"

Show host: Good evening, ladies and gentlemen. I am Dieter Sielinsky, and I am your host of our show Fortune Wheel Fortuna. Who is going to <u>win tonight</u>—and what? That is the big question. <u>Now</u>, here is our first <u>guest</u> today: What is your name, please?

Guest: Lentz, Gertrud Lentz.

Show host: Where are you from, Frau Lentz?

Guest: From Augsburg.

Show host: Frau Lentz, what do you do?

Guest: I am an architect.

Show host: Do you have any <u>hobbies</u>, Frau Lentz?

Guest: Yes, <u>many</u>. <u>Reading</u>, <u>traveling</u>, <u>dancing</u>, <u>hiking</u>, and <u>crossword puzzles</u>.

Show host: How do you like Berlin?

Guest: <u>Very</u> interesting, <u>really</u> fascinating.

Show host: Thank you very much, Frau Lentz.

Guest: You are welcome.

Show host: <u>Have</u> <u>fun</u> and <u>good</u> <u>luck</u> to you!

FIGURE 3-5 Descriptive adjectives
(Source: Zayas-Bazán and Bacon (2004), p. 42.)

FIGURE 3-6 Salt or sugar

(Source: C. Flumian et al., *Rond-Point*, 3rd. ed. (Upper Saddle River, NJ: Pearson Prentice Hall, 2007), pp. 62–63.)

APPENDIX 3.1

Spanish calendar

Vida y Estilo

Domingo, 5 de octubre de 1997   Las Noticias

Agenda

Miscelánea

PASADENA. . . . .

Evento: exhibición y venta de artesanía americana nativa y del oeste

Lugar: Pasadena Center, 300 East Green Street

Fecha: viernes 10 de octubre, de 1:00 de la tarde a 7:00 de la noche; sábado 11 de octubre, de 10:00 de la mañana a 7:00 de la noche; domingo 12 de octubre, de 11:00 de la mañana a 5:00 de la tarde

Teléfono: (213) 770-4444

Precio: $6 adultos, $5 ancianos, $2 niños de 6 a 12 años, gratuito para menores de 6 años

SAN MARINO. . . . .

Evento: presentación de la ópera Tosca

Lugar: residencia del señor y la señora Gilbert y Margaret Moret, 1570 Shenandoah

Fecha: domingo 19 de octubre, a las 6:30 de la tarde

Teléfono: (818) 988-2387

Precio: $20

SAN PEDRO. . . . .

Evento: aventura hacia las islas Channel.

Lugar: la actividad se inicia en el acuario marino Cabrillo, 3720 Stephen White Drive

Educación

SYLMAR. . . . .

Evento: exhibición grupal de pinturas y esculturas de formas derivadas de la naturaleza New Organic Forms

Lugar: galería Century del condado de Los Angeles, Veterans Memorial Park, 13000 Syre Street

Fecha: domingo 5 de octubre

Teléfono: (818) 362-3220

Precio: gratuito

WILMINGTON. . . . .

Evento: clases de inglés para adultos

Lugar: ESL del colegio Harbor, 1111 Figueroa Place

Fecha: las clases se ofrecen odos los sábados, de 9:00 de la mañana a 4:30 de la tarde según los niveles

Teléfono: (310) 784-0701

Precio: gratuito

Salud

COMMERCE. . . . .

Evento: seminario dirigido a profesionales en Recursos Humanos para aprender cómo detectar a empleados—problema durante al entrevista de contratación y cómo tratar a empleados—problema ya contratados

Lugar: Wyndham Gardens Hotel, The Citadel, 5757 Telegraph Road

Fecha: martes 14 de octubre, de 11:30 de la mañana a 1:30 de la tarde

Precio: $20 con reservación, $22 a la puerta

Teléfono: (818) 964-6411

SAN GABRIEL. . . . .

Evento: Día Nacional de Exámenes para detectar la Depresión

Lugar: edificio CHEC del centro médico del Valle de San Gabriel, 261 Junípero Serra Drive

Fecha: jueves 9 de octubre, de 2:30 a 5:00 de la tarde

Teléfono: (818) 570-6663

Evento: clases sobre la diabetes

Lugar: centro médico del Valle de San Gabriel, 218 South Santa Anita Street

Fecha: las clases se inician el primer miércoles de cada mes y se ofrecen durante cuatro miércoles consecutivos, a las 9:30 de la mañana o a las 6:30 de la tarde

Teléfono: (626) 570-6508

Evento: clase ofrecida a futuras madres con técnicas de masaje y relajamiento

Lugar: centro médico del Valle de San Gabriel, 218 South Santa Anita Street

Fecha: lunes 6 de octubre, de 7:00 a 9:30 de la noche

Teléfono: (626) 457-3232

APPENDIX 3.2

Research findings

Here are summaries of research findings that document how information is stored in the brain. What pedagogical implications can you draw from these findings regarding how to introduce vocabulary and how to optimize the long-term retention of this information?

- The brain seems to organize a great variety and breadth of partial activities, in a parallel and simultaneous fashion, that are by and large bundled in the language-dominating, left-brain hemisphere (Götze 1995).
- "Comprehension and language do not take place in a clearly defined language center, but in widely scattered areas that get interconnected and are most likely organized, based on language, with each individual in a different way (Götze 1995).
- The right brain hemisphere seems to hold the most influence over the production and comprehension of emotional prosody,[3] the tone of voice or the emotional content of speech. It contributes to our understanding of humor and metaphor, higher forms of social communication. Patients with right-hemisphere lesion have been found not to understand metaphors; when people in one group were asked to choose a picture that matched the phrase "give someone a hand," they picked a picture of a platter with a hand on it. These patients also had impairments in regard to understanding humor; when given a choice of endings to fun stories, they often chose bizarre conclusions instead of appropriate punch lines (Ratey 2001).
- Regarding brain research, the following results are relevant (Götze 1995):
  - It is easier to remember specific characteristics of a word (e.g., colors [banana = yellow], or generic terms [eagle = bird]).
  - The retention of formula and frameworks (dates, telephone numbers; idiomatic phrases; "How are you?") is easier than single words.

APPENDIX 3.3

Introducing fruits (teacher direction of a sample script)

Steps	Teaching routines	Comment/rationale
1	Introduce three to four pieces of fruit. show a piece of fruit write the word for this item on the board have students pronounce the new word	
2	Have students pick up a piece of fruit from a basket. For example, tell a student to give you—or pick up—the banana.	
3	Have students draw, on separate pieces of paper, each piece of fruit being introduced.	
4	Have students hold up each piece of paper with the drawing of the fruit that you ask for in the target language (TL).	
5	Send a student on a shopping spree. Spread the fruit around the classroom. Hand students a shopping list that you made up earlier. The student is to pick up each item in the order it appears on the list. Post the shopping list on the board for all the students to see.	
6	Ask students either/or questions. Example: Would you like to have an apple or a pear?	
7	Ask students to name each item of fruit in chorus.	
8	In pairs, one student names the fruit item, and the other holds up the corresponding drawing.	
9	Ask individual volunteers to name the fruits being learned. If they name each fruit correctly, offer them a piece of the fruit and invite them to eat it.	

Endnotes

1 The ultimate goal of a Total Physical Response Storytelling (TPRS) lesson would be to get the students to retell a story. In the example given in Illustration 5, the vocabulary the instructor introduces leads up to the following story. [translation] "There is a woman. Her name is Cogi. Cogi has a big cat. There is a man. He is a very bad man. The man runs toward Cogi, grabs her, and throws her on the ground. The cat escapes."

2 (in reading) a type of speed reading technique that is used when the reader wants to locate a particular piece of information without necessarily understanding the rest of the text or passage. (For example, the reader may read through a chapter of a book as rapidly as possible in order to find out information about a particular date, such as when someone was born.)

3 The study of the metrical structure of verse.

CHAPTER 4

Grammar and Language Learning

There is no quick fix to mastering grammar.

REFLECTION

What does the word *grammar* mean to you? Write down all the words that come to mind.

_____

_____

_____

What role did grammar play in the classroom when you were a learner? Would you teach grammar the way you were taught? Why or why not?

_____

_____

_____

_____

In this chapter you will learn about

- the role of grammar teaching in the classroom.

- cognitive processes that impact the learning of language structures.

- inductive/deductive, guided discovery, and explicit/implicit grammar teaching.

- different methodological options to teaching grammar.

- teacher intervention and noticing strategies.

- processing instruction.

- TPR-based grammar introductions.

Introduction

With the inception of communicative language teaching (CLT), most advocates of this approach have come to an agreement that the teaching of grammar as an end in itself is considered unacceptable. However, as grammatical accuracy plays a pivotal role when used to receive and produce interesting and purposeful meanings within the context of real-life language use, the teaching of grammar constitutes an integral part of foreign language instruction. The question remains concerning how to go about it in the current communication-oriented and standards-based climate. In other words, what are effective instructional strategies of introducing grammatical structures that support the learner's second language acquisition process? That is the focus of this chapter.

Issues in Grammar Teaching

For years, the literature on foreign language teaching has been concerned with whether grammar structures and rules should be made explicit to the learners, or whether the learners themselves are able to pick up on forms merely from being exposed to contextualized situations. **Explicit grammar instruction** is a form of instruction in which grammar rules are clearly defined and explicitly stated. On the contrary, an **implicit** form of instruction rejects the need for any kind of explicit focus on form. This is based on the belief that learners can acquire language naturally if they receive sufficient comprehensible input from the teacher (Krashen 1985a; Dulay and Burt 1973; Terrell 1977).

Explicit
a) Fully and clearly expressed, defined or formulated
b) Readily observable

Implicit
a) Implied or understood though not directly addressed
b) Contained in the nature though not readily apparent

Although some scholars argue that explicit grammar knowledge does not support the language acquisition process (see Krashen 1982; Lee and VanPatten 2003), many practitioners believe that making rules explicit is not only beneficial but also imperative in a classroom environment (see Doughty 1991; Schmidt 1990). In addition, in recent years research has provided us with ample evidence in favor of the benefits of some formal grammar instruction (for a synthesis and meta-analysis of studies, see Norris and Ortega 2000).

Ellis (2002) provides some compelling arguments in favor of making rules explicit:

[E]xplicit knowledge serves to (1) monitor language use and thereby, to improve accuracy in output; (2) facilitate noticing of new forms and new form-function mappings in the input; and (3) make possible "noticing the gap" (i.e., comparing what is noticed in the input with what learners are producing themselves). (p.164)

Despite ample evidence in support of instructed grammar, the question of how to teach grammar has met with little agreement (DeKeyser and Sokalski 1996; Fotos and Ellis 1991; Salaberry 1997; Shaffer 1989; VanPatten and Cadierno 1993). Essentially, there are numerous curricular options in introducing grammar structures and making rules explicit to the learners. These range from teacher-centered and deductive to student-centered discovery and self-study approaches in preparation for or as a follow-up to a lesson. In particular, the following questions raise some of the issues teachers face when planning grammar lessons:

- Should new forms be introduced as isolated examples or presented through meaningful contexts?
- Should new input be introduced through authentic or teacher-created materials, situations, or contexts?
- How many new rules should be presented in a lesson?
- Should input be presented in oral or written form?
- How should rules be made explicit, and what is the role of the teacher?
- How do rules differ, and which approaches work best?
- When and how—that is to say, in what modality (e.g., in writing, orally, or through nonlinguistic responses)—should learners apply the new forms?

The following section addresses each of these questions in more detail.

Presentation of Input: Some Principles and Guidelines

Most lessons begin with the presentation of some form of input to demonstrate how the target language (TL) structures operate. There are numerous methodological options to do so.

Traditionally, as was the case with the audiolingual and grammar-translation methods, teachers would present grammatical structures in isolation and explain the rules of the language to their learners. With the advent of communicative-based methodologies, however, the basic understanding of language instruction changed. No longer was language considered to be merely a set of rigid structures imposed upon the learner; instead, it was viewed as a primary means of communication. Grammar rules were no longer considered the main focus of instruction, but were seen as a means to an end that allowed students to express themselves in meaningful ways. This new emphasis on communication also caused a shift toward presenting grammar forms embedded as they occur in meaningful communicative contexts. The swing toward whole language and contextualized language input was further endorsed by claims positing that only through contexts and natural discourse can the actual and full range of language use be demonstrated. Furthermore, for students to acquire new language structures, they need to be exposed to an input-rich environment, that is, a wide variety of contexts (Doughty and Long 2003).

Essentially any source of input can be used to demonstrate how language structures operate for the purpose of language learning. The most immediate source of input at a teacher's disposal is the classroom itself. The classroom environment provides a wealth of situational and functional contexts that can be exploited to introduce grammatical structures. For example, social interactions include greetings; introducing oneself and each other; and talking about and describing one's personal life, school events, and daily life or classroom routines. For instance, many instructors find Total Physical Response (TPR; see sample lesson below) an ideal way to introduce command forms—such as *open*, *show*, *take*, *go*, *be quiet*, *read aloud*, *give*, and *pick up*—or to demonstrate the use of prepositions by describing classroom objects.

In addition, teachers can draw from multiple text and discourse types—short stories, children's stories, newspaper articles, advertisements, poems, dialogues, and speech bubbles as well as textual or aural/video-based representations of real-life discourse. For example, short stories or narrative texts are commonly used in first-year language programs to introduce past tense forms (see sample lesson below). Any communicative materials or task-based situations essentially lend themselves to introducing a new TL structure. However, the choice of materials and contexts needs to be based on the premise that they embed numerous examples allowing focused demonstration of the new grammatical forms. In many instances, despite the emphasis on using authentic materials and tasks in CLT, authentic resources and contexts require special adaptation in task design or textual editing to make them usable in beginning language classes.

For presenting input with new grammatical structures, the following guidelines suggested by Lee and VanPatten (1995a) are useful:

1. Introduce one grammar aspect at a time.
2. Keep meaning in focus.
3. Move from sentences to connected discourse.
4. Use both oral and written input.
5. The learner must do something with the input.
6. Keep the learner processing strategies in mind.

One of the most important principles to keep in mind is the **meaningful principle**. As pointed out in a previous chapter, a fundamental principle of learning is that input has to be meaningful and comprehensible. Thus, before students can analyze how language structures determine meaning, it is imperative for them to understand the meaning of the input itself. In other words, the initial focus of the presentation phase needs to be on meaning. Many strategies allow an instructor to enhance the comprehension process (e.g., by using pictures, performing actions, and incorporating explanations; see Chapters 1 and 3). In addition, the task design may further support the learners to keep meaning and the targeted grammar forms in focus while processing the language input (see sample lesson and instructional processing below; Lee and VanPatten 2003).

Another guideline to be considered has to do with the learners' **processing demands**. Learners' processing demands are affected not only by the number of rules presented but also by how the learners are asked to apply the new rules. In many textbooks, it is still common to introduce whole sets of rules at once, as they are found organized in nominal/adjectival paradigms and conjugation tables in grammar references. Such an approach places high processing demands on the learners. As Sousa (2000) points out, a brain's working memory can handle only a few items at once. With an average of five to nine items for most adult language learners, the introduction of a whole verb paradigm or six different conjugation rules that are followed by immediate production exceeds this capacity for most learners. Moreover, the presentation of paradigms sends the message that grammar is best learned in this way, which is not the case (see Bybee 1991). To alleviate this problem and to make the delivery of the input more efficient, Lee and VanPatten (1995a) propose introducing "One thing at a time." For example, they suggest that nominal/adjectival paradigms be broken and that rules are focused on, one at a time, as they are used to serve the communicative function. In more detail, VanPatten and Glass (1999) describe this strategy in the following way:

> "To illustrate, rather than presenting the entire verbal paradigm of the Spanish imperfect tense along with all of the uses of the imperfect, the instructor would isolate a single form (e.g., third-person singular) and a single use (e.g., habitual actions in the past) at a given moment, subsequently adding more forms and rules of usage to the picture as the lesson continues." (p. 99).

A task-based approach supports this way of grammar teaching as only those rules or structures are introduced as they are required to perform a task. For example, the task of introducing oneself in German requires students to know only the first person singular form of the verb *heißen* [to be called]. If the task were extended to introducing their peers, they would also need to know the third-person form. Or, to demonstrate another example, if a task requires the arrangement of a group of people at dinner tables, by taking into account the peoples' commonalities and interests, only some prepositional phrases such as "next to," "on the left," "to the right," and "across from" will be required to describe the arrangement.

Students' processing of TL structures can be further constrained if learners are asked to apply new grammar rules immediately, in particular in oral contexts. To make this process less constraining, the teacher has the option of initially delaying oral or written production or keeping the focus on comprehension. This can be done through activities that initially engage students in a series of nonverbal or minimally verbal responses, with a primary focus on comprehension of meaning. This is what is meant by the guideline, "Learners should do something with the input." Examples include either/or, T/F, agree/disagree, yes/no, multiple-choice, or matching activities, or activities that allow the students to demonstrate comprehension through actions or gestures as promoted through the TPR technique. This method has a further advantage because it prolongs the exposure of the new forms and thus aids in assimilating the new target forms.

Another strategy that supports the learning process is to provide written and oral input. As pointed out earlier, presenting the target structures exclusively orally and asking students to apply the new forms immediately often leads to confusion and anxiety. Such practices will most likely cause students to produce new language structures by imitating the instructor's examples, since the students have little opportunity to notice new forms or gain some conceptual understanding of how the target rules operate. Particularly during grammar presentation, when teachers make use of a classroom-based situation, presenting examples of the new target structures in writing is a vital strategy that alleviates the learners' processing constraints. Many learners benefit from seeing the language (i.e., having it provided in written form) in addition to hearing it (VanPatten and Glass 1999). This strategy gives learners more time to process the new language forms and makes it easier to hypothesize about and identify some underlying patterns. It also accommodates a wider variety of learner types.

ANALYSIS AND DISCUSSION

Read through the lesson scripts of a French and Finnish lesson in Appendix 4.4. How does the design of these lessons meet the guidelines just mentioned? In other words, how much "grammar" is introduced in each lesson? How and through what modalities (oral, written)? At what phases of the lesson do students apply the new forms? How is the grammar made explicit? Which psycholinguistic constraints might students experience?

Making Rules Explicit: From Teacher- to Student-Centered Approaches

As most practitioners agree, the issue is not whether to make rules explicit to the learners, but how to go about it. In general, all textbooks include explanations or descriptions of grammar rules, and they provide overviews in the form of **paradigms**—that is, representations displaying the various forms of a grammatical structure, such as verb charts or a summary table of case endings. Ideally, this strategy allows students to study and review rules on their own, or to use such grammar references when needed. The question remains, what are pedagogically sound practices for making grammar points explicit to the learners? Several curricular options exist to achieve this goal; they include teacher-centered and deductive, teacher-guided, student-centered, and inductive and self-instructional approaches.

In traditional language instruction, it was common practice for teachers to begin grammar lessons with a deductive approach. The instructor presented the rules first and then followed up with many examples. In other words, instruction moved from the general to the particular—that is, from a rule statement to the application of the rule in specific cases. Assessment of students' comprehension of the rules did not take place until they applied the rules in language learning activities. Examples were normally decontextualized and consisted of random lists of disconnected sentences. Many arguments can be made against such an approach to grammar presentations. For example, it implies a direct instructional and authoritative role by the teacher. It places the teacher into the role of an atlas, which suggests that the teacher is the sole transmitter of information and who is solely responsible for student learning (Lee and VanPatten 1995a; Adair-Hauck, Donato, and Cumo-Johannsen 2000). This practice assigns a passive role to the learners, who consequently are often less engaged. Furthermore, a deductive approach places grammar structures at the core of instruction so they become the main goal and organizational principle of a lesson, instead of focusing on the communicative use of language itself.

An alternative to a teacher-centered approach to making rules explicit is a student-centered and inductive/implicit approach. In this approach, the new target structures are presented implicitly, within a context, to demonstrate through many reoccurring examples how the grammar rule operates. The students are asked to infer the rule of generalization from a set of examples. The process of learning involves going from the particular to the general. The primary goal of implicit grammar presentation is to actively engage the learners in formulating their own hypothesis about the target rule. Such an approach is based on the principle of discovery or inductive reasoning, which is believed to promote a deeper level of processing and to have the highest impact on the student's learning process. For example, Bruner (1961) hypothesizes that students do better when having to discover underlying patterns themselves rather than being told them. Or, as Götze (1997, p. 10) puts it, "Am wirksamsten sind grammatische Regeln dann, wenn der Lernende selbst unmittelbar vor der Erkenntnis steht, diese Regel zu formulieren." [Grammatical rules are most effective, if the learner is getting close to formulating a rule by himself.]

Despite some of the positive effects of an inductive approach, there are also some drawbacks. Herron and Tomasello (1992) state that the inductive method cannot guarantee that the learner will discover the underlying concepts or that the induced concepts will actually be correct. This can be frustrating to adolescent or adult learners, many of whom have already become analytical regarding the rules that govern their native languages. Research also has shown that some learners do not attend to or notice the teacher's grammatical agenda in implicit, inductive lessons, because the stimulus domain—that is, the language contexts—is too rich.

For example, in a series of studies carried out on French immersion students, it was found that French native language (L1)/English second language (L2) learners who received focused instruction on English adverb placement and question formation achieved and sustained correct production of these structures to a greater degree than did learners in classrooms who were exposed to the new structures by solely engaging in communicative or drill and practice activities (Lightbown and Spada 1990; Lightbown, Spada, and Ranta 1991; White 1991).

In another study, conducted by Jessica Williams and Jacqueline Evans (1998), one group was provided with an increased number of artificially enhanced examples of the participial adjective structure in English, such as "He is interesting." Another group was given an explicit explanation of the adjectives' "form, meaning, and use"; a third group was simply exposed to examples of these structures but had no special teaching. The group that was given explanations for the adjectives did indeed do better than the other groups did. There was no difference between the other two groups, which had been flooded with examples only.

The results of some of these studies show that some grammar structures may require a more direct approach to making rules explicit. That is to say, in many instances students may require help with noticing grammar forms and understanding explanations about how rules operate. Many arguments can be made for why this help is necessary. In many cases, rules are too complex or the language structure is not transparent enough for students to figure out an underlying rule, as is the case with many **syntactical** (e.g., word order rules) aspects of the language or with exceptions to the rule. Some L2 grammatical features are so close to the learners' L1 structure that it is difficult for learners to notice the differences. Other rules are so context specific or so rare in the L2 input that they need to be explicitly pointed out and explained.

Interestingly, grammar items that are considered easy to learn—that is, items that have a straightforward form-function relationship but are somewhat imperceptible in oral input—may also benefit from more explicit grammar instruction. For example, Pica (1994) found that, in comparing learners of English who received explicit instruction in the use of plural –s with those who had never received classroom instruction, the first group used the plural –s more accurately than did the uninstructed learners. The second group of learners often used a strategy of attaching quantifiers rather than –s to their nouns, as in utterances such as "three book" or "a few house."

Another factor to be considered is the learner group itself. For example, the learner's age has to be considered. The younger the learner, the less effective a cognitive-based or explicit approach will be to grammar instruction. While age determines cognitive readiness with younger learners, individual readiness with adult learners may also make a difference. This factor plays an important role in the effectiveness of any kind of grammar instruction and thus predicts success in the acquisition process (Pienemann 1989; Bardovi-Harlig 1995). As pointed out previously, readiness implies that the learners are able to make a "comparison between their internal representation of a rule and the information about the rule in the input [i.e., feedback] they encounter" (Chaudron 1988, p. 134). Several studies support this claim. For example, in Pica's study (1994) mentioned earlier, beginning students of English who received focused instruction or only implicit exposure on the progressive *–ing* form did not show very positive results in either group of the study. The instructed learners tended to overgeneralize, producing utterances such as "I liking the movie," "Every day I going home for lunch," and "I want to seeing you." The uninstructed learners, on the other hand, often omitted *–ing* altogether from their verb production. Williams and Evans's (1998) study also revealed similar findings showing that explicit instruction of fairly complex and non-transparent forms in English, such as the passive, had provided no advantage as a form of grammar instruction. Similarly, a finding by Bardovi-Harlig (1995) "suggests that instruction on the use of the pluperfect is futile unless the learner has demonstrated stable use of the simple past and has begun attempts to express reverse-order reports, that is, to establish a context that would require the use of the pluperfect" (quoted in Williams and Evans 1998).

Besides the learner's cognitive development, his or her cognitive style may also make a difference. For instance, a study of English as a Second Language (ESL) students by Abraham (1985) investigated the relationship of field dependence and field independence. **Field-dependent learners** are defined as those who pay more attention to what they see than what they feel. Their perceptions are influenced by their environment. They use their entire surroundings to process information and focus on the whole rather than on its parts. They are externally motivated, prefer to work collaboratively rather than independently, are people oriented, and are affected by instructor interaction and communication style. On the other hand, **field-independent learners** are believed to pay more attention to what they feel than what they see. Their perceptions are not influenced by their environment. They focus on the parts rather than the whole. They are intrinsically motivated, prefer to work independently or competitively, and take a more impersonal approach to learning. Abraham (1985) discovered that field-independent learners performed better on a posttest when they were exposed to lessons that used a deductive approach, while field-dependent learners did better with an inductive approach.

Teacher-guided approaches: Intervention and noticing strategies

There are several instructional strategies to compensate for some of the challenges of implicit/inductive grammar instruction and further guide the learners to discovering the rules themselves. One such approach is known as a "guided participatory or co-constructive" approach (Donato and

Hauck 2002). The application of such strategies normally requires teacher guidance, hence the term *co-constructive*, and a sequence of scaffolded tasks. Such tasks involve the students' active involvement in noticing, deciphering, and formulating underlying rules, while the teacher facilitates the students' inductive processes. In other words, the teacher leads the students to discover[1] the rules themselves, and the teacher and the students become the co-constructors of grammatical explanations. The following section provides several strategies that support such an approach.

A strategy that can further enhance the students' learning process is the use of noticing or awareness-raising tasks. Students may be asked to find, underline, and organize similar patterns of grammatical structures and then formulate the rules before the teacher confirms or rejects their hypotheses. Recent findings in second language acquisition (SLA) research have shown that, in particular, those strategies that explicitly draw the learner attention to target forms appear to have positive effects on their performances (e.g., see Alanen 1995; Izumi 2002; Jourdenais 1998; Leow 1997, 2001; Overstreet 1998; White 1998). Such practices are well supported by Schmidt's noticing hypothesis (1990), which claims that only when students notice the targeted forms can they also process the new forms. In other words, active strategies such as identifying and underlining not only promote a higher level of engagement but also engage the noticing process, and they are thus more likely to lead to deeper levels of processing.

ILLUSTRATION 1

Consciousness-raising

The following activity (Ellis 1998, p. 48) provides an example of a consciousness-raising task directed at helping learners discover when to use *at*, *in*, and *on* in adverbial time phrases. First, the students are to underline the time expressions in the passage, and then they must write them into the table. As a follow-up task, the teacher might ask questions about the underlying rules for using these prepositions.

1. Underline the time expressions in this passage.

   I made an appointment to see Mr. Bean at 3 o'clock on Tuesday the 11th of February to discuss my application for a job. Unfortunately, he was involved in a car accident in the morning and rang to cancel the appointment. I made another appointment to see him at 10 o'clock on Friday the 21st of February. However, when I got to his office, his secretary told me that his wife had died at 2 o'clock in the night and that he was not coming into the office that day. She suggested I reschedule for sometime in March. So I made a third appointment to see Mr. Bean at 1 o'clock on Monday the 10th of March. This time I actually got to see him. However, he informed me that they had now filled all the vacancies and suggested I contact him again in 1998. I assured him that he would not be seeing me in either this or the next century.

2. Write the time phrases into this table:

at	in	on
at 3 o'clock		

ILLUSTRATION 2

Organizing data

Figure 4-1 demonstrates how a teacher has organized language input so students can notice underlying patterns. The goal of this lesson is to help students decipher the rule on how to express the concept of "knowing" in German, for which either the verb *wissen* or *kennen* is used[2] (see Appendix 4.2 for the complete lesson). In step 1 of the lesson, the teacher introduces and models the new verb form, provides several examples, and writes them on the board. Next, students work in pairs (A/B), performing a communication gap activity. In step 2, the teacher follows up with numerous questions using the different verbs expressing the meaning of "knowing." Next, in step 3 the teacher organizes her input in the form of a tabular display to draw students' attention to the syntactic structures so they can notice underlying patterns. Continuing the lesson in a co-constructive way, the teacher might ask the following questions based on the set of aggregated sample sentences: "What is the difference between use of the verb in column A and B? Which of the two lists of questions expresses factual knowledge? Which verb expresses the meaning in the sense of being familiar, acquainted, or associated with somebody or something?"

In step 3, organizing data, the teacher writes several sample sentences in two separate columns on the board or overhead projector.	
Column A	**Column B**
1. Ich weiß, dass er Heinz heißt.	1. Ich kenne ihn gut.
2. Ich weiß, dass er drei Kinder hat.	2. Ich kenne auch seine Frau.
3. Ich weiß, woher sie kommt.	
4. Ich weiß nicht, ob sie schon lange hier lebt.	

Column A

1. I know that his name is Heinz.
2. I know that he has three children.
3. I know where she comes from.
4. I do not know whether she has been living long here.

Column B

1. I know him well.
2. I also know his wife.

FIGURE 4-1 Sample chart of organized data

The following section presents two different lessons that both demonstrate how teachers make use of noticing and guided participation strategies in helping the learners figure out the rules. In the German lesson below, the teacher uses an authentic story as the basis of the input. In the second example, the French lesson, the teacher makes use of situational contexts guiding the students toward figuring out past tense forms.

Lesson Sample 1: Using a Text-Based Approach and Guided Participation

Grammar topic: *weil*– clause in German

Content/input: authentic text (poem)

Noticing: Instructor draws students' attention to new forms.

Rule formulation: Instructor aids students in co-constructing underlying rules.

Application: Students move from written input to oral application.

The following lesson design is based on the PACE Model [P=Presentation; A=Attention; C=Co-construction; E=Extension] (Donato and Hauck 2002). This lesson demonstrates how a teacher uses a poem to introduce the *weil*– clause in a German class. In the first lesson phase, the presentation (P) of the input, the teacher introduces the poem. Next, in phase two, the noticing or awareness-raising phase, the teacher draws the students' attention (A) to the new forms by having them underline the conjunction *weil* (because) and the verbs. Following is the co-construction or guided participation phase, in which the instructor invites the students to hypothesize about how the rule operates. The lesson continues with several extension (E) activities.

Description and rationale for choice of text

The lesson is based on a poem by Eric Fried, entitled "Was geschieht?" [What is happening?] The poem consists of six stanzas and deals with the theme of indifference. The text is highly repetitive in its use of the *weil*– (because) phrase, which makes it ideal to introduce this language structure in German. For example, the poem contains statements such as: "Poor people do not notice anything, because they are too poor and the rich ones do not notice it because they are…" Since the poem uses language that is by and large easy to understand, it is well suited to the first-year college or second-year high school level.

Presentation

Introduction

Step 1

Teacher elicits the meaning of the word *geschehen* [to happen]. She might present a scenario such as: "Dein Freund liegt im Krankenhaus!" [Your friend is in the hospital!] "Was ist geschehen?" [What do you think happened?] "Was heisst 'geschehen'?" [What does the word 'geschehen' mean?]

Step 2

The instructor reads the poem out loud, and along the way explains, models, and/or demonstrates unknown vocabulary. These include words such as *guilty*, *raising one's shoulder*, *care*, and so forth.

Step 3

This step is a comprehension check and discussion of meaning. Students in pairs answer the following questions: "Was geschieht mit den Unschuldigen? Den Armen? Den Dummen? Den Jungen? [What happens to the innocent, the poor, the dumb, the young people?] "Welche Wörter kommen oft vor? Welche Rolle spielen Gegensätze in diesem Gedicht?" [Which words do occur frequently? What is the role of contrasts in this poem?]

Attention

Step 4

Students are asked to underline the conjunction *weil* and all the verbs in the *weil*– (because) clause using one color, and all the verbs in different phrases with a different color. Here are some possible teacher-guided questions: What do all the *weil*– (because) clauses have in common? As an alternative strategy students may be asked to write all the *weil*– clauses in one column, and the other sentences in another column on the board. If necessary, the teacher asks students to focus on the position of the verbs and to compare where the verb occurs in a *weil*– clause and a regular sentence.

Co-construction

Step 5

The teacher asks the students to form the rule in pairs. Then he rejects or confirms the students' hypothesis.

Extension

Step 6

Part 1: Pedagogical Tasks

Students do two assimilation activities:

1. Students combine two sentences. For example: "Ich gehe jetzt nach Hause. Ich bin so müde." [I am going home now. I am so tired.] (Answer: Ich gehe jetzt nach Hause, weil ich so müde bin. [I am going home now, because...]).
2. Students do a sentence completion exercise. For example, "Die Schüler üben die Sprache, weil..." [Students practice the language, because...]. "Ich lerne Deutsch, weil..." [I study German, because...].

Part 2: Real-life Tasks

In pairs, students write a similar poem making up all kinds of excuses. They then present the poems to the class. Peers vote on the best poem and have to say why they like it most.

Lesson Sample 2: Using Situational Contexts and Guided Participation

> Grammar topic: agreement of past participle in French
>
> Content/input: conversational, communicative context
>
> Noticing: Instructor draws students' attention to new forms.
>
> Rule formulation: Instructor aids students in co-constructing underlying rules.
>
> Application: Immediate oral application; students move from written input to oral application.

The following lesson is an example of an implicit grammar presentation on the topic of the agreement of the past participle in French. The lesson consists of these three phases:

Step 1: Give students an advance organizer so that their attention is focused on examples containing the grammatical structure. This allows students to form a hypothesis about what the rule is and to test the hypothesis through the examples.

Step 2: Guide students to form the rule of the structure.

Step 3: Give students meaningful practice with the structure.

Step 1

Advance organizer

A. Prepare oral questions on a given topic, for example, "Qu'avez-vous fait hier soir?" [What did you do last night?]
   1. *Avez-vous regardé la télé hier soir?* [Did you watch television last night?]
   2. *Avez-vous fait vos devoirs?* [Did you do your homework?]
   3. *Avez-vous fini les exercices de français?* [Did you finish the French exercises?]
   4. *Avez-vous écrit votre rédaction de français?* [Did you write your French composition?]
   5. *Avez-vous écouté la radio?* [Did you listen to the radio?]
   6. *Avez-vous lu le journal?* [Did you read the newspaper?]

B. Write answers on the board/overhead as they are given by the students.
   1. *Oui, j'ai regardé la télé hier soir.* [Yes, I watched television last night.] *Non, je n'ai pas regardé la télé hier soir.* [No, I did not watch television last night.]
   2. *Oui, j'ai fait mes devoirs. Non, je n'ai pas fait mes devoirs.* [Yes, I did my homework. No, I did not do my homework.]

C. After each student response, give the answer using a pronoun.
   1. *Moi aussi, je l'ai regardée. Moi non plus, je ne l'ai pas regardée.* [I watched it too. I did not watch it either.]
   2. *Moi aussi, je les ai faits.* [I did it too.]

3. *Moi aussi, je les ai finis.* [I finished them too.]
4. *Moi aussi, je l'ai écrite.* [I wrote it too.]
5. *Moi aussi, je l'ai écoutée.* [I listened to it too.]
6. *Moi aussi, je l'ai lu.* [I read it too.]

Step 2

Guided induction (discovery)

In the second phase, the instructor provides a conscious focus and makes the rule explicit by helping the students to induce the rule.

Ask either/or questions, such as the following, about the agreement of the object pronoun and the past participle ending:

Regardez le participe passé (pointing). [Look at the past participle (pointing)].

Savez-vous pourquoi il y a un "e" à la fin? [Do you know why there is an "e" at the end?]

Savez-vous pourquoi il y a un "s" à la fin? [Do you know why there is an "s" at the end?]

Est-ce que le "l'" remplace un nom masculin ou féminin?
Je l'ai regardée.

[Does the "l'" replace a masculine or feminine noun? I saw it.]

Pourquoi est-ce que nous avons un "e" dans le premier et pas dans le deuxième? [Why do we have an "e" in the first and not in the second one?]

Est-ce que le "l'" précède ou suit le verbe? [Does the "l'" precede or follow the verb?]

Pourquoi le "s" dans le deuxième exemple? [Why is there an "s" in the second example?]

Step 3

Practice[3]

A. Written class practice: Ask students to write 6 to 10 sentences making agreement [between the object pronoun and the past participle ending] if necessary.

Ex: J'ai vu les deux films français. [I saw the two French movies.]
Reponse: Je les ai vus. [I saw them.]

B. Listening discrimination: Dictate 6 to 10 sentences to students.

Ex: Je l'ai ouverte. [I opened it.]

Write the answers on the board/overhead. As students give the answers, show the correct response.

Assign homework on the agreement of the past participle in the textbook.

(Source: Mitchell and Redmond (1993), pp. 17–18.)

Instructional processing

Another curricular option that has been promoted in recent years has become known as **processing instruction** (Lee and VanPatten 1995). The goal of this particular focus-on-form technique is to repeatedly draw the learners' attention to the new forms without engaging the learners in pro-ducing the target items. As is often the case during the input phase of gram-mar presentations, students feel overwhelmed because they are expected to produce the target language (TL) structures right away or have to cope with too many new structures at once. Hence students have little time to pay attention to target forms and cannot actively process them. What beginning language learners need, as VanPatten and Cadierno (1993) argue, is structured input activities that enable them to focus on meaning while attending to form before they are expected to use the language to produce output. In these authors' view, the input may be more beneficial to the learners when they are not engaged in producing the target item but are engaged in processing it actively, and when they manipulate the input in certain ways so form/meaning connections become more salient to them.

The following example (Ellis 1998, p. 44) of a grammar task demon-strates such a structured-input task (also see sample lesson below). The target structure is predicate adjectives (e.g., the distinction between *boring* and *bored*). L2 learners have been observed to confuse these words, producing sentences such as "I am boring with you" (Burt 1975). In this task, the learners simply have to indicate whether they agree or disagree with a series of statements.

Do you agree or disagree with these statements?

1. Quiet people are boring.
2. I am bored when someone tells a joke.
3. People who gossip a lot are very irritating.
4. I get irritated with small talk.
5. It is interesting to talk about yourself.
6. I am interested in people who always talk about themselves.

Lesson Sample 3: Using Processing Instruction

Grammar topic: third-person plural verb forms in Spanish

Content/input: structured input activities

Noticing: implicit in the design of the activity

Rule formulation: not demonstrated in this lesson

Application: Students move from nonverbal or minimally verbal (e.g., matching, T/F statements) responses to written and oral application.

The following excerpt demonstrates the beginning of a lesson adapted from *¿Sabías que...?* (VanPatten, Lee, and Ballman 1996, p. 60). First, the instructor begins the lesson by making the rule explicit. He either briefly explains the new grammar rule, or has the students read through the rule description in the textbook. Next, he begins a series of input processing activities. During this input phase, students engage in a matching activity (Activity A). Next they decide on whether weekend activities are typical for students by providing a true or false statement (Activity B). The activities are designed to require the students to keep meaning in focus. Furthermore, students' attention is repeatedly drawn to verbal inflections, the targeted language structure, by processing the input. Only then, in the next activity, are students asked to actively produce the new forms.

Note that **se** is used before the third person plural form of verbs like **acostarse.**

El sábado, Ramón y sus amigos **sacan** vídeos y **se quedan** en casa por la tarde.

— context
— meaningful

Actividad A   ¿Qué hacen y por qué?

Ramón and his friend from work have lots of weekend plans. Match their activity in column A with a logical reason in column B.

Ramón y un compañero de trabajo...

A	B
1. _____ sacan un vídeo porque...	**a.** necesitan ropa nueva (*new*).
2. _____ van al cine porque...	**b.** quieren ver la nueva película (*film*) de Spike Lee.
3. _____ van de compras porque...	**c.** necesitan hacer ejercicio.
4. _____ corren porque...	**d.** quieren ver una película en casa.
5. _____ se levantan tarde porque...	**e.** no tienen que trabajar por la mañana.

Actividad B   ¿Quiénes?

For each statement, decide whether the weekend activity is typical of students, of people who work full-time, or could easily refer to both groups.

1. Juegan a los videojuegos.
2. Limpian la casa.
3. Se quedan en casa y miran la televisión por la noche.
4. Lavan la ropa.
5. Visitan a parientes (*relatives*).
6. Trabajan en el jardín (*yard*).
7. Duermen más que (*more than*) durante la semana y se levantan más tarde.
8. Van de compras.
9. Dan un paseo con su perro.
10. Salen a bailar.

---

5. They visit relatives.
6. They work in the yard.
7. They sleep more than during the week and get up late.
8. They go shopping.
9. They go for a walk with the dog.
10. They go out dancing.

FIGURE 4-2 Sample processing instruction activity
(Source: VanPatten, Lee, and Ballman (1996), p. 60.)

On Saturday, Ramon and his friends get some videos and stay at home in the evening.

Activity A. What to do and why?

Ramon and his friend from work have lots of weekend plans. Match their activity in column A with a logical reason in column B.

Ramon and a friend from work...

A	B
1. _____ get a video because	a. need new clothes.
2. _____ go to see a movie because.	b. want to see the new movie of Spike Lee
3. _____ go shopping because	c. need to exercise
4. _____ run because	d. to see a movie at home
5. _____ get up late because	e. don't have to work in the morning.

Activity B. Who?

For each statement, decide whether the weekend activity is typical of students, of people who work full-time, or could easily refer to both groups.

1. They play video games.
2. They clean the house.
3. They stay at home and watch TV at night.
4. They do laundry.

Total physical response: An alternative technique to modeling language structures

An instructional strategy that lends itself well to modeling language structures in context is the Total Physical Response (TPR). TPR in its simplest terms refers to learners carrying out the actions commanded by the instructor. Although TPR has actually been formalized as a method developed by James Asher of San Jose State University in the 1970s, TPR is presented here only as an alternative technique to presenting input. Many grammatical structures such as command forms, prepositions, pronouns, singular and plural forms, or reflexive verbs can be introduced through TPR.

Figure 4-3 outlines the instructional steps of a TPR-based input segment of a lesson. In phase 1, the instructor first performs the actions while learners listen and watch. Then, in phase 2, the learners perform the same actions with the instructor. The goal of these two phases is to give the learners repeated exposure to the targeted language structures. In phase 3, "the instructor subsequently 'tests' the binding[4] of the commands by stopping simultaneous performance of the command and allowing learners to act it out as a group on their own" (Lee and VanPatten 2003, p. 41).

Description of a TPR-based sample lesson. The following lesson script demonstrates a TPR-based lesson introducing the two-way prepositions in German. Please note, this lesson assumes that the accusative and dative cases have already been introduced. For this reason, the input phase is shorter than normal, and students are asked to produce these forms orally relatively early on in the lesson. Furthermore, this lesson makes use of the TPR-based technique in phase 1, 2A, 2D, and 3 and combines it with other strategies as previously described in this chapter.

1. Input phase
   A. Modeling of new vocabulary

   (sample script)

   Ich möchte euch alle zum Essen einladen. Aber bevor ich das machen kann, möchte ich euch erst einmal zeigen, wie man in Deutschland den Tisch deckt. Ich brauche nämlich eure Hilfe. Ich habe euch alles, was wir dafür brauchen, mitgebracht. *[Teacher takes out a fork and shows it to the students.]* Das ist eine Gabel. *[Teacher writes the word on the board and has everybody repeat*

Phase 1: The instructor performs the actions while learners listen and watch.

Phase 2: Then the learners perform the same actions with the instructor.

Phase 3: The instructor tells the learners what actions to perform without performing the actions. The students perform the actions.

FIGURE 4-3 Outline of instructional steps of a TPR-based input segment of a lesson

the word a couple of times.] Jeder von euch, nehmt bitte eine Gabel. *[Teacher gives one student a bag with forks and says...]* Nimm die Gabeln und teile sie bitte aus.

I'd like to invite you all for dinner. But before I can do so, I'd like to show you how we set the table in Germany, because I need your help. I brought along everything that we need. *[Teacher takes out a fork and shows it to the students.]* This is a fork. *[Teacher writes the word on the board and has everybody repeat the word a couple of times.]* Each of you, please take a fork. *[Teacher gives one student a bag with forks and says...]* Take the forks and hand them out.

[Teacher repeats the same with knife, spoon, glass, napkin, and plate.]

B. Modeling of new prepositions in the accusative case (input flooding)

(sample script)

Ich zeige euch jetzt wie man in Deutschland den Tisch deckt. Schaut mir erst mal alle zu! Zuerst stellt man den Teller auf den Tisch. Die Gabel legt man neben den Teller, ich meine natürlich, links neben den Teller. Das Messer, das legt man rechts neben den Teller. Das darf man nicht verwechseln, also deswegen sage ich das noch einmal, das Messer muss man rechts neben den Teller legen. Ok! Wohin legt man jetzt den Löffel? Den Löffel legt man entweder neben den Teller, das heißt, rechts neben das Messer. Oder man kann ihn allerdings auch vor den Teller legen. Wohin kommt das Glas? Das stellt man normalerweise rechts, ein bisschen schräg, vor den Teller. Und als letztes, was mache ich mit der Serviette? Die legt man auf den Teller. Fertig! Damit ist der Tisch gedeckt.

I am going to show you now how to set the table in Germany. First, watch what I do! First, you put the plate on the table. You put the fork next to the plate...what I actually want to say is, on the left side of the plate. You put the knife on the right side of the plate. You must not confuse this. So let me say this once more. You must place the knife on the right side of the plate. Ok! Where do we put the spoon? You can put the spoon either next to the plate, I mean, next to the right of the knife. Or you can also put it in front of the plate. What about the glass? Normally, you place the glass in front of the plate, slightly to the right. And last, what do I do with the napkin? You put it on the plate. Done. Then your table is set.

---

2. TPR-based (comprehension) phase
   A. Teacher tells the students to follow along and do as he models.

   (sample's script)

   Jetzt macht mir das bitte einmal nach. Nehmt den Teller und stellt ihn auf den Tisch.

> Now please do exactly as I do. Take the plate and put it on the table. *[All students follow along and do as the teacher models.]*

B. Next, so students can see some of the structures in writing, he writes some of the phrases into the right column on the board.

(sample sentences)

Stell den Teller auf den Tisch.
Leg die Gabel neben den Teller.

> Put the plate on the table.
> Put the fork next to the plate.

C. Next, working in pairs and taking turns, the students tell each other how to set the table.
D. Then, the teacher asks the students to tell him how to set the table in the United States.
3. Input phase
A. Modeling of new prepositions in the dative case

(sample script)

Wie würden wir jetzt beschreiben, wie wir den Tisch gedeckt haben. Das schaut so aus. Der Teller steht auf dem Tisch. Die Gabel liegt neben dem Teller, d. h., sie liegt links neben dem Teller. Das Messer liegt rechts neben dem Teller. Und der Löffel liegt vor dem Teller. Und die Serviette, die dürfen wir nicht vergessen. Sie liegt auf dem Teller.

> How would we describe how we set the table? That goes like this. The plate is on the table. The fork is lying next to the plate, i.e., it is lying to the left of the plate. The knife is lying to the right of the plate. And the spoon is lying in front of the plate. And the napkin, you cannot forget about it. It is placed on the plate.

B. Next, so students can see some of the structures in writing, the teacher writes some of the phrases into the left column on the board.

(sample sentences)

Der Teller steht auf dem Tisch.
Die Gabel liegt neben dem Teller.
Der Löffel liegt vor dem Teller.

> The plate is on the table.
> The fork is lying next to the plate.
> The spoon is lying in front of the plate.

4. Controlled practice

Next, the teacher checks on students' comprehension of the new vocabulary and further probes to see if students can apply the dative prepositions. He moves around some of the objects, for example, he puts the fork on the plate and asks some either/or display questions such as "Ist die Gabel auf dem Teller oder auf dem Tisch?" [Is the fork on the plate or on the table?] Or, he asks, "Wo liegt das Messer?" [Where is the fork?]

5. Guided participation/co-construction of rules

The instructor asks questions about the difference between the sentences in the left and right column. He further explains the rule about when to use the accusative and when to use the dative case with the two-way prepositions.

6. Guided practice

Pedagogical Task

A. Fill-in-the-blank

The students fill in the correct prepositions in either the accusative or dative case.

B. Communication gap activity

In pairs, students describe the location of objects in a room or tell each other where to put things. Students A and B have different images of rooms in which objects are scattered throughout.

7. Extension

A. Students talk to two to three students in class and find out how they have organized their rooms. They draw a simple layout of their classmates' arrangements. Then, they decide which of them is more organized.

B. By email, each student provides advice on organizing to the student who is least organized.

TPR is an excellent technique for introducing some language structures in classroom-based contexts. This technique has great potential because it aids learners in building comprehension skills while repeatedly exposing them to the targeted language forms. Furthermore, many students normally find it very engaging because they physically get to perform actions. At the same time, this technique involves several caveats that are often reported by teachers. TPR is an aural-based technique, so it favors auditory learner types. Moreover, not all learners like to act out parts, and some personality types only reluctantly participate in these activities. In conclusion, while TPR allows the teacher to create meaningful input in a physically engaging way, it has most potential during the input phase of a lesson. TPR is most successfully applied when combined with other techniques such as the presentation of written input and some form of rule noticing and guided discovery strategies that aid learners with the rule formulation process. Needless to say, TPR-based activities are only one form of pedagogical tasks that are meant to prepare the students for communicative and task-based language activities.

Self-instructional approaches

An alternative and a complementary practice for teachers explaining grammar is to have students read, learn, and use targeted grammar structures on their own. This can be done as a preparation for a new lesson or as a follow-up to the teacher's grammar instruction. As a preparatory strategy, this practice has many advantages. It serves as an advance organizer of the grammatical forms, thus foreshadowing the new content. Furthermore, it supports the goal of freeing up class time that can otherwise be used for communicative application. In other words, when students come to class, they are assumed to be ready to apply the language in communicative-based learning activities.

When adopting such a strategy, the question to be asked is how effective it is—or in other words, how much learning can students achieve outside of class without teacher intervention? Unfortunately, little research exists to provide us with detailed information about this question. One such study by Scott and Randall (1992) revealed that a self-study approach works best when the learning of new grammatical structures involved some content-based words—such as *more*, *less*, or *same as*—which is the case when learning comparatives. The subjects of the authors' study showed less success with more complex and abstract grammatical rules such as relative pronouns. Though only in limited ways, this study presents some evidence that students can do rule learning outside the classroom. Besides, this strategy promotes student autonomy and responsibility in the foreign language learning process.

From Declarative to Procedural Knowledge

As pointed out at the beginning of this chapter, ample research supports the arguments that adult language learners benefit from knowing how grammar rules operate (see Ellis 2002; Doughty 1991; Schmidt 1990). Conscious knowledge or awareness of grammar rules constitutes an essential part of the early language learning process. However, conscious knowledge of grammar is not to be confused with the ability to use language. In communicative language teaching (CLT), the primary goal is not explicit knowledge of grammar, but the communicative ability to use it correctly and automatically. Thus grammar knowledge plays a vital role, but only inasmuch as it serves as a facilitator for making language skills automatic, which is the case during early stages of the acquisition process in a formal learning environment.

To further highlight this point, in the literature on skill acquisition theory, knowledge about language and the ability to use language are traditionally distinguished as declarative, procedural, and automatizing or fine-tuning procedural knowledge (Anderson 1982; 1995a). DeKeyser (1998) explains the difference in the following way: "Declarative knowledge is factual knowledge, for example, knowing … that most English verbs take an –s in the third person of the present tense when the subject is singular" (p. 49). On the other hand, procedural knowledge consists of encoded behavior. For instance, "fully automatized procedural knowledge means […] that one uses a third person –s for singular verbs without having to think about it" (p. 49).

The important question concerns how to move from declarative knowledge to procedural or at least partially procedural knowledge. Inexperienced teachers often overlook the fact that to attain fully automatized knowledge, an extended period of total immersion is normally required, and it cannot be compensated for by an exclusively grammar-based approach. A more realistic goal in a foreign language classroom environment is that students at best will be able to achieve only partial control of most grammatical structures, whose degree of mastery will vary depending on some of the factors mentioned earlier, on the length of study, and on student ability. The goal of developing procedural knowledge is best achieved during extensive communicative language application. For this reason, the learners need to be provided with opportunities that engage them in a wide range of meaningful and communicative contexts, where they can apply these skills in multiple ways. In addition, for learners to develop procedural skills, lessons need to be structured and designed to incrementally lead them toward developing these skills. Instructional strategies and guidelines to reach this goal are the focus of Chapter 6.

Conclusion

This chapter has presented several approaches to second language (L2) grammar teaching. Because grammar teaching has met with little agreement among teachers, educators, methodologists and ESL/EFL professionals, this overview supports the notion that grammar teaching not only enhances learner proficiency and accuracy, but that there are many effective ways to go about such kind of instruction. While there is no panacean approach that meets all the challenges in grammar teaching, factors such as rule complexity, learner types, and age need to be taken into account to guide instructors in their decisions on which strategy to apply.

In light of different rule complexities and learner types, introducing grammatical structures or making rules explicit is best achieved through a combination of teacher- and student-centered approaches. As DeKeyser and Sokalski (1996) remind us, not all grammatical concepts and rules are the same. Some forms are easy to notice and comprehend, but difficult to produce. Other forms may be difficult to notice but, once noticed and learned, are produced rather easily. In other words, the degree and form of instructional intervention (e.g., through teacher help or strategy) required may depend on the complexity and degree of transparency of a grammar rule, as well as on individual learner differences.

While many arguments can be made in favor of inductive approaches, findings reported in SLA research comparing the effectiveness of deductive and inductive approaches are somewhat mixed (see summary in Erlam 2003). In general, however, there seems to be a trend in favor of those strategies that make use of inductive reasoning. While in some cases the deductive approach has been reported to be more effective in the short term, in the long run there was not only a higher decrease in effectiveness but also a greater variability among students (Erlam 2003; Zoble 1995; VanPatten 1996). In other words, some students who were instructed through the deductive approach forgot much faster what they had learned than did those students who had experienced an inductive approach. Based on such findings, it can be concluded that approaches making use of rule discovery, teacher-student co-constructive strategies, awareness-raising, and noticing strategies help learners in general to ingrain information more deeply—thus having a more lasting effect on their acquired language system.

No one particular way of grammar teaching is suitable for all learners. Hence, to maximize the learning outcome, teachers need to choose varying modes of grammar presentations so all learner types will benefit. The incorporation of visual, auditory, kinesthetic, and tactile learning stimuli allows learners to decipher patterns of language structures by themselves and while interacting with each other. Furthermore, grammatical concepts vary in complexity—another reason teachers need to be flexible and adaptive when teaching grammar. With most learners, a multiple approach is necessary for deeper levels of language learning to take place. Such an approach includes self-study, teacher explanation, and most of all, meaningful, engaging, and motivating learning tasks. In most cases, the teacher initially plays a pivotal role in helping learners understand grammatical concepts. In the long run, however, what is ultimately most important is how and in what contexts the learner gets to apply the new forms. In other words, the linguistic richness of the learning environment and the design of a learning task that requires the learner to focus on form and meaning will make a difference in the learner acquisition process. Furthermore, ongoing teacher intervention in the form of feedback that confirms or rejects a student's notion of the correctness of a grammatical structure will be necessary to gradually lead a student from conscious toward automatic language processing.

Checking chapter objectives

Do I know how to. . .

- ❏ describe the role of grammar teaching in the classroom
- ❏ define inductive/deductive, guided discovery, and explicit/implicit grammar teaching
- ❏ describe different methodological options to teaching grammar

❏ describe cognitive processes that impact the learning of language
  structures
❏ describe teacher intervention and noticing strategies
❏ describe instructional processing activities
❏ describe TPR-based grammar introductions

Explorations

TASK 1: MYTH AND REALITY OF GRAMMAR TEACHING

Grammar plays a fundamental role in language learning. At the same
time, it is also one of the least understood and most complex skills to
learn. Read the statements in Figure 4-4, and indicate to what degree you
are in agreement with such assumptions. What are your current beliefs
regarding the teaching and learning of grammar?

_____

_____

_____

	not at all			very much	
The teaching of grammar is necessary to learn a language.	1	2	3	4	5
Conscious knowledge of grammar rules is necessary to speak a language proficiently.	1	2	3	4	5
Accurate use of grammar is essential to communicating effectively.	1	2	3	4	5
Students internalize grammar rules in a developmentally linear way.	1	2	3	4	5
Easy grammar rules are easier for students to internalize than conceptually difficult ones.	1	2	3	4	5
The presentation of paradigms (e.g., organization of rules in reference tables) helps students internalize rules more efficiently.	1	2	3	4	5
A teacher's explicit explanation of how grammar operates is fundamental to students' internalizing grammar.	1	2	3	4	5
Foreign language learners eventually master all grammar rules in the same way.	1	2	3	4	5
Presenting grammar in a motivating and interesting way is more important than precise explanations.	1	2	3	4	5
Native speakers have an advantage in teaching grammar rules because they know how rules operate intuitively.	1	2	3	4	5
Nonnative speakers have an advantage in teaching grammar rules because they themselves had to learn the rules.	1	2	3	4	5
The more grammar structures are drilled, the better learners master these forms.	1	2	3	4	5

FIGURE 4-4 My beliefs about learning and teaching grammar

TASK 2: ANALYSIS AND DISCUSSION

As DeKeyser and Sokalski (1996) point out, not all grammatical concepts and rules are the same. Some forms are easy to notice and comprehend, but difficult to produce. Other forms may be difficult to notice but, once noticed and learned, are produced rather easily.

In the language you teach, identify grammatical concepts whose forms are easy to understand, but whose underlying rule patterns are difficult to formulate. Discuss and develop strategies on how to introduce such grammatical concepts.

TASK 3: DISCUSSION

1. What kind of grammar instruction do you believe is most effective? Which one do you think is easiest to teach?

    _____

    _____

    _____

2. What kind of grammar instruction do you think students prefer most and consider easiest to learn?

    _____

    _____

    _____

TASK 4: ANALYSIS AND DISCUSSION

Project yourself into a language classroom where the instructor introduces verb forms in an implicit/inductive and deductive way to beginning language students. Discuss the pros and cons of each instructional strategy.

TASK 5: DISCOVERY LEARNING ACTIVITY

To experience a guided discovery activity from the perspective of a student, do the activity presented in Appendix 4.1 or Appendix 4.3. What are the pros and cons of this approach? In case you had a hard time deciphering the rule yourself, what kind of teacher "intervention" strategies might have helped you in formulating a much clearer hypothesis about this rule?

TASK 6: DISCUSSION AND ANALYSIS

Compare a TPR-based grammar introduction to other approaches such as processing instruction or a story-based approach. What are the pros and cons involved in each of these approaches?

Task 7: Discussion

What are arguments in favor of, or against, making grammar presentations more teacher centered than learner centered?

Task 8: Textbook Analysis

Select two different grammatical topics, for example, "inverted word order," present perfect, and so on. Then look at the instructor's editions of at least two different textbooks of your choice and describe (1) how these grammatical structures are introduced in the book and (2) what instructional strategies the authors suggest. Make sure to provide specific examples.

Task 9: Classroom Observation

Observe the approach an experienced language instructor uses when introducing a new grammatical topic to the class. Preferably, choose a beginning class in a language other than the one you teach.

Application

Task 10: Developing a Lesson Script

Choose a grammatical topic, and select a particular approach of grammar teaching that you believe would be the best fit for introducing the grammatical topic you have chosen. For example, TPR is known as a technique that is especially effective in the teaching of command forms. Prepare a brief lesson script, and demonstrate how you would introduce this grammatical topic.

APPENDIX 4.1

Discovering rules

Example of Guided Discovery
(adapted from Funk and Koenig 1991)

The goal of this activity is for the learner to decipher a set of underlying patterns (rules) regarding word order in German from the text in Figure 4-5. Please note that the learners should be familiar with the meaning of this text. To guide the learners along the process of discovering these rules, Funk and Koenig suggest a three-phase lesson: (1) Students collect or look for sentences or phrases that make use of the grammatical structure or item to be analyzed; (2) students organize their materials based on similarities or differences; and (3) students attempt to decipher an underlying pattern and possibly formulate a rule.

NOTE!
The rule that you are trying to discover has to do with word order.

> Peter treibt gerne Sport. Er spielt am Montag Fußball. Dienstags geht er zum Schwimmen. Am Mittwoch spielt er Handball und jeden Donnerstag geht er zum Squash. Er arbeitet samstags an einer Tankstelle, am Sonntag Nachmittag spielt er wieder Fußball.
>
> Peter likes to do sports. He plays soccer on Monday. He goes swimming on Tuesdays. On Wednesday, he plays handball, and every Thursday he plays squash. He works at a gas station on Saturdays, and on Sunday in the afternoon he plays soccer again.

Figure 4-5 Sample German text

Step 1. Introduction

To do this activity, first familiarize yourself with the meaning of the German text in Figure 4-5.

Step 2. Analysis

Together with a partner, look at Peter's weekly time schedule (see Figure 4-5). Compare the sentences and identify similarities.

Step 3. Data collection

Underline all sentences that contain time phrases.

Step 4. Organize the data

List those sentences that contain similar structures in separate columns based on where the time phrase, the subject, and the verb appear in the sentence.

Step 5. Discover the rules

Formulate a rule.

NOTE!

Before you continue with the task of formulating the rules in your own words (obviously this is best done in everybody's native language), your teacher should elicit and summarize the results of the pair-work activity on the board or overhead projector. Next, she will mark words or phrases using symbols to further enhance students' awareness of the similarities between sentences.

APPENDIX 4.2

Introducing 'wissen' and 'kennen' (know)

Presentation of content/input

Note: This grammatical concept is similar in many other languages (e.g., see "conocer" and "saber" in Spanish, or "connaître" and "savoir" in French).

Step 1: Presentation and modeling of verb forms of — "wissen" and 'kennen'

A. *The teacher introduces and models the new verb form providing several examples and writes them on the board.*

1. Wie gut kennen Sie ihre Nachbarn?
2. Ich kenne meinen Nachbarn nicht gut.
3. Ich weiβ nur wenig von meinem Nachbarn.
4. Ich weiβ, dass er Müller heiβt.
5. Ich weiβ, dass er einen Mercedes fährt.
6. Ich weiβ nicht, wie alt er ist.
7. Ich weiβ nicht, was er von Beruf ist.
8. Ich weiβ nicht, woher er kommt.

1. How well do you know your neighbors?
2. I do not know my neighbor well.
3. I only know a little about my neighbor.
4. I know that his name is Müller.
5. I know that he drives a Mercedes.
6. I do not know how old he is.
7. I do not know what he does.
8. I do not know where he is from.

B. *Students work in pairs (A/B) and answer questions about each other neighbors. Students follow the questions and cues as provided on their handout.*

Model
Student A asks:
Weiβt du, woher dein Nachbar kommt?
Student B looks up the answer and says:
Ja, er kommt aus Deutschland.

Model
Student A asks:
Do you know where your neighbor is from?
Student B looks up the answer and says:
Yes, he is from Germany.

Student A handout:

1. Wie gut kennst du deinen Nachbarn?
2. Weiβt du, wie er heit?
3. Weiβt du, wieviele Kinder er hat?
4. Kennst du seine Frau?
5. Weiβt du, wie sie heit und woher sie kommt?
6. Weiβt du, ob sie schon lange hier lebt.

Student A handout:

1. How well do you know your neighbors?
2. Do you know his name?
3. Do you know how many children he has?
4. Do you know his wife?
5. Do you know what her name is and where she is from?
6. Do you know whether she has been living here for long?

Student B handout:

1. gut
2. Name: Heinz
3. Kinder: 3
4. Name der Frau: Anne
5. Herkunft: Bonn
6. 10 Jahre

Student B handout:

1. well
2. Name: Heinz
3. Children: 3
4. Woman's name: Anne
5. Origin: Bonn
6. 10 years

Step 2: Follow-up questions using the verb *kennen*

Teacher models the verb *kennen* asking the following questions.

1. Kennst du deine Groβeltern?
2. Wie gut kennst du deine Klassenkameraden/ Klassenkameradinnen?
3. Hast du einen Freund/eine Freundin? Wie gut kennst du ihn/sie?

1. Do you know your grand parents?
2. How well do you know your classmates?
3. Do you have a boyfriend/girlfriend? Howell do you know him/her?

Step 3: Organizing data

The teacher writes several sample sentences in two separate columns on the board or the overhead projector. She also sets the main and the subordinate clauses slightly apart in column A.

Column A		Column B
1. Ich weiß,	dass er Heinz heißt.	1. Ich kenne ihn gut.
2. Ich weiß,	dass er drei Kinder hat.	2. Ich kenne auch seine Frau.
3. Ich weiß,	woher sie kommt.	
4. Ich weiß nicht,	ob sie schon lange hier lebt.	

Column A	Column B
1. I know that his name is Heinz.	1. I know him well.
2. I know that he has three children.	2. I also know his wife.
3. I know where she comes from.	
4. I do not know whether she has been living long here.	

Step 4: Student discover rules

In pairs, students try to formulate a rule about the use of the two different verb forms. The teacher asks guiding questions, if necessary. For example, which of the two lists of questions expresses factual knowledge.

Step 5: Follow-up and confirmation

The instructor summarizes the rules explicitly and follows-up on the students' hypotheses, confirming or rejecting their current understanding.

APPENDIX 4.3

Sample French lesson demonstrating self-discovery approach

The goal of this lesson is for the learners to figure out the how the rule of noun-adjective agreement in French operates.

Step 1: Underline all the adjectives in the sentences in Figure 4-6.

Step 2: Fill in all the masculine adjectives in column A of Figure 4-7, the adjectives in masculine plural in column B, the feminine adjective in column C, and the feminine adjectives in plural in column D.

Step 3: Compare all the adjective endings in each column of Figure 4-7. What do they have in common? Formulate a rule.

Français I   Nom: La date:

Comparez les formes des adjectifs de nationalité dans les phrases suivantes:

1. Le président Clinton est américain.
2. Mme Clinton est américaine aussi.
3. Chelsea et Mme Clinton sont américaines.
4. Monsieur Jacques Chirac est le président de la République française. Il est français.
5. Mme Chirac est française.
6. Monsieur et Mme Chirac sont français.
7. Jean-Claude Van Damme est belge.
8. La fiancée de Jean-Claude est belge aussi.
9. Claudia Schiffer est allemande.
10. Detlef Schrempf est allemand.

FIGURE 4-6 French adjective endings

Compare the forms(endings) in the <u>adjectives</u> in the following phrases:

1. President Clinton is <u>American</u>.
2. Mrs. Clinton is also <u>American</u>.
3. Chelsea and Mrs. Clinton are <u>American.</u>
4. Monsieur Jacques Chirac is the president of the French Republic. He is <u>French</u>.
5. Mme Chirac is <u>French</u>.
6. Monsieur and Mme Chirac are <u>French</u>.
7. Jean-Claude Van Damme is <u>Belgian</u>.
8. Jean-Claude's fiancée is also <u>Belgian</u>.
9. Claudia Schiffer is <u>German</u>.
10. Detlef Schrempf is <u>German</u>.

A. Les adjectifs masculins	B. Les adjectifs masculins et pluriels	C. Les adjectifs féminins	D. Les adjectifs féminins et pluriels

FIGURE 4-7 Organizing adjectives

APPENDIX 4.4

Lesson scripts

Sample Finnish Lesson

The goal of this lesson is to introduce the static locative cases (–ssa/ssä, –lla/llä) in Finnish. The students have already been introduced to the following words and should be familiar with them: **kissa** [cat]; **talo** [house]; **lintu** [bird]; **hiiri** [mouse]; **lasi** [glass], **malja** [bowl].

(Source: Original lesson script designed by Lola Rogers; modified by Klaus Brandl.)

Step 1: Review of vocabulary

Teacher shows the picture of a house and asks the students: Mikä tämä on? [What is this?]

She shows the picture of a cat and asks: Mikä tämä on? [What is this?]

Step 2: Input phase and demonstration of the locative case (–ssa/ssä)

Rationale: The purpose of this phase is to demonstrate the meaning of the phrase (…in the house) by providing several examples of the locative case (–ssa/ssä).

Example 1: Teacher shows a picture with the cat in the house and says: "Kissa on talossa." [The cat is in the house.] She writes the phrase "Kissa on talossa." [The cat is in the house.] into column 1 on the board (see next page).

Example 2: The teacher reviews the word *mouse* (see above). Then she shows a picture with a mouse in the house and says: "Hiiri on talossa." [The mouse is in the house.] She adds the phrase "Hiiri on talossa." [The mouse is in the house.] to column 1 on the board.

Example 3: The teacher reviews the word *lintu* (see above). Then she shows a picture with the bird in the house and says: "Lintu on talossa." [The bird is in the house.] She adds the phrase "Lintu on talossa." [The bird is in the house.] to column 1 on the board. To demonstrate further examples, she shows a picture with a mouse or a bird in a glass and also writes these phrases into the column.

Column 1	Column 2
Kissa on talossa. [The cat is in the house.]	
Hiiri on talossa. [The mouse is in the house.]	
Lintu on talossa. [The bird is in the house.]	
Hiiri on lasissa. [The mouse is in the glass.]	
Lintu on lasissa. [The bird is in the glass.]	

Step 3: Input phase and demonstration of the locative case (–lla/llä)

Rationale: The purpose of this input phase is to demonstrate the meaning of the phrase (…on the house) by providing several examples of the locative case (–lla/llä).

Example 1: Teacher shows a picture with the cat on the house and says: "Kissa on talolla." [The cat is on the house.] She writes the phrase "Kissa on talolla." [The cat is on the house.] into column 2 on the board (see below).

Example 2: The teacher *shows a picture with the bird on the house* and says: "Lintu on talolla." [The bird is on the house.] She adds the phrase "Lintu on talolla." [The bird is on the house.] to column 2 on the board (see below).

Column 1	Column 2
Kissa on talossa. [The cat is in the house.]	Kissa on talolla. [The cat is on the house.]
Hiiri on talossa. [The mouse is in the house.]	Hiiri on talolla. [The mouse is on the house.]
Lintu on talossa. [The bird is in the house.]	Lintu on talolla. [The bird is on the house.]
Hiiri on lasissa. [The mouse is in the glass.]	Hiiri on lasilla. [The mouse is on the glass.]
Lintu on lasissa. [The bird is in the glass.]	Lintu on lasilla. [The bird is on the glass.]

Example 3: The teacher shows a picture with a mouse on the house and says: "Hiiri on talolla." [The mouse is on the house.] She adds the phrase "Hiiri on talolla." [The mouse is on the house.] to column 2 on the board (see previous page). To demonstrate further examples, she shows a picture with a mouse or a bird on top of a glass and also writes these phrases into the column.

Step 4: Aural comprehension check of new grammar structures

Rationale: In this step, students are to demonstrate comprehension of the new phrases and be further exposed to the new grammar structure.

The teacher shows two pictures and describes one of the two. The students have to point at the one she describes. For example,

Kissa on talolla. [The cat is on the house.]	Kissa on talossa. [The cat is in the house.]
Lintu on talolla. [The bird is on the house.]	Lintu on talossa. [The bird is in the house.]

Step 5: Rule formulation

Rationale: The goal of this activity is for students to decipher the rule by themselves. If necessary, the teacher asks some additional guiding questions.

In pairs, students try to figure out and formulate a rule based on the data provided in the two columns. The teacher follows up and confirms or rejects the students' hypothesis on how the new rules operate.

Step 6: Written application and practice

Rationale: The students apply the rules in writing and in pairs first. In this way they can work cooperatively at their own pace, producing the new rules and forms for the first time.

Written application: In pairs, students describe pictures provided on a handout in writing. For example, the handout contains pictures depicting a cat on a house, a bird inside a cat, a mouse on a cat, a bird on a house, and so on. The teacher follows up on this activity by providing feedback on the students' answers.

Step 7: Oral application and practice

Rationale: First the teacher models the learning activity for the students, checking their comprehension. Next, the students apply the new forms orally in pairs.

Modeling: The teacher hands out glasses, bowls, and pictures of a mouse, a bird, and a cat. For example, placing the mouse on top of or inside the cup, she asks a student about the location of the object. For example, "Missä hiiri on?" [Where is the mouse?]

Oral application: In pairs, students ask each other about the location of the objects, following the teacher's model. For example, placing the bird on the cat, a student would ask his partner in Finnish: "Where is the mouse?"

3. Comprehension check: Showing the following picture, the teacher asks: "Missä lintu on?" [Where is the bird?]

(Source: Original lesson script designed by Lola Rogers; modified by Klaus Brandl.)

Sample French Lesson

T	Alors, Raphael. Tu viens. Alors. Regardez bien Raphael. Voici. *[Raphael is mimicking buttoning up his shirt.]* Qu'est-ce qu'il fait?
S	*[in chorus]* Il met sa chemise.
T	Il met sa chemise. Qu'est-ce qu'il fait? *[Raphael is mimicking putting on his shoes.]*
S	*[in chorus]* Il met son pantalon.
T	Voila. Il met son pantalon. Qu'est-ce qu'il fait?
S	*[in chorus]* Il met ses chaussettes. Oui…
T	Qu'est-ce qu'il fait?
S	*[in chorus]* Il met *[mumbling]* ses chaussures.
T	Qu'est-ce qu'il fait?
S	*[in chorus]* Il met son *[error]* cravate.
T	Oui, la cravate.
S	*[in chorus]* Oui, la cravate.
T	C'est tout. Bien, merci, merci. Alors, moi, quand il fait froid, je mets un pull-over. Et, Chantal, qu'est-ce que tu mets quand il fait froid? Froid. *[Teacher mimics shivering.]* Je mets un pull-over, et toi?
S	Je mis *[error]* un anorak.
T	Je mets *[correcting]*.
S	Je mets un anorak.

T	D'accord. Qu'est-ce que tu mets? Marie-France?
S	Je mets … *[mumbling in an unintelligent way]*.
T	Qu'est-ce que tu mets, Philippe?
S	*[hesitantly]* Uh, uh, …
T	une robe?
S	non, non, une *[error]* costume
T	Un costume. D'accord. Pour aller dîner, qu'est-ce que tu mets, Annick? Pour aller dîner au restaurant?
S	Je mets une robe.
T	Alors, moi aussi. Pour aller dîner au restaurant, Annick et moi, nous mettons une robe. Qu'est-ce que il met quand il fait froid, Nicole?
S	Il met une *[error]* anorak.
T	Un *[correcting]* anorak. D'accord. Et, qu'est-ce que Marie-France met quand il fait chaud? Qu'est-ce que elle met quand il fait chaud, Raphael?
S	Elle met un bikini?
T	Un bikini. C'est ça. Qu'est-ce que nous mettons pour aller dîner au restaurant, Chantal?
S	Vous mettez une robe.
T	Une robe. Une robe très élégante, n'est-ce pas. Répétez après moi. Je mets une robe.
S	*[in chorus]* Je mets une robe.
T	Tu mets une robe.
S	*[in chorus]* Tu mets une robe.
T	Il met un pantalon.
S	*[in chorus]* Il met un pantalon.
T	Nous mettons un pull-over.
S	*[in chorus]* Nous mettons un pull-over.
T	Vous mettez un anorak.
S	*[in chorus]* Vous mettez un anorak.
T	Ils mettent un pantalon.
S	*[in chorus]* Ils mettent un pantalon.

T	Well, Raphael, come here. Look at Raphael. *[Raphael is mimicking buttoning up his shirt.]* What is he doing?
S	*[in chorus]* He is putting on his shirt.
T	He is putting on his shirt. What is he doing? *[Raphael is mimicking putting on his shoes.]*
S	*[in chorus]* He is putting on his pants.
T	He is putting on his pants. What is he doing?
S	*[in chorus]* He is putting on his shoes.
T	What is he doing?
S	*[in chorus]* He is putting *[mumbling]* on his shoes.

T	What is he doing?
S	*[in chorus]* He is putting on his *[error]* tie.
T	Yes, the tie.
S	*[in chorus]* Yes, the tie.
T	That's all. Well. Thank you. Well, when it is cold, I put on a pullover. And, Chantal, what do you put on when it is cold? Cold. *[Teacher mimics shivering.]* I am putting on a pullover, and you?
S	I …*[verb error]* a coat.
T	I wear *[correcting]*.
S	I wear a coat.
T	Ok. What do you wear, Marie-France?
S	I wear… *[mumbling in an unintelligent way]*
T	Ok. What do you wear, Philippe?
S	*[hesitantly]* Uh, uh, …
T	a dress?
S	no, no, *[gender error]* suit
T	a suit. Ok. To go out for dinner, what do you wear, Annick? To go out for dinner.
S	I wear a dress.
T	Well, me, too. Going out for dinner to a restaurant, Annick and I wear a dress. What does he wear when it is cold, Nicole?
S	He wears *[error in French]* a jacket.
T	A *[correcting]* jacket. Ok. And, what does Marie-France wear when it is hot? What does Marie-France wear when it is hot, Raphael?
S	She wears a bikini.
T	A bikini. That's it. What do we wear when to go out for dinner, Chantal?
S	You all wear a dress.
T	A dress. A very elegant dress. Repeat after me. I am wearing a dress.
S	*[in chorus]* I am wearing a dress.
T	You are wearing a dress.
S	*[in chorus]* You are wearing a dress.
T	He is wearing a pair of pants.
S	*[in chorus]* He is wearing a pair of pants.
T	We are wearing a pullover.
S	*[in chorus]* We are wearing a pullover.
T	You (all) are wearing a jacket.
S	*[in chorus]* You (all) are wearing a jacket.
T	They are wearing a pair of pants.
S	*[in chorus]* They are wearing a pair of pants.

(Source: Teaching with Allons-y! Transcription of video materials (Boston: Heinle & Heinle, 1988).)

Endnotes

1 The idea of a guided or self-discovery approach in grammar presentation dates back to the early 1900s. It was proposed by Jespersen (1904), who called it an "inventional grammar" because in discovery procedures the students write their own little grammars.

2 This concept is the same in many other languages, such as Spanish (*saber* versus *conocer*), or French (*savoir* versus *connaître*).

3 The activities in this practice section demonstrate types of pedagogical tasks that can be found in many traditional textbooks. When implementing such activities, particularly the one as in activity B, Listening discrimination, the teacher needs to ensure that the students demonstrate the comprehension and meaning of these phrases.

4 Terrell (1986) uses the term *binding* in describing the cognitive and affective mental process of linking meaning to form. The concept of "binding" is what language teachers refer to when they insist that a new word ultimately be associated directly with its meaning and not with a translation (p. 214).

CHAPTER 5

Feedback and Error Correction in Language Learning

In this chapter you will learn about

- the role of feedback.

- dilemmas and challenges when dealing with errors in the classroom.

- different error correction techniques and their effectiveness.

- practical guidelines on how to provide error treatment.

"But I have taught them so many times and they are still getting it wrong!"

(anonymous teacher)

REFLECTION

Thinking back about your own experience as a foreign language learner, how did you feel when your instructor corrected your mistakes in class? What kind of strategies did your teachers employ? How do you believe errors should be dealt with?

_____

_____

_____

Introduction

The role of feedback, more commonly known as "error correction" and "positive comments," has been one of the most controversial topics in the history of foreign language teaching as well as second language acquisition (SLA) research. Though feedback is considered in general a fundamental principle of learning, the pedagogical pendulum has swung back and forth between positive and negative perceptions about the need and effect of error correction. The Audiolingual Method promoted a no-tolerance approach to learner errors and tried to eradicate them to avoid bad habit formation. Traditionally, it was also argued by some scholars that learners' errors fossilize if they are not treated (Vigil and Oller 1976). Later methods such as the Natural Approach considered error correction as too anxiety-inducing and counterproductive and thus supported only limited use of error correction.

In recent decades, with numerous advances in SLA and the advent of communicative language teaching (CLT) methodologies, attitudes toward learner errors have gradually changed. However, classroom-based research on the effectiveness of error correction still remains highly controversial. While learner errors have been considered a part of the learning process for a long time, one strand of research contends that many errors are developmental and can only be rectified over time. This stance suggests that the effectiveness of error correction may be limited. Some scholars have even argued that there is no guarantee that learners benefit from feedback on grammatical errors at all (see Hammond 1988; Krashen 1985, 1999; Truscott 1996, 1999). Hence, some practitioners believe that devoting valuable classroom time to providing feedback to students' errors is of little value. Then, there are those who claim that grammar correction can be useful in enhancing and accelerating adolescent and adult foreign language learning, if it is done in an appropriate way (Doughty and Williams 1998a; Lightbown 1998; Long and Robinson 1998; Lyster, Lightbown, and Spada 1999). Furthermore, many learners believe in the benefits of receiving and learning from feedback (see Brandl and Bauer 2002; Schulz 2001). For such reasons, students normally expect their teachers to provide feedback for them.

Making errors is part of any learning process, so teachers are faced with the dilemma and decision how to deal with errors and how to go about providing feedback. This chapter examines the types of evaluative feedback that can be useful in responding to learner oral and written tasks of various types. The role and benefits of feedback, as well as the advantages and disadvantages of corrective strategies, are discussed. In addition, a set of guidelines are provided on how to go about providing feedback in different learning contexts.

Error Correction in Second Language (L2) Learning

Teachers face numerous decisions and questions when dealing with learner errors in the classroom. What is the role of feedback, and how feasible is it to provide effective feedback? Should all errors be corrected, or should some errors be left untreated? If so, which errors are to be corrected? Who should make the corrections, the teacher or the students? Should individual learner differences be taken into account? And finally, are some strategies more effective than others? (See page 150 for information on the role of feedback.)

Defining Feedback

In a general sense, feedback can be categorized in two different ways: as 'positive' feedback and 'negative' feedback. The purpose of **positive feedback** is to confirm the correctness of a student's response. Teachers do so by agreeing, praising, or showing understanding. **Negative feedback** is generally known as **error correction** (see Chaudron 1988). Its function is to correct students' faulty language behavior. Some scholars further distinguish between the term *correction* and *feedback on error, corrective* *feedback*, or *error treatment*. The preference for the latter terms reflects an "observation made by Long (1977) that what the teacher can do is to provide information to the learner, but it is the learner who will (or will not) eventually correct the error" (Lyster, Lightbown, and Spada 1999, p. 457). Feedback can be provided by the teacher or the students. In beginning language classrooms, it is common for teachers to make most corrections, guide students toward corrections, or to invite student peers to aid with the correction process. Student-initiated peer corrections are less common in beginning language classes. If instructors choose to employ student-initiated peer corrections, they must be approached with the proper support—such as clear guidelines and correct answer sheets.

Types of Oral Feedback Strategies

The following list provides an overview of the most commonly employed feedback strategies during students' oral language performances.

Positive feedback

Positive feedback plays an important role in learning. Teachers provide positive feedback in acknowledging a learner's utterance for many reasons. The most common one is to confirm a learner's utterance regarding features such as grammatical correctness, word choice, or any particular content. Other reasons for doing so are to praise learners for their performance or to encourage them for their attempts in using language. Many teachers also make ample use of positive feedback even if a learner's utterance was only partially correct, or if a learner's pronunciation assimilated the target language (TL) sound.

- Confirmations
  The teacher confirms that a student's utterance was correct (e.g., by saying "well done, correct, etc.").

- Encouragements
  A teacher provides positive feedback to acknowledge a learner's improvement, progress or attempt. For example, a teacher might say, "I like how you pronounce *x* [target sound]. Can you try it once more to see if you can make it sound even more like the way it is pronounced in [target language]?"

- Praise
  The teacher praises the learners for their performance (e.g., for what and how they said something in the TL).

- Teacher's request to repeat
  The teacher asks the student to repeat what she or he said, due to the quality of the response. In this way, the teacher applauds the student in front of the whole class and simultaneously reinforces model language use.

Negative or error corrective feedback

A teacher's negative or error corrective feedback can be categorized as **direct/explicit** or **indirect/implicit corrective strategies.** Indirect strategies implicitly provide a correct model of the student's error without telling the student overtly what the mistake was. Explicit strategies point directly to a learner's error. The following paragraphs provide a brief description and example of each strategy.

Indirect/implicit strategies.

There are two types of indirect/implicit strategies. These are recasts and clarification requests.

- Recasts

  A teacher reformulates all parts of a student's utterance minus the error.

      Example:

      T: What did you do yesterday?
      S: I *go* shopping.
      T: Oh, I went shopping myself. Where did you go?

- Clarification requests

  The teacher uses phrases such as "Pardon me?" or "I don't understand." Or, the teacher asks another question, such as "What do you mean by x?" This request signals to the students that there was some kind of error, or something was not clear in their language use, and invites them to reformulate their utterance. Teachers normally make use of clarification requests when students make meaning related errors while the focus is on communication.

      Example:

      T: How old are you?
      S: thirteen
      T: Pardon me? (Clarification request)
      S: thirty

Direct/explicit strategies. The purpose of the direct/explicit type of error correction is to make an error overt and provide a correct answer. There are several ways to do so. The teacher can either provide correct answer feedback (i.e., models), help the learner notice the error, or if necessary, guide the learners toward self-repair.

1. Correct answer feedback

The teacher directly tells a student what the mistake was and provides the correct answer. For example, she might say, "oh, you mean . . .," or "you should say . . .," or "the correct form of this verb form is . . . ." An alternative of this strategy is to ask a peer student, other than the one who committed the error, to provide the correct answer.

Example:

T: Where did you go after class yesterday?

S: I *go* home.

T: *Go* is not the correct past tense form. You need to say, "I went home."

2. Guided feedback

A more effective strategy than direct correction is to provide the students an opportunity to self-repair and guide them toward the correct answer. Strategies that allow the teacher to do so are normally referred to as elicitation techniques. The purpose of such strategies is to help the students notice that something was wrong, locate the mistake(s), and/or provide metalinguistic feedback, that is, some information about the mistake. Depending on the learner, the error, or instructional context, the teacher may have to employ numerous strategies to guide the learner toward self-repair.

Metalinguistic feedback.   **Metalinguistic feedback** contains either comments, informations regarding the accuracy of a student's utterance without providing the correct form.

Example:

T: Where did you go after class yesterday?

S: I *go* home.

T: How do you say this in simple past tense?

The teacher can also provide general reminders simply by referring to a particular lesson or class. In doing so, the teacher activates grammatical rules the student has dealt with before.

Example:

T: Where did you go after class yesterday?

S: I *go* home.

T: Do you remember the grammar we focused on in class yesterday?

A teacher can also use a variety of **noticing strategies** to get the student to produce a correct form or self-repair an existing error. These techniques include asking students to repeat their utterance again, asking questions, or pinpointing.

Teacher's request to repeat (with corrective intent).   The teacher asks the student to repeat with an error corrective intent in mind. This response may indicate that the teacher did not understand what the students had said, or that the students' utterances contained a mistake.

While the intention of this strategy is to let the students know that there was an error in their response, it does not point out what was wrong.

Example:

T: Where did you go after class yesterday?

S: I *go* home.

T: Where did you go? Can you say this again? Your answer was not grammatically correct.

Asking questions.   The teacher asks a particular question about the mistake. For example, "How do we say this in Spanish?" By asking specific questions, most teachers indirectly provide some information about what a student's actual mistake was. This strategy is also a form of metalinguistic feedback.

Example:

T: Wohin gehst du später? [Where are you going later?]

S: Später *ich* *gehe* einkaufen. (*erroneous word order) [I am going shopping later on.]

T: What should be the correct word order in your sentence?

Pinpointing.   There are different ways of pointing out which part of a student's utterance is wrong and in need of repair. One strategy is to echo the faulty utterance. The teacher repeats the student's ill-formed utterance without correction, but pronounces the feature with exaggeration.

Example:

S: En la mesa hay *una taza rojo**. *(error). [On the table there's a red cup.]

T: Um hmm, pero tú dijiste "una taza ROJO" (EMPHASIZING). ¿Qué mas? [Um hmm, but you said "a red cup" (EMPHASIZING). What else?]

Pausing.   Another strategy involves pausing. The instructor repeats the learner's utterance up to the point of the error, where the student needs to self-correct.

Example:

T: Where are you going later?

S: I am go to the supermarket?

T: I am . . .

S: I am going to the supermarket.

Types of Written Feedback Strategies

1. How did you feel about receiving written feedback as a learner? What kind of written feedback was most useful to you as a learner? Which one did you consider least effective?

   _____

   _____

2. Now take the attitudinal questionnaire in Appendix 5.1. First, take it from the point of view when you were a learner of a foreign language. Then, take it again, but this time from the point of view as teacher. Compare the results of both questionnaires. Are there any differences?

Written feedback can be provided in different ways. Such feedback includes positive and negative comments, and error corrective information. As with positive oral comments, the purpose of positive written feedback is to confirm the correctness of students' responses as well as to praise and encourage students on their performance. On the other hand, the purpose of negative written feedback is to let students know about their errors. This can be done by providing the correct answer to a student's error or by giving information about the kind of error or its location, so students can engage in self-correction. The most common written error corrective strategies constitute:

Overt error correction

This kind of correction is also known as correct answer feedback. The teacher indicates the error and provides the correct answer. For example, the teacher crosses out the incorrect ending of a verb form and writes in the correct form. Or, in case of a meaning-related error (e.g., wrong word choice), the teacher reformulates the learner's utterance, in part or as a whole.

Error location and metalinguistic feedback

The teacher using this strategy indicates the location of an error without providing the correct answer. In addition to the location of an error, metalinguistic information about the type of error can be provided. Metalinguistic feedback may entail lengthy verbal explanations or references as provided by an **error correction code (ECC)**. An ECC is a list of commonly occurring errors that are given a specific abbreviation that allows the teacher to give feedback more efficiently (see Appendix 5.2 for an example). Here are some options for applying this kind of feedback:

- highlighting an error (e.g., by circling the erroneous part of a word or underlining the whole word).
- taking a marginal tally of the number of errors in each line, without explaining the type of error(s).
- using a marginal ECC and indicating the location of an error
- using a marginal ECC without indicating the location of an error

Selective error correction

Instead of marking all errors, a teacher also has the option to be selective and mark only errors of a particular type. A teacher may choose either to locate the errors or to indicate only that a student's work contains errors of a particular type. For example, a teacher may say, "Check all your past tense forms of the verb *to be*."

Role of feedback

Why do teachers provide feedback on learners' grammar errors? The standard view of correction can be described in the following way: "Learners find out that they are wrong in regard to a particular grammatical structure and are given the right form (or directions for finding it); they then have correct knowledge about that structure, so they should be able to use it properly in the future, assuming that they understand and remember the correction" (Truscott 1996, p. 342). While such an intuitive and common view is quite a compelling argument in favor of correction, it is also simplistic and idealistic. As many teachers have experienced, the reality in the classroom often looks quite different. The following description provided by a teacher illustrates such experiences in more detail:

There were two incidents that happened in class today that made me think about the effectiveness of error correction. The first had to do with an exercise in which the students, in groups of three, had to write a classified ad for a roommate or boy- or girlfriend using the present subjunctive tense after indefinite antecedents, which is part of the lesson right now. As students read their ads, there were two repeated mistakes. The first one had to do with the use of *tener que* + infinitive to describe particular qualities they were looking for in a person. The students kept leaving out the infinitive verb after *que*. They would say, "una persona que tenga que paciente" instead of "que tenga que ser paciente." I verbally corrected the mistake as it happened, but it kept being repeated; so at one point I took a moment to write the two usages: *tener que* + infinitive and *ser* + adjective, on the overhead projector's transparency roll and explained to them as clearly as I could that they must always use the infinitive after *tener que*, and also an adjective with *ser* when describing a personal quality, that these were rules that simplified the task for them. Of course, the next person made the same mistake almost immediately after I pointed this out.

Based on the teacher's experience just described, what conclusions would you draw about learners' acquisition processes?

_____

_____

_____

The teacher's example demonstrates what instructors frequently experience—namely, that their students, after receiving feedback, often keep making the same mistakes. Even after getting it right initially, they may still fall back into their previous faulty language behavior. While there are many reasons for such erratic language behavior, it is often unclear what kind of feedback, how much feedback, or if any kind of feedback makes a difference in the learners' language development at all. Thus, it comes as no surprise that some teachers often feel confused about the role of feedback and doubt the effectiveness of the entire process.

What is the role of negative feedback, and how does negative feedback support the learning process? Primarily, feedback has an informative role. Its provision constitutes a first step toward letting the learners know that something is not in agreement with their current TL use. Taking the perspective of learners, it allows them to accept or reject a hypothesis, assuming they are testing one, about how the TL operates. Subsequently, this aids them in making an attempt toward successfully repairing an error.

Given that SLA is not a linear but a dynamic and individual process, in some cases, the immediate effect of feedback can be observed. In other cases, feedback and interaction are not always the locus of immediate learning, but must be seen as a catalyst for later learning (Mackey and Philp 1998). Often feedback is simply needed to digest the new linguistic input (Mackey, Gass, and McDonough 2000) and students may make the same or similar mistakes again, even after successful repair. This has to do with the fact, as Doughty and Williams (1998) remind us that "acquisition is a process that is not usually instantaneous" (p. 208), and achieving positive effects with error corrective feedback involves a long-term process. Only by continuously receiving corrective feedback until it is assimilated will students be in a position to ultimately acquire the correct forms. The purpose of feedback is thus to impact the learner's acquisition process gradually. Therefore, the provision of feedback must be considered not only important, but indispensable.

Providing oral feedback in the classroom has other goals and benefits. While feedback is primarily directed toward the learner who committed an error, it allows other students in a classroom setting to benefit from it as well. We know from research that any kind of overt interaction between a teacher and a student in a classroom provides learning opportunities for the learner who is directly receiving feedback as well as the other learners (see Slimani 1989, 1992). For example, when a student makes an error, peer students can test their own hypothesis of correct language use and further match it with the teacher's feedback or correct response. In some cases, error corrective feedback may even be more beneficial to nonparticipating students than to those who committed an error, as they often feel less affected by the correction process. Indeed, Slimani (1989, 1992) and Dobinson (1996) support such a hypothesis, reporting that low-participating and even non-participating students often recalled as much or sometimes even more from lessons as did their high-participating peers.

Considering that language acquisition is an individual process, the challenge about providing effective feedback is that it is difficult to know when, how, and what to correct in classroom L2 teaching. For feedback to be effective, it would have to be tailored to individual learners. For a teacher to do so, however, he or she would have to know about a variety of individual learner factors. These include the actual source of an error, a learner's ability and developmental readiness, and other affective characteristics.

Challenges: decisions and dilemmas

To provide precise feedback on a learner's error, teachers must determine what the error is. That is to say, they must understand the error and know the source of the error. Considering the inherent complexities of many grammars, this task is challenging. For example, in many languages that distinguish between genders and have a complex case system as well, it is often difficult to determine whether the origin of a learner's error has to do with lack of knowledge about gender or a case ending. In many situations, with increasing experience teachers are normally able to understand the nature of students' errors. However, in some cases, the source of a learner's error may always remain a mystery.

Learning ability and developmental readiness determine whether learners are able to incorporate feedback, and how they respond to error treatment. As far as learner ability is concerned, first of all, learners need to notice interactional feedback. This means they need to be aware that something was wrong. Unfortunately, in many learning situations learners do not realize their mistake and thus require further help in "noticing" (Schmidt 1990, 2001). In these cases, one benefit of negative feedback lies in drawing learner attention to some problematic aspect of their interlanguage (Lyster and Ranta 1997). Furthermore, learners need to know what was wrong. This means the correct answer or metalinguistic information about an error in many situations can be potentially useful. For some learners, exposure to the mistake is sometimes sufficient for them to identify and avoid similar mistakes in the future. In many other cases, however, a single exposure is not enough to overcome the faulty behavior.

Drawing attention to an error or letting the learner know that something was wrong are useful strategies only if the learner is also developmentally ready. This means, for feedback potentially to make an impact, learners have to entertain some kind of hypothesis that they are testing. This is generally referred to as the learner readiness hypothesis. As believed by many foreign language educators, **learner readiness** may be the most decisive factor in predicting success in the acquisition process. Readiness implies that the learners are able to make a "comparison between their internal representation of a rule and the information about the rule in the input [i.e., feedback] they encounter" (Chaudron 1988, p. 134). Simply put, if a learner makes a mistake and has no clue that he made a mistake, nor does he know what he did wrong, nor does he entertain some kind of hypothesis, then any kind of error corrective feedback may simply be ineffective because the learner is not yet ready to receive this kind of assistance. Brandl (1995) argues that this is often the case with low-level learners. He finds they are more likely to engage in trial-and-error behavior and randomly guess about a correct answer, while not being able to benefit from any kind of feedback that is given to them.

The decision on whether and how to correct can be further impeded by learners' affective reactions. Oral feedback is normally provided within the context of a student's learning environment and involves student-to-teacher and student-to-student interactions. As pointed out in long-established literature, during any kind of interaction emotions such as affect, anxiety, fear, arousal, and self-esteem are present. When negative feedback is provided, the learners' emotions, in particular, often become increasingly salient. As clearly documented by research, negative feedback may cause stress and embarrassment among some learner types (Horwitz and Young 1991). Walker (1973) also reports that some students believe that receiving frequent corrections destroys their confidence, and they prefer to be allowed to communicate freely without constant intervention from the teacher. In other words, there are potentially negative side effects of error correction; particularly regarding the impact it may have on the learners' learning experience. The following teacher comment illustrates this issue:

> Several students had previously taken French, and had come away traumatized by the experience, saying that they were afraid to even talk in class or ever use French because they were so harshly criticized for bad pronunciation. So I just let this aspect develop naturally, and I think they are all doing very well.

Research on written feedback also has shown that some students feel discouraged and stressed when they receive a great deal of error corrections (Semke 1984). This response is what has become known as the red-pen effect. For such reasons, some scholars have gone as far as suggesting that correcting students' errors directly does not help students, may frustrate them, and causes them to focus on language use rather than meaning.

Despite the potential harmful side effects of negative feedback, several studies have documented that most students normally want to receive feedback on their errors (Schulz 1996, 2001; Courchêne 1980; Conrad 1997, 1999; Brandl and Bauer 2002). This means students' attitude toward error corrections in general not only supports a teacher's decision but also requires them to do so. Good language learners always want to know about the quality of their oral and written language performance. This motivates them to make corrections and to work harder on their language skills. The absence of any kind of oral feedback strategies can be equally as confusing and damaging as receiving error corrections that are taken too far.

Teacher behavior and effectiveness of strategies

Considering the plethora of strategies on how to go about correcting, the question that has been the repeated focus of research is whether some strategies are more effective than others. Most scholarship that has addressed this question uses observational studies of student behavior. These have primarily focused on the effects of feedback in terms of how learners react to different feedback strategies and how they make use of the error corrective information. Several studies also look at actual teacher behavior to find out which strategies they consider most effective and which they make use of most.

Teachers go about correcting in different ways. For example, Breen (2001) states that "many teachers selectively correct errors depending upon who makes them and on the basis of their judgment of a learner's ability, resilience and emotional state" (p. 120). Many teachers also claim that they do not correct every student mistake, which is supported by Doughty's (1994) finding that teachers provided feedback only a little more than 40 percent of students' utterances.

Teachers also have been observed to employ a wide range of strategies. The most frequent types of feedback included clarification requests, repetition, and recasts (see Doughty 1994). Among these, the most popular form of feedback preferred by teachers is the recast (Doughty 1994; Lyster and Ranta 1997; Havranek 1999). In some cases, recasts made up nearly 75 percent of all teacher responses used (Ellis, Loewen, and Basturkmen 1999). The least popular strategies seem to be those that tell learners directly and explicitly that their utterances are incorrect. As Seedhouse (1997) suggested, teachers try to avoid telling learners directly that they made an error. Finally, teachers also have been shown that they to distinguish between different errors; that is, they respond with different feedback to different learner utterances. For example, Doughty (1994) observed six hours of lessons for beginners of French at the university level. She found that teachers used recasts as the form of error correction in nearly 60 percent of cases when they provided negative feedback. Other alternatives were repetitions and clarification requests.

The widespread behavior of recasts and its use as a communicative strategy has drawn a great deal of attention to recasts as a form of negative feedback. In the SLA literature, recasts have been of particular interest because, as Long (2007) points out, "if recasts turn out to be sufficient (and better yet, efficient) as a means of delivering negative feedback, their implicit and genuinely unobtrusive qualities will allow teachers and learners to continue their joint focus on meaning . . . while still dealing with linguistic problems (p. 103)." In general, many scholars consider recasts as beneficial to learners' L2 language development (e.g., see Leeman 2003; Long 2007; Long, Inagaki, and Ortega 1998; Mackey and Philp 1998). Such claims are based on findings that students exposed to recasts outperform students who received no feedback at all. Or, as Ohta (2000) has observed, learners sometimes repeated softly to themselves recasts of other students' errors, which demonstrates that many students are aware of a teacher's recast of student utterances.

Some scholars also have compared the effects of recasts to the use of other feedback strategies. For example, a study by Loewen and Philp (2006) investigated the distribution of different types of corrective feedback in communicatively oriented classrooms and their effect on uptake with adult English as a Second Language (ESL) learners. By **uptake**, they were referring to students' response to feedback. An uptake was considered successful if it incorporated the production of the correct linguistic form (i.e., the repair of the original utterance). The results of their study shows that of the 465 focus-on-form episodes, the teachers' error corrective moves involved recasts (50 percent), elicitations (14 percent), and some form of explicit information (metalinguistic) about the error (37 percent). Figure 5-1 shows the percentages of the various feedback types that led to uptakes.

Loewen and Philp's (2006) findings are consistent with other studies in general (e.g., see Lyster and Ranta 1997), which suggest that elicitations

Feedback type	Use by teachers	Uptake (successful repair of original utterance)	No uptake (original utterance still needs repair)
Recasts	50%	60%	19%*
Elicitations	14%	83%	11%*
Metalinguistic	37%	46%	31%*

Figure 5-1 Uptake following feedback type

(Source: Loewen and Philp (2006).)

*Percentage of error corrective moves to which students did not respond are not listed here.

have the highest potential as feedback strategies. When given time, through an elicitation move, learners are often able to draw on their explicit knowledge to help them produce the correct form. As such, elicitations are more engaging than all the other strategies because they involve the learners in the self-correction process. Furthermore, elicitations normally include information about the location of an error, thus further facilitating the self-repair process. Conversely, metalinguistic feedback can be beneficial although its immediate effect is normally not as high. This may have to do with the fact that metalinguistic feedback normally includes explicit information about the problematic linguistic form, which may require the learner to understand the grammatical explanation. This is not to forget that such feedback is often generic, and teachers often refer to learner errors in categories. For example, a teacher's comment such as "How would you say this with the correct word order?" or "How do you say this in past tense?" requires the learner to locate the error and interpret her or his error, which may easily result in another unsuccessful repair. It may also be the case that teachers tend to use metalinguistic feedback with errors that do not lend themselves as well to elicitation moves. This tendency would also explain why students' responses to metalinguistic feedback yielded the highest number of unsuccessful uptakes, as shown in Loewen and Philp's (2006) study.

Despite the value of elicitation and metalinguistic feedback strategies, there are some disadvantages. One is that these strategies inevitably interrupt communication. In many cases, they also require the use of the native language (L1). This may explain why teachers use metalinguistic feedback and elicitations less frequently than recasts. They are time-consuming and often create an opportunity for teachers to become side-tracked. Being overt and direct, they may also negatively influence the affective side of learning (see later discussion). Finally, the most detrimental drawback may be a psycholinguistic one, as suggested by Long (2007). Drawing on the work by Doughty (1999, 2003), he reports, "there is reason to believe that interruption of their attempts at communication in order to divert learners' focal attention to form impedes form-function mapping" (p. 103). In sum, it might be best to limit the use of elicitation and metalinguistic feedback strategies with targeted linguistic forms or when a particular grammar topic is in focus.

The question remains regarding how to go about using recasts effectively. The problem with and disadvantage of recasts is that students do not recognize them as correctional feedback, especially when teachers repeat students' utterances that are frequently identical to affirmative repetitions (Lyster 1998). Often, students have difficulties with perceiving recasts as corrective feedback; or more specifically, identifying what part of a teacher's recast is corrective or what signals the student's error. On the other hand, recasts have the advantage of providing error correction in an unobtrusive way that allows the teacher to maintain the flow of communication and furthermore prevents the teacher from getting sidetracked into lengthy error corrections.

Several suggestions can be provided on making more effective use of recasts. There appears to be more likelihood of a positive effect on learning when specific features, such as a particular grammar form, have been targeted for recasts (Doughty and Varela 1998). Or, as Havranek (1999) maintains, recasts with no special focusing element are unlikely to lead to interlanguage change. Such claims are supported by several studies. For example, Ellis, Lowen, and Basturkmen (1999) showed that 75 percent of teachers' responses to student errors were recasts. The researchers also found a 75 percent uptake, which they contribute to the fact that students received one hour of specific grammatical instruction preceding the data collection of their study. In other words, the hour of grammatical instruction may have enhanced the learners' ability to notice their errors. Another study by Iwashita (2003) also demonstrated the positive effect of recasts on targeted structures. In her study, 3 out of 5 subjects received treatment through intensive recasts once a week for an hour over the period of 12 weeks while performing communicative tasks. The two subjects who did not receive intensive recasts improved slightly, but not as much.

Learners do perceive recasts as corrective feedback in classrooms where the focus is primarily on language forms (Ohta 2000). Some scholars also recommend that the recasting technique involve an initial attention-getting phase, because some students need guidance in noticing (see Doughty 1999). This would suggest that error-noticing strategies such as echoing or a change in stress while recasting have a beneficial effect. Loewen and Philp's study (2006) supports such a claim. They found that uptake was more likely when recasts were characterized by additional pausing, change in pitch, or declarative intonation. However, as Leeman (2003) has shown, the simple strategy of helping students notice is often not sufficient, and more guidance and additional cues by the teacher may ultimately be necessary in many instances (Doughty 1999).

Recasts also seem to be effective with **phonological errors** (Mackey and Philp 1998). As observed by Mackey, Gass, and McDonough (2000), learners do not always perceive recasts of grammatical errors as corrective feedback in communicative interaction, but they do so in most cases when the error is of a phonological nature. In other words, learners seem to more easily notice sound discrepancies between their own pronunciation and a teacher's pronunciation, which makes pronunciation errors more salient than morphological errors. Such errors also can be more easily repaired since they require only the matching of sound patterns, which is generally a low-level cognitive skill. Despite the beneficial effects of recasting with regard to pronunciation errors, teachers should be aware that recasting a student's pronunciation error is often more beneficial to auditors (peers) than it is to the student who committed the error. Havranek (2002) found that those who are corrected learn most from the correction of grammatical errors and least from the correction of pronunciation errors. It seems that in a communicative and

- They are unobtrusive and do not interrupt the flow of communication.
- They may include an invitation to the learner to give another response to the teacher.
- They allow the teacher to stay in the target language.
- They inform the teacher whether the feedback was heard.
- They are most effective, if the teacher's recast focuses on only one error.
- They may be more effective if they include stress/emphasis of the recast utterance.
- Recast of phonological errors may be most effective to other students in the classroom (Havranek 2002).
- Their emphasis is primarily on language form (i.e., they are not beneficial in classrooms where the emphasis is primarily on meaning and content).
- There is no guarantee whether the student picks up on the error.

FIGURE 5-2 Summary of benefits and drawbacks of recasts

performance-based situation, students give less attention to the correction of pronunciation errors than to other types of errors—in particular, meaning-related errors. This would also explain why peers, as Havranek further reports in her study, scored best on pronunciation items and gained least from correction of lexical errors.

In sum, this section has presented advantages and disadvantages of different types of feedback, including their effects on a learner's successful repair of an error. The positive effects that teachers can achieve by using different kinds of negative feedback demonstrate that such feedback may be facilitative to a learner's language acquisition. Regarding the potential benefits of recasts (see Figure 5-2), it must be further noted that that successful uptake to an error correction move is not a measure of acquisition, as suggested by many researchers (see Ellis et al. 2001; Lightbown 1998; Loewen 2004; Lyster and Ranta 1997). That is, the presence or absence of uptake, even successful uptake, does not indicate the extent to which the learner notices the recast or benefits from it.

Effectiveness of written feedback on grammar errors

Written feedback is different from oral feedback in the classroom in many ways. First there is the issue of timing and delay. When students receive delayed feedback, they may no longer remember their initial thought processes or hypotheses for using a particular language structure. This reduces any potential effect of immediate feedback.

Second, the absence of the teacher brings along other challenges. Follow-up questions on students' understanding of the source of their errors or what the correct form should be, and any scaffolded teacher guidance, cannot be applied. The teacher has to decide on whether and what form of feedback to provide, assuming the kind of written feedback he or she provides will be the most effective. Then, it remains up to learners to cognitively engage with their teacher's corrective feedback and discover or look up the correct answer.

Unfortunately, when students are left in control of their own learning, other problems often arise that diminish the effectiveness of feedback. For example, one issue involves students' limited engagement. Unfortunately, as teachers often realize after hours of marking students' assignments, students often appear to pay little or no attention at all to error corrective feedback. Some research studies have also shown that students do not know how to interpret their teacher's error corrective feedback (Cohen 1987; I. Lee 1997). This is often the case when a student lacks not only understanding of an error, but sufficient tailored teacher feedback to bridge this gap. This difficulty is further compounded by students' limited understanding of commonly used grammatical terms in an error correction code (ECC), as pointed out by I. Lee (1997). Furthermore, even if students figure out the right answer by means of feedback, they often still do not fully or only superficially comprehend a problem.

Given some of the issues just mentioned, the question about the efficacy of written feedback on grammatical errors has been repeatedly addressed in the literature. Numerous research studies have attempted to investigate the short- and long-term effects of feedback (Cardelle and Corno 1981; Fathman and Whalley 1990; Kepner 1991; Rieken 1991; Semke 1984; Sheppard 1992).

There are few doubts about the short-term effects of feedback. For example, several studies have shown that if students are given the time to correct, and if teachers point out their errors, they do better on their follow-up versions (e.g., on essay assignments). One such study was done by Cardelle and Corno (1981), who found that students receiving correction or a combination of correction and praise on their homework surpassed those receiving only praise but no negative feedback at all. Another study by Rieken (1991) showed that explicit, direct corrections resulted in more accuracy of the passé compose (French past tense form) than did indirect or no corrections. Conducting experimental classroom studies on the effects of different types of feedback on follow-up writing assignments, Fathman and Whalley (1990) and Ashwell (2000) also reported positive effects of corrective feedback. Fathman and Whalley (1990) demonstrated that when teachers underlined grammatical errors in their students' texts, students made fewer grammatical errors in rewriting their compositions than when no such feedback was provided. Similarly, Ashwell (2000) found that when revising their essays, students took into account three-fourths of the feedback (e.g., on grammar, lexical, and mechanical errors) they had received on their first draft.

Some studies have also attempted to measure long-term effects of feedback on grammatical accuracy in students' compositions (see Semke 1984; Kepner 1991, Sheppard 1992). None of these studies found any significant effect of corrective feedback on language form. This lack of clear empirical evidence on long-term effects has made feedback a repeated subject of controversy, leading some scholars to go as far as to call it a waste of time and argue that it only takes away valuable time from other types of instruction (Truscott 1996, 1999).

Given the differences in research designs, and the controversial findings of some of the studies just reported, it is impossible to pronounce one type of feedback as being clearly more effective than another. Needless to say, classroom situations vary; and there are different curricular goals and learner needs that may ultimately warrant a varied approach to providing feedback. Coming back to the question regarding whether corrective feedback works, the answer is affirmative. There is little doubt that corrective feedback plays a beneficial role in a learner's acquisition process. The strongest empirical evidence in support of this claim to date comes from a meta-analysis that investigated the effect sizes of 15 different studies of corrective feedback on oral and written performance (Russell and Spada 2006). Russell and Spada's findings strongly support the effectiveness of corrective feedback in general for L2 grammar learning. Nevertheless, the results of studies with a delayed posttest design do not show effect sizes as strong as those studies that have measured the immediate impact of corrective feedback. This may have to do with the fact that long-term effects of corrective feedback are categorically difficult to measure. Furthermore, it has to be emphasized that the acquisition of a grammatical structure is a gradual process. It is not a sudden discovery (Long 1991). During this process, learners need repeated feedback on some linguistic features. In some cases, learners should not be expected to make immediate changes based on a single correction (Williams 2005). In other cases, it cannot be assumed that the positive effect of immediate corrective feedback results in a permanent change of a learner's interlanguage. "It seems unlikely," as Williams (2005) points out, "that long-term changes will take place in the absence of short-term improvement" (p. 156). For this reason, any kind of feedback that has the benefit of achieving short-term change must also be considered essential for the long run.

When and How to Provide Feedback: Some Practical Guidelines

Despite the indispensable role of feedback in a language-learning environment, the pragmatic side of providing feedback poses many challenges. On the spur of the moment, a teacher must make copious decisions such as whether to correct and, if so, when and how to correct; which error type (e.g., a meaning-related, grammatical, or pronunciation error); whom to correct; and how much feedback to provide. These decisions affect the lesson pace, use of time, affective climate, and learners' cognitive engagement. Many pitfalls also can occur, such as a teacher getting sidetracked or providing overly lengthy explanations. This section provides a set of practical guidelines to further aid in understanding the ins and outs of engaging in the correction process in the classroom.

Be mindful of when and when not to correct

Questions often arise concerning whether all errors should be corrected, which errors should be brought to the learners' attention, and which type of feedback should one choose when providing correction. Teachers have to make choices, while considering that it is not only impossible but also unwise to correct all the errors they might encounter. Cohen (1975) suggests a list of criteria that may further support a teacher's decision-making process. These include the pedagogical focus of a learning task, the intelligibility of a student's utterance, an individual student's requests, the frequency of specific errors, the stigmatizing and irritating effects of errors, and errors due to exceptions of rules. Another criterion that helps with making this decision is to consider whether students can be expected to self-correct, because they have the ability or the resources to figure out the correct answers themselves. Last, the decision whether or not to correct may also depend on individual learner characteristics. This issue is discussed in more detail later.

Purpose of the learning task. There seems to be general consensus among scholars and practitioners that the primary decision regarding whether and how much to correct should correspond with the purpose of the learning task (see Omaggio-Hadley 2001; Harmer 2001). When learners are focused on mastering particular features of the language, they will probably benefit most from fairly direct and immediate feedback on the correctness of their responses (Omaggio-Hadley 2001). In the language curriculum, such learning tasks include skill-getting phases where the focus is on accuracy, and where feedback is needed to facilitate the language-learning process in moving learners toward more precise and coherent language use. On the other hand, during open-ended tasks with a focus on creative language use, communication, and development of fluency, any error corrective feedback should either be avoided, provided only indirectly, or reserved for a later time. Obviously, when communication breaks down—for example, due to the lack of learner intelligibility—feedback in the form of clarification requests is indispensable to making communication possible. This observation applies to oral and written tasks alike. Examples of such oral tasks include group work activities or oral presentations. Examples of writing tasks that warrant a selective or limited approach to error feedback are online chats or daily journal writing.

Error type and pattern. Error type is another important criterion that needs to be taken into account. The assumption that all errors are equal is obviously not correct. Grammar rules vary in type and complexity, and error types vary as well and require different kinds of feedback. For example, surface errors such as spelling or some types of morphological errors lend themselves to self-correction better than do meaning-related errors, which normally require a teacher's intervention (I. Lee 1997).

Some errors may also have a stigmatizing or irritating effect. Across languages, some words when slightly mispronounced or used wrongly in context may yield such effects. Such meaning-related errors normally require special attention. Although it is widely accepted that learner errors do not generally stem from L1 (see Corder 1967) but are rather due to developmental processes in second language acquisition (SLA), some patterns of errors (e.g., pronunciation errors) still find their roots in L1. These errors may also require special treatment. Finally, there are exceptions to grammatical rules that often require the teacher's expertise and intervention.

Ease of correction. A teacher may decide not to correct many of the errors made in a language class. Such decisions may be based on the fact that some errors take too long to explain and would be interrupting the lesson flow. As pointed out earlier, language learning is developmental, and it is often a misconception of teachers that lengthy explanations will prevent students from making the same mistakes again. In most such cases, in particular with complex language structures, ongoing teacher modeling of correct language use may be the most effective and efficient strategy.

Engage the learners in the correction process

Another question often arises regarding who should correct errors: the teacher or the learners themselves? Traditionally, it has been the teacher's role to provide all the error corrective feedback. At the same time, it is common practice among teachers to involve the learners in the correction process. From a cognitive viewpoint of learning, it can be argued that self-corrective and self-discovery strategies are most engaging and potentially beneficial to the learning process. As Williams (2005) puts it, "It is thought that when learners register the gap between their own production and the target form by themselves, they process the information more deeply, perhaps transferring the correct form to long-term memory, than if the teacher leads them to it (p. 156)." Students who are able to correct their own errors may also experience an enhanced feeling of success.

The caveat about self-corrections is that learners often are not able to detect their own mistakes. In many cases, students require their teachers' expertise and do better when being guided in their correction process (Fathman and Whalley 1990). The goal of guidance is to lead the learners toward self-repair by providing additional help and thus maximizing their engagement in the correction process. On written assignments, this can be done by providing error feedback in the form of an ECC or by pinpointing (underlining or circling) the location of an error. Similarly, oral correction techniques such as clarification requests, providing metalinguistic feedback, repetitions, pinpointing, and pausing allow the teacher to help students self-repair.

In the classroom, a teacher can apply several other strategies to facilitate the learner's correction process. One such strategy is to allow for ample response time. Many teachers have intolerance for what they may feel to be a long period of silence. They often expect immediate responses and do not allow for sufficient response time. In particular, when asking students to self-correct, teachers need to be patient in allowing them ample time to reflect upon their utterance.

Another strategy is to display oral errors in writing on the board or overhead and underline the key features. The advantage of such practice is that the written modality of a student utterance allows for deeper processing and more time to discover an error. From a pragmatic point of view, this strategy is very time inefficient; it is best used only when it supports the pedagogical purpose of a lesson. Furthermore, the displaying of a student's erroneous language should be dealt with respectfully. Research has shown that some students consider the task of writing on the board as inducing high anxiety (Young 1990). Therefore, the display of student errors may be best done anonymously.

Last, teachers can encourage learners to meet with them in person to discuss their errors. This technique allows for tailoring feedback to a student's individual needs and is the most engaging.

Use multiple techniques

Omaggio-Hadley (2001) points out that "The assumption that all learners receive corrective feedback in the same way and with the same degree of enthusiasm is [. . .] problematic. [. . .] we need to keep in mind that they may work differently with different learners (see for example DeKeyser 1993) and should therefore not be used in a rigid or prescriptive fashion" (p. 276). Needless to say, learners vary widely in their personalities, learning styles, preferences, and abilities; they require individually tailored feedback for it to be most effective. For example, as Brandl (1995) finds, low-achieving students ask for different kinds of feedback than high achievers do when given an option in a computer-based environment. There is no panacean approach to dealing with errors, so teachers need to vary in their use of strategies. Depending on error or learner type, the use of multiple or a combination of strategies is normally necessary.

Make use of peer corrections

The purpose of providing feedback is to assist not only the one student who committed a mistake but also all participants involved in the learning environment. Therefore, all students should be integrated in the correction process. They should be encouraged and taught to be active monitors of their peers' utterances. This requires them to actively listen and stay engaged. When asking student peers to aid with the error correction process, teachers need to be sensitive to the students' feelings. Students normally notice when they cannot self-repair and others are called on to help.

Keep the learners' affective reaction in mind

Learning is about making mistakes. While most learners are aware of the importance of making mistakes in order to learn, they still may feel uncomfortable about being corrected. For most learners, this is only a normal emotional reaction. Some learner types feel more embarrassed than others do after making a mistake; to them, making a mistake poses the possibility of threatening their self-esteem in a public situation. In some extreme cases, the fear of making errors or embarrassment may block some learners from speaking up in class at all. The fear of making errors has also been claimed to have a stifling effect on what and how much students are going to say in a written assignment (Sheppard 1992).

In most cases, however, the way students feel about being corrected depends on their motivation and on how comfortable they feel in their learning environment. That is, how comfortable students feel is often also determined by a teacher's response to student participation and performance. Some scholars believe that students' positive attitude toward correction may be the most influential factor in leading to successful use of the corrected forms (Havranek 2002). Teachers need to be sensitive to the needs and individual concerns of their students and their preferences for feedback (see Walz 1982). Furthermore, feedback needs to be conveyed in such a way that learners do not feel impeded from speaking up freely in the classroom; nor should feedback be provided so that it stifles their effort on written assignments.

Discuss your error correction strategies with your students

Numerous studies report that students expect to be corrected and prefer consistent feedback (see Brandl and Bauer 2002; Cathcart and Olsen 1976; Courchêne 1980; Schulz 2001). However, there may be occasions when a teacher does not want to correct, or only use a particular strategy. For this reason, it is important that the instructor discusses error correction with her students and informs her students about her correction strategies. Students should be informed when they are corrected, and in which situations they are not, or only to a limited degree, to avoid any kind of confusion.

Furthermore, the instructor should ask her students how they feel about the teacher's error correction strategies. This has several advantages. The teacher finds out whether her students consider the corrections informative and valuable, and what strategies the students prefer most. In addition, it provides an opportunity to discuss the importance of self-correction with the students. An alternative to asking students in class directly is to provide a brief questionnaire about how they feel about error correction. Possible questions that a teacher can ask are: 1) Is my feedback clear and informative enough? 2) What kind of error corrective feedback helps you most? 3) How do you want me to correct your errors? For example, do you want me to provide correct answers or mark errors only? 4) How do you feel about self-corrections?

Be mindful of students' inquiries

A question that often arises is whether a teacher should correct and provide feedback, in particular when an individual student inquires about the nature of an error. Generally speaking, the answer is yes, because it suggests that a student has noticed an error and could benefit from some kind of clarification. However, a teacher has to be cognizant of the kinds of errors students ask about. In many instances, particularly in CLT classrooms where students are exposed to rich input, students inquire about language structures to which they have not yet been introduced. When this happens, it is better to avoid any kind of explanations, at least during regular class time. Let students know that the topic will be introduced at a later stage in the curriculum. This is not to say that discussing advanced grammar features should be avoided during class time. Ultimately, the teacher makes this choice; but often these concerns should be addressed at an individual level, outside of class.

Conclusion

This chapter has provided an overview of a wide range of oral and written error corrective strategies that teachers have at their disposal. It has also looked at the role of feedback in general and discussed the effectiveness of different oral and written feedback strategies. The position taken in this chapter is that feedback constitutes a vital part of learning. Existing research predicts, at least for the short term, positive effects for written and oral error correction. In addition, recent second language acquisition (SLA) research on *focus on form* strongly suggests that adult language learners need their errors made salient and explicit to them, so that they can avoid fossilization and continue developing language competence. As such, negative feedback has an awareness-raising effect. It lets the learner know that something is wrong. If the learner is ready, and if feedback is repeatedly provided, it can be useful in facilitating the progression of a learner's skills toward more precise and coherent language use and thus create a lasting impact. There is also some evidence that feedback is most effective if the learner is actively engaged in the repair and monitoring process.

The pragmatic side of providing feedback involves numerous decisions. Feedback should not be provided in an ad hoc way. Instead it should be based on a conscious rationale, taking into account learners' needs, backgrounds, and instructional contexts. Given the dynamics of social interactions in the classroom and other complex learning processes, teachers need to prepare themselves for an environment where feedback does not always result in a learner's instantaneous or continuously correct use of language. By creating an environment that allows students to have positive attitudes toward rectifying errors and to receive mindful error corrections, nevertheless, teachers can maximize their learners' progress.

Checking chapter objectives

Do I know how to . . .

- ❏ discuss the role of providing feedback and error correction
- ❏ deal with challenges that occur when providing error correction in the classroom
- ❏ define different error correction techniques and discuss their effectiveness
- ❏ describe some practical guidelines for providing error treatment

Explorations

TASK 1: TEST YOURSELF

Match the description, definition, or example with the type of error corrective feedback.

MF	metalinguistic feedback
REC	recast
REP	repeating (asking students to repeat)
P	pausing
CR	clarification requests
NF	no feedback
E	echoing
AQ	asking questions

1. Teacher says: "Can you say this again?"	MF REC REP P CR NF E AQ
2. A teacher reformulates all parts of a student's utterance minus the error.	MF REC REP P CR NF E AQ
3. T: Where are you going later? S: I am go to the supermarket? T: I am . . . S: I am going to the supermarket.	MF REC REP P CR NF E AQ

4. Such feedback contains either comments, information, or questions about the accuracy of a student's utterance. For example, regarding a student's wrong use of verb form, the teacher might provide grammatical information by saying: "You need the first-person singular of [this particular] verb form."	MF REC REP P CR NF E AQ
5. S: En la mesa hay una taza rojo* (*ERROR). [On the table there's a red cup.] T: Um hmm, una taza roja. ¿Qué mas? [Um hmm, a red cup. What else?]	MF REC REP P CR NF E AQ
6. The teacher uses phrases such as "Pardon me?" or "I don't understand?"	MF REC REP P CR NF E AQ
7. S: En la mesa hay una taza rojo* (*ERROR). [On the table there's a red cup.] T: Um hmm, ¿Qué mas? [Um hmm, What else?]	MF REC REP P CR NF E AQ
8. When using this strategy, you would say: "What is the correct word order of this sentence? What is the correct article of word 'X'?"	MF REC REP P CR NF E AQ
9. The teacher repeats the student's ill-formed utterance without correction but pronounces the feature with exaggeration.	MF REC REP P CR NF E AQ
10. S: En la mesa hay una taza rojo* (*ERROR). [On the table there's a red cup.] T: Um hmm, pero tú dijiste "una taza ROJO" (EMPHASIZING). [Um hmm, but you said "a red cup" (EMPHASIZING).]	MF REC REP P CR NF E AQ

TASK 2: DISCUSSION

Discuss the following questions: Where do errors come from? Or, why do learners make mistakes?

TASK 3: DISCUSSION

What learner types may have problems being corrected? What are potential reasons for this?

TASK 4: DISCUSSION

Read the statements in Figure 5-3, in which teachers describe their error correction strategies and their beliefs about their effectiveness. Based on their error corrective behavior, what assumptions do the teachers make about the impact of oral error correction on student learning? Do you agree with these assumptions? Why or why not?

1. If I want my students to speak freely, then I must not do a lot of overt correction. They would be afraid to speak if they knew they were going to be corrected all the time.

2. In activities where I am emphasizing a grammar point, then I correct more, especially the grammar point we are working on.

3. In communicative activities, the purpose is for the students to express their ideas. When they make errors, I just rephrase and correct the errors, but I do not want to break the flow. They have the information to think about later.

4. When and how I correct depends on the level of the student. For the weaker students, I just rephrase to correct the error, because I am just happy that they are talking. For the better students, I might actually correct the error because they will know what I am getting at.

5. Correcting students' pronunciation takes so much time. Now I correct my students' pronunciation only if I cannot understand at all what they are trying to say.

6. Although pronunciation is important to me, I never correct my students on it. I sometimes remind them of certain sounds as a class, but I don't use explicit correction for this.

7. I believe that, with my help, the students realize that they made an error . . . at least for a time . . . of course they will not stop making that error all of a sudden. It is a process. And only by working on it again and again, until it is assimilated, will they get the correct structure.

8. When I correct exercises in class, I ask every student to read the sentences aloud and then I write the answers on the board. I deliberately make mistakes when writing and then ask students to correct me.

FIGURE 5-3 Teachers' beliefs about error correction

TASK 5: ANALYSIS AND DISCUSSION (WHEN AND HOW TO CORRECT)

How would you describe the teacher's role in providing oral feedback on students' errors? Should a teacher correct all of the students' mistakes? Can you think of situations when a teacher should not correct a student's mistake? Provide a rationale for your answer.

TASK 6: SELF-ANALYSIS

Briefly describe how you go about correcting your students' errors in your classroom. Before you do so, fill out the questionnaire in Appendix 5.1. If you do not teach at this point, describe how you think you would approach error correction in the classroom.

TASK 7: ANALYSIS (OBSERVATIONS/ACQUISITION PROCESS)

What kind of challenges have you experienced in providing error corrections?

TASK 8: EXPERIMENTING RECASTING

Read the following dialogue between a teacher and student out loud. Dialogue in the classroom:

> T: Could you tell me something about your family?
> S: I have two *brother* and two sisters.
> T: Oh, there are four children in your family.
>   I have three brothers. What are your brothers like?
> S: My *brother* are 4 and 7 years old. Their *name* are . . .

What was the student's mistake? You may not have noticed the student's mistake at first. What conclusion would you draw from this experiment about the significance of these errors? How do you feel about the technique of recasting?

TASK 9: CASE STUDY

In Mrs. Anderson's class her students gave short presentations, which they had prepared on the Day of the Dead. All of the students who gave presentations made mistakes in using the verbs *estar* and *ser* (both verbs mean "to be" but are used in different ways in Spanish). The teacher did not interrupt their presentations, but commented on a few errors after the end of each presentation. The pronunciation of certain words was the only thing she corrected them on. She also made comments such as "You guys really need to watch how you use the verbs *estar* and *ser*."

When asked about her rationale for error corrections, the teacher said she chooses to focus more on pronunciation errors than on grammatical ones. She corrects her students' grammar, but lets it slide a bit more than their pronunciation. She said that her students would tend to remember the correct pronunciation of something after only a single correction.

What are Mrs. Anderson's assumptions about the effectiveness of error correction? Do you agree? How would you have dealt with the learners' errors in the case just described?

TASK 10: OBSERVATION

Observe an experienced language teacher. What kind of error correction techniques does he or she make use of? At the same time, focus on the learners. What are their reactions to their teacher's way of providing oral feedback? Last, interview the instructor and ask approximately what percentage of his or her students' errors he or she corrects. How does the teacher's report match with her or his practices?

TASK 11: BENEFITS AND DRAWBACKS OF ORAL FEEDBACK STRATEGIES

Discuss the benefits and drawbacks of different types of oral feedback such as recasts, clarification requests, metalinguistic feedback, elicitations, or a teacher's explicit corrections. How do you best apply such error corrective moves in different classroom situations?

TASK 12: BENEFITS AND DRAWBACKS OF WRITTEN FEEDBACK STRATEGIES

Discuss the benefits and drawbacks of different types of written feedback such as overt error corrections, different error location strategies, using an error correction code, and metalinguistic feedback.

TASK 13: FINDING OUT STUDENTS' PREFERENCES

Develop a short questionnaire and find out your students' preferences regarding your use of error corrections strategies on their written or oral performances. Ask questions such as 1) Is my feedback clear and informative enough? 2) What kind of error corrective feedback helps you most? 3) How do you want me to correct your errors? For example, do you want me to provide correct answers or mark errors only? 4) How do you feel about self-corrections? Based on what you are learning from your students' comments, how can you make your oral or written correction strategies more effective?

TASK 14: FOLLOWING-UP ON WRITTEN FEEDBACK

How important is it to follow-up on error corrections with your students; for example, feedback that you provided on homework or a test? What are pros and cons of going over error corrections in class? How can you get your students to attend to your feedback, self-correct, and learn from their errors?

TASK 15: OVERT ERROR CORRECTION IN THE CLASSROOM

The strategies below demonstrate different ways of engaging learners in error correction in the classroom: Discuss the pros and cons of each of these strategies. Can you think of any other strategies?

1. As part of a warm up, the teacher writes two sentences on the board that each contain several grammatical and spelling errors, and asks to students to find the errors, and provide the correct answer.
2. The teacher writes five sentences on the board that each contain a variety of different types of errors. She asks to students to work in pairs to find the errors and provide the correct answer.
3. The teacher provides two versions of a written text (e.g., a student homework): Version A contains errors, and Version B is error free. She asks the students to work in pairs and compare the correct with the faulty version.
4. The teacher announces that they are going to play an error correction game. The teacher provides an uncorrected sample of a student homework. For each error the students can find, they get 1 point, for

the correct answer they receive 2 points. She asks the students to work in pairs and limits this activity to 5 minutes.
5. The teacher provides the following scenario on an overhead.
Miriam and Claudia just met in the parking lot of the apartment complex where they both live. Miriam is from Kuwait, and Claudia is American.

Claudia: "It was really nice to meet you. Let's have dinner some time."

Miriam: "Nice to meet you, too. When? I can come by tomorrow. What is your apartment number?"

Claudia: (*looking confused*) "I'll let you know. Bye."

Then, she assigns the following task to her students. In pairs, analyze and discuss the error situation in this situation. Then, write a dialog or a story about a misunderstanding that occurred between somebody from your own culture and somebody from another culture.

Application

TASK 16: WHEN AND HOW DO I CORRECT?

Part 1: Self-analysis

Fill out the following questionnaire and identify when and how you correct. Describe your error corrective behavior.

Questionnaire

1. What is your tendency in correcting your students' errors? Mark your answers from 5 (a great deal) to 1 (very little).

   During open-ended tasks   5 4 3 2 1

   During activities with a narrow focus   5 4 3 2 1

2. What kind of errors do you tend to correct?
   - pronunciation
   - grammar (morphosyntactic)
   - lexical
   - pragmatic
   - content

3. Who corrects in your class?
   - the teacher
   - the learner who made the error
   - other learners

4. When do you correct most of the time?
   - immediately after a student made a mistake
   - at the end of a student's response or presentation
   - during a dedicated correction phase (e.g., at the beginning or the end of a lesson)

5. How often do you encourage your learners to self-correct?
   - all of the time
   - most of the time
   - sometimes
   - hardly ever
   - never

6. How do you engage your students in self-corrections?
   - I say that something is wrong.
   - I say where the error is.
   - I give nonverbal cues indicating that something is wrong.
   - I provide additional metalinguistic comments (e.g., I indicate which grammar structure, such as third-person singular, needs to be used).
   - I say when and where we learned and talked about the linguistic phenomenon currently under scrutiny.

7. How do you normally correct, in case you prefer to provide the error correction yourself?
   - I only provide the correct form, and point out what the mistake was.
   - I repeat the learner's wrong utterance, but in the correct way.
   - Other.

8. How do you follow up on your error correction?
   a. in response to a student's self-correction:
      - I continue with my task.
      - I have the learner who made the mistake repeat the correct utterance.
      - I repeat the corrected utterance myself.
      - I provide additional information.
   b. in response to peer correction:
      - I continue with my task.
      - I have the learner who made the mistake repeat the correct utterance.
      - I repeat the corrected utterance myself.
      - I provide additional information.
   c. in response to your own correction (teacher-corrected):
      - I continue with my task.
      - I have the learner who made the mistake repeat the correct utterance.
      - I repeat the corrected utterance myself.
      - I provide additional information.

9. What language do you use when correcting errors?
   - only the TL
   - only English
   - English and the TL

10. How do you react when a student makes an error?
   - friendly
   - ironic
   - neutral
   - frustrated
   - humorous
   - other:

Source: Kleppin (1998, 75–77); translated and modified by Klaus Brandl.

TASK 17: WHEN AND HOW DO I CORRECT?

Part 2: A closer look at different lesson phases and task types

Although many teachers find it challenging to change their error correction practices, particular lesson phases or task types lend themselves well either to enhancing or reducing error corrections, or to employing a particular strategy.

Do you correct during the following lesson phases or task types? If so, how? Fill out the following survey.

	Yes	No	Only if . . .	How do you correct?
Students read out loud				
Group/pair work				
Guided grammar exercises				
Student presentations				
Role-playing, skits				
Communicative language practice (e.g., open-ended or personal questions with unpredictable answers)				
Pre-communicative language practice (e.g., guided teacher questions with predictable answers)				
Authentic communication (e.g., free discussions)				

Source: Kleppin (1998, p. 91); translated and modified by Klaus Brandl.

TASK 18: WHEN AND HOW DO I CORRECT?

Part 3: Follow-up analysis

To receive verification about your actual error correction behavior in class, pair up with another instructor and observe each other's language classes. Choose the questionnaire from either part 1 or 2 above, and answer all of the same questions for your peer instructor during the observation. Compare your self-analysis with your partner's recording. What differences do you notice?

Questionnaire

1. What is your tendency in correcting your students' errors on written assignments? Mark your answers from 5 (a great deal) to 1 (very little).

During open-ended tasks	5 4 3 2 1
During activities with a narrow focus	5 4 3 2 1

2. What kind of errors do you tend to correct?
   - grammar (morphosyntactic)
   - lexical (word meanings)
   - pragmatic
   - content
   - spelling/punctuation

3. Who corrects in your class?
   - the teacher
   - the learner who made the error (self-correction)
   - other learners (peer correction)

4. How often do you encourage your learners to self-correct?
   - all of the time
   - most of the time
   - sometimes
   - hardly ever
   - never

5. How do you normally correct?
   - I only comment that something is wrong.
   - I provide the correct answers.
   - I mark the errors (by circling or underlining).
   - I indicate the margin of the line where an error has occurred.
   - I use an error correction code (ECC).
   - I provide informative comments about what was particularly good.
   - I provide informative comments about the areas needing improvement. For example, "You need to review your past tense conjugation forms . . ."
   - I provide positive comments such as "Good job! Well done!"
   - I mark only one type of error.

6. How do you follow up on your error correction?
   - I encourage students to self-correct the assignment.
   - I ask students to self-correct the assignment, and I correct it again.
   - I have students correct each other's errors in class.
   - I do not do anything.

APPENDIX 5.1

Sample error correction

1.	WOmC	word order in main clause
2.	WOiC	word order in dependent [subordinate] clause
3.	G	gender
4.	Pl	noun plural form
6.	GenC	genetive case
7.	NC	noun capitalization
8.	AdjE	adjective ending
9.	PerPro	personal pronoun
10.	PossPro	possessive pronoun ending
11.	PossAdj	possessive adjective ending
12.	RefPro	reflexive pronoun
13.	IntPro	interrogative pronoun
14.	VT	verb form, tense
15.	VE	verb form, irregular
16.	VE	verb form, ending
17.	AC	accusative case
18.	DC	dative case
19.	WCh	word choice
20.	Prep	preposition
21.	TE	time expressions (e.g., adverbial phrases)
22.	Sp	spelling

APPENDIX 5.2

My attitude toward error correction

1. My previous attitude toward correcting and feedback as a student.

	very	<->	little
I loved to be corrected. It gave me a sense that the teacher cared for my learning.	3	2	1
I thought of it as a waste of my time, because I never looked at the feedback my teacher provided.	3	2	1
I thought it was a waste of time, because I kept making the same errors.	3	2	1
I considered it important, because it gave me a sense of what I needed to learn.	3	2	1
I considered it important, because it provided me with some valuable information on how to improve.	3	2	1
I considered it important only when I asked for it.	3	2	1
I considered it harmful, because it had a frustrating and discouraging effect on me.	3	2	1

2. My attitude toward correcting and feedback as a teacher.

	very	<->	little
I love to correct. It gives me a sense of power.	3	2	1
I think of it as a waste of my time, because my students never look at my feedback.	3	2	1
I think of it as a waste of time because my students keep making the same errors.	3	2	1
I think of it as a waste of time because it is too time-consuming in relation to what my students gain from it.	3	2	1
I consider it important, because it gives me a sense of what my students have learned.	3	2	1
I consider it important, because it allows me to provide some valuable feedback to my students.	3	2	1
I consider it important, because my students ask for it.	3	2	1
I consider it harmful, because it has a frustrating and discouraging effect on my students.	3	2	1

Instructional Sequencing and Task Design

Tell me and I will forget; teach me and I will remember; involve me and I will learn.

Chinese proverb

REFLECTION

As a learner of another language, which exercises or activities worked best for you? Which ones did not work at all? Explain your answer.

_____

_____

Introduction

Performing a communicative language task in the target language (TL) normally involves a range of language skills. Depending on the task, these may require the learners to engage in different skill areas such as speaking, listening, reading, or writing. While doing so, they have to apply knowledge of vocabulary, grammar structures, and—most importantly—demonstrate the ability to express meaning, fluently and accurately. Differently put, communicative language teaching (CLT) requires the teaching of skills in an integrated versus an isolated manner, as is the case with traditional methods of teaching. Such a multiple-skills-encompassing endeavor, however, poses many challenges. Learners may feel easily overwhelmed if they are asked to perform language tasks that involve too many different skills at once—or, on the other hand, they may get bored if tasks are too repetitive, too narrow in scope, or exclusively focus on formal features of a language. Here are some questions that arise: How are communicative tasks to be designed to address the range of different language skills? How are skills to be combined while incrementally leading the learners toward open-ended language application? How are tasks to be sequenced so they optimize the language learning process? The purpose of this chapter is to explore the topic of task design and sequencing in more detail.

Description of Lesson Phases and Characteristics of Communicative Tasks

Language lessons can be divided into different segments: a noncommunicative learning segment, an input phase, an assimilation phase, and the final extension or application stage. Lessons may vary in length of time. While some lessons take learners through all lesson phases in a single class period, others are arranged over a period of several days.

Figure 6-1 provides an overview and illustrates the progression from pedagogical to real-life tasks along these lesson phases. Noncommunicative learning tasks that have a strong focus on processing or learning skills, such as grammar "awareness-raising" or "discovery learning" tasks, normally fall toward the left side of the continuum. They primarily have an enabling character; that is, they aid the learners in their understanding of how language works as well as in the development of learning skills and strategies in general. While such noncommunicative learning tasks normally precede or are part of the presentation of the input, they may be integrated into any lesson phase.

Input phase

The input phase constitutes the initial segment. Its main focus is the presentation of the new content through textual resources (e.g., stories, dialogues, authentic ads, scripted or semi-scripted texts), audio- or video-based language situations, communicative language acts (e.g., introductions, telling time), or instructional processing activities.

As discussed in previous chapters, this phase normally involves the introduction of new vocabulary and grammar structures. The primary purpose is to expose learners to model structures of language in context, while keeping meaning in focus, and to lead the learners towards comprehension of the target language input. To keep meaning in focus, students' comprehension should be consistently monitored. At beginning levels, comprehension checks may be limited to strategies such as yes/no, true/false, either/or questions, or nonlinguistic responses (e.g., gestures). With students' increase in language proficiency, such instructional strategies involve complex language tasks such as open-ended comprehension questions or summaries (see Chapters 7, 8, and 9 on the development of listening, speaking, and reading skills).

Assimilation phase

The second phase, assimilation, consists of a cycle of controlled and guided practice. The goal at this stage is to provide students with a variety of learning tasks that allow students to incrementally build skills with the teacher's help.

Noncommuni-cative learning	Input Phase (pre-communicative language practice)	Communicative Language Application
		assimilation tasks <————————> real-life tasks

		focus on
		process <————————————————————————————> product

| noncommunicative learning tasks are integrated in all lesson phases | nonlinguistic tasks limited student output | **Progression of student output during task performance**
 predictable <————————> unpredictable <br> teacher controlled <————————> student controlled <br> reduced choices <————————> open-ended content <br> non-creative <————————> creative language use <br> narrow context <————————> broad context |

FIGURE 6-1 Overview of task characteristics and skill progression

Source: Adapted from Littlewood (2004).

The initial activities in this segment should require that students attend to both meaning and form of the new linguistic features. Tasks are designed so students zoom in on isolated aspects that are required to perform a communicative task. For example, initial activities may deal with receptive skills (listening or reading), so that students are not required to produce the new features. Language is applied within a narrow communicative context, in small chunks (e.g., focusing on only one or two grammar rules), and the task is usually controlled and guided by the activity and the teacher. Tasks may also focus on listening, speaking, or writing only. Students' language production moves from yes/no to one-word to longer discourse answers. The contents of their answers are initially predictable while they become increasingly more communicative. Students usually work in pairs or in small groups, although some activities may be teacher centered.

Some researchers also suggest that a longer input phase may enhance learner internalization of the new features (VanPatten and Cadierno 1995). For this reason, some methods (i.e., Total Physical Response) promote and apply prolonged input and guided participation lesson phases that initially deemphasize active, productive skill activities. Before students move on to the final lesson phase, a lesson may also cycle through the input and assimilation phase several times, so they can assimilate all the skills that are needed to perform successfully in the final lesson phase. Feedback and error correction play an enhanced role during this phase as well.

Application and extension phase

Extension is the last of the different lesson phases. This final lesson segment is also known as the phase of open-ended communicative application, or when students perform the targeted lesson goals and tasks. Ballman (1998) describes this segment as follows:

> Extension requires students to participate in a culminating activity in which much, if not all, the lesson's target vocabulary, grammar and content are used. The language produced by students is more open-ended and creative, with spontaneous language use a likely phenomenon. It is during the Extension segment where most learner/learner interaction occurs, and where learners take on the responsibility for their participation. These extension activities are likely to be found at the midpoint, and they are always found at the end of a lesson. (pp. 101–102)

The final phase usually integrates multiple skills. The teacher does not control or guide the student language anymore. Most activities consist of student-centered learning tasks. Examples include roleplay, discussions, debates, writing emails. Feedback and error correction play a reduced role, while the assessment of learning is demonstrated through students' achievement of communicative goals.

Teacher Roles

Several roles are assumed of language teachers in the communicative classroom. These roles constantly change during different segments of a lesson phase. In earlier chapters, you were introduced to vocabulary and grammar presentation techniques, during which the teacher takes on the role of the presenter. Following or integrated into the presentation (input) phase of a lesson, the teacher also functions as a designer, organizer, and guide. In these roles, the teacher leads the students along the sequence of different learning tasks in order to meet the different pedagogical goals of the lesson. Normally, once the students have gained enough linguistic expertise, they move on to perform and demonstrate these skills during pair or group work activities, or working individually. When shifting from teacher- to student-centered activities, the teacher's role changes to that of a facilitator. Ballman (1998) describes the facilitator's role in the following way:

> By facilitator, it is meant that the teacher sets up and models each student-centered activity. If during a lesson on the topic of family students are asked to work in pairs, for example, with Student A drawing Student B's family tree, the teacher would briefly explain what each student is to do. The teacher would also model the beginning of the activity with a student in the class. (p. 100)

During a student-centered activity, the teacher also assumes the role of a resource provider, group process manager, and needs analyst who assesses the students' performance. She walks through the classroom, monitoring student work and answering any questions. Immediately, following a student-centered activity, the focus of the class returns to the teacher, since she must lead the class in a follow-up or synthesis activity. The teacher's role changes again to a discussion leader, classroom manager or facilitator, and evaluator who draws conclusions about the students' performance.

The Role of "Repeated" Practice

The notion of repeated practice in learning and skill acquisition permeates all strands of education. As expressed in educational slogans such as "practice makes perfect" or "repetition is the mother of all studies," the importance of practice to learning is a necessity. Needless to say, effective teachers recognize the need for repetition and review and integrate these activities in their daily and long-term instructional practices. For example, most teachers start their lessons with some form of review or repetition of previously introduced materials (see Chapter 2, Short-term and Daily Lesson Planning). Or, well-structured lessons recycle language-learning content in different segments of the lesson. The assimilation phase is marked by repetition. The extension period of a lesson segment is essentially also a review and repetition of different skills at a more encompassing level (Ballman 1998).

From a neurobiological perspective, the role of repetition is very important. For learning to occur, neural networks and associations need to be formed. Furthermore, repeated activation of patterns is necessary to strengthen such links (Myles, Hooper, and Mitchell 1998). Another advantage of repetition is that it helps with freeing up memory. While learners start feeling more at ease with one component, it allows them to pay attention to other processes, and thus integrate procedural and declarative knowledge at a deeper level (see Chapter 4, Grammar and Language Learning).

Nevertheless, in both applied linguistics and language education, repetition is a problematic concept. The term itself is often negatively associated with the kind of mindless act of repeating language patterns that learners are tempted to engage in, when the need to keep meaning in focus is not required. This was often the case with many audiolingual drills (see "Mechanical drills") due to their often exclusive focus on forms. For this reason, referring to the concept of repetition as 'retrial' (Johnson 1996) or task 'recycling' (Lynch and McClean 2000) might be more appropriate. Both of these concepts imply a more hands-on and learner-centered approach and encourage cognitive engagement at each retrial attempt. These concepts also imply that learning takes place in incremental stages. Hence, learners need many opportunities for retrials, which makes the strategy of task recycling necessary.

Task recycling means that learners perform communicative language tasks in some varied forms. The communicative goal may remain the same; but some content may change—the mode (e.g., orally or in writing), the conditions (e.g., spontaneous language application or built-in planning time, either individually or in groups), or the communicative partner. This process may also involve the exact duplication of a task if implemented in a different communicative context or with different communicative partners.

When teachers are planning daily and long-term lessons, the instructional practices of recycling and retrial raise many questions. For example, what is it that is to be repeated? Is it isolated language patterns or complete communicative tasks? How should learning tasks be designed, so they are engaging to the learners? Can tasks be designed so learners attend to form and meaning? What characteristics of task design promote the learning process? How can effective task recycling be achieved? In what sequence should learning tasks be arranged?

The following section looks at design features of learning tasks that motivate the learning process. It also analyzes linguistic and cognitive processes and conditions that influence task design.

Characteristics of Communicative Learning Tasks

One fundamental principle of second language acquisition (SLA) is that learners need access to input that is meaningful. "Input [here] is defined as meaning-based language that learners hear or see in context" (Wong and VanPatten 2003, p. 408). To elaborate more on the definition of **meaningful**, this principle means that the language being attended to by the learner involves comprehension of an intended message. In learning, 'meaning' plays an important role, because only something that conceptually makes sense can be integrated into existing mental structures, retrieved and manipulated, and reapplied in other contexts. In this sense, the meaningful principle distinguishes itself from traditional rote learning. Through rote learning, information can also be stored in memory—but only as a whole, not as a concept.

A second design principle is that learning tasks are **communicative**. The aspect of being 'communicative' has become a hallmark of many communicative learning tasks, underlining the purpose of language as communication. Above all, as many proponents of CLT believe, it is major forces such as language exchange, negotiation of meaning, and interaction that drive the SLA process.

To further interpret these principles, let us take a look at the design of traditional and more recent textbook activities. A traditional form of exercises is the drill type. A **drill** is defined as a "technique commonly used in language teaching for practicing sounds or sentence patterns in a language, based on guided repetition or practice. A drill which practices some aspect of grammar or sentence formation is often known as **pattern practice**" (Richards, Platt, and Platt 1992, p. 117). Examples of such drills are substitution drills, repetition drills, or transformation drills.

1. Substitution drill:		
Teacher asks:	**Student says:**	**Substitutions provided in the textbook**
What does Hans speak?	Hans speaks <u>German</u> and lives in <u>Germany</u>.	German—Germany
1. What does Marie speak?	. . .	French—France
2. What does Eduardo speak?	. . .	Spanish—Spain

2. Transformation drill:	
Instructions: Transform the following statement into a question.	
Teacher's cue:	**Student says:**
I bought a car.	What did you buy?
1. I speak English	. . .
2. I study French.	. . .

Another classification of such traditional grammar exercises is known as "mechanical," "meaningful," and "communicative" drills (Paulston 1972). Lee and VanPatten (1995a) summarize these differences in the following way:

> The classification of drills as mechanical, meaningful, or communicative is based on the degree of learner control over the response: whether or not there is one right answer, and whether or not the answer is already known to those participating in the interaction (see Paulston 1972 for the origin of this classification). The classification is based also on whether or not learners need to understand either what is said to them or what they themselves are saying in order to complete the drill successfully. (pp. 91–93) .

Mechanical drills

Mechanical drills exclusively focus on grammatical forms. They are defined as exercises for which there is only one correct response, and the outcome is controlled. To complete an exercise, students do not have to attend to meaning. The following illustrations demonstrate such drill types.

ILLUSTRATION 1

The purpose of this exercise is to drill the inverted word order in German. Students are to insert adverbial phrases, such as *später* [later], *jetzt* [now], and so on.

Model:

1. Ich gehe nach Hause. [I go home.]

Cue: später [later]

Answer: Später gehe ich nach Hause. [I go home later.]

2. Ich lese ein Buch. [I am reading a book.]

Cue: jetzt [now]

Answer: Jetzt lese ich ein Buch. [I am reading a book now.]

ILLUSTRATION 2

The purpose of this exercise is to drill conjugation forms in French.

Jon [revenir] justement d'une nouvelle arrestation policière musclée. Lui et ses hommes avaient pu intervenir et empêcher un autre drame passionnel. Mais Jon [se demander] pourquoi autant de mystères entourent l'organisation pour qui il [travailler]. Pourquoi, en effet; leur méthode pour combattre le crime n'[être]'-elle pas reconnue légalement?

As seen from these two illustrations, the learners do not have to understand what the language means. Students can perform the exercise simply by manipulating forms.

Meaningful drills

The difference between a mechanical and **meaningful drill** is that learners have to attend to meaning in order to perform the activity. There may still be only one correct answer, and the answer is also controlled. For example, one way of turning the French conjugation drill in Illustration 2 into a meaningful exercise would be to list the verbs in infinitive forms in a separate column. Then, for the learners to fill in the correct verb forms, they would need to understand the meaning of these verbs and the text.

Illustration 3 is an example of a meaningful activity. The purpose of this activity is for the students to demonstrate the use of prepositions and the dative case. In this example, the teacher places different objects around the classroom, before he asks the students about the location of these objects. To answer the questions, the students have to understand the meaning of the objects the teacher asks about. They further have to know the name of the location where the object was placed. The advantage of this exercise is that a student's answer is predictable, which allows the teacher to assess a student's knowledge of a targeted language structure. During a meaningful activity, meaning and form are always kept in focus.

ILLUSTRATION 3

The teacher asks the students to describe the location of each object. Calling on students, he asks questions such as:

1. Wo ist die Tasche? [Where is the bag?]

[The teacher places the bag on the table.]

The student answers:

Die Tasche ist auf dem Tisch. [The bag is on the table.]

2. Wo ist der Bleistift? [Where is the pencil?]

[The teacher places the pencil on the book.]

The student answers:

Der Bleistift ist auf dem Buch. [The pencil is on the book.]

Communicative drills

A **communicative drill** distinguishes itself from a meaningful and a mechanical exercise in as far as the learner's answer is unknown. In a communicative drill, the learners always have to attend to meaning. The example in Figure 6-2 demonstrates a communicative drill to practice object pronouns.

Communicative learning tasks

Although the design characteristics "meaningful" and "communicative" are nothing new, communicative language-learning activities distinguish themselves from traditional drill types in several ways. The meaningful principle is fundamental and is strongly adhered to. Furthermore, the primary focus is not the practice of grammar structures, but the actual use of language and the development of communicative skills. While such a goal does not exclude a focus on form, it emphasizes contextualized language practice. In other words, communicative language tasks are situated within an authentic context. Walz (1989) provides the following three criteria that define a well-contextualized **communicative learning** task: It connects exercise sentences with the same situation or theme; it provides additional information concerning people, activities, and descriptions; and it combines cultural aspects with language practice within the exercise. Walz argues that contextualization is conducive to learning, as "connecting sentences within the same situation, theme or semantic

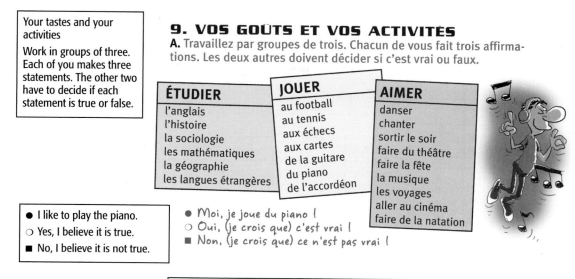

Your tastes and your activities

Work in groups of three. Each of you makes three statements. The other two have to decide if each statement is true or false.

9. VOS GOÛTS ET VOS ACTIVITÉS
A. Travaillez par groupes de trois. Chacun de vous fait trois affirmations. Les deux autres doivent décider si c'est vrai ou faux.

ÉTUDIER	JOUER	AIMER
l'anglais	au football	danser
l'histoire	au tennis	chanter
la sociologie	aux échecs	sortir le soir
les mathématiques	aux cartes	faire du théâtre
la géographie	de la guitare	faire la fête
les langues étrangères	du piano	la musique
	de l'accordéon	les voyages
		aller au cinéma
		faire de la natation

- I like to play the piano.
- Yes, I believe it is true.
- No, I believe it is not true.

- Moi, je joue du piano !
- Oui, (je crois que) c'est vrai !
- Non, (je crois que) ce n'est pas vrai !

study...	play...	like...
English	soccer	dance
history	tennis	sing
sociology	chess	go out in the evening
mathematics	carts	etc.

FIGURE 6-2 Sample of communicative drill
(Source: Flumian et al. (2007a), p. 17.)

field may help students retain information better" (p. 161). His argument is well supported by research on how the brain stores information (see Chapter 3, Getting Started: Introducing Vocabulary). Furthermore, while there is no concrete evidence that contextualized learning activities affect learning, unlike decontextualized grammar exercises, however, a context creates a coherent framework that more likely will lead to meaningful and communicative use of language.

Two common strategies that allow students to use language in a meaningful and communicative way are to make activities personalized and to give students a choice of answers. Being able to express one's own opinions, feelings, and interests has a positive effective on students' attitudes toward learning. Such expression keeps them more engaged, motivated, and interested (Terrell 1982). Allowing students to choose from a list of answers still makes a student's answer communicative. At the same time, the communicative context is narrowed, and the students' answers are somewhat pedagogically manageable.

The following example demonstrates these strategies:

Activity A: What do you usually wear?
Instructions: Say what you normally wear in the following situations.
Example: I usually wear jeans and a T-shirt to the university. At work I wear a sports shirt, a pair of pants, and a jacket.

to work	to a rock concert
to the university	with friends
in bed	at home
on the weekend	on an airplane
at the concert or opera	at a birthday party
to a formal party	at the beach
on a rainy day	in winter at 0° Celsius

Although some practitioners claim (see Lee and VanPatten 2003) that all activities should adhere to the two principles of being meaningful and communicative, "true" communicative activities, in the sense that students exchange unknown information with each other, have some caveats. A disadvantage of such activities is that the teacher cannot control the content and form of students' answers. As seen from the example above, the teacher can anticipate a student's answer in only limited ways. Consequently, there is no guarantee that the student necessarily understands all the listed items from which he chooses. Or, as demonstrated by another example, a learner's personal response to the fill-in-the-blank activity "Como _____ y _____ a cualquier hora del día. [I eat _____ and _____ at any time during the day.]" allows for a wide range of answers. Although the context of such an activity clearly asks for a food item as an answer, a student can mention practically any food item without clearly demonstrating that he understands the meaning of these words. Besides, in open-ended activities, some students may have a tendency to avoid answering a question because they are not confident enough to say it.

Occasionally, in particular during initial phases of instruction, there is a need for activities calling for a student response that is predictable and controllable. Such activities have previously been referred to as "pre-communicative," because their function is to lead up to a communicative activity (Richards 1988). They allow for easier control of a student's meaningful use of language, and for more controlled practice of target forms. As such, they make it easier for a teacher to pay attention to a student's accurate use of language and provide tailored feedback. Needless to say, the more open-ended and communicative a student's response, the harder it is for the teacher to anticipate that student's understanding, responses, and possible errors.

The following example demonstrates a meaningful activity with a highly controlled response:

Activity B: In which sequence?

Read over the list of activities that Ramón did yesterday. Number each item from 1 to 8, with 1 being the first activity Ramón did in the day and 8 as the last activity he did.
Ramón…

____ left for the office.	____ had lunch with a client
____ woke up	____ got up
____ left the office	____ went to class
____ watched a video at night	____ studied before class

Source: Adapted from VanPatten, Lee, and Ballman (1996), p. 80; translated by Klaus Brandl.

Another characteristic of a communicative language task is that the learner has to do something with the information she has learned. This design feature distinguishes traditional communicative activities from tasks and makes it what is generally referred to as task based. Many such tasks often also have a concrete outcome that learners have to achieve (see definitions of a task in Chapter 1). Consider the following lists of communicative activities:

1. Ask five people in class what their names are and where they are from.
2. Ask five people in class why they study Spanish.
3. A classmate invited you to his party. Find out directions to get to his place.

Now read the descriptions again:

4. Ask five people in class what their names are and where they are from. Write their names on the different states on a U.S. map.
5. Ask five people in class why they study Spanish. Now compare and rank the five reasons in terms of which reason is most compelling.
6. A classmate invited you and your friends to his party. Find out directions to get to his place, and share this information with your friends.

A close look at both sets of activities shows that they all are communicative in nature. The second descriptions, however, require the listeners to do something with information that they just gained and then complete a task. As examples 4 through 6 illustrate, the learners have to write down information, compare and rank the information, and exchange the information with somebody else via email or in person. This element of a communicative task design is important for several reasons: For students to complete a task, they have to negotiate meaning. In negotiating meaning, they have to listen, speak up, repeat, rephrase, and maybe even show each other information that they have written down, to get a message across. Language is not used for the sake of practice. Whatever information the students exchange has to be clear and comprehensible enough to enable them to do something with it. Futhermore, having to do something with the information reengages the students cognitively and requires them to apply additional skills. In essence, such task design represents one of the most vital elements of communicative language learning. It is the need to push output that supports the acquisition process. The fact that the task requires the students to reach an outcome further allows teachers to observe and measure achievement.

Overview of characteristics of communicative tasks

- The learner has to do something with the target information (e. g., list, rank, compare, or share it with somebody else in writing or orally).
- There is an outcome or product that learners have to achieve.
- A task involves multiple communicative language acts.
- A task engages cognitive processes.

Instructional Sequencing of Communicative Tasks

Performing a communicative function or task usually involves employing language in an open-ended, creative way in which much, if not all, the lesson's target vocabulary, grammar, and content are used. This also requires the simultaneous use of a combination of skills. Traditionally, these skills have been categorized as listening, reading, speaking, or writing. Modes of instructionally grouping these skills are often based on contrasting oral and written skills and/or productive and receptive skills (see Table 6.1).

TABLE 6.1   Traditional grouping of skills

	oral	**written**
productive	speaking	writing
receptive	listening	reading

A more recent approach classifies the use of skills based on the mode of communication (Brecht and Walton 1994), and characterizes them as (1) interpersonal, (2) interpretive, and (3) presentational. For example, two Students talking to each other in the classroom while performing a pair-work activity make use of an **interpersonal mode of communication**. This means they take turns talking and listening, and when the communication breaks down, they have the opportunity to negotiate meaning. They can tell each other to clarify misunderstandings, to repeat, to rephrase, or to follow up on what has been said. An interpersonal mode of communication takes place when two speakers talk to each other in person, over the phone, or through written modes of correspondence (e.g., in chat rooms or via e-mail).

Unlike during the interpersonal mode of communication, the **interpretive mode of communication** does not allow for any kind of possibility of negotiation of meaning with the writer or speaker. Examples of this kind of mode include (1) listening to people talk on the radio, on TV, or in movies; and (2) reading a text. As Shrum and Glisan (2000) point out, this mode of communication may often "require a deeper knowledge of culture to gain an appropriate cultural interpretation of a text," as "clarification of meaning is not possible since the creator of a text is absent or not accessible" (p. 120).

Similar to the interpretive mode of communication, the **presentational mode** also constitutes one-way communication. "Speaking and/or writing skills are involved, and no direct opportunity exists for active negotiation of meaning between the presenter and audience. Examples include giving a speech or oral report, preparing a paper or story, and producing a newscast. Substantial knowledge of the language and culture is necessary since the goal is to ensure that the audience will be able to interpret the message (NSFLEP 1996)" (cited in Shrum and Glisan 2000, p. 120).

In contrast to the traditional grouping of skills, Brecht and Walton's approach to skill description is vital to organizing task-based instructions. This is so because it is the mode of communication, not the skills in isolation, that need to serve as the basis for planning and designing learning tasks that prepare the learners for communicative language performance. For example, students who interact in pair or pair-work activities have to be prepared to function in their roles as listeners as well as speakers. Or, to mention another example, when students are asked to listen to peer presentations, the mode of communication puts them into the role of the listener, who tries to interpret the presenters' message. As both examples demonstrate, different modes of communication often require different preparation and instructional strategies in order to create an engaging and successful learning experience. This approach also requires an understanding of the mental processes involved when the learners engage in speaking, writing, listening, and reading tasks, in addition to the cognitive complexity of a task itself; and last, the conditions under which learners perform these tasks. (Please note that these mental processes are discussed in more detail in later chapters.)

Applying different modes of communication that involve multiple skills raises the questions: How should different skills be introduced, how can they be broken down into manageable subtasks, and how should learning tasks be scaffolded? By **scaffolding** is meant the process of sequencing learning tasks into subtasks so that one activity becomes the basis for the subsequent one. In addition, it is necessary to ask what factors influence task performance—that is, what makes one task more difficult than another?

Skill progression and task sequencing

To demonstrate and better understand some of the issues involved, look at the case study in Figure 6-3 below. Then, answer the questions in "Analysis and Discussion."

To avoid some of the problems that the instructor encountered in Figure 6-3, let us briefly analyze what happened. Conducting an impromptu interview with a fellow student in the beginning foreign

---

ANALYSIS AND DISCUSSION

1. Why did this activity break down?

   _____

   _____

   _____

2. What would you have done differently?

   _____

   _____

   _____

Mr. Garfield starts a beginning class of German by introducing family and kinship terms. He uses a chart of a family tree to introduce and explain all the kinship terms. In his next activity, he spends about 10 minutes asking his students various questions about their families. Next, he gives his students the following assignment: Choose a partner and interview one another in German about your families. He gives them 15 minutes to complete the interviews. However, as Mr. Garfield begins to circulate in the class, he notices that students are confused. They have no idea how to form the questions in German, they are speaking in English, they are searching through vocabulary lists in their books, and they look very frustrated.

FIGURE 6-3 Sample lesson script

language class requires students to immediately apply a variety of skills. They have to think of the contents of the questions to ask. They have to apply the language code—for example, choose the vocabulary, apply all the grammatical rules (formulating questions, conjugating verbs, etc.), and pronounce the questions.

Furthermore, interacting with their interviewing partner involves listening comprehension skills, in other words decoding their fellow students' oral answers. Last, the impromptu nature of this task may also have enhanced the task difficulty by creating potential performance pressure for students. That is to say, some students can function better under pressure; others feel more anxious and nervous.

The reason the class broke down is that students were asked to perform too many skills at once and under conditions for which they had not been prepared. As the case above illustrates, numerous factors may play a role impacting task difficulty. A general scheme proposed by Candlin (1987) assesses task difficulty based on linguistic code and cognitive complexity, as well as on communicative stress experienced by learners. As Figure 6-4 demonstrates, the interaction of these variables may either facilitate or impede the performance of learning tasks.

The **linguistic code** refers to the language factors (Skehan 1996) that learners have to process and produce in a given task. These include the range and complexity of vocabulary (knowledge and usage, pronunciation, etc.), grammar (syntactic and morphological knowledge), and text structures, that is, skills and knowledge involving the language itself.

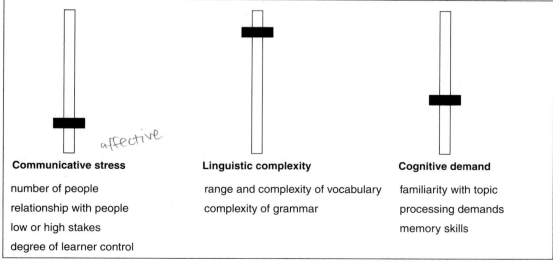

Communicative stress

number of people

relationship with people

low or high stakes

degree of learner control

Linguistic complexity

range and complexity of vocabulary

complexity of grammar

Cognitive demand

familiarity with topic

processing demands

memory skills

FIGURE 6-4 Interaction of variables affecting task difficulty

ANALYSIS AND DISCUSSION

Read the task description in Figure 6-5. What are some of the factors that make this task difficult?

_____

_____

_____

At a workshop on computerized testing, the presenters wanted to demonstrate a computerized testing task. Since the example involved watching a one-minute speech given by the former German chancellor Helmut Kohl on his political achievement during his time in office, they asked for a proficient speaker of German as a volunteer from the audience. The German volunteer watched the video clip, and then was asked to summarize Helmut Kohl's major achievements.

FIGURE 6-5 Case study: A computerized test

The **cognitive** complexity of a task is determined by a variety of factors. One set of factors has to do with the mental processes that are required by the task assignment. For example, repeating information, describing a situation, ranking, sorting, comparing, analyzing or interpreting data involve mental processes that are different and vary in cognitive complexity. Another set of factors involves the input itself, that is, the aural or written texts or visual input, that we process. Being familiar with the topic of a conversation or having background knowledge in a content area facilitates the process of the interpretation of an oral or written message or text, and thus makes it easier to understand (Bernhardt 1993; Carrell 1992). The amount of input and the density of contents of the information that we have to process further adds complexity. For example, listening to a one-word answer is cognitively less challenging than a paragraph-long answer. This has to with how much information we can retain in our working memories, and how fast we can process this information. The way the input is organized further makes a difference. For example, information that is coherently structured is easier to understand than information that is loosely structured. Whether an idea is presented in an abstract or a concrete way also plays a role. In light of such factors, the amount of time that is available when processing input can either increase or alleviate task difficulty. It usually takes quite a bit of time and experience to build a mental foundation that allows learners to process big chunks of information in the target language.

A third factor impacting task difficulty has to do with the conditions under which the students are performing a learning task. Some conditions create **commmunicative stress** that leads to anxiety and stress among learners and influence how well they can complete a task. Such conditions depend and vary based on the following factors (Skehan 1996): language mode (e.g., speaking, listening, reading, writing), language channel (e.g., voice of a native or nonnative speaker, audio or video-based, level of background noise), and the level of immediacy in responding to the task, scale (number of participants or relationship involved, e.g., during group work), stakes (either low or high, depending on how important it is to do the task and to do it correctly), and control (how much learners can "control" or influence the task). Interpersonal factors such as shyness, status, or cultural differences may also be reasons causing communicative stress. As we have seen from the case study in Figure 6.3, an oral interview involves interpersonal modes of communication (speaking and listening)—that is, immediacy-task skills, which in general cause students more stress than reading and writing tasks do. Because of the high processing demands of most speaking tasks, the format of pair and small-group work has become a commonly applied instructional practice, as a means of preparation and practice time, that reduces stress for beginning language learners. Imagine how the communication demand changes when students have to perform an impromptu speaking task in a testing situation, either in front of the whole class or for an official testing board.

ANALYSIS AND DISCUSSION

Appendix 6.1 describes two sets of randomly chosen first-year learning activities as language instructors sometimes teach them. Considering the design of the learning tasks—that is, the cognitive processing and communicative skills, including the conditions that are involved—what makes the design of some of the activities easier or more difficult than others?

Compare these activities and place them along a continuum based on their relative degree of difficulty. Choose one or two examples and explain your answer.

Description of a Sample Lesson Plan

To further demonstrate a sequence of learning activities, this section presents a lesson plan to be taught at the secondary school level and covering about two to three periods. Table 6.2 describes the pedagogical procedures for each lesson step in detail and furthermore presents the teacher's rationales for implementing and sequencing each activity. The lesson plan also lists the modes of communication using Brecht and Walton's framework (1994) and points out the skills of speaking (S), listening (L), reading (R), writing (W), and kinesthetic involvement (K).

The goals of this lesson are the following that students will be able to:

- give directions to various destinations using a map
- follow directions given, using a map
- use basic courtesies when asking for directions
- recognize the differences between American and German city maps

The following new content knowledge and skills that are required to perform the lesson tasks will be introduced:

links, rechts, geradeaus [left, right, straight ahead]
basic questions (review)
Strasse, Ampel, Platz [street, traffic light, square]
polite questions
names of buildings (review)
prepositions: vorbei, entlang, hinunter [passed, along, down]
command forms (review)

TABLE 6.2   Lesson steps, rationales and skill description

Lesson phase	Description of activity and pedagogical rationale for design, implementation, and sequencing.	Modes of communication/ skills
Day 1		
1 input	**Introduction of vocabulary.** The instructor introduces new vocabulary (adverbial phrases of place, such as *links, rechts, geradeaus*, etc. [left, right, straight ahead] using Total Physical Response (TPR). Unlike during a traditional TPR lesson, the teacher also writes the new words on the board. TPR involves students actively in the vocabulary introduction activity. Students demonstrate nonverbal comprehension through TPR movements. Seeing the words in writing further helps students to make a connection between the meaning of the new words and their written representations.	interpretive, L, K
2 assimilation	**Vocabulary activity:** The students label traffic signs, describing in which directions they are pointing. This activity provides written reinforcement of vocabulary items. Students get to produce the words in writing themselves.	interpretive, R, W
3 input	**Dialogue: Different people asking for directions.** The teacher introduces the dialogue by role-reading each line. Along the way, she explains, models, or acts out unknown vocabulary. Next, she follows up with comprehension questions. Last, she has students role-read the dialogue in pairs, and then asks for volunteers to read (out loud) the dialogue in front of the class.	interpretive, R, interpersonal, L, S, one-word answers

TABLE 6.2   Lesson steps, rationales and skill description

Lesson phase	Description of activity and pedagogical rationale for design, implementation, and sequencing.	Modes of communication/ skills
	The purpose of using this dialogue is to introduce and model polite phrases students need to know to ask for directions. The focus is mostly on written input, but answers of comprehension questions provide oral application of one-word answers. Requesting information demonstrates cultural and sociolinguistic language skills.	
4 assimilation (review)	**Fantasy trip around city**. The classroom is decorated with pictures from various shops. The teacher takes the students around the room, telling and asking them what they can do and buy at each shop. This activity provides a review of previous material in a communicative way while the teacher acts like a tour guide. The purpose of this activity is furthermore to review the names of the shops and prepositions that require either the dative or accusative case.	interpersonal, L, S, short answers
5 assimilation (homework)	**Fill-in-the-blank activity**. For homework, the students are asked to do a fill-in-the blank activity and a matching exercise. The students match different phrases used in asking directions. This activity provides reinforcement of vocabulary in context, which students will be producing later.	interpretive, R, W (one-word answers)
Day 2		
6 assimilation	**Scavenger hunt**. In pairs or small groups, students follow prearranged directions around the school to find other clues to ultimately find a prize. The activity is done as a race between teams. The Scavenger hunt activity is a fun way of getting students involved in applying reading skills. Doing this activity in pairs encourages cooperative learning. Written directions provide further examples of the language the students have to produce later. This is a simulated, hands-on activity, which also makes use of a competitive learning style.	interpretive, R
7 assimilation	**Vienna map activity**. Teacher hands out maps of Vienna, including written directions to particular authentic destinations. Students, in groups, must figure out the destination. This activity integrates authentic cultural materials, which provides further practice in and reinforcement of reading directions.	interpretive, R
8 assimilation	**Cultural comparison**. Students compare German and American city maps and discuss similarities and differences. This activity integrates culture. The activity is done in English.	cultural understanding

(Continued)

TABLE 6.2   Lesson steps, rationales and skill description

Lesson phase	Description of activity and pedagogical rationale for design, implementation, and sequencing.	Modes of communication/ skills
9 assimilation	**TPR shower-curtain map activity**. The students sit around a shower curtain that displays a map of an authentic German city. The teacher gives directions, and volunteers follow the route to various destinations. The students demonstrate listening comprehension skills by following the direction. This performance-based skill is one of the goals of the lesson.	interpretive, L, K
10 assimilation	**Shower-curtain map activity (part 2)**. Students take turns giving others directions using the shower-curtain map. Students apply language in a communicative way. This performance-based task is the goal of the lesson. As the students give oral directions for the first time, it is a good strategy to do this activity in a teacher-fronted format, so the teacher can provide feedback and assistance if necessary.	interpersonal, S, L, K, short phrases
Day 3		
11 assimilation	**Information-gap activity**. Working in pairs, students take turns asking for and giving each other directions to locations on a map. The listener fills in the name of the building on his or her map. This activity provides further practice in pairs, which involves all the students and reduces the stress to produce oral language. It involves requesting and giving information; in other words, it focuses on interpersonal communication skills.	interpersonal, L, S, short phrases and answers
12 assimilation	**Listening assessment**. Students show comprehension by following directions on a map and writing down the name of the destination. This activity functions as a direct or indirect assessment as one of the lesson objectives. Students listen to paragraph-long directions. For logistic reasons, the listening section is done first.	interpretive , L, short paragraph
13 extension/simulated real-life application	**Taxi activity** from "Games with Aims"—Each student has a destination on a card that she or he draws. Students must hail the taxi (teacher), and using their map, give the taxi driver directions to the destination. This oral, performance-based assessment tests another objective of the lesson.	interpersonal or presentational, S
14 extension/simulated real-life application	Students write down the directions to places on a map. The lesson concludes with a final assessment. This written, performance-based task tests the objective of the lesson. For instructional purposes, the sequence of activities 13 and 14 could be reversed, since students would get additional practice in writing before demonstrating this functional objective orally.	presentational, W

(Source: Pat Branson, "Instructional Planning," *GOLDEN Online Course*, 2001, http://golden.unl.edu.)

Guidelines For Instructional Sequencing and Task Design

In the previous sections, we have pointed out some of the skills involved in processing information in a second language. The following instructional strategies provide some suggestions that aid in reducing a learner's processing demands. Applying these guidelines further helps with scaffolding and sequencing different learning tasks.

- **Introduce one thing at a time**

  In traditional language teaching, it was common practice among language teachers to introduce whole sets of grammatical rules such as verb conjugation paradigms at once, while the learners were expected to memorize and apply these rules thereafter. This kind of instructional practice has its roots in the audiolingual era, when language was perceived as a set of structures that the learners needed to master first. With the inception of communicative language learning, "the message to be conveyed" has become the primary focus, which subsequently determines what vocabulary and grammar rules are to be introduced. For example, if a student is to talk about himself, the first person singular may be the only rule that he needs to learn from the whole verb paradigm to accomplish the communicative task. In other words, the trend has shifted away from introducing whole grammatical paradigms toward isolating and introducing single forms (e.g., first person singular or third person singular verb conjugation forms) at a given moment, subsequently adding more forms and rules of usage to the picture of a lesson (see Ch 4, Grammar and Language Learning). In this way, the cognitive overload is reduced and is less demanding and stressful, especially for learners with lower memorization skills.

- **Move from nonlinguistic to linguistic output**

  The initial segment of a language lesson involves the introduction of new materials through written or oral input. In traditional language teaching, many teachers immediately move from input to output, testing their students' comprehension of the newly introduced materials. As reality shows, this instructional sequencing is often too overwhelming for most beginning language learners, as it asks the student to apply too many skills at once. One instructional strategy that reduces the attentional demands of a task is the initial use of nonlinguistic tasks. These are tasks that do not require active production of language for output. Such tasks allow for more exposure, more examples, deeper anchoring, and are less demanding on the language processing faculty. Non-linguistic tasks are raising hands, pointing, acting out, drawing, and so on. Tasks with reduced linguistic output are true/false, yes/no answers, matching, and multiple-choice activities.

- **Move from words to sentences to connected discourse**

  The development of oral communicative skills is challenging for language learners due to high processing demand, which involve linguistic and cognitive skills and whose application is further impeded by different conditions. Structuring activities so students move from single words to longer discourse answers allows students to gradually build speaking skills and reduces the linguistic demands. Examples range from yes/no, short answers (single words/sentences, phrases), to paragraph-long discourse.

- **Break down an activity into manageable subtasks**

  Another strategy that helps learners to reduce stress created by cognitive overload is to break down an activity into a sequence of subtasks. The tasks should isolate skills and be narrowly focused, keeping the attentional demand of each task manageable. For example, when using audio- or video-based materials divide the materials into small listening and thinking segments because it helps reduce the amount of information students have to process. Allowing for repeated listening or viewing, and telling the learners what to focus on during the listening process, gives the learners an opportunity to attend to a different listening task or focus on information they missed before (see Ch 7, Developing Listening Skills, for further discussion).

  Another example taken from the methodology of teaching reading skills further highlights this teaching principle. A common instructional practice among teachers is to ask students to read a text out loud while expecting students to process the meaning of the text at the same time. When students focus their attention on pronunciation, they often cannot recall any information about what they have read. The attentional demands of processing the meaning of a text while reading out loud are simply too high for most beginning language learners. The instructional strategy that works much better is to divide the attentional demands by first asking the students to read the text silently, so they can focus their attention on the meaning of the text. Then, in a later activity, once the meaning of a text has been clarified, students could read a text aloud and thus attend to practicing the pronunciation (see Ch 9, Developing Reading Skills, for further discussion).

- **Allow for ample preparation and planning time**

  Most communicative speaking tasks are challenging for beginning language learners because of the level of immediacy in responding to the task and anxiety that is invoked by talking with or in front of other students in a class. In many occasions, this challenge can be alleviated by allowing for planning and preparation time. By building in a preparatory step, it gives the learner an opportunity to think about what he wants to say and how to formulate his utterance. This reduces stress and anxiety and an early break down of an activity. For example, interviewing tasks work best if students have time to brainstorm and develop the contents of interview questions in separate steps. Ample time should also be provided for most learning tasks that involve reading or writing. Depending on the complexity of the text or the writing task, most reading and writing tasks require more time to accomplish.

- **Allow for student collaboration to work on tasks**

  Ample research supports the benefits of instructional strategies that promote social interaction and collaboration among learners. Students by and large perform more effectively when working in pairs or small groups than when being called on in front of the class. Tasks also need to be designed so students have to respond to each other's output. In this way students attend to each other. It increases social interaction and thus learning among the students. It is also helpful for the speaker if the sender has information that the listener does not have, but that the listener, for some reason, needs. This puts the speaker firmly in control of the information and motivates her to communicate that information (Brown & Yule, 1983) (see Ch 8, Developing Listening Skills, for further discussion).

Conclusion

This chapter has provided an overview of different lesson segments and described the different pedagogical goals and purposes of each segment. Furthermore, it has presented characteristics of communicative language activities and discussed factors that make task performance easy or difficult. Understanding such factors is vital as it allows a teacher to accommodate for task difficulty when sequencing, scaffolding and implementing lesson activities. A step-by-step approach to task design and implementation is indispensable. It helps prevent students from feeling overwhelmed and lost, makes a lesson run more smoothly, and is most conducive to maximizing student learning. However, it must be noted, a gradual scaffolding of learning activities does not suggest that learning, in particular the development of different skills occurs in a linear fashion. As repeatedly pointed out, language acquisition does not occur in linear but in developmental stages. In other words, just because grammatical concepts have been introduced and practiced, students will not have mastered them. Most likely they will only have gained some level of partial control. For ultimate mastery, it takes many situations and exposures within a variety of contexts, reintroducing and reinforcing grammatical forms. With regard to some grammatical topics, the acquisition comes late; some forms can never be mastered, not even by advanced students. Because skills acquisition and learning involve individual learner processes, it is difficult to promote a universal framework of a language lesson design that meets all language learners to the same degree. Besides, lessons have different goals and learners vary in their aptitude. Ultimately, it remains for the teacher to decide how to scaffold lesson tasks, when to insert additional lesson steps, modify or skip a lesson task, in preparation for or even while teaching a lesson.

Checking chapter objectives

Do I know how to. . .

- ❏ describe the goal and purpose of different lesson phases?
- ❏ define different teacher and learner roles in the communicative classroom?
- ❏ explain the role of "repeated" practice?
- ❏ describe characteristics of communicative learning tasks?
- ❏ list the skills involved in processing different information when speaking, listening, reading, or writing?
- ❏ sequence and scaffold learning tasks?

Explorations

TASK 1: HOW BENEFICIAL IS A DRILL?

'Communicative drills' have experienced some controversies. Due to their enhanced focus on grammatical structures, some practitioners consider any drill-type activities as "traditional" (Lee and VanPatten 2003). Others believe that the application of these activities is in accordance with skills acquisition and cognitive learning theories (DeKeyser 1998), which makes them a valuable contribution to the language learning process as currently characterized.

Which of these positions do you agree with? Provide a rationale for your answer.

TASK 2: IDENTIFYING STRESS FACTORS

Rank the level of stress experienced by learners of any of the activities in Figure 6-6. (The results of this research study are provided in Appendix 6.7.)

What can you do to reduce the level of stress in the activities that you have ranked most stressful?

(Source (for task): Shrum and Glisan (2000), p. 115.)

Scale from MODERATELY RELAXED (5) to MODERATELY ANXIOUS (1)	
1. Read orally in class.	5 4 3 2 1
2. Repeat individually after the instructor.	5 4 3 2 1
3. Speak in front of the class.	5 4 3 2 1
4. Read silently in class.	5 4 3 2 1
5. Open discussion based on volunteer participation.	5 4 3 2 1
6. Work in groups of three or four.	5 4 3 2 1
7. Write your work on the board.	5 4 3 2 1
8. Interview each other in pairs.	5 4 3 2 1
9. Present a prepared dialogue in front of the class.	5 4 3 2 1
10. Compete in class games by teams.	5 4 3 2 1
11. Write a composition at home.	5 4 3 2 1
12. Listen to questions and write answers to the questions.	5 4 3 2 1
13. Role-play a situation spontaneously in front of the class.	5 4 3 2 1
14. Repeat as a class after the instructor.	5 4 3 2 1
15. Work on projects (i.e., newspapers, filmstrips, and photo albums).	5 4 3 2 1
16. Speak individually with the instructor in his/her office.	5 4 3 2 1
17. Give an oral presentation or skit in front of the class.	5 4 3 2 1
18. Do exercises in the book.	5 4 3 2 1
19. Work in groups of two and prepare a skit.	5 4 3 2 1
20. Write a composition in class.	5 4 3 2 1

FIGURE 6-6 Ranking of Anxiety Level
(Source (for questionnaire): Young (1990), p. 545.)

TASK 3: THE DINNER TABLE (TASK ANALYSIS)

In Appendix 6.5, you find an earlier version of the Dinner Table Organizing task. Analyze and compare this set of learning activities with the more recent version in Appendix 1.3 of Chapter 1. What changes did the textbook authors make? How are both versions pedagogically different?

TASK 4: IDENTIFYING COMMUNICATIVE TASK CRITERIA

Analyze and compare several activities from the textbook of your choice or use the ones in Appendix 6.3:

1. Identify the pedagogical goal of each activity. In which phase of a lesson (e.g., input, assimilation, extension) would you find this learning task?
2. To what degree does the design of the activity meet the criteria of a well-constructed communicative language-learning task? (If necessary, review design criteria such as being meaningful, contextualized, having a choice, etc.)
3. In case you were to adopt any of these activities, which ones would you discard? What changes would you suggest in implementing the activity?

TASK 5: UNDERSTANDING SKILLS AND SEQUENCING

The following three activities dealing with the teaching of numbers are similar to those often found in first-year foreign language textbooks. Critique the design and sequence of these learning activities. What skill(s) does each activity focus on? In which sequence would you teach these activities? If necessary, would you suggest any changes?

Activity 1. Read the following numbers out loud.

33	47	17	18	29	44
24	50	36	62	21	58

Activity 2. Now, listen to the conversations and write down any numbers that are mentioned.

——— ——— ——— ——— ——— ——— ———

Activity 3. The following math problems are not quite complete: the signs + and − were left out. Combine the numbers below to match the totals. Write down the numbers so you can explain your solutions to the class.

Model: $6 + 10 - 2 = 14$

a. 5__7__10=22   b. 56__8__9=57
c. 66__3__25=44   d. 23__42__19=46

TASK 6: ANXIETY FACTORS

In Appendix 6.7, you find the results of the anxiety questionnaire that is presented in Figure 6.6. Which task design factors (e.g., "How much language do students have to produce?" or "In which manner do students have to perform a learning task?") may be responsible for causing more anxiety in performing one learning task than another?

Task 7: Understanding communicative activities and tasks

Analyze the learning activities in Appendix 6.4. To what degree do these activities

- focus on forms rather than actual language use?
- require the learners to keep meaning in focus?
- allow for communicative language use?

Argue in favor of (or against) using any of these activities in a communicative language classroom.

If necessary, how would you teach any of these activities to engage the learners in processing the meaning of language?

Task 8: Activity or task?

Analyze the learning activities in Appendix 6.3. Which ones are best aligned with the definition of a task? Why?

Task 9: Understanding skill complexity

In posing questions, it is important for the instructor to understand the complexity of the answer to the question. For example, asking a question such as "At what time did you come home last night?" requires the student to produce significantly less language than describing exactly what she did until 10 p.m.

Describe the skills required in responding to these two questions.

Task 10: Understanding instructional sequencing

Part A
The following seven instructional activities present a set of possible steps for teaching a dialogue. Arrange these activities in a sequence, as you would apply them. Omit any of the strategies you would not use, or add any others if necessary. Provide a rationale for your choice of sequence.

The instructor:

1. plays the dialogue on the tape
2. reads each line out loud, having students repeat each line
3. reads the dialogue out loud while students are listening
4. asks the students about words they do not understand
5. explains unknown words
6. presents comprehension questions
7. asks students to respond to questions

Part B

In a follow-up discussion with her supervisor, the instructor provided the rationale claiming that it helps the students to understand the words better if they hear them pronounced first. Based on the research findings about how meaning is anchored in the brain (see "Guidelines for Instructional

Sequencing and Task Design," as well as Chapter 3, Getting Started: Introducing Vocabulary), do you agree with the instructor's comment? If any, what suggestion for change would you make to the instructor?

TASK 11: PRACTICING INSTRUCTIONAL SEQUENCING

In Appendix 6.2 (Part 1), you will find a language lesson whose pedagogical learning tasks are in mixed order. This lesson was designed to teach "how to say the time" to a level one German class. Determine the sequence these learning tasks should follow in the order that reflects the theory as delineated in this chapter. Work by yourself or with one other student to determine the rationale for the sequence you decide. Furthermore, identify the skills and modes of presentation and write them down in the worksheet of Appendix 6.2, Part 2.

TASK 12: TEXTBOOK ANALYSIS

Look at one chapter of a textbook and make a list of the number of mechanical, meaningful, and communicative drill exercises. Assess the opportunities the learners have to develop communicative language ability. What skills are practiced? How are they practiced? Using examples from the book, explain your rationale.

TASK 13: CASE STUDY

Mr. Smith starts his beginning language class by presenting a 15-line-long dialogue. In the dialogue, three friends talk about their plans for the weekend. The dialogue is tightly structured around *Wh*– questions: Where do you like to go? What do you like to do? As the dialogue includes three different roles, Mr. Smith invites his native speaker–teaching assistant and a student volunteer to assist him in reading the dialogue out loud. As a follow-up, Mr. Smith spends about 10 minutes at the board, explaining and commenting on the meaning of unknown words. Next, he asks his students to develop a similar dialogue in groups of three. While Mr. Smith is circulating around the class, he notices that students are busy looking up the meanings of words in their textbooks and rereading the dialogue. After about 10–15 minutes, he interrupts the activity by saying: "We won't have time to finish the dialogue today. We'll continue with this tomorrow."

Comment on Mr. Smith's sequencing of activities and choice of learning tasks. What would you have done differently?

Application

TASK 14: ADAPTING A LESSON PLAN

Adapt the lesson plan on giving directions (see Table 6.2) to a different learning environment, such as a class at a middle school, university, or community college level. Would you teach any of these activities in a different way when teaching in a different environment?

TASK 15: LESSON PLAN DEVELOPMENT

Develop a lesson plan. Identify clear objectives, and outline clearly sequenced activities that lead to fulfillment of the objectives. Furthermore, for each activity identify the mode of communication used in this activity to accomplish the task, and provide a rationale for your instructional sequencing.

APPENDIX 6.1

Sample of First-Year Learning Activities

List I: L = low   M = medium   H = high

		linguistic code	cognitive code	communicative demand
1	Students listen to a dialogue and indicate if the following statement is correct. Tante Uschi hat in Heidelberg studiert. richtg/falsch [Aunt Uschi studied in Heidelberg. true/false]	L M H	L M H	L M H
2	Based on a tape that students listened to, the instructor asks the students questions, such as: Was hat Uschi in Hamburg gemacht? [What did Uschi do?]	L M H	L M H	L M H
3	Students are taking turns reading out loud, one sentence at a time, from a fairy tale. When they finish, the instructor immediately asks the students comprehension questions on the text.	L M H	L M H	L M H
4	Students are taking turns reading out loud, one sentence at a time, from a dialogue. The instructor tests the students' comprehension by asking them to fill out T/F questions.	L M H	L M H	L M H
5	Students read a fairy tale silently and, in pairs, answer a set of comprehension questions.	L M H	L M H	L M H
6	Students match items from column A with items from column B. Column A: / Column B: / Du hast eine Erkältung. / Danach haben wir geheiratet. / [You have a cold.] [Then we got married.] / Er hat mich geküßt. / Du hast mir leid getan. / [He kissed me.] / [I felt sorry for you.]	L M H	L M H	L M H
7	For practice with numbers, the teacher gives the students math problems, which they have to do perform orally. For example, the teacher would ask in the target language: How much is 48 divided by 8?	L M H	L M H	L M H

List II: L = low;   M = medium;   H = high

		linguistic code	cognitive code	communicative demand
1	The instructor asks his students to interview two students in class about their families and orally report their findings to the class.	L M H	L M H	L M H
2	The instructor involves her students in a basic conversational scenario by asking miscellaneous questions about their families. For example, the teacher says: "John, tell me a little bit about your family. How many brothers and sisters do you have? How old are they? … parents?"]	L M H	L M H	L M H

(continued)

3	An instructor asks her students to talk about what they did over the past weekend.	L M H	L M H	L M H
4	The instructor asks his students, in pairs, to make a list of items they need to take along when they go on a summer vacation.	L M H	L M H	L M H
5	Students watch a video about students describing themselves. Students fill out multiple-choice answers to check their comprehension.	L M H	L M H	L M H
6	As part of a test, students listen to a conversation between a tourist and resident of a real city in the target country; the speakers discuss how to get from one place to another. Students trace the path on an authentic map.	L M H	L M H	L M H
7	Students listen to a phone message on the answering machine. In the message, Daniela asks her girlfriend Andrea whether she has time to go out on Friday night. Unfortunately, Andrea is busy that night, but she would like to go out on Saturday. Write up a brief email message to Daniela and explain the situation.	L M H	L M H	L M H

APPENDIX 6.2
Scrambled lesson plan

Part 1:

List of Scrambled Activities

1. Teacher introduces numbers 1–24 using TPR using body parts:[1]

   1 = student shows one finger
   2 = student shows two fingers
   3 = student shows three fingers
   4 = student shows four fingers
   5 = student shows five fingers
   6 = student shows six fingers
   7 = student shows seven fingers
   8 = student shows eight fingers
   9 = student shows nine fingers
   10 = student shows ten fingers
   11 = student holds two hands out and then shows one finger
   12 = student holds two hands out and then shows two fingers

2. Information-gap activity—students in pairs practice time expressions.
3. Introduce a song, "Zehn kleine Mädchen" ["Ten Little Girls"] to reinforce learning of numbers.

   Ein kleines, zwei kleine, drei kleine Mädchen
   Vier kleine, fünf kleine, sechs kleine Mädchen
   Sieben kleine, acht kleine, neun kleine Mädchen
   Zehn kleine Mädchen tanzen
   (sung to the tune of "Ten Little Indians")

4. Students write out their school schedules as homework—recording their daily schedule.
5. Teacher disseminates homemade "watches" created by previous students (last year). Each watch has a different time, and the swatch

watch is paper-clipped onto each student's wrist. Students are given a list of all students in the classrooms, and they have 10 minutes to interview one another regarding what time it is according to their watch.

6. Using these schedules in pairs, students interview one another to determine five facts about their partner's schedule.

7. Teacher introduces one page from an authentic telephone book that she uses for an information-gap activity. Partner A has five names whited out; Partner B has five telephone numbers whited out. A has to ask B for the telephone numbers, and B has to ask A for the names of the individuals to whom the telephone numbers belong.

8. Using this TPR technique, the instructor can teach colors while teaching numbers as well as adverbs and prepositions such as *unter, über, neben, links, rechts, oben, unter* [under, above, next to, etc]. The students place the numbers on their desks and then point to the numbers as the teacher calls them out (the same can be done with colors).

9. The teacher introduces a popular German nursery rhyme:

Eins, zwei, Polizei	[one, two, …]
Drei, vier, Offizier	[three, four, …]
Fünf, sechs, alte Hex	[five, six, …]
Sieben, acht, gute Nacht	[seven, eight, …]
Neun, zehn, schlafen gehn	[nine, ten, …]
Elf, zwölf, kommen die Wölf	[eleven, twelve, …]

10. The students are provided with their own set of laminated, colored numbers and do as the teacher models.

11. Students scramble numbers and place in the order as called out by teacher, e.g.:

Finde Nummer 3, leg sie mitten auf den Tisch, Nummer 5 is rot, leg sie unter Nummer 3, etc.[2]

[Find number 3, put it in the middle of the table, number 5 is red, place beneath number 3, etc.]

12. The teacher introduces time-frame phrases by modeling with clock concepts such as 9:30 and quarter to using the context of the school day: for example, Wann beginnt die Schule? Wann ist zu Schule zu Ende? Wann beginnt die Deutsch Klasse?

[When does school start? When is it over? When does the German class start?]

13. The teacher provides students a handout containing written math problems, for example, eins und vier minus zwei ist _____ [one and four minus two is _____].

14. Pair-work activity: Students dictate their favorite five numbers to one another.

15. Wild card 1: Please specify and describe this activity.

16. Wild card 2: Please specify and describe this activity.

(Source: Prof. Aleidine J. Moeller, University of Nebraska, Lincoln.)

Part 2

Sequence of activities/rationale	Skills	Modes
#1: lesson starts with the instructor's presentation of numbers	comprehension (listening)	

APPENDIX 6.3
Sample Textbook Activities

Activity 1

A. Look at the list of activities below and complete the chart.

Liste d'activités: jouer au rugby, le jazz, la politique, les restaurants chinois, voyager en avion, l'hiver, les plages désertes, l'histoire, Bach et Vivaldi, sortir la nuit, visiter un parc thématique, faire du shopping, faire du ski, voir des monuments historiques, faire de l'équitation, le calme, voyager seul (e), faire une randonné, la pêche, faire du camping, faire de la plongée

Translation

A. Look at the list of activities below and complete the chart.

List of activities: playing rugby, jazz, politics, Chinese restaurant, traveling by plane, winter, sand beaches, history, Bach and Vivaldi, going out at night, visiting theme parks, shopping, skiing, visiting historic monuments, horse riding, quiet time, traveling alone, going for a walk, fishing, camping, diving

B. Now, choosing from the same list and using the same expressions, write five sentences indicating the likes and dislikes of your father, your mother, your siblings if you have any, some friends, etc.

_____

_____

_____

_____

(Source: Flumian et al. (2007b), p. 48.)

+++ j'aime beaucoup	+ j'aime bien	− je n'aime pas beaucoup	−−−je n'aime pas du tout

Activity 2

In a lesson about things to do in a city, you have to help out with making arrangements for the arrival of foreign exchange students. First, read the messages of some of the exchange students, which they have posted on the Internet, and find out what they like to do. Then, make list of things you have in common with them. Next, with two other classmates, decide which exchange student each of you wants to take around, and plan what you will do. Last, present your plan to the class.

Activity 3

A friend is coming from out of town to spend a few days with you. Make a list of five interesting places that are to be found in your city and of five things that are right in your neighborhood.

> Modèle: Dans ma ville, il y a un stade de football.
> [Translation: In my town, there is a football stadium.]

APPENDIX 6.4

Six Language Activities

Activity 1

Il y avait une bonne raison! Vous avez remarqué l'absence de certaines personnes à la réunion familiale. Donnez une bonne excuse pour expliquer cette absence.
[Translation: There was a good reasons! You noticed the absence of certain people at the family reunion. Provided a good excuse to explain the absence.]

MODÈLE: toi	
É1: Tu n'étais pas là.	
É2: Bien sûr ! J'étais malade.	
1. notre cousin Serge	faire un voyage
2. Grand-père Mathieu	être à l'hôpital
3. notre oncle Charles	avoir trop de travail
4. notre cousine Camille	se préparer à des examens
5. nos grands-parents	se reposer
6. la sœur de Philippe	attendre une invitation
7. notre fille Chantal	finir un projet
8. vous	avoir des invités

Example: you		
E1: You were not there.		
E2: Of course. I was sick.		
1.	our cousin Serge	make a trip
2.	grandfather Mathieu	be in the hospital
3.	our uncle Charles	have too much work
4.	our cousin Camille	prepare for exams
5.	our grandparents	rest
6.	Philip's sister	accept an invitation
7.	our daughter Chantal	finish a project
8.	you	

(Source: Fouletier-Smith, (2004), p. 303.)

Activity 2

Packing your suitcases
Act out the dialogue in groups of four to five persons. This is how it works:

Example:

S1: I am packing five bikinis in my suitcase.

S2: I am packing five bikinis and sneakers in my suitcase.

S3: I am packing five bikinis, sneakers and sandals in my suitcase.

The person who forgets or says something wrong drops out.

Activity 3

A. Read the following statements about the life of Chilean poet and Nobel Prize winner Pablo Neruda, and write the verbs in their correct form in the preterit.

1. En el año 1965 (obtener) _____ el título de Doctor Honoris Causa en Filosofía y Letras de la Universidad de Oxford.

2. En 1938 (comenzar) _____ a escribir Canto General, obra referida a todo el continente americano.

3. El 6 de diciembre de 1930, el poeta (casarse) _____ con María Antonieta Hagenaar, una holandesa criolla de Java.

4. El 12 de julio de 1904 (nacer) _____ en la ciudad de Parral, Chile, Neftalí Ricardo Reyes Basualto, conocido en todo el mundo con el nombre de Pablo Neruda.

5. En junio de 1927 (comenzar) _____ su carrera diplomática al ser nombrado cónsul honorario en Rangún, Birmania. Entre 1927–1928 (viajar) _____ por toda Asia.

6. La primera publicación con el nombre de Pablo Neruda (aparecer) _____ en octubre de 1920 y el 28 de noviembre de ese mismo año (recibir) _____ el primer premio en la fiesta de la Primavera de Temuco.

7. A mediados del año 1923, Neruda (abandonar) _____ sus estudios universitarios para dedicar todo su tiempo a la creación literaria. Este mismo año (producir) _____ Crepusculario. El año 1924 (aparecer) _____ su famoso libro Veinte poemas de amor y _____ una canción desesperada.

8. El 23 de septiembre de 1973, Neruda (morir) _____ en la ciudad de Santiago.

9. En 1945 (comenzar) _____ su carrera política. Ese mismo año (ganar) _____ el Premio Nacional de Literatura.

10. El 21 de octubre de 1971 (obtener) _____ el Premio Nóbel de Literatura. En 1972 (regresar) _____ a Chile gravemente enfermo.

B. Now put all the information from the previous exercise in chronological order, starting with the earliest event. Include six connectors to give coherence to the biography.

(Source: De la Fuente et al., (2007b), pp. 109–110.)

---

1. In 1965, he (receive) _____ the title Doctor Honoris Causa in Philosophy and Literature from Oxford University.

2. In 1938, he (begin) _____ to write Canto General, a work referring to the whole American continent.

3. On December 6, 1930, the poet (marry) _____ María Antonieta Hagenaar, a Dutch Creole from Java.

Activity 4

Here are two excerpts from a photo-novella. Some sentences are missing, and you need to identify them to complete the dialogues. Then, listen and check.

a. Sit down, please. (formal)

b. But please, sit down.

c. Come in, please.

d. etc.

(Source: Flumian et al. (2007a), p. 135.)

Activity 5

3-10 Fill in the blanks with appropriate words to complete the following sentences:

(Words: 叫, 會, 說, 是, 不, 也)

1. 我 ＿＿ 中國人 。
2. 她 ＿＿ ＿＿ 英文 ，也 ＿＿ ＿＿ 一點兒法文 。
3. 他 ＿＿ 李中 ，他 ＿＿ 美國人 。
4. 我 ＿＿ 吳英 。我 ＿＿ 法國人 。我 ＿＿ 法語 。
5. 小文 ＿＿ 英國人 。他 ＿＿ ＿＿ 說日文 ，他 ＿＿ ＿＿ 英文 。
   他 ＿＿ ＿＿ ＿＿ 一點兒中文 。

Words jiao (call), hui (can), shuo (speak), shi (is or am), bu (no), ye (also).

I am Chinese. [Wo shi zhongguo ren.]

She can speak English, (she—implied) also can speak a little French. [Ta hui shuo yingwen, ye hui shuo yidianr fawen.]

He is called Li Zhong. He is American. [Ta jiao Li Zhong. Ta shi Meiguo ren.]

I am called Wu Ying. I am French. I speak French. [Wo jiao Wuying. Wo (shi) faguo ren. Wo (shuo or hui fawen).]

Xiao Wen is English. He no can (cannot) speak Japanese. He can speak English. He also can speak a little Chinese. [Xiaowen shi Yingguo ren. Ta bu hui shuo riwen. Ta hui shuo yingwen. Ta ye hui shuo yi dianr zhongwen.]

(Source: Wu et al., (2006), p. 39.)

Activity 6

Formulate sentences.

sollen / er / ausmachen / das Licht / um elf Uhr / .
im Deutschkurs / Anna / müssen / aufpassen / .
wollen / seinen Vater / er / einladen / zum Geburtstag / .
Zeitung / lesen / nicht / Petra / möchten / .
aufräumen / wir / müssen / leider / die Wohnung / .
können / nicht / warum / Heidi / einkaufen / heute abend / ?
der Film / um halb acht Uhr / anfangen / .

---

should / he / turn off / the light / at eleven o'clock / .

in the German class/ Anna / must / pay attention / .

want / his father / he / invite / for his birthday/ .

read / the newspaper/ not / Petra / like to / .

clean up / we / have to / unfortunately / apartment/ .

can / not / why / Heidi / go shopping / tonight / ?

the movie / at seven thirty / begin / .

APPENDIX 6.5

Three-day sample lesson plan

Day 1

Setting the Stage

Pictures of several families are displayed in the classroom. Students are asked to unscramble the following words written on the board: al limo-fai > la familia (family).

Providing Input

The instructor gives a simple description of a nontraditional family of the United States, with "step" and "half" relations. Students draw the family tree, along with the teacher. To follow up, the teacher asks true or false (¿cierto o falso?) questions (e.g., "John Smith tiene dos hermanas y un medio hermano." [John has two sisters and one half-brother.]), as well as specific questions (e.g., "¿Como se llama el medio hermano de John?" [What is the name of John's half-brother?]).

The instructor repeats the previous input activity, but now the input focus is a traditional Hispanic family (los García). The activity is again followed up with true/false and specific questions.

Guided Participation

In pairs, students are provided with true/false written statements based on the Smith family and the Garcia family, which they read to each other, e.g., "En la familia Smith hay hermanos y medio hermanos." (Cierto) [In the Smith family there are brothers and half-brothers. (True)]

In pairs, students do a matching activity in which partners alternate between reading a brief description and identifying to which of the two families it pertains. ("¿Es la familia Smith o la familia Garcha?" [Is it the Smith family or the Garcia family?])

Providing Input

Students are given a chart taken from a Spanish-language almanac in which average family size is given for the United States and for several Spanish-speaking countries. The instructor points out a few of the statistics.

Guided Participation

To expand on the last activity, the instructor asks the class, "¿Son Uds. típicos o no?" Students are directed to divide into groups of four and to determine the average family size for their group. The instructor writes a model question on the board: "¿Cuántos hay en tu familia nuclear?" [How many are there in your nuclear family?], and mentions that half- and step-relations count. After the instructor tallies the reported averages of each group on the board, the instructor and students determine whether the class approximates the average family size in the United States or in one of the Spanish-speaking countries.

Providing Input/Review

The class listens to a tape of a young Hispanic man describing his immediate family members. The tape is played two or three times, with students drawing a family tree based on the description. To conclude, the instructor shows what the family tree should look like and asks several related questions in Spanish.

Day 2

Setting the Stage

Students are asked to unscramble words and to complete a sentence based on the family trees presented on Day 1 (e.g., ster jshoi > tres hijos [three children]; "En la familia García hay tres hijos." [In the Garcia family there are three children.]

Providing Input

The instructor describes the Spanish royal family. The class, along with the instructor, draws the family tree. The instructor follows up with true/false and specific questions.

The instructor explains that, similar to England, Spain is a democracy with a royal family, *una monarquía parlamental* (a parliamentary monarchy). The instructor mentions that Spain has had a democratic system since 1975.

The instructor describes his or her immediate family, including some personality descriptors. Students draw the family tree as the description is given. The instructor follows up with either/or and specific questions.

The instructor explains how possessives are expressed in Spanish, and gives examples:

El príncipe Felipe es el hijo _____ de _____ y (Juan Carlos, Sofía).

[Prince Phillip is the son of Juan Carlos and Sophia.]

Guided Participation

Students take a pop quiz in which they must complete five sentences using information based on the Spanish royal family and the instructor's family, e.g.:

La esposa del rey Juan Carlos es _____. (la reina Sofía)
   [King Juan Carlos' wife is (Queen Sophia).
El esposo de la profesora se llama _____.
   [The husband of the professor is called_____.]

Possessive constructions are used in all five sentences.

After the instructor and the class go over the correct answers for the quiz, students are told to work in pairs and write their own questions based on the Spanish royal family and the instructor's family. They are told to be careful with the formation of the Spanish possessive. Later, individual students orally answer questions written by their classmates.

Guided Participation/Review

The instructor asks the class several true/false questions based on today's lesson. In the follow-up, the instructor elaborates on each statement to make sure the class has understood. Sample items include:

1. En España, no hay presidente; sólo hay un rey. (Falso. En España hay una monarquía y un presidente. Es decir, la monarquía coexiste con el sistema democrático....) [In Spain, there is no president; there is only a king. (False. In Spain there is a monarchy and a president. In other words, the monarchy coexists with the democratic system....]
2. Hay más personas en la familia nuclear del Rey Juan Carlos que en la familia nuclear de la profesora. [There are more people in the nuclear family of King Juan Carlos than in the professor's nuclear family.]

Day 3

Setting the Stage

Students, from memory, draw and label the family trees of the Spanish royal family and of their instructor. Afterward, students use Spanish to compare their family trees against the model family trees shown by the instructor.

Guided Participation

Students are shown pictures of several families to include families of famous personalities, for example, Gloria Estefan and Rubén Blades. They are instructed to pick one family but not reveal which it is. In pairs, one partner asks yes/no questions to figure out which picture his or her partner has chosen (e.g., "¿Hay cuatro personas en la familia?" [Are there four people in the family?]).

Providing Input/Review

The instructor reviews the meanings and uses of the possessive adjectives *su/sus* (his, her, your, their), giving examples.

Guided Participation

In an activity called *Relaciones famosas* (Famous relations), students answer questions by supplying the names of the famous relatives, for example:

1. El príncipe Carlos y la princesa Diana: ¿Quiénes son sus hijos? [Prince Charles and Princess Diana: Who are their sons?]

2. Martin Sheen: ¿Cómo se llaman sus dos hijos, también actores?
   [Martin Sheen: What are his two sons' names, also actors?]

In the follow-up, the instructor checks for correct responses and reviews the meanings of *su/sus* (his/her/your/their).

Providing Input/Review

The instructor reviews interrogative words and question formation, focusing on the students' families, e.g., "¿Cuántos hermanos... /¿Cuántas hermanas tienes.? ¿Cómo se llama..?,/¿Cuál es e/ nombre de... ?" [How many brothers/sisters do you have? What is the name of....?]

Guided Participation

Students prepare a brief oral description of their own family. First, students orally give their description to a partner who draws the family tree. The partner asks clarification questions in order to draw and label the family tree accurately. After each partner has given a description and has drawn the other's family tree, the partners check the family trees for accuracy.

The instructor selects two or three volunteers to give their descriptions aloud to the class. The class draws each family tree and asks clarification questions as needed. The instructor may ask students to turn in the family trees they have drawn and labeled.

Extension Activity

Famous families game. The instructor asks students to write down the names of famous families in television programs, world politics, world history, or world literature. The instructor then gives one name to a volunteer, and teams of students alternate asking questions of the volunteer student. All questions must pertain to nuclear family members. This is played for several rounds, with the team with the highest number of correct guesses winning.

(Source: Ballman (1997), pp. 174–186.)

APPENDIX 6.6

Dinner Game

2 gente con gente ◆ TAREAS

2-14 **Un crucero por el Mediterráneo**
Todas estas personas van a hacer un crucero por las Islas Baleares.
Otro/a compañero/a y tú trabajan en la agencia de viajes "OLATOURS"
y tienen que organizar el grupo. ¿Puedes reconocer en la imagen a
los pasajeros de la lista? Escribe en las etiquetas su número.

2-14 A Mediterranean Cruise
1. All these people are going on a cruise to the Baleares Islands. You and your partner work in a travel agency "Olatours" and have to arrange these people in groups. Can you recognize the passengers from the pictures and *match them with the descriptions on your list.*

1. Sr. López Marín
Biólogo jubilado.[3]
67 años.
Sólo habla español.
Colecciona
mariposas.

2. Sra. López Marín
Jubilada.
65 años.
Habla español y
francés.
Muy aficionada al
fútbol.

3. Sra. Marina Toledo
51 años.
Profesora de música.
Habla español e
inglés.
Soltera.

4. Manuel Gálvez
Profesor de gimnasia.
50 años.
Separado.
Habla español y
francés.
Colecciona mariposas.

5. Keiko Tanaka
Arquitecta.
35 años.
Habla japonés y un
poco de inglés.
Casada.

6. Akira Tanaka
Pintor.
40 años.
Habla japonés y un
poco de español.

7. Ikuko Tanaka
6 años.
Habla japonés.

8. Celia Ojeda
Chilena.
Arquitecta.
32 años.
Habla español y un
poco de inglés.

[3] También se dice "retirado".

1. Mr. Lopez Martin
retired biologist
67 years old
Only speaks Spanish.
Collects butterflies

2. Manuel Galvez
HS teacher
50 years old
Separated
Speaks Spanish and
French

6. Ikuko Tanaka
6 years old
Speaks Japanese

TAREAS ◆ **gente con gente** 2

9. BLAS RODRIGO
Chileno.
Trabaja en una
  empresa de
  informática.
20 años.
Habla español, inglés
  y un poco de alemán.
Muy aficionado al
  fútbol.

10. BERND MÜLLER
Suizo.
Pianista.
35 años.
Soltero.
Habla alemán, italiano
  y un poco de
  francés.

11. NICOLETTA TOMBA
Italiana.
Estudia informática.
26 años.
Soltera.
Habla italiano, francés
  y un poco de inglés.

12. VALENTÍN PONCE
Funcionario.
43 años.
Casado.
Sólo habla español.
Muy aficionado al
  fútbol.

13. ELISENDA GARCÍA
  DE PONCE
Ama de casa.
41 años.
Casada.
Sólo habla español.

14. JAVI PONCE GARCÍA
8 años.

15. SILVIA PONCE GARCÍA
Estudia biología.
18 años.
Habla español, inglés
  y un poco de
  italiano.

Compara tus conclusiones con las de tu compañero/a. ¿Son iguales?

2-15 **La distribución de los turistas en el restaurante**
  Ustedes quieren que los clientes lo pasen bien: ¿cómo van a
distribuirlos en las mesas? Escucha a otros empleados de la empresa
para tener más información.

Y otra cosa: ¿con quién van a sentarse ustedes?

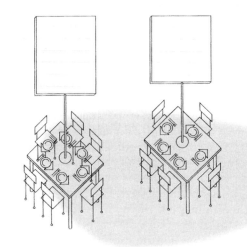

LES SERÁ ÚTIL

En la mesa 1: A, B...

A al lado de B porque...

Tienen { la misma edad.
         la misma profesión.
         el mismo hobby.

Los dos...

A habla francés y B, también.

2-16 **La propuesta**
  Tienen que explicar y razonar la distribución a toda la clase.

> **2–15.** *Making table
> arrangements.*
>
> You want your
> passengers to get
> along. How are you
> going to arrange
> them at the dinner
> table? Listen to
> other employees to
> find out more
> information.
>
> With whom will you
> sit down?

> **2–16** *Explain your
> rationale to the
> whole class.*

(Source: Martín, Sans, and Caballero (2003), pp. 26–27.)

APPENDIX 6.7

Results of the anxiety questionnaire

The subjects, high school students, ranked their anxiety level (5 = most relaxed to 1= least relaxed) for the following activities. The results are listed in order, ranging from moderately relaxed to moderately anxious.

Moderately relaxed: 1–Read silently in class. 2–Repeat as a class after the instructor. 3–Write a composition at home.

Neither anxious nor relaxed: 4–Do exercises in the book. 5–Work in groups of three or four. 6–Work on projects (i.e., newspapers, filmstrips, and photo albums). 7–Compete in class games by teams. 8–Repeat individually after the instructor. 9–Open discussion based on volunteer participation. 10–Interview each other in pairs. 11–Work in groups of two and prepare a skit. 12–Read orally in class. 13–Listen to questions and write answers to the questions. 14–Speak individually with the instructor in his/her office. 15–Write a composition in class.

Moderately anxious: 16–Write your work on the board. 17–Present a prepared dialogue in front of the class. 18–Give an oral presentation or skit in front of the class. 19–Speak in front of the class. 20–Write a composition in class.

Endnotes

1 When students touch a body part while hearing the numbers spoken by the teacher, the learning increases from 30 percent to 90 percent because they are "doing" what they are "hearing." Such a kinesthetic approach anchors meaning for students and connects spatial and tactile experience with hearing to enhance learning. This TPR approach to teaching numbers is equally successful for elementary learners and adult learners—they enjoy the active nature of the learning process and are surprised to see how quickly they can learn this way.

2 The primary focus of this activity is to practice students' comprehension of the numbers. At the same time, although the prepositions are not the focus of this lesson, the teacher introduces prepositions naturally. While calling out the numbers (e.g., "leg Nummer zwei unter Nummer drei")—at this point the teacher should wait a moment to make sure students are taking the number being called out—the teacher places the numbers on the overhead projector to model the activity. Students will internalize the prepositions quickly in the form of "incidental learning."

CHAPTER 7

Developing Listening Skills

Without hearing, there is no listening.
Without listening, there is no comprehension.
Without comprehension, there is no communication.

REFLECTION

How did you develop listening skills as a learner of another language? What sources of input helped you most? For example, your teacher's use of the target language (TL), songs, movies and TV, language lab materials, or people speaking in TL environments. What did not help you at all? Provide a rationale for your answers.

_____

_____

_____

_____

Introduction

In the history of foreign language teaching, the teaching of listening has undergone many changes. With an increasing emphasis on communicative approaches, the recognition of the importance of listening skills in the foreign language curriculum has become more prevalent. Some comprehension-based approaches (e.g., see the Natural Approach, or Total Physical Response—TPR) even believed that mere exposure to comprehensible and meaningful input might be sufficient and lead to the acquisition of language skills. Nevertheless, listening has been treated as the "Cinderella of language learning" for many years (Nunan 2002, p. 238), and only in recent years applied linguists have started to agree that listening deserves equal attention, both in the classroom and in teacher preparation. The development of listening skills must not be seen as separate from the development of communicative competence, but as a vital prerequisite and an essential part at all stages of instruction.

The purpose of this chapter is multifold: First, it will describe the nature of listening and discuss factors that affect the listening comprehension process. Second, taking into account how people listen and, as supported by research in SLA and cognitive psychology, the chapter will explore principles and guidelines for the design of listening tasks and materials that aid the learners in their development of listening skills in a foreign language learning environment. Third, the chapter will demonstrate how to integrate scripted and authentic listening materials in and outside the classroom in a variety of ways. The need for the integration of such materials is based on the view that "in-class listening alone cannot provide sufficient input either for language acquisition or the development of listening skills" (Joiner 1997, p. 99).

Defining Listening

What is listening? **Listening**, in most general terms, is simply described as the act of hearing. While such a definition merely alludes to listening as a neurological event, listening involves many invisible mental processes of understanding speech in a second or foreign language (Rost 2002). No single definition exists that captures the complexity of these mental processes and thus what constitutes listening comprehension. Nevertheless, several aspects have emerged from an evolving body of research over the last few decades that have contributed to better understanding of the nature of listening comprehension. These aspects include (1) receptive, (2) constructive, (3) collaborative, or (4) transformative. Rost (2002) describes these orientations in the following way: Listening is "receiving what the speaker actually says." These involve elements such as "'getting the speaker's idea', 'decoding the speaker's message', and 'receiving the transfer of images, impressions, thoughts, beliefs, attitudes and emotions from the speaker'" (pp. 2–3). Listening also means aspects such as 'catching what is in a speaker's mind', 'finding out what is relevant for you', or 'noticing what is not said'" (p. 2). In this sense, listening is constructive. In many situations, the negotiation of meaning requires collaboration between the speaker and listener. In this sense, listening means "'responding to what the speaker has said', or 'acting interested while the speaker is talking', or 'signaling to the speaker which ideas are clear and acceptable to you'" (pp. 2–3). Such a view makes listening an interpersonal skill and active part of communication[1]. Lastly, listening is also transformative. It is "'involvement with a speaker without judgment', 'empathizing with the speaker's motivation for speaking', or 'the process for altering the cognitive environment of both the speaker and listener'" (p. 3).

How Do We Comprehend and Process Information?

As echoed by Lee and VanPatten (2003), "Scholars agree that listeners are active participants during the communicative act and that listening is a dynamic process drawing on a variety of mental processes and knowledge sources" (p. 195). One way of describing this process is by looking at the kind of strategies that are activated to help the listener comprehend. This model is generally referred to as bottom-up and top-down processing. Another way to understand the comprehension process is by analyzing what kind of and how information is processed. This so-called **information-processing model** describes the listening comprehension by breaking it down into three different phases: perception, parsing, and utilization (Anderson 1995).

    Bottom-up comprehension refers to the part of the listening process in which "understanding" of incoming language is worked out proceeding from sounds, into words, into grammatical relationships and lexical meanings. The **bottom-up processing model** assumes that in the first phase of the process, we perceive and decode the acoustic signals. Based on the perception of these aural stimuli, we analyze the smallest meaningful units (phonemes), for example, whether a word has a long or short vowel (*wann* [when] versus *Wahn* [delusion]), a voiced or voiceless consonant (*two* versus *due*). From the stream of input, we set word boundaries based on the sound script of a word that we recognize. During this process, we match the new sound with a data bank of sound scripts that we have stored in our echoic or phonologic memory. This memory, which is part of our background knowledge, is established when we hear, pronounce, and use words or phrases in meaningful contexts over and over. The quality of the acoustic signal and the amount of background noise, and the degree of familiarity with a speaker's accent or dialect, strongly affect the perception process.

ANALYSIS AND DISCUSSION

1. "Listening in a foreign/second language"—write down what comes to mind.

    _____

    _____

2. What makes listening comprehension easy or difficult? First, list all the factors you can think of that may affect or support the listener's comprehension process. Next, compare your list with the one provided in Figure 7-3 in task 2 at the end of the chapter.

    _____

    _____

In the next phase, the **parsing phase**, we construct meaning by decoding this new input. Decoding occurs while the new information is parsed and matched against a huge data bank of pre-stored words and phrases based on semantic and syntactic cues. Because listening takes place in real time and under severe processing constraints, and because there is too much information to process, not every piece of information of the input is processed. When assigning meaning, we focus only on key units (e.g., words or components of a word), which allows us to preempt larger idea units (propositions) that we then cross-reference against pre-stored information. In other words, not all semantic, syntactic, or phonologic parsers need to be fully and equally activated. For example, the word *yesterday* as a past tense referent makes past tense verb markers in many instances redundant. We also do not have to recognize every word or sound in the input, because we hear words not in isolation but in specific contexts, which allows us to infer information to complete an interpretation (Goh 1998a; 1998b). The comparison of low-and high-proficiency listeners shows that the latter can do all this easily because they have "a recourse to hundreds of thousands of memorized phrases, partial sentences, and complete sentences. Many of these complete sentences accumulated over a life-time are accessed and used as whole[s] [chunks] as they have been on previous occasions" (Tschirner 2001, p. 314). Hence, recognition and accessing of such phrases occurs very quickly.

With more incoming information, and a short-term memory that keeps filling up, information is processed or pushed out. During this process, the **utilization phase**, some information gets lost while some makes it into the long-term memory for later retrieval. Some information is stored there a short while; other information, if further elaborated and revisited, is reintegrated into the existing knowledge structures and may be stored for the rest of someone's life. Please note that this description of how information is stored is only a metaphor; the three processes—perceiving, parsing, and utilizing—do not take place in a linear way. They take place recursively within a very short period of time, while some processing occurs simultaneously or parallel, or even retroactively. An incoming stream of new information allows and causes the listeners to continuously change and update the interpretation of the input.

While words and phrases take on different meanings when used in different contexts, a listener's broader background knowledge further determines how he interprets a message. In this regard, as Celce-Murcia and Olstain (2000) point out, "It is generally acknowledged that bottom-up information, i.e., physical signals or clues, cannot operate with any accuracy or efficiency on its own and that it requires the interaction with

ANALYSIS AND DISCUSSION

To experience different phases involved in the listening processes, do Task 1 in "Explorations."

top-down information to make discourse comprehensible to the listener" (p. 103). Making use of top-down information is generally referred to as **top-down processing**. Top-down knowledge is evoked from an internal source, from a bank of prior knowledge, which is generally known as schemata, and global expectations about the language and the world.

Schemata can refer to various possible knowledge areas including cognitive strategy use, prior knowledge of the subject matter, or familiarity with rhetorical features (Alexander, Schallert and Hare 1991; Swaffar, Arens, and Burns 1991). One particularly important area is that of specific knowledge about the context itself. This knowledge is necessary so the listener can successfully reconstruct an intended message. In a particular listening situation, such knowledge may require information about the setting (where the speakers are), the topic (what they talk about) and purpose (why they talk), and the participants (who they are). Familiarity with the content area and details pertaining to the listening situations may further ease the comprehension process (Chiang and Dunkel 1992; Markham and Latham 1987). A listener's topical knowledge is further influenced by his sociocultural experiences and backgrounds.

During the comprehension process, bottom-up and top-down processes interact with each in nonlinear and complex ways. They also have a compensatory effect, meaning that if one process fails, the listener switches to another.[2] Other factors that further affect the comprehension process are the listener's cognitive abilities, including linguistic and sociolinguistic skills, reasons for listening, and what we have to do with the information. All this makes the act of assigning meaning to multi-defined words and phrases a very individual and interpretive matter. Let us now look at some other factors in more detail.

Listening Situations and How We Listen

Besides the listener's background knowledge, numerous other factors also affect the comprehension process. Some of these have to do with the listening situation itself—for example, whether we are active participants engaging with a speaker, whom we are listening to, and why we listen all play an important role in determining how we listen. The cognitive demand of the listening content and what we have to do with

ANALYSIS AND DISCUSSION

Read through the list of situations in Figure 7-1. How are people listening in these situations? What kind of tasks are the listeners in these situations likely to attempt?

1. You are interviewing for a job.

2. You are listening to the announcement of the lottery numbers on the radio.

3. A friend you haven't heard from in a long time calls you up on the phone.

4. You are talking to your doctor, describing how you feel.

5. You listen to the news on the radio.

6. A teacher provides instructions for the test.

7. Your students work in pairs or groups.

8. Discuss any other situations that you have encountered recently:

_____

_____

FIGURE 7-1 Listening situations

the aural input—that is, the task we perform while or in response to listening—further affects how much and which information we comprehend and retain.

Lynch (1998) points out that all listening experiences can be placed along a continuum from collaborative to non-collaborative. By **collaborative** is meant listening that occurs when two or more speakers engage with each other in face-to-face situations, over the phone, or via video-conferencing tools. **Non-collaborative** listening occurs when there is no interaction between the speaker and the listener, and the listener acts as an observant listener. Examples of non-collaborative listening experiences are listening to a lecturer, the news on TV or radio, music, or being in the role of a bystander while others engage in a conversation.

Unlike non-collaborative listening situations, collaborative situations have the advantage that the listener, as an active participant in the conversation, has some control over the communication process. The listener can respond by switching to the speaker role, and she can provide prompts to the speaker to continue the discourse. Speakers and listeners can negotiate meaning. Through this collaboration of listening, the listener becomes a co-constructor of the discourse. Listeners use global, local, and transitional cues and queries to demonstrate their comprehension and to guide further conversation. They can alert the speaker if they are not processing the input and are not able to interpret and thus comprehend the information. In other words, during interpersonal communication, where listening is part of the communicative act, collaboration allows the listener and the speaker to make use of communication strategies such as asking questions. Asking the speaker to slow down, to repeat, or to clarify all aid in the comprehension process. Collaborative situations are normally more engaging and allow us to avoid misinterpretation.

Listening situations can also be divided into whether the listener has aural and visual perception or aural perception only (Lee and VanPatten 2001). In **aural perception** situations, the listener hears only the language and receives no visual cues. An example would be listening to the radio. **Visual perception**, on the other hand, occurs when a listener can see the speaker live, on TV, or while video-conferencing and can therefore receive information not just through the words themselves, but through nonlinguistic visual cues such as facial expressions, gestures, lip movements, and signs. From an early age, we learn how to make use of such cues (Green and Kuhl 1989; 1991), which contribute to our interpretation of a message. Although visual perception may aid with the comprehension process, at the same time it can lead to the misinterpretation of a message, if the speaker's and listener's interpretations of visual clues such as gestures or facial expression are not in agreement.

Whether we are involved in a collaborative or non-collaborative situation, how we listen is an important factor that influences each listener's comprehension process. This makes listening, as opposed to simply hearing, an intentional act that involves attention. Whether to pay attention or not is under the listener's control, which is one reason listening is best described as an active rather than merely a receptive skill (see Lee and VanPatten 2003). Understanding how attention determines listening is central to understanding the listening process. Indeed, it is only the information that we focus on, that we can process and ultimately retain (Rost 2002). How we listen and what information we attend to in different situations are also influenced by a range of other factors. In general, these have to do with the situational context, that is, whom we talk to, why we listen to somebody or a message, and what we have to do with this information. While the act of listening is different in all of these situations, the degree of attention and concentration also varies in these situations and is determined by the importance of the message or the listener's interest. For instance, in small-talk situations we often listen to make a conversation. To keep the conversation alive, we ask questions or acknowledge what the other person is saying. The purpose for listening becomes more a social act than an informational one. Last, the listener's cognitive ability and the listening content further influence the comprehension and the retention of the information.

Cognitive Ability and Listening Content

Many factors that affect the comprehension process have to do with the listener's **cognitive ability**. In part, this factor has to do with a listener's memory and processing skills, that is, how much information a listener can retain and process in his working memory within a limited period of time. Cognitive ability becomes evident through the task type and its demand. For example, ask yourself how many times you had to listen to a phone number, the last time one was left as a voice message in your native language, until you finally managed to write down the whole number.

While at the surface level you may have understood every single digit, your retention capacity may have manifested itself through your mental and processing ability. This difference, needless to say, allows some people to recall a seven-digit phone number easily after listening only once, while the average person most likely has to listen several times.

The cognitive aspect is tightly linked to the contents of the aural input—that is, the conceptual complexity of a whole text or discourse, or also individual words. For example, you may have heard a particular word being used many times before, but have only a vague idea of its actual meaning. If this word is a key word, and you cannot conceptualize its meaning, other supporting information may be of little help during the process of constructing its meaning.

The text type and discourse, and our degree of familiarity with it—for example, whether we listen to a story, an interview, or political speech—contribute to the ease or difficulty of understanding it (Rost 2002). For example, let us look at the discourse structure of a job interview. What kind of questions will a dialogue between a job applicant and an interviewer entail? Most likely the interviewer will ask questions such as "Why do you want this job? What have you done before that qualifies you for this job?" While not every single question can be foreseen, some general questions, however, are predictable. A listener's background knowledge and familiarity with the discourse structure normally assist her in predicting and inferring information that aids the comprehension process.

How a text type or discourse is organized also makes a difference. To illustrate this point, a story that is presented in excerpts as flashbacks and out of order is more difficult to understand than one presented in a chronological sequence of events. But the most central feature affecting the difficulty and understanding of a text is the content, or its intrinsic, cognitive subject matter (G. Brown 1995). Implicit, ambiguous, or abstract information is more difficult to interpret than information that is clearly stated (Brown and Yule 1983; Brown et al. 1984).

Developing Listening Skills in Second Language Learning

Considering the complexity underlying the development of listening skills, foreign language learning environments are not ideal. Whereas L1 speakers have been exposed to thousands of hours of aural input gradually building up a knowledge bank of structures and words that

ANALYSIS AND DISCUSSION

What problems do students encounter when processing listening (aural) texts?

allows them to develop listening skills, FL learners face a tough challenge to achieve the same goal with limited exposure and within a short period of time.

It seems only obvious, but the most prominent factor that accounts for why listening comprehension is difficult for foreign or second language learners has to do with aspects of language (Brown, 1995; Rost, 2002) and bottom-up processing (Goh, 2000). For example, Anderson and Lynch (1988) report that various grammatical forms (e.g., particular syntactic forms that caused difficulty for young native speakers) were also often misinterpreted by lower-level L2 learners, while older L1 listeners and more advanced L2 learners had no such problem. Goh (2000), in a study on the cognitive perspective of language learners' listening comprehension problems, reports that "half of them were perceptual processing problems arising from failure in word recognition and ineffective attention" (p. 68). In other words, students, in particular at beginner levels, cannot recognize the words fast enough to establish meaning that further allows them to construct meaning of the whole message.

To maximize the development of listening skills, several strategies are necessary: 1. Teachers need to take full advantage of in-class listening situations. 2. Teachers need to expose students to a wide range of listening materials and provide opportunities to the students that allow them to access materials that would otherwise not be possible without the guidance of an instructor. 3. Students need to be provided with outside listening practice that is necessary to make up for shortcomings in the classroom.

The following sections discuss strategies and guidelines to maximize exposure to aural input and the development of listening skills in and outside the classroom environment.

Listening Situations in the Foreign Language Classroom

Though the classroom is hardly ideal for developing listening skills, it is nonetheless a starting point, where a teacher can create a learning environment that maximizes the exposure to aural target language (TL) input. This can be achieved by using the TL extensively and by integrating collaborative and interpersonal communication activities (see Chapter 8, "Developing Oral Communication Skills") and non-collaborative learning situations such as the use of audio-video-based resources. Face-to-face interactions allow students not only to develop interpersonal skills (i.e., listening and speaking) but also to use communication strategies such as asking questions, asking for clarification, asking to slow down and repeat, or making oneself understood through nonlinguistic strategies (see the section on creating input in Chapter 1). All of these activities may function in support of the comprehension process.

REFLECTION

Based on your experience as a teacher or learner, make a list of listening practices that students normally engage in. What kinds of opportunities for listening practice are available in the classroom? How engaging are these?

_____

_____

With students' increasing language abilities, many classroom-based situations such as giving classroom instructions, providing explanations, and conducting regular classroom business provide excellent opportunities for students to develop listening comprehension skills (Flowerdew and Miller 2005; Lee and VanPatten 2003). In addition, the teacher can have an informal chat with the student, which creates a situation that provides excellent listening practice for the students. Such a strategy can be interpolated at any stage of the lesson, serving as a relaxing break from more intensive work. Chats are live, personal and easy to listen to and students normally like them. Ur (1984, p. 62) gives suggestions for such informal teacher talk topics: a member of your family, a friend of someone you have met, something you like doing, a place you know from your childhood, a film or play you have seen.

Classrooms also provide many listening opportunities that allow "students [to] act as an eavesdropper rather than as a participant in the interaction" (Underwood 1989, p. 32). Although this role occurs less frequently in real life, when adapted as a teaching/learning strategy, it helps students to develop monitoring and evaluating skills. Teacher, student, or guest speaker presentations provide further opportunities (see "Integrate Real-Life Listening Scenarios," below, for details on using active listening strategies during non-collaborative tasks). Teachers can also integrate audio- or video-based materials to expose students to noninteractive listening situations (see "Integrate Video/DVD-Based Materials," on page 254, on using technology and video/DVD).

Despite the many potential opportunities for exposing students to a range of input that supports the development of listening comprehension skills, L2 classrooms are inadequate and limited in many ways. For example, for students to develop communication strategies, such as giving turn-taking signals, asking questions, asking for clarification, or becoming co-creators in a dialogue, they have to participate in real-life listening situations. It is real-life situations—such as when we are actually talking to a stranger because we are lost, or to a doctor while trying to make sure we are understood when explaining our physical problems—that allow us to develop the strategies we need to negotiate meaning. In the classroom, students rarely negotiate meaning when interacting with each other. This is because, as pointed out by Lee and VanPatten (2003), normally only the teacher has the skill "to provide a model of the fullest range of skilled listener behavior" (p. 203).

Furthermore, considering what it takes to become a successful listener in the TL, in-class listening is not sufficient in terms of the amount of aural input that can be provided. That is, extensive exposure and practice outside the classroom are required so the learner can build up a huge data bank that demonstrates how words and phrases are used in a wide range of contexts. Nevertheless, the classroom is an excellent environment in which learners can develop the groundwork, under the guidance of an instructor, that allows them to build on and evolve from initially controlled to automatic processing skills.

Guidelines For Integrating And Implementing Listening/Viewing Materials And Tasks

The successful integration of listening materials and the implementation of listening tasks require taking into account numerous factors. One set of factors has to do with the input of the listening materials. These include the content (e.g., linguistic complexity, density of information, organization and structure of the information, degree of implicitness of information), the sound quality, and the speakers' speech rate. Another set of factors concern the design of a listening task and how it is implemented. For example, the purpose of listening, what the listeners are to do with information (e.g., repeat, retain, or reproduce), how listening/viewing tasks are sequenced and scaffolded, and how the input is presented (e.g., multiple times; with introductions, with or without written support). A third factor involves the learners, for example, their cognitive and linguistic ability, level of proficiency, and interest in content and motivation. All of these factors play an important role and may contribute to the success or lead to the demise of a learner's listening experience in the classroom. The focus of the following section is to discuss these factors in detail.

Consider the pedagogical purpose of using an aural text/viewing segment

The pedagogical purpose and goal for using an aural/viewing segment determines the choice of the materials, the design of the listening/viewing task, and how to present the input. For example, if a dialogue or a speech pattern—whether it is presented in the form of audio, video, or teacher input—is to serve as a model for later speech production, its linguistic

If you are currently teaching a language class, how do you go about developing your students' listening skills? What practices or materials do you use?

If you are not teaching, what practices have you observed, or how would you go about developing your students' listening skills? Make a brief list of strategies.

_____

_____

content needs to be aligned with the learners' ability and level of proficiency. For this reason, most listening/viewing materials are normally made up of scripted or semi-scripted content in beginning language curricula. The input also needs to be presented so that it allows for the comprehension of most details. This normally requires multiple repetitions and additional written input.

If the primary purpose of a listening task is to comprehend communicative content, the listening/viewing process is more selective, and the learners may not have to understand every detail nor every single word. With this purpose in mind, the listening materials do not have to be scripted, and authentic resources can be integrated as well. Examples include simulated voice messages, brief lectures on a cultural topic, or excerpts from movies or other authentic audiovisual resources. Considering the learners' listening skills and level of proficiency, the teacher needs a clear understanding of the kind of information the listeners can elicit from a text and should design the task accordingly.

Make listening or viewing task based

A communicative or task-based approach to language teaching encourages active listening or viewing (Brown 1987). **Active viewing/listening** means the viewers/listeners cognitively engage with the input, i.e., they do something with the input. For example, students mark off words they recognize, answer questions, sequence, or write a summary in L1 or the TL (see examples below). A task-based approach also has the benefit of holding students accountable for an outcome. As Mayer (2001) reminds us, "Meaningful learning outcomes depend on the cognitive activity of the learner during learning rather than on the learner's behavioral activity during learning" (p. 1). In other words, the task design is more important than the learner simply doing something.

Illustration 1 demonstrates a task-based approach to listening. Students are given a line drawing of a public telephone. They then listen to a recorded conversation and label the drawing to show the steps in using the phone.

ILLUSTRATION 1

Learning how to use a public telephone

Listening task: Listen to the following conversation and label the drawing to show the steps in using the phone.

Extract of the CD script

June: Okay. This is a public telephone. We have two kinds of telephones:the blue one is for international calls, while the red one is for local calls.

Carlos: I see.

June: Erm … do you often use public phones in Mexico?

Carlos: Yes, but I think they are a bit different from here.

June: Okay. Now, what you need to do is first get some coins, and, erm, lift the receiver and wait till you hear the dial tone. Then you put the coin in the slot and wait till you hear a different tone. Okay. Now once you hear the change in tone you can dial your number.

Carlos: Ah, yes. And do I need a local code?

June: Eh, no. Not if you are calling within the city. But if you want to call outside the city, then you need to use the other city code first. See, here next to the phone there is a list of codes.

Carlos: Okay. That is useful.

June: After you dial the number then wait till someone speaks and then press this button. Then you can speak.

(Source: Flowerdew and Miller (2005), pp. 14–15.)

In real life, many listening situations require, by nature of the task, a communicative response to the aural input. In other words, the response to a listening task is inherently part of the task itself. For example, this could be the answer to a question, a request that is made on an answering machine, or a problem-solving task. The student's ability to perform the task becomes an indirect assessment of his comprehension of the listening script. The example in Illustration 2 demonstrates such a listening task.

ILLUSTRATION 2

Problem-solving and decision-making listening task

I've got a problem. An old auntie of mine, who lives a long way away, gave me her piano three years ago. When it arrived at my flat, I realized that it was a very poor piano not nearly as good as the old one I already had. Auntie thought her piano was wonderful, of course. Anyway I decided not to keep her piano and I sold it. I didn't tell her what I'd done because I thought it would upset her. When she asked "How's the piano?" I always said "Oh, fine" or "It's wonderful!" Now she's coming to visit me! Another aunt of mine is bringing her to my flat next Saturday. I never dreamed that she would ever come to my place. What am I to do?

(Source: M. Underwood (1989), p. 79.)

As suggested in Chapter 1, tasks fall along a continuum of pedagogical to real-life tasks. Ultimately, the goal is to get students to perform tasks that resemble real-life listening behavior and that result in a real-life product. For example, in an academic environment while listening to a short lecture, students take notes. Or, when people write down information based on a voice message, they do so based on what they consider important. The simulation of such tasks in a foreign language curriculum is very desirable since they emphasize the process students employ in finding a successful outcome to the task.

Along the way, students need help with practicing targeted listening skills. A traditional approach to dealing with listening skills—by asking questions about the content, requesting spoken or written replies, expecting students to reproduce some language from a video, or stress only listening comprehension—has raised many concerns (Swaffar and Vlatten 1997) and is certainly not enough. The development of listening skills requires special attention to isolated listening processes. For example, learners need to engage in selective listening tasks that aid them in comprehending at the phonemic, word, phrase, or gist level. This kind of listening includes noticing linguistic as well as nonlinguistic nuances of language. The examples in illustrations 3 and 4 demonstrate two tasks that focus on selective listening skills. In addition, students need help with the development of listening strategies.

The following list of potential instructional strategies focuses on the process of developing listening skills at different levels.

General strategies and response types of listening activities (Please note that many of these strategies can be used when working with audio or DVD-based materials.)

- distinguishing between homonyms
- distinguishing between phonemic differences (e.g., short or long vowels, tones, etc.)
- listening for keywords pointed out in advance
- checking off items in a list related to content
- checking off items in a list related to grammar
- listening/viewing a segment and stopping the CD/DVD/speaker when the answer to a previously posed question or a particular word or expression is heard
- circling an answer, a picture, or an object
- writing the answer

- filling in or labeling a picture
- completing fill-in exercises
- sequencing items or pictures
- following oral directions (nonlinguistic)
- signaling (by standing, raising hand, clapping, etc.) recognition of grammatical features (tense, gender, etc.)
- filling in gaps in a dialogue (e.g., students listen to two or three lines of dialogue and guess the next line, or they assume a speaker's part and produce his/her lines)
- giving or selecting a title
- identifying the main idea based on visual inputs (e.g., pictures, photos, short video scenes), T/F or multiple-choice statements
- writing the main idea
- sequencing or matching items or pictures (e.g., in chronological order)
- giving summaries
- making an outline
- filling in graphic organizers (see Chapter 9, "Developing Reading Skills")
- developing questions (e.g., for peers to answer)

Some video-specific strategies

- watching a silent clip and making inferences based on extralinguistic and paralinguistic information
- watching a silent clip and scanning for specific extralinguistic information in the setting or paralinguistic details such as gestures or body language
- watching a silent clip and predicting the dialogue (e.g., students write and act out the dialogue as a role-play)
- predicting the next segment in a story line
- clarifying ambiguous messages (at the word and sentence level)

ILLUSTRATION 3
Beginning level

Est-ce qu'ils font du sport?

Écoutez les interviews. Est-ce que toutes les personnes interrogées font du sport? Si oui, quel sport?

> Do they exercise?
> Listen to the interviews. Do all these people exercise? If yes, what sport do they do?

Sample listening script

Interviewer: Excuse me. I'd like to ask you all a question. Do you do sports?

Speaker 1: No, not really. I used to play tennis once in while. Now I don't have time any more.

Interviewer: What about you, Sir?

Speaker 2: I play soccer. I play soccer twice a week, every Tuesday and Saturday.

Interviewer: And you? Do you do any kind of physical activities?

Speaker 3: Oh, yes. I ride my bike every weekend with my friends.

Interviewer: How many kilometers do you bike?

Speaker 3: At least 30 to 40 kilometers.

Interviewer: Thank you very much.

(Source: Flumian, Labascoule, Lause, and Royer (2007a), p. 35.)

ILLUSTRATION 4

Intermediate level

Écoutez maintenant la conversation d'Emma avec un vendeur. Qu'est-ce qu'elle cherche? Elle devra finalement acheter ce produit par correspondance. Vous remplir pour elle le bon de commence?

Now listen to this conversation with Emma and a salesman. What is she looking for? She will eventually have to buy this product by mail. Can you fill out the order slip for her?

BON DE COMMANDE

QuantitÈ	RÈfÈrence	Nom de líarticle	Prix unitaire	Total

Frais de port et díemballage: 7,50Ä

TOTAL

(Source: Flumian et al. (2007a), p. 125.)

Prepare the listener/viewer

Most selective or non-collaborative listening tasks need some kind of preparation. The instructional segment in which the teacher is trying to get the students prepared is generally referred to as the **pre-listening phase** (Underwood 1989). Generally speaking, the goal of pre-listening tasks is to aid the listeners with their listening processes, that is, to reduce the information-processing load on listeners so they can maximize their comprehension (Anderson and Lynch 1988). The use of pre-listening activities is vital and has been found to facilitate L2 listening comprehension (see Berne 1995; Herron 1994; Herron, Hanley, and Cole 1995).

Pre-listening/viewing work can be done in many different ways, ranging from a simple question to a sequence of activities. Often it is integrated in a prior lesson segment. For example, a reading, writing, or pair-work activity may have a preparatory function leading up to a listening task. The level of preparation that is required needs to be gauged against the students' linguistic skills, their background knowledge, the task difficulty, and the goal of the lesson.

Most pre-listening tasks fall into two categories: those that support top-down and others that help with bottom-up processing. In general, these tasks are implemented for the following purposes:

- activate and elicit relevant background knowledge that may help in contextualizing the listening
- help with anticipating the contents
- motivate the students
- review and preview—clarify important information in advance that might interfere with comprehension (e.g., cultural information, key words, idiomatic expressions)

The preparation phase also requires the teacher to implement metacognitive strategies. The strategies may involve these activities:

- checking whether students understand how the listening activity should be done (i.e., making sure that students understand what is required of them)
- making clear to the learner the specific task details—what they are going to listen to and the listening purpose (Anderson and Lynch 1988; Mendelsohn 1998)
- providing general information (e.g., if a listening text is to be repeated a number of times, and what the definite purpose of each listening task involves)

Here are a few other examples of pre-listening tasks.

ILLUSTRATION 5
Anticipating discourse structures

In a video scene from the movie *Billy Elliot* (see whole video lesson in Illustration 9), Billy Elliot and his father appear in front of a panel when applying to the Royal Dance Academy in London. The preparation task prior to watching this scene could involve students to generate a list of questions one might expect to be asked by the members of the admissions panel. The rationale for such a task design is multifold: It reviews the discourse structure of an interview; it allows the students to anticipate potential questions to be asked; and it allows the teacher to preview and review vocabulary pertinent to the particular context of applying to a ballet school.

ILLUSTRATION 6
Asking personalized questions

In an intermediate listening activity on the topic of travel, the teacher may ask the following types of questions:

Q1: Has anyone traveled to Spain before?
Q2: What was it like?
Q3: Who else has traveled to Spain?
Q4: Can you tell the class what it was like?

These questions are open and personalized questions that can be used to activate the relevant students' schemata for the listening part of the lesson. While such open questions lend themselves well as a general introduction to a topic, the types of questions asked nevertheless need to be specific enough so that they not only activate general background knowledge on the topic, but create a direct connection to the specific content of the listening text.

ILLUSTRATION 7
Using visuals (pictures, graphics, or photos)

The following list of focused questions demonstrates how a teacher might introduce an audio or video-based lesson on flamenco dancers.

Look at the picture on page eight of your textbook (picture of a flamenco dancer).

Q5: What can you see in the picture? (focused)
Q6: What is she wearing? (focused)
Q7: Can you describe what the man is wearing? (focused)

(Source: Flowerdew and Miller (2005), p. 190.)

Here are some more general ideas for pre-listening/viewing tasks:

- stating the topic
- using content-related pictures (e.g., labeling a picture, asking questions about it, comparing pictures)
- looking at a list of ideas, thoughts, items, and so on (for an example, see the video script of the French video lesson based on the movie excerpt from *L'Argent de Poche* in Appendix 7.2)

- brainstorming (see Illustration 8 on brainstorming and Illustration 9, the sample lesson based on the transcript from *Billy Elliot* in Appendix 7.3)
- reading a content-related text
- reading through questions to be answered while listening/viewing
- predicting and speculating
- previewing the work that will be heard in the listening text/viewing segment

---

ILLUSTRATION 8

Brainstorming

Now, individually or in pairs, make a list of possible ideas/suggestions, questions, items, advantages/disadvantages, pros/cons, or positive/negative aspects that are related to a specific topic. For example, think about things you have at home in your room, items you pack for a trip, and so on.

Adapt the task to the learner's listening and cognitive ability

A goal of CLT is to maximize input in the foreign language curriculum. One way of achieving this is by integrating authentic materials as early as possible. Most authentic materials, even with increasing language skills, make the interpretation of a message appear like an unfinished puzzle—some parts are recognizable and others are only fragmented pieces. In other words, while learners may understand some words or phrases verbatim when listening to an authentic text, other segments may remain totally incomprehensible. To gradually move away from scripted or semi-scripted texts, it has been repeatedly suggested that through task design it is possible to bridge the gap between the learner's proficiency level, the difficulty of the text, and the embedded cognitive complexes of the content, thus allowing for an increased integration of authentic materials.

Numerous strategies lend themselves well for adapting and designing tasks that support such an alignment approach (Figure 7-2).

Underwood (1989) suggests that "The level of difficulty of listening work can be adjusted by a) the selection of less/more difficult texts or b) the setting of less/more difficult tasks or c) giving less/more support to the students" (p. 34). Support can also be provided during the pre-listening or preparation phase (see "Prepare the Listener/Viewer"), and at the task level.

At the task level, several strategies can be used to facilitate the comprehension process. One such strategy is to divide a listening of a text into subtasks. This allows for presenting the listening task in steps and assigns to each subtask a different goal and purpose for listening. The further advantage of such a selective listening or viewing approach is that it

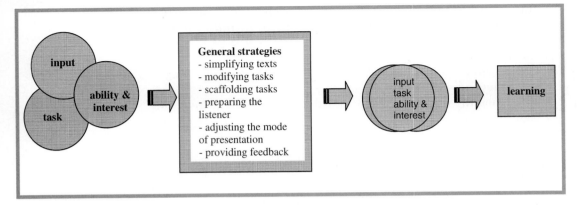

FIGURE 7-2 An alignment model for maximizing listening comprehension
(Source: Model adapted from Lawrence and Brandl (2006); Wulff (2006).)

encourages focused attention on one feature at a time. This method helps with reducing cognitive overload (Swaffar and Vlatten 1997) and, at the same time, allows for recursive and repetitive listening or viewing.

Another advantage to breaking down the listening of a text into subtasks is that it allows for scaffolding the listening process. The idea behind **scaffolding** is that information gained from a previous task leads to better success in accomplishing the following, more challenging task. One form of scaffolding is to sequence comprehension tasks from general to specific. This strategy is beneficial if the whole listening script is aligned with the listener's level of proficiency skills. That is to say, sequencing comprehension tasks toward detailed understanding works only if the learners have the knowledge and skills to pick up on these details.

When using authentic resources, teachers find this strategy becomes more difficult to apply because authentic texts normally are not consistent in the level of difficulty. That is to say, different textual segments often vary in the degree of difficulty. Students may be able to understand some sections verbatim and be able to grasp only the gist of other parts. In that case, task adjustment becomes necessary. For this reason, the subdivision of tasks should not be viewed as a rigid hierarchy, in which tasks are to be sequenced in a particular order. More importantly, appropriate adjustments in the task demands need to coincide with learners' listening abilities regarding a particular section or the whole listening script.

Here are some useful guidelines for sequencing and task adjustments:

- Establish the topic/context.
- Isolate/focus on key words. The first steps in a sequence of tasks need to aid the listeners in decoding isolated key words. These words need to be chosen based on how essential they are in establishing the

topic and basic understanding. Doing so helps free up students'
capacity for top-down processing.
- Focus on the gist or main idea.
- Focus on the level of details.

Task difficulty can be increased or reduced by providing different
degrees of textual or visual support. Examples constitute responding to
multiple-choice exercises, true/false statements, or sequencing activities,
which may be provided in the L1 or the TL. Such instructional strategies
have a multiple effect: they expose students to expressions (1) that they
need to understand; and (2) that they need to talk about after they have
perceived the aural input, such as the listening or video segment (Swaffar
and Vlatten 1997). The design of such tasks also allows the teacher to
provide the learners with descriptive statements or summaries of the content in simplified language.

Illustration 9 presents a listening lesson that was adapted at a low
and intermediate level of proficiency. Each lesson is divided into three
phases: pre-viewing/listening, listening task, and extension or post-
viewing/listening. Listening tasks for the lower level are further graded
and broken down into subtasks to simplify the listening process at this
level. This lesson is based on the interview scene in the movie *Billy Elliot*.
In this scene, Billy and his father appear in front of the admissions com-
mittee for an interview. Billy is applying to the Royal Academy of Ballet.

ILLUSTRATION 9
Video-based lesson for low- and intermediate-level listeners

Lower level	Intermediate level
Listening tasks	**Listening tasks**
Pre-viewing/listening	**Pre-viewing/listening**
Think about the structure of an interview. How does an interview begin and end? Who normally asks the questions? What questions would you expect in an interview? Make a list.	Think about the structure of an interview. How does an interview begin and end? Who normally ask the questions? What questions would you expect in an interview? Make a list.
Listening tasks	**Listening tasks**
Note: The questions would be in English; some of the statements could be provided in French. **Subtask 1.** Which of the following statements are true or false? T F Billy says he is excited about dancing.	*The following questions would be in French:* 1. Match the questions that you came up with the ones that were asked by the committee? Which ones did the committee ask? Which ones were similar? Which ones the same?

(Continued)

Lower level	Intermediate level
Listening tasks	**Listening tasks**
T F His father says that he dances all the time. T F Billy's father is an expert in dancing. T F Billy asks a question about the school. **Subtask 2.** How does Billy describe how he feels while dancing? He says: T F He feels like a bird. T F He feels nothing. T F His heart is changing. T F He forgets about everything. T F He feels electricity. **Subtask 3.** What does the head of the admissions committee wish Billy's father on his way out?	2. What does the school expect from his father? 3. How does Billy's father describe his son's attitude towards dancing? 4. Describe how Billy feels when he dances. What images does he use?
Post-viewing/listening (extension)	**Post-viewing/listening (extension)**
Use a still-picture of admissions committee. Guess how you believe each member might rate Billy's interview. Say why each member might or might not accept Billy.	Imagine you were part of the admissions committee. Are you in favor or against accepting Billy? Prepare a statement (written or oral) and share it with the other committee members?

Learners also benefit from help in the form of visual support material (Anderson and Lynch 1988; Mueller 1980; Pratt, Bates, and Wickers 1980; Underwood 1988). The strongest support comes from research on the effectiveness of multimedia learning. Such research claims that "words and pictures [...] can complement one another and that human understanding occurs when learners are able to mentally integrate visual and verbal representations" (Mayer 2001, p. 45). Nevertheless, it is important to bear in mind that the effectiveness of different types of visual aids, as in the case of speech modifications, varies according to learners' degrees of L2 listening proficiency and their spatial learning ability (Blau 1990; Chaudron 1985; Chiang and Dunkel 1992; Mayer 2001; Mueller 1980). Examples of tasks providing visual support are identifying, matching, or sequencing pictorial objects, pictures, or picture stories. Video and multimedia applications offer multiple ways of presenting visual information (e.g., images, written verbal text) and aural information (e.g., music, spoken verbal text) while taking advantage of the availability of visual information in support of the comprehension process of verbal input (see the following guidelines).

Lynch (1988) points out that making task-based adjustments also has its disadvantages. The difficulty with task modification lies in designing a task that is challenging enough and that meets the learning goal, or what Krashen referred to as 'i+1' (Krashen 1982), while pushing the learner to exert all his mental capacities to maximize the comprehension process. Some questions are simply too easy, such as "How many speakers are taking part in a conversation?" (Lynch 1988), which listeners can normally figure out without having understood much of the text. Others are often too difficult and can become frustrating for students. It is often difficult to predict whether the type and demand of a task are aligned with the learner's listening ability, and include the cognitive challenges, without frustrating him. In such cases, it is often best to try out the task with the learners.

Keep the listener's processing capacity in mind

Listening is an **immediacy-task** skill—meaning the stream of incoming and ongoing information allows only minimal processing time. This kind of task puts tremendous constraints on the working memory. The linguistic and cognitive complexity of the input, or additional visual content when watching film, may further create and increase overload for the working memory. In other words, the more information, including aural and visual input, learners are required to process and retain in their working memory, the higher are the capacity constraints, and the more the listeners/viewers are going to split their attention. Splitting attention means that the listener/viewer becomes selective by being able to attend to only some of the aural or visual information. What the listeners/viewers have to do with the input, such as answering a multiple-choice, true/false, or open-ended question further affects their cognitive demands. Illustration 10 demonstrates a task in which the learners are asked to check off lists of vocabulary or items of objects after watching a video scene in silent mode. The purpose of this task is to foreshadow these words and stimulate the language use of what the students see on the screen. Drawing the learner's attention initially to the images only, reduces their cognitive demands.

Here are some general strategies for dealing with processing constraints:

- Use short listening segments. A 30-second to 3-minute video or audio-based segment is normally sufficient (Stempleski and Tomalin 2001).
- Stop frequently, and repeat the audio/video CD segment (see "Make Use of Repetition and Pausing," p. 247).
- Discuss only a few comprehension tasks at a time. About 3–5 questions are the most the average student can handle at a time.

- Design tasks that focus on visual and aural input separately.
- Use check-off or marking tasks for while-viewing/listening tasks. The more multitasking is involved, such as additional reading and writing, the higher are the processing demands.

ILLUSTRATION 10

Excerpt from the video-based lesson *L'Argent de Poche* (see Appendix 7.3 for the whole lesson).

2. Cochez (√) les objets que vous observez chez Sylvie:

un lit   un animal en peluche
une brosse   un sac en forme d'éléphant
un sac noir de dame   une commode
un appareil photo   un mégaphone
un bol avec deux poissons des portes
une fenêtre   des cahiers
une clé

---

2. Mark off (√) the objects that you observe in the scene with Sylvie:

a bed   a stuffed animal
a brush   a handbag in the shape of an elephant
a black handbag   a chest of drawers
a photo camera   a megaphone
a bowl with two fish   doors
a window   notebooks
a key

Consider differences between spoken and written texts

Spoken discourse or texts are very different from written ones, and they need to be taught in different ways. For example, written texts are more densely structured, and sentence structures are normally longer and more complex than those of spoken texts. As Flowerdew and Miller (2005) suggest, placing spoken genres along a continuum by marking different degrees of "spokenness" and of "writtenness" (p. 48) helps us understand their differences and complexities (see Appendix 7.4). For example, a casual interactive conversation would fall on the right side of the continuum, while political speeches, written academic lectures, sermons, or newscasts would fall on the other end of the continuum. Whether a spoken text is carefully planned and written out, as opposed to unplanned and spontaneous, in most cases changes the degree of "spokenness" and of "writtenness" (Flowerdew and Miller 2005; Ochs 1979).

In a foreign language learning environment, it is common for teachers to use carefully planned and scripted aural texts. The advantages of using scripted materials are multifold. The contents of scripted texts can be geared to targeted learner levels and needs. Furthermore, it is normally quite challenging to find authentic discourse that is not too difficult for beginning language learners or that does not require a great deal of adaptation on the teacher's side. Nevertheless, there are numerous disadvantages with the use of scripted texts for the development of listening comprehension skills. While many scripted texts are meant to simulate natural speech, unfortunately they rather resemble versions of simplified written discourse. That is, they lack the many features that are normally present in natural speech—pausing, speech redundancies, repetitions, contractions, slowing down, changing intonations, and emphasis (see Appendix 7.1), which play vital roles in understanding oral discourse. When working with such texts, teachers need to bear in mind the nature of aural discourse. They need to present these texts in a way that makes up for the lack of natural discourse features. One way of achieving this is by presenting an aural text (e.g., a dialogue or giving directions) themselves, in a way that resembles natural discourse, rather than playing a CD.

ANALYSIS AND DISCUSSION

Make a list of features that distinguish aural from written texts. Then, go to Appendix 7.4 and compare your list. How do such differences affect the listening comprehension process?

_____

_____

_____

Make use of repetition and pausing

Repetition and pausing are two important strategies that facilitate the comprehension process. Indeed, teachers commonly use such strategies when presenting aural input. As research suggests, the repetition of passages appears to facilitate listening comprehension more than other types of modifications and thus should be encouraged (Berne 1995; Cervantes and Gainer 1992; Lund 1991). The practice of pausing is also vital. As Rost (2002) points out, "By pausing the spoken input (the tape or the teacher) and allowing for some quick intervention and response, we in effect 'slow down the listening process' to allow the listener to monitor their listening more closely" (p. 145). The use of repetition and pausing also allows for opportunities to make the listening process interactive.

This means the instructor can pause at an important moment, redirect the students' attention to key sections of the input, ask follow-up questions, provide feedback, and negotiate the meaning of the contents. As far as processing demands are concerned, the more details the listener/viewer has to attend to, the more repetition and pausing are normally required.

Follow up on the listening/viewing tasks

Providing feedback on the students' listening/viewing task is an essential strategy for supporting the development of listening skills. Feedback is normally given as part of the listening/viewing phase as a follow-up to the listening task. It allows the learners to see how successfully they interpreted a message or completed a task. Furthermore, checking on students' answers to comprehension questions and tasks gives the teacher an opportunity to provide diagnostic feedback and identify listening problems. In particular, feedback is important during scaffolded listening tasks—when information gained from one listening tasks supports the comprehension of the next.

The question remains, how can teachers provide feedback on learner's comprehension? During collaborative listening situations such as conversational exchanges, the speakers can use active clarification strategies to negotiate meaning. During non-collaborative situations, the teacher must take on the role of guiding students along the comprehension process and making the listening process interactive. A traditional and somewhat minimalist approach to providing feedback is simply to let the students know whether their answers to the listening tasks are right or wrong. On the other hand, an alternative and constructive approach is for the teacher to provide feedback in form of guidance that allows students themselves to reconstruct the meaning of the listening task. As pointed out by Field (2002), students improve their listening ability most if they get to construct their own representation of meaning from what they hear. Strategies that allow for a constructive approach include allowing students to relisten and then discuss and compare what they understood. From a practical standpoint this strategy is not always possible as a follow-up to every listening task, because it is a time-consuming. From a pedagogical standpoint, however, it a valuable strategy that the teacher should employ whenever the listening task asks for it.

Teach real-life listening strategies

Research suggests that an initial focus on training in listening comprehension facilitates L2 development to greater degrees than does an initial focus on oral practice (Postovsky 1981). Rost (2002, p. 155) provides the following list of strategies that are often practiced by successful L2 listeners.

Predicting:	Predicting information or ideas prior to listening
Inferencing:	Drawing inferences about complete information based on incomplete or inadequate information.
Monitoring:	Monitoring one's own performance while listening, including assessing areas of uncertainty.
Clarifying:	Formulating clarification questions about what information is needed to make fuller interpretation.
Responding:	Providing a personal, relevant, response to the information or ideas presented.
Evaluating:	Checking how well one has understood, and whether an initial problem has been solved.

Many of these strategies can be incorporated into listening activities. In this way, the teacher indirectly models such strategies and gives the students an opportunity to practice them.

Integrate real-life listening scenarios

In many instances the task itself—particularly those that embed communicative functions such as 'requests, or asking for information'—integrates performance-based behavior as a natural follow-up. Lee and VanPatten (2003) suggest leaving voice messages on answering machines or voice boxes to provide students additional noninteractive and out-of-class practice. An alternative—for those who consider this practice instrusive—this strategy can also be easily implemented through online learning and course management systems[3] such as MOODLE (see Brandl 2005 for an overview) or Blackboard.

ILLUSTRATION 11
Sample online listening assignment

Mia, my good friend, and I are having a party next Saturday. Mia is in charge of contacting everybody, but unfortunately, she is not very well organized. Below you see her guest list for the party. The sound file contains the recording of the voice-mail message that I left for her last night (see sample voice message below). Listen to my message, and provide an updated and complete guest list for Mia.

Mia's guest list

Iben Andersen	tlf. 98 ????
Mikael Petersen	tlf. 98 15 33 33
Randi ????	tlf. 86 12 12 17
Marianne ????	tlf. 72 45 60 28
Preben Hovbjerg	tlf. ????
Lotte Carlsen	tlf. ?? 39 19 40
Søren ????	tlf. 98 45 82 19

Listening script

Hey Mia. I am returning your call because you asked to me to call you back and give you again the list of phone numbers of everybody we want to invite. It seems like you got some missing or wrong numbers. I am sorry for this confusion. Anyway, here is the list again. Iben's number is 98 53 12 14. Mikael's telephone number is 98 15 33 34. Make sure you got his number right. You mentioned that there was something wrong with the number you had. Randi's number is 86 12 12 17. Make sure to double-check his number. You can look it up in the phone book or also online. His last name is Vestergaard. Marianne Kirstegaard's number is 72 45 60 28. Preben Hovbjerg's number is 98 11 43 24. Lotte's number is 98 39 19 40, and her sister's is 98 45 82 19. I hope you can understand all these numbers. Call me back if you have any other questions. My number is 67 71 42 83. Thanks again for contacting everybody. I'll see you on Saturday.

ILLUSTRATION 12

Performance-based listening task (beginner level)

You and your friend need to buy a list of different paraphernalia for the classroom. To find the store where you get the best deal, you both decided to check out different stores. You just came home from visiting a department store, where you found all your items (see list below). Your friend checked out the prices in a different store and left you a voice message on your answering machine. Listen to her message and compare the prices. Which store is a better deal for you?

Your list:		Your friend's list
Pen	$ 1.50	_____
Notebook	$ 2.95	_____
Eraser	$ 0.90	_____
Pencils	$ 0.25	_____
Calculator	$ 11.80	_____

Extend the listening tasks

Tasks related to a particular listening or viewing segment, which are done after the listening/viewing is completed, are generally referred to as **post-listening tasks** (Underwood 1989). There are two categories of tasks: (1) those in response to the listening/viewing work and (2) those whose purpose it is to exploit and extend the information the students heard or learned in the listening/viewing section of the lesson (Flowerdew and Miller 2005). Primary pedagogical reasons for doing extension tasks are

- to use the input to anchor or consolidate the language by integrating other skills

- to use the input as a springboard for other activities
- to demonstrate what students have learned

There are myriad ways to follow up on teacher or student, audio or video-based input. Here are some general ideas and strategies for follow-up tasks:

- Expand the content of the listening text to another or related topic or context (Underwood 1989).
- Have students apply the new information they have learned or what they have listened to in a more individual way.
- Analyze and explore the speakers' way of communicating (e.g., accents and dialects, structural and lexical use, sociolinguistic and pragmatic use, nonlinguistic aspects (facial expressions, emotional reactions, attitudes, manners).

The lessons in Appendixes 7.3 and 7.5 demonstrate examples of post-listening/viewing extension tasks.

While all listening tasks—in interactive as well as noninteractive contexts—need to be followed up to check on the learners' comprehension, not all listening tasks lend themselves well to post-listening communicative extension. These include tasks with a particular focus. Thus, the decision whether to follow up with post-listening work depends on the purpose and design of a listening task and on its pedagogical and curricular goal. On the other hand, many real-life tasks, by nature of the design, often require a communicative response (see illustrations in "Make Listening or Viewing Task Based") as a follow-up.

Integrate multimedia- and internet-based listening materials in the curriculum

As Joiner (1997) reminds us, "It is evident that in-class listening alone cannot provide sufficient input either for language acquisition or the development of listening skills" (p. 99). Due to the shortcomings of in-class listening in terms of time and limited opportunities, providing students with outside and independent listening practice is a necessity. Traditionally, it has been the role of language labs to provide access to additional resources, such as satellite TV or multimedia applications in recent decades. In recent years, however, the role of the centralized language lab has changed, while the delivery of learning programs has gradually shifted from local desktop to online-based multimedia applications.

Despite this shift, multimedia applications continue to play an important role in the development of language learning skills. As noted by Joiner (1997), "The most obvious advantage of such computer-assisted multimedia applications is instantaneous random-access to any sentence or segment on the sound source [. . .] and the ability to replay and relisten with ease to difficult passages" (p. 88). The design of interactive multimedia programs also allows adding text or any other visual support to further help with the comprehension process. For example, these programs include online scripts, built-in glossaries, immediate feedback capabilities, and the integration of other skills (e.g., reading and writing) via one application. Such features can provide considerable help to the listeners in various ways, and they can be more effective than audio- or video-based media. For example, in a comparative study of three media—audio, video, and multimedia—Brett (1997) discovered that "performance on task showed more effective comprehension and recall while using multimedia than either audio or video plus pen and paper" (p. 39).

The shift toward online delivery programs also brought forth the development of many open-source and free applications such as online course management and learning systems (e.g., MOODLE[4]) or audio recorders (e.g., audacity[5]). Unlike most desktop applications, the advantage of such systems is that they are very user friendly, fairly easy to learn, and allow teachers to use the Internet as "part telephone, part interactive television," or answering machine (Warschauer and Healey 1998, 64). Further, they permit teachers to adapt this environment to their own instructional goals by creating and integrating authentic listening tasks for their students. Such online systems also allow for out-of-class synchronous and asynchronous interactions among students, thus providing further opportunities to practice interpersonal oral communication skills.

The following are several illustrations of such listening tasks for beginning and intermediate language classes.

ILLUSTRATION 13
Listening to a voice message

You are invited to attend a party. Your friend, who is organizing the party, has called you up and left a message on your answering machine. Listen to her voice message and find out information about the party. Send her an e-mail or leave a voice message and let her know what you are going to bring.

Listening script

Hi everybody! You have reached 555-8912. I am sorry I cannot come to the phone right now. If you are calling about the party next Saturday, this is what we still need. Some appetizers, green salads, and vegetarian main dishes. No need to bring meat dishes, drinks, and desserts. We'll have enough already. Feel free to come by any time after 3. Looking forward to seeing you all.

ILLUSTRATION 14
Listening to directions

You are looking for a Danish restaurant. You know you are close, but cannot find it. You are asking somebody on the street where to find it.

Listen to the stranger's description. Draw a map so you can remember where to go.

Listening script

This street is Martin Luther Boulevard. Go straight ahead till the next traffic light. Then walk one more block, and turn left on 18th street. Go all the way until you get to Jackson Street. Then take a right. The restaurant is on the left side of the street, about half a block away.

ILLUSTRATION 15
Responding to an authentic voice message

You just arrived at home after attending classes at the university. You managed to go to all your lectures except the geography lecture. You find the following voice message from a classmate on your answering machine. Listen to the voice message, and write down essential information about what you need to do.

Listening script

Hi, this is Klaus. It's Tuesday afternoon and I'm calling to see if you have notes from the geography lecture today. I missed it because of a dental appointment; so if you have notes, just bring them tomorrow so I can borrow them. Hmm. If not, call me back at 213-555-4201 tonight so I can call someone else. Okay, thanks. Bye.

(Source: Adapted from Celce-Murcia and Olstain (2000), p. 209)

Integrate listening materials in support of the affective side of learning

Music and songs play an important role in language learning, and there are many benefits to integrating music. Popular music can serve as a gateway to culture and has a strong influence on the affective side of learning. Students also normally respond well to the use of music in the language classroom. Using songs to develop listening comprehension skills, however, has many challenges. Songs are like poems, and the lyrics represent the artistic freedom of the song writer, which is why they are often difficult to understand. The language in songs is also often very different from the conventional language use. The acoustic representation also makes songs difficult to hear and understand. For such reasons, not all songs lend themselves well to the development of listening skills. The songs need to be well chosen, and in most cases working with songs requires textual support. Nevertheless, students who like target culture songs and are given opportunities listen to these songs over and over on their own time most likely benefit from this experience.

1. Not all songs lend themselves well to the development of listening skills; yet many do, and teachers like to use them. Discuss some general strategies on how to integrate songs in the classroom in different ways.
2. Do Task 10 in the "Application" section.

Integrate video/DVD-based materials

Many teachers still make use of audio-based materials. For quite some time, however, in their own lives students have been predominantly using visual-based technology (e.g., videos, DVDs [digital versatile discs], TV, life-video streaming, and recently also video-enhanced handheld devices). This trend has also made its way into the FL classroom. For more than 50 years teachers have been using film, both inside and outside the classroom. In recent decades, language-edited video materials have also become an integral part of many textbook materials. There are many advantages to using video/DVD-based materials. In contrast to audio-only materials, when students can see people speak they have a visual context for what is being said. A bimodal input—that is, visual and auditory—also has been found to support speech perception (Green and Kuhl 1989). Authentic film-based materials expose students to varied language, such as to voice, dialects, and registers other than their teacher's (Swaffar and Vlatten 1997). Furthermore, as Stempleski and Tomalin (2001) put it, "The medium of film is excellent at communicating cultural values, attitudes and behaviors" (p. 1) and provides cultural contexts for the target language (TL). Video/DVD-based materials also serve to motivate, and students are more interested in them than in audio materials (Hennessey 1995). They also provide a rich source for classroom communication and discussion.

DVDs, the Internet, and increasingly evolving computer-based technologies also allow access to richer information and to a more versatile use of film-based materials than ever before. For example, many DVDs contain theatrical trailers, director's comments or voice-overs, or documentaries about the making of a film or historical periods, and they often include captions and subtitles in one or many languages. In particular, the use of TL captioning has been repeatedly reported as having a positive effect on intermediate and advanced learners' development of listening comprehension (Borrás and Lafayette 1994; Markham 1999; Pusack and Otto 1995; Smith and Shen 1992). DVDs can be played back on any computer and be easily integrated with other multimedia presentation tools such as PowerPoint (see the preceding discussion on advantages of using multimedia tools).

Nonetheless, the use of video/DVD materials has been met with reluctance and uncertainty by language teachers. In particular, questions on how to use video most effectively—whether to ask questions about

What are advantages and disadvantages of using video/DVD-based materials?

_____

_____

the content, whether to request spoken or written replies, expect student to reproduce some language from a video, or stress only listening comprehension—have raised many concerns (Swaffar and Vlatten 1997).

While the use of video has many advantages, from a cognitive viewpoint the simultaneous processing of visual and auditory information is often overburdening. Consequently, in most cases, authentic video materials require adaptation to make them usable in the classroom. Stempleski and Tomalin (2001, pp. 2–5) provide some specific video-based techniques that lend themselves well to exploring visual and auditory contents in different ways. The following sections discuss these techniques in detail.

Silent viewing (vision on/sound off). One of the most powerful techniques is silent viewing. In other words, the teacher plays the scene with the sound turned off. This technique is "useful for highlighting visual content, for stimulating student language use about what they see on the screen, and for getting students to guess or predict the language used on the soundtrack" (Stempleski and Tomalin 2001, p. 2). From a cognitive point of view, this technique is especially powerful since it reduces the learners' cognitive overload by splitting their attention and focusing only on the visual input first. The video lesson based on *L'Argent de Poche* (*Small Change*) in Appendix 7.2 demonstrates how silent viewing is used as preparation for the listening phase. Silent viewing can also be used for a wide range of other pedagogical tasks. For example, in general, silent movies or video scenes presented with the sound turned off are a great source of nonlinguistic visual input that can be used for writing or speaking practices.

Sound on/vision off (sound only). When working with video, teachers also have the option to work with sound only. To prevent the students from seeing any visual images, one can adjust the brightness on the monitor or simply cover up the screen. Working with sound only allows students to further divide their attention to the background music and noises, sound effects, voices or language. For example, asking viewers to attend to the background music lends itself well as a pre-viewing strategy to introduce a film genre or the mood about a film sequence that is conveyed by its accompanied soundtrack. Illustration 16 (Brandi, 1996, p. 19) demonstrates this technique and proposes some questions that can be used for any kind of film sequence. Similar information can also be elicited from the tone of speakers' voices. Focusing on speaker voices and a specific characteristic is an excellent strategy for making predictions or introducing the main characters. When working with sound only, teachers also can use film just like a CD. For example, they can have students listen to the sound only and match it with the images. This technique, however, works well only if the visual input supports the comprehension process of the language input.

ILLUSTRATION 16

Sample questions regarding background music

1. What kind of emotions does the music evoke?
2. Which of the following characteristics do you associate with this film sequence? Mark all that apply.

(Source: Brandi (1996), p. 19, translated by Klaus Brandl.)

Pause/still/freeze-frame control. Whether we watch or listen, due to the transitory nature of auditory or visual signals, we selectively attend to information that we perceive. Guided by our background knowledge as well as interests, we see and hear information individually in different ways. In foreign language learning, it is hence often necessary to make the learner aware of particular aspects of the auditory or visual input. A useful technique for doing so is using still pictures. During any segment of a video lesson—that is, as part of the preparation phase, integrated in the while-viewing phase, or as part of an extension task—still pictures lend themselves well in a variety of ways. When used at a decisive moment, pausing or freezing a frame on the screen is a powerful technique for grabbing the students' attention and creating expectations. More general strategies include asking questions about objects, people, their relationship, the setting, past and current actions, predictions about

suspenseful	lively
exciting	adventurous
romantic	fast
sad	slow

future events, or film-related aspects. For example, "Who are the people? What are they doing? How are they dressed? What is going to happen next? What happened before? Where does the scene take place? What is the effect of showing people from this angle?" Illustration 9, the sample lesson based on the interview scene from *Billy Elliot*, demonstrates the use of a still picture as part of the extension task.

Sound and video on (normal viewing). The normal way of viewing a video scene is to watch it with the sound and the pictures turned on. See the guidelines and principles described earlier for information on implementing and developing viewing tasks.

Split viewing. The strategy of split viewing is similar to what is generally known as "jigsaw" reading or listening (for further examples, see Chapter 8, "Developing Oral Communication Skills"). There are various ways of applying jigsaw viewing. For example, Stempleski and Tomalin (2001) suggest letting some students watch a video sequence without the sound. Others hear the same soundtrack without seeing the pictures. Next, both groups of students can compare notes and build a complete picture of what happened. They can then watch the video with both picture and sound. A variation is to show a video scene to only half the students of a class. In pairs or groups, students who have seen the video segment then describe the scene to those who have not seen it. As a follow-up, students watch the scene again to see how well they understood or how well the scene was described. Essentially, any short film or brief film segment lends itself to this technique. If the language itself is too difficult for the students, the video segments can be presented with subtitles or silently, while students focus on developing interpersonal (listening and speaking) skills.

Jumbled sequence. An instructional strategy that stimulates discussion and work with story lines in different ways is to divide up a scene or to play short segments out of order (Stempleski and Tomalin 2001). Stempleski and Tomalin provide the following list of sequencing ideas (p. 4):

- Show the beginning and end of a sequence and ask students to guess [orally or in writing] in the middle.
- Show a number of sequences out of program order and ask students to order them.
- Choose two short sequences each from three different films and show them in random order; students must allocate the sequences to the films and decide on the order of the sequences in each film.

Using whole movies. It takes many years of foreign language study before learners are able to follow a whole motion picture with ease. Whereas showing a whole movie with subtitles most likely has little impact on the learners' listening comprehension skills, there are nevertheless many ways of integrating whole movies into a foreign language curriculum. As pointed out earlier, movies are a great source of input. Whether it is because of an entertaining or intriguing story, or because of its cultural information, a movie allows students to write and talk about the movie or its various aspects, give presentations, or use it as the basis for research projects. In this way, the movie's content gives students an incentive to apply the TL for communicative purposes. For example, students can do movie reviews, narrate or summarize main events, and talk about or describe individual characters.

Conclusion

The purpose of this chapter was to discuss the many factors affecting the listening comprehension process and to provide strategies and guidelines on how to compensate for such factors. Listening skills play a vital role in a learner's language acquisition process. Listening skills and strategies, as needed for interpersonal communication or in non-collaborative situations, must be addressed and integrated in the curriculum at all stages of instruction. This is not to say that the teacher's use of the target or the integration of textbook-based materials in the classroom are enough. Ultimately, and the earlier the better, students need to be exposed to authentic input both inside and outside the classroom. The teacher plays a key role in the learners' success or failure. It is the teacher who decides on the listening materials, designs listening tasks, and chooses how to implement them in a foreign language curriculum.

Checking chapter objectives

Do I know how to . . .

- ❏ define bottom-up and top-down processing
- ❏ identify and describe problems that learners encounter when practicing listening
- ❏ identify and describe factors that affect listening/viewing comprehension
- ❏ align listening/viewing tasks, texts, and listening ability
- ❏ identify textual characteristics that make an aural text easier or more difficult
- ❏ identify and describe differences between spoken and written texts
- ❏ implement a wide variety of instructional strategies that aid the learners in their listening comprehension
- ❏ describe and design tasks that focus on different types of listening skills
- ❏ design a lesson plan based on an excerpt from an authentic movie and adapt it to different learner levels

Explorations

TASK 1: HOW DO WE COMPREHEND? SIMULATING PROCESSING STEPS OF AURAL INPUT

The following experiment simulates different steps and parsers that are activated while learners are processing aural input and attempting to assign meaning. To review these steps read the section, "**How do we com-prehend and process information?**" at the beginning of this chapter. To experience how your comprehension of the aural input is gradually updated, follow the experiment step by step. The experiment works best if you do not look at the written texts and your instructor or a classmate reads the information in the input boxes that is provided for each step. (The text used in this task was adapted from R. C. Anderson et al. 1977).

Step 1: Assigning word boundaries
Assign word boundaries to the open phrase of listening text below.

Rockyslowlygotupfromthemat

Step 2: Running the phonetic parser
When you hear the sound [tu:] in English, what comes to your mind? Write down all the different possibilities.

Step 3: Running the phonetic and semantic parser
Spell out the following sound [tu:] in the English phrase "too well," and assign meaning.

Step 4: Assigning and inferring meaning based on individual words and sense units
(This example demonstrates a lower-level comprehension, which makes assigning and inferring meaning difficult.)
Without looking ahead to step 5, guess the meaning of this text.

Rocky _____ got up _____ planning
_____ moment _____ Things _____
too well. _____ held, _____ _____
situation. _____ _____ strong _____

Step 5: Assigning and inferring meaning based on individual words and sense units

Now read the same text, while some of the essential key words were added to the text.

Revise your initial hypothesis above.

_____

Rocky _____ got up _____ mat, planning
_____ escape. _____ moment _____
Things _____ not _____ well. _____
held, _____ charge _____ weak. _____
situation. _____ lock _____ strong _____
thought _____ break _____

Step 6: Matching against background knowledge such as differently experienced contexts and schemata

Reread the text below. Can you think of any different contexts that change the interpretation of the text?

_____

Rocky slowly got up from the mat, planning his escape. He hesitated a moment and thought. Things were not going too well. What bothered him most was being held, especially since the charge against him had been weak. He considered his current situation. The lock that held him was strong, but he thought he could break it.

TASK 2: ANALYSIS AND DISCUSSION

Factors that affect listening comprehension

1. Read through the list of factors that may affect or support the listening comprehension process in Figure 7-3. Discuss how any of these factors may affect low- or high-proficiency speakers.

_____

_____

2. Based on the factors listed in Figure 7-3, what arguments can be made that listening must be considered an active rather than a passive dimension of language? Write down your arguments.

_____

_____

1. background noise
2. a speaker's accent (including phonetic quality or prosodic patterns)
3. body language (gestures, etc.)
4. interaction with another speaker
5. seeing somebody's face and lip movement
6. prior knowledge of context, the world, topic, situation, culture
7. speaker's control of topic or conversation
8. number of times you hear something
9. knowledge of phonology, vocabulary, grammar
10. type of aural text (e.g., story, instructions, small talk, political speech, lecture, etc.)
11. the purpose of listening (e.g., test-taking situations; interest in topic)
12. a listener's memory skills (including short-term memory capacity)
13. supporting information (e.g., images, subtitles, written information, etc.)
14. a speaker's speech rate
15. age
16. condition
17. chewing food
18. a speaker's number of pauses
19. other:_____
20. other:_____

FIGURE 7-3 Potential factors affecting the listening comprehension process

TASK 3: ANALYSIS AND DISCUSSION

A tourist guide wants to make an announcement (in English) about Westminster Abbey to a group of tourists. Which of these two versions would be easier for them to understand, and why? Are there any disadvantages in choosing the "easy" version?

Version A

"Now next we're going to see the most famous church in Britain, the place where all the kings and queens have been crowned, Westminster Abbey. We'll have about half an hour or so to look around this lovely old building. If you get lost, we'll all meet at the west door at four o'clock. Remember it's also a holy place, so behave yourself."

Version B

"Now next we're going to see Westminster Abbey. Westminster Abbey is where all the kings and queens have been crowned. We'll have about half an hour to look round the Abbey. If you get lost, we'll meet at the west door of the Abbey at four o'clock. Remember, it is an Abbey, so behave yourself."

(Source: Anderson and Lynch (1988), p. 54.)

TASK 4: ANALYSIS AND DISCUSSION

Most native speakers of English are able reach the intermediate level after at least one year of language instruction at a college environment (about 2–3 years in secondary schools) in languages such as Spanish, French, or German. (Note: This normally takes longer in Japanese, Arabic or Chinese.) Read through the ACTFL Proficiency guidelines describing listening skills at the intermediate level in Appendix 7.1. Discuss the development of listening skills with foreign language learners based on the description of these skills.

TASK 5: TEACHING LISTENING TECHNIQUES

Look at the list of instructional practices. Discuss the potential strength and weakness of each strategy.

Instructional technique	strength	weakness
1. Teacher dictates random texts.		
2. Teacher plays weather broadcasts, news, and so on.		
3. Students work on specific listening skills such as distinguishing minimal pairs, identifying grammar errors, answering comprehension questions.		
4. Teacher does a listening activity without any kind of introduction.		
5. Teacher brings in a guest speaker at least once every other week.		
6. Teacher asks students to tell her what they did not understand.		
7. Teacher maps out students' ideas on the board before listening. After listening, she asks them to compare their own thoughts with the map and revise their thoughts.		
8. Teacher plays one sentence at a time and asks her students to translate each sentence into their L1.		
9. Teacher plays a short passage and then asks comprehension questions orally.		

(*continued*)

Instructional technique	strength	weakness
10. Teacher plays a short passage several times and each time gives a different listening task.		
11. Teacher asks students to read along while listening.		
12. Teacher tells her students the rationale for listening.		
13. Teacher asks students to discuss the answers to the listening tasks in pairs.		
14. Teacher asks students to summarize in their native language what they understood.		
15. Teacher asks students to predict the contents before listening.		
16. Teacher goes through the listening materials, explaining word by word at the post-listening stage.		

Application

TASK 6: LESSON ANALYSIS

Read the lesson description in Figure 7-4. Trio 2 (Radley and Sharley 1999) claims to use a communicative approach. However, a closer analysis of the lesson shows that the lesson activities suggest an audiolingual-based approach. Do you agree or disagree? Redesign this lesson, so it supports principles of communicative language teaching (CLT).

TASK 7: TASK DEVELOPMENT

Adapt Illustration 11, a task-based listening activity on revising the guest list, to the language that you teach. First, make all the appropriate changes in the guest list. For example, present the telephone numbers the way they are listed in a target culture that you teach. Next, record a sample text.

TASK 8: CASE STUDY ANALYSIS

Consider the following teaching scenario. In a third-year German high school class, the teacher introduced a listening activity, in which the students had to fill in the blanks with prepositions and articles. Figure 7-5 presents the actual listening script that the students were using. This is what the teacher said: *We are going to listen to several dialogues in which people describe directions. Listen carefully! I'll play each dialogue only twice. First, however, I want you to read through the dialogues, so you know what to listen for.*

The students had a lot of difficulty carrying out the activity. Why do you think this is so? How would you go about teaching this activity?

Unit 3, Lesson 4: What's her name?

Listen and read: Students listen to a taped recording and read a dialogue between two men talking about finding a suitable milkman to deliver milk. They talk about two possible assistants, a boy and a girl. The dialogue is tightly structured around giving personal information in reply to *Wh*– questions: What's her name? Where does she live? The listening activity lasts around three minutes.

Answer: Students listen to the conversation again and complete a chart about the girl and the boy. They listen for name, age, address, hobbies, and description.

Listen and repeat: Students listen to the question format on the tape and repeat what they hear: What's her name? What's his name?

Write and speak: Students are directed to look at the dialogue in Activity 1 and find all the questions. They need to write the questions in their notebooks. Then they practice asking each other the questions and giving the appropriate reply for the boy and the girl in the textbook.

Write and speak: Students copy a chart similar to that in Activity 2. They fill in the chart with information about themselves first; then they interview a partner and fill in his/her information.

Listen: Students listen to a new conversation about a film producer looking for a boy and a girl to act in a new movie. The producer has a conversation (similar to that in Activity 1) to find out information about two possible candidates. Students listen only and complete a personal information form.

Write: Students are given a cloze passage about the girl the producer in Activity 6 was enquiring about. Then they write a similar paragraph about the boy.

FIGURE 7-4 Description of lesson
(Source: Flowerdew and Miller (2005), pp. 103–104.)

What would you change to create a successful and meaningful learning experience for the students?

TASK 9: TEXTBOOK ANALYSIS

Choose a first-year language textbook. By yourself or with a partner, analyze a unit or chapter of a textbook. Make a list of activities describing how listening skills are practiced, and in what contexts. For example, students respond to *Wh*– questions about personal information, or students fill out missing information in an address book. Then, further analyze these listening tasks according to what listening skills the learners engage in (e.g., they listen for specific information, they make inferences, they listen for stress and intonation and mimic). Evaluate these tasks for their "closeness" to real-life situations.

TASK 10: LESSON DEVELOPMENT

Depending on factors such as the learner level, the type and quality of a song, and use of language, songs require special adaptation. Choose a contemporary song that is appropriate in the language classroom, and

Carmina und Victoria sind in Würzburg und suchen die Stadtbibliothek.

Carmina: Entschuldigen Sie bitte, können Sie uns sagen, wo die Stadtbibliothek ist?

Fremder: Da sind Sie ganz falsch hier. Laufen Sie hier zurück _____ zweiten Kreuzung. Gehen Sie zuerst _____ Kreuzung und dann nach rechts _____ Pfannenstrasse entlang. Nach ungefähr ein bis zwei hundert Metern, sehen Sie Fubgängerzone _____ linken Seite. Laufen Sie der Fubgängerzone entlang _____ Marienweg. Auf der rechten Seite sehen Sie dann die Post, und diagonal _____ Post im Gebäude, da ist die Bibliothek. Das können Sie gar nicht verfehlen.

Carmina and Victoria are in Würzburg and are looking for the city library.

Carmina: Excuse me, could you tell us how, where the city library is?

Stranger: Oh, you are totally wrong here. Go back until you get [*to the*] second intersection. First, [*go across the*] intersection and turn right onto the Pfannenstrasse. After about one to two hundred yards, you can see passenger zone [*on the*] left side. Walk along the passenger zone [*until the*] Marienweg. On the right side, you'll see the post office, and diagonally [*across from*] the post office is the library. You cannot miss it.

Note in German, this task requires modifying articles in the accusative or dative case. The German listening script shows the original text. The text in English translation includes the answers marked in brackets.

FIGURE 7-5 Listening script

develop a brief lesson. For those songs that are appropriate to the level, include pre-listening, listening, and extension tasks.

TASK 11: TEXTBOOK ANALYSIS

Choose a first-year language textbook. Look at several chapters. How are listening activities scaffolded? For example, are they sequenced to move from yes/no and true/false questions via display to open-ended questions? What listening tasks and skills do students engage in at the beginning, middle, and end of the book? Is any listening support provided, for example, by embedding a task in context or by preparing learners through pre-listening activities such as visuals?

TASK 12: DEVELOPING PRE-LISTENING AND LISTENING TASKS

Develop a set of pre-listening and direct assessment tasks based on the following listening script.

Listening script:

I've got a problem. An old auntie of mine, who lives a long way away, gave me her piano three years ago. When it arrived at my flat, I realized that it was a very poor piano not nearly as good as the old one I already had. Auntie thought her piano was wonderful, of course. Anyway I decided not to keep her piano and I sold it. I didn't tell her what I'd done because I thought it would upset her. When she asked "How's the piano?" I always said "Oh, fine" or "It's wonderful!" Now she's coming to visit me! Another aunt of mine is bringing her to my flat next Saturday. I never dreamed that she would ever come to my place. What am I to do?'

(Source: M. Underwood (1989), p. 79.)

TASK 13: DEVELOP A VIDEO-BASED LESSON FOR AN INTERMEDIATE-LEVEL LANGUAGE CLASS

1. Choose a short (3–5 minutes) excerpt from a movie, documentary, TV show, or any other authentic source. Give a brief summary of the scene, and explain your rationale for choosing the segment. What skills do you want your students to practice?
2. Develop a set of learning activities that guide students toward comprehension of the video-based materials. The set is to include the following learning activities:

   - Pre-viewing activities: Introduce the theme of the video segment, cultural and/or linguistic information (vocabulary or grammar) if necessary. Note: The theme of the whole movie may be different from your video clips.
   - Listening tasks that test the students' comprehension at a global and detailed level
   - Post-viewing activities that allow students to further apply what they have learned
   - Provide information demonstrating how you will go about teaching each phase.

APPENDIX 7.1

ACTFL Listening Guidelines

Novice–Low

Understanding is limited to occasional isolated words, such as cognates, borrowed words, and high-frequency social conventions. Essentially no ability to comprehend even short utterances.

Novice–Mid

Able to understand some short, learned utterances, particularly where context strongly supports understanding and speech is clearly audible. Comprehends some words and phrases from simple questions, statements, high-frequency commands and courtesy formulae about topics that refer to basic personal information or the immediate physical setting. The listener requires long pauses for assimilation and periodically requests repetition and/or a slower rate of speech.

Novice–High

Able to understand short, learned utterances and some sentence-length utterances, particularly where context strongly supports understanding and speech is clearly audible. Comprehends words and phrases from simple questions, statements, high-frequency commands, and courtesy formulae. May require repetition, rephrasing, and/or a slowed rate of speech for comprehension.

Intermediate–Low

Able to understand sentence-length utterances which consist of recombinations of learned elements in a limited number of content areas, particularly if strongly supported by the situational context. Content refers to basic personal background and needs, social conventions and routine tasks, such as getting meals and receiving simple instructions and directions. Listening tasks pertain primarily to spontaneous face-to-face conversations. Understanding is often uneven; repetition and rewording may be necessary. Misunderstandings in both main ideas and details arise frequently.

Intermediate–Mid

Able to understand sentence-length utterances which consist of recombinations of learned utterances on a variety of topics. Content continues to refer primarily to basic personal background and needs, social conventions and somewhat more complex tasks, such as lodging, transportation, and shopping. Additional content areas include some personal interests and activities, and a greater diversity of instructions and directions. Listening tasks not only pertain to spontaneous face-to-face conversations but also to short routine telephone conversations and some deliberate speech, such as simple announcements and reports over the media. Understanding continues to be uneven.

Intermediate–High

Able to sustain understanding over longer stretches of connected discourse on a number of topics pertaining to different times and places; however, understanding is inconsistent due to failure to grasp main ideas and/or details. Thus, while topics do not differ significantly from those of an Advanced level listener, comprehension is less in quantity and poorer in quality.

(Source: http://www.sil.org/lingualinks/LANGUAGELEARNING/OtherResources/ACTFL ProficiencyGuidelines/ACTFLGuidelinesListening.htm.)

APPENDIX 7.2

Sample video lesson based on *L' Argent de Poche*

Nom _____

Before viewing

Introduce the theme of the video, e.g., you might say in French, "I am going to show you a video clip about a girl who has an argument with her parents."

Introduce unknown vocabulary from the list used in task 2 (e.g., *une clé*, [a key], etc.)

Scene I

Part 1: Silent viewing task
Choisissez la réponse correcte.

1. Le papier peint dans la chambre de Sylvie est:

   • bleu, blanc et rouge
   • bleu, blanc et rose
   • bleu, blanc et jaune

2. Cochez (√) les objets que vous observez chez Sylvie:

un lit	un animal en peluche
une brosse	un sac en forme d'éléphant
un sac noir de dame	une commode
un appareil-photo	un mégaphone
un bol avec deux poissons	des portes
une fenêtre	des cahiers
une clé	

2. Mark off (√) the objects that you observe in the scene with Sylvie.

a bed	a stuffed animal
a brush	a handbag in the shape of an elephant
a black handbag	a chest of drawers
a photo camera	a megaphone
a bowl with two fish	doors
a window	notebooks
a key	

Viewing Instructions
1. Explain the listening tasks.
2. Make sure the subtitles are covered.
3. Show the following scene silently. Stop the scene before the girl speaks into the megaphone.
4. Discuss the answers of activity 1 and 2.

Rationale for design
The purpose of showing this scene the first time with the sound turned off is to draw the students' attention to the visual information only. Furthermore, the contents of the video are foreshadowed in this way. The instructor introduces or reviews the meaning of vocabulary items in the written, interpretive mode which aids the comprehension process before students hear some of these words in context.

Scene I:

Part 2: Listening task (sound-on)

Choisissez la réponse correcte.

3. Sylvie habite dans:
   a) an appartement
   b) une maison

4. Les poissons de Sylvie s'appellent:
   a) Plic et Ploc
   b) Ric et Roc
   c) Lic et Loc

5. Les parents de Sylvie vont:
   a) au café
   b) au restaurant
   c) chez les amis

Scene I: Choose the correct response.
3. Sylvie lives in:
   a) an apartment
   b) a house
4. The names of Sylvie's fish are:
   a) Plic and Ploc
   b) Ric and Roc
   c) Lic and Loc
5. Sylvie's parents go:
   a) to a cafe
   b) to a restaurant
   c) out with friends
6. Sylvie does not want to go with her parents because she:
   a) prefers to play
   b) would like to eat fast food
   c) refuses to carry her mom's bag
7. What does Sylvie put into the fish bowl?

6. Sylvie ne va pas avec ses parents parce qu'elle:
   a) préfère jouer
   b) voudrait manger au fast-food
   c) refuse d'apporter le sac de sa mère

7. Qu'est ce que Sylvie met dans le bol des poissons?

Rationale for design

The focus is on comprehending the main ideas of this scene. As the language is fairly challenging for first- or second-year or second-year students, using a multiple-choice format provides the students some information about the contents of the scene, and furthermore allows testing the students' comprehension.

Scene II

Viewing Instructions
1. Explain the listening tasks including unknown vocabulary in questions 8–10. Have students read the questions.
2. Play the scene with the sound turned on.
3. Replay the scene again, if necessary.
4. Discuss the answers of questions 8-10.
5. Play the whole video clip one more time with the subtitles uncovered.

Prédiction. Cochez (√) la réponse que vous trouvez logique.

8. _____ Les parents vont retourner.
   _____ Sylvie va pleurer.
   _____ Sylvie va utiliser le mégaphone et elle va crier par la fenêtre.
   _____ Sylvie va téléphoner la police.
9. Qu'est-ce que Sylvie crie par la fenêtre? _____
10. Cochez (√) les choses à manger que vous observez dans le panier.

---

du pain	du vin
des pommes	du fromage
des bonbons	un Orangina
un poulet	du rosbif

Scene II:
Predicting: Choose the most logical response.
8. The parents are going to come back.
   Sylvie is going to cry.
   Sylvie is going to use the megaphone and yell out of the window.
   Sylvie is going to call the police.

9. What is Sylvie going to yell out of the window?
10. Select the items you can eat that you have seen in the basket.

bread	wine
apples	cheese
candy	soft drink (Orangina)
chicken	beef

Rationale for design

The purpose of question #8 is to practice predicting strategies. The comprehension of question #9 is essential to understanding this video. That is why we ask the students to write down what Sylvie says. Question #10 focuses on the review of food vocabulary. Presenting a list of vocabulary items aids the comprehension process as the students only have to match visual images and the sound with the correct word from the list.

Post-viewing extension tasks

Optional variations for follow-up to the video activities:

First year:
With a partner, write a sentence telling what the parents, Sylvie, and the neighbors will do.

Second year:
Write one paragraph about how the story continues.

First or second year:
Discuss cultural differences in English. What would have happened if this scene had taken place in the U.S.?

(Source: Judy Davis, Seattle Preparatory School, Seattle, WA.)

APPENDIX 7-3

Transcript of chapter 15 of *Billy Elliot,* 25 sec into the scene.

CHAIR:	Just, well, just a few questions then. Billy, can you tell us why you first became interested in ballet?
BILLY:	Don't know. *[pausing]* Just was.
CHAIR:	Well, was there any particular aspect of the ballet which . . . caught your imagination?
BILLY:	The dancin'.
FATHER:	He dances all the time. Every night after school.
CHAIR:	Yes, well, we have a very enthusiastic letter *[pausing]* from Mrs. Wilkinson, and, uh, she has told us all of your personal circumstances. . . . Mr. Elliot, are you a fan of ballet?
FATHER:	I wouldn't exactly say I was an expert.

CHAIR: *[pausing]* Do you realize that all pupils must attain the highest standard, not just in ballet but also in their ordinary academic work. No child can succeed without the 100% support of his family. *[pausing... very low voice]* You are completely behind, Billy? Are you not?

FATHER: Yes, yes of course.

PANEL MEMBER: Do you want to ask us any questions?

FATHER: *[clears throat]* No, not, not really, no.

CHAIR: In that case, we shall let you know in due course.

ANOTHER MEMBER: Just one last question, Can I ask you, Billy. What does it feel like when you're dancing?

BILLY: Don't know. Sort of feels good. It's sort of stiff and that, but once I get goin', then I forget everything . . . and . . . sort of disappear sort of disappear. Like I feel a change in me whole body. Like there's fire in me body. I'm just there, flyin'. . . like a bird, like electricity, *[pausing]* yeah, like electricity.

CHAIR: Have a safe journey home. *[pausing]* Mr. Elliot, good luck with the strike.

APPENDIX 7.4

Characteristics of Spoken and Written Texts

Linguistic features of spoken text

- phonological contractions and assimilations
- hesitations, false starts, and filled pauses
- sentence fragments rather than complete sentences
- structured according to tone units rather than clauses
- frequent occurrence of discourse markers at beginning or end
- tone groups
- high incidents of questions and imperatives
- first and second person pronouns
- deixis (reference outside the text)

Linguistic features of written text

- longer information units
- complex relations of coordination and subordination
- high incidence of attributive adjectives
- wider range and precise choice of vocabulary
- high lexical density (nominalization)
- longer average word length
- more frequent use of passive voice
- high use of coherence and cohesive devices

(Source: Flowerdew and Miller (2005), p. 48.)

APPENDIX 7.5

Sample Video Lesson

(Source: Motyl-Mudretzkyj and Späinghaus, (2005), pp. 147–151)

D Film: *Schwarzfahrer von Pepe Danquart*

In diesem Abschnitt werden Sie mit dem Kurzfilm *Schwarzfahrer* arbeiten. Der Film wurde 1993 von Pepe Danquart gedreht.

Schwarzfahrer

Übungsbuch
Einheit 4, Teil D

1 Wortschatz: Das Wortfeld „schwarz" Lesen Sie die folgenden Ausdrücke, in denen das Adjektiv **schwarz** vorkommt. Vermuten Sie zunächst, was sie bedeuten könnten. Ihr Kursleiter/Ihre Kursleiterin hilft Ihnen anschließend.

der Schwarzmarkt _____

schwarz auf weiß _____

schwarzes Gold _____

schwarze Zahlen schreiben _____

schwarzarbeiten _____

schwarzes Schaf _____

schwarz sehen _____

schwarze Kasse _____

schwarzer Tag _____

sich schwarz ärgern _____

warten, bis man schwarz wird _____

schwarzfahren _____

In einigen dieser Ausdrücke hat **schwarz** die gleiche Bedeutung: die schwarze Kasse, der Schwarzmarkt, schwarzarbeiten und schwarzfahren. Durch welches andere Adjektiv kann man **schwarz** in diesen Ausdrücken ersetzen? Was ist dann wohl ein Schwarzfahrer?

Film sehen

2 Erste Sequenz sehen Sehen Sie die erste Sequenz. Beobachten Sie die Leute, die Sie in der Sequenz sehen. Stellen Sie Vermutungen an.

Filmsequenz
Sequenz: 1
Start: Anfang
Stopp: Alle Leute an der
ersten Haltestelle sind
in die Straßenbahn
eingestiegen.
Länge: circa 3.30

Person	Hat welchen Beruf?	Sieht wie aus?
_____	_____	_____
_____	_____	_____
_____	_____	_____
_____	_____	_____
_____	_____	_____

3 Hypothesen aufstellen Arbeiten Sie mit Ihrem Partner/Ihrer Partnerin. Sehen Sie sich das Bild auf Seite 149 an und beantworten Sie die Fragen.

◇ Wo sind die Leute? In welcher Situation befinden sie sich?

_____

◇ Was denkt die alte Frau? Was denkt der Mann neben ihr? Schreiben Sie die Gedanken auf.

Die alte Frau denkt: _____

_____

Film: Schwarzfahrer by Pepe Danquart

In this sequence you will work with the short film "Schwarzfahrer." The film was made by Pepe Danquart in 1993.

1. **Vocabulary: Lexical field "black."** Read the following expressions using the adjective "black." Guess their meaning first. Your instructor will help you.

   black market _____

   black on white _____

   black gold _____

   etc.

   In some of these expressions "black" means the same: black market, etc. Which different adjective would you use to substitute "black" in these expressions? What is a "Schwarzfahrer"?

2. **Viewing the film** Viewing the first sequence Watch the first sequence. Look at the people that appear in this sequence. Make assumptions about them.

person	profession	looks like
_____	_____	_____
_____	_____	_____
_____	_____	_____

3. **Hypothesizing.** Work with your partner. Look at the photo on p. 149 and answer the questions.
   Where are the people? In which situation do they find themselves?

   _____

   What does the old woman think? What does the man next to her think? Write down your opinion. The old woman thinks:

   _____

Der Mann denkt: _____
_____
_____

Filmsequenz
Sequenz: 2
Start: Alle Leute an der
ersten Haltestelle sind
in die Straßenbahn
eingestiegen.
Stopp: Der Junge Mann mit
dem Kopfhörer steigt in
die Straßenbahn ein.
Länge: circa 3.00

4 **Zweite Sequenz ohne Ton sehen** Sehen Sie die zweite Sequenz
vorerst ohne Ton und konzentrieren Sie sich auf folgende Aspekte.

◊ Was sehen Sie? Was passiert hier?
◊ Was macht die alte Frau? Beachten Sie ihre Mimik und Gestik.
◊ Wie reagiert der schwarze Junge? Beachten Sie seine Mimik und
Gestik.

5 **Ansichten antizipieren** Lesen Sie die Aussagen hier und auf Seite
150, bevor Sie die Sequenz mit Ton sehen. Unterstreichen Sie die
Sätze, die Ihrer Meinung nach in dieser Sequenz von der alten Frau
gebraucht werden.

„Als ob man sich nicht an unsere Sitten[1] anpassen[2]
könnte."
„Ich bin sehr zufrieden mit meinem Leben."

„Ich habe keine Angst, deshalb gehe ich abends oft
allein aus dem Haus."
„Man müsste wenigstens verlangen können, dass
sie ihre Namen ändern, bevor sie zu uns kommen, sonst hat man ja gar keinen Anhaltspunkt[1]."
„Leider kann er nicht gut Deutsch, aber das macht
ja nichts."
„Und dann arbeiten die alle noch schwarz. Als ob
das jemand kontrollieren könnte, wo von denen
einer aussieht wie der andere."
„Ich vertraue auf meine Mitmenschen."
„Warum kommt ihr überhaupt alle hierher, hat
euch denn jemand eingeladen?"
„Wer von unseren Steuern profitiert, könnte sich
wenigstens anständig[2] benehmen[3]."
„Mit so vielen verschiedenen Menschen fahre ich
immer gern in der Straßenbahn."
„Wir haben es alleine geschafft, wir brauchen keine
Hottentotten[4], die uns auf der Tasche herum-
liegen[5], jetzt, wo wir selber so viele Arbeitslose
haben."

6 **Zweite Sequenz mit Ton sehen** Sehen Sie dieselbe Sequenz
noch einmal, dieses Mal mit Ton. Was haben Sie gehört? Was sagt die
Frau? Fassen Sie ihre ausländerfeindlichen Bemerkungen zusammen.
Ausländer passen sich nicht an die deutschen Sitten an.
_____
_____
_____
_____
_____

The man thinks: _____
_____

4. Watch the second sequence with the sound
   turned off and focus on the following aspects:
   • What do you see? What is happening here?
   • What is the old woman doing? Watch her
     mimic and gestures.
   • How does the black man react? Watch his
     mimic and gestures.

5. **Anticipating.** Read over the statements on this
   and the following page, before watching the
   sequence with the volume turned on. Underline
   those statements that the old woman makes.
   "As if it is not possible to adapt to our
   customs."
   " I am very happy with my life."
   " I am not afraid, that is why I often leave home
   alone at night."
   "You could at least expect them to change their
   names before they come over
   here. Otherwise you have no point of
   orientation."
   "Unfortunately, he cannot speak German well,
   but that's ok."
   "And they all do work under the table. As if this
   could be controlled, considering they all look
   alike."
   "I trust my fellow men."
   "Why do you all come here? Did somebody
   invite you?"
   "Whoever benefits from our taxes, could at least
   behave in a decent way."
   "I always like to take the streetcar when there
   are so many different people."
   "We made it on our own. We do not
   need 'Hottentotten" (insults for blacks), who cost
   us a lot of money, in particular, now since we
   have so many unemployed people."

6. **Watching the second sequence with sound.**
   Watch the same sequence again, this time with
   the sound turned on. What did you hear? What
   does the woman say? Summarize her comments
   against foreigners.
   Foreigners do not adapt themselves to
   German costumes.
   _____

Filmsequenz
Sequenz: 3
Start: Der junge Mann mit
dem Kopfhörer steigt ein.
Stopp: Der Fahrkarten-
kontrolleur steigt ein.
Länge: circa 2.30

7 **Dritte Sequenz sehen** Lesen Sie vor dem Sehen die folgenden
Fragen. Diskutieren Sie nach dem Sehen mit Ihren Kommilitonen/
Kommilitoninnen.

 ◇ Warum hat die alte Frau Ihrer Meinung nach solche Vorurteile[1]
gegen Ausländer?
 ◇ Warum reagiert der Mann nicht darauf?
 ◇ Wie reagieren die anderen Fahrgäste auf die ausländerfeindlichen
Bemerkungen der Frau? Warum?
 ◇ Wenn Sie an der Stelle des jungen Schwarzen wären, wie würden Sie
reagieren?
 ◇ Wie wird der Film Ihrer Meinung nach weitergehen?

Filmsequenz
Sequenz: 4
Start: Der Fahrkarten-
kontrolleur steigt ein.
Stopp: Ende
Länge: circa 3.30

8 **Vierte Sequenz sehen** Sehen Sie das Ende des Films und
besprechen Sie danach:

 ◇ Was macht der junge Schwarze?
 ◇ Was passiert mit der Frau?
 ◇ Wer ist der eigentliche Schwarzfahrer?
 ◇ Wie reagieren die Fahrgäste auf die Situation?
 ◇ Warum ist der Titel des Films ironisch?

Weiterführende Aufgaben

9 **Diskussion** Keiner der anderen Fahrgäste hat verbal auf die ausländerfeindlichen Bemerkungen der Frau reagiert. Diskutieren Sie die
folgenden Fragen.

 ◇ Wie würden Sie reagieren?
 ◇ Würden Sie etwas zu der alten Frau sagen oder würden Sie sie
ignorieren?
 ◇ Wie sollte man sich in so einer Situation verhalten?

Übungsbuch
Einheit 4, Teil D

10 **Zusammenfassung schreiben** Fassen Sie den Film zusammen.
Schreiben Sie aus einer der folgenden Perspektiven.

 ◇ aus der Perspektive des Schwarzen
 ◇ aus der Perspektive der alten Frau
 ◇ aus der Perspektive eines anderen Fahrgastes

7. **Watching the third sequence** Read over the following questions before watching. Discuss the following questions with your peers.
Why does the old woman have such prejudices against foreigners? Why does the man not react? How do the other passengers react? Why? If you had been in the black man's place, how would you have reacted? How will the film continue?

8. **Watching the fourth sequence.** Watch the ending of the film and discuss the following: What does the black man do? What happens to the woman? Who is actually illegally riding the streetcar? How do other passengers react? What makes the title of the film ironic?

Extension tasks

9. **Discussion.** None of the other passengers reacted to the woman's "anti-foreigner" comments. Discuss the following questions.

How would you react?

Would you say something to the old woman, or would you ignore her?

How should one behave in such a situation?

10. **Summary.** Summarize the film based on one of the following perspectives.

 • from the black person's perspective
 • from the old woman's perspective
 • from another passenger's perspective

Endnotes

1 See the section on Standards, in particular how *communication* is defined, in Chapter 1, Principles of Communicative Language Teaching and Task-Based Instruction. Furthermore, see Chapter 8, "Developing Oral Communication Skills," for a discussion of the interaction of listening and speaking skills.

2 The claim that top-down and bottom-up processes have a compensatory effect was made by Stanovich (1980) in the context of reading research. Chapter 9, "Developing Reading Skills," discusses this research in more detail.

3 A course management system (CMS) is an online application that facilitates the teaching and management of a course. In their most basic form, such systems allow the user to post syllabi, assignments, multimedia resources, and discussion forums. Many also have built-in record-keeping features and allow for the administration of different test types. A learning management system (LMS) is a software application or Web-based technology that is used to plan, implement, and assess a specific learning process. It allows an instructor to create and deliver content, monitor and assess a student's performance, and guide the learner along a predetermined learning path.

4 For a detailed description of MOODLE and some examples, see Brandl (2005).

5 See www.audacity.org.

CHAPTER 8

Developing Oral Communication Skills

Speaking involves the oral expression of thought and mind.

In this chapter you will learn about

- communicative competence.

- optimal conditions that foster the development of speaking skills.

- instructional strategies that support the development of speaking skills.

- different pedagogical designs of speaking activities and group work.

- instructional strategies that accommodate for linguistic and cognitive demands of speaking tasks.

- instructional strategies that allow for a range of different student interactions.

- instructional strategies that introduce, prepare for, and follow up on group and pair activities.

- strategies that reduce anxiety among learners.

REFLECTION

1. How would you assess your oral fluency in relation to other skills in one of the languages you speak?

   _____

   _____

2. What experience was most useful to you in developing speaking skills?

   _____

   _____

Introduction

Today's pedagogical approaches to learning a foreign language consider communication not only as the reason for learning the language but also as the way to do so. Communication can be characterized in many different ways (Schriffin 1987). Historically, communicative ability has been described in terms of four skills: Speaking, listening, reading, and writing. Clearly, speaking has a central function in the process of communication. However, speaking cannot occur in isolation. For example, having a conversation involves at least two persons. Furthermore, interacting with other people involves many other skills. It entails listening and/or making use of nonverbal communicative strategies such as using gestures or facial expressions. Furthermore, there is usually a context and a purpose for communication, whether it simply involves small talk or sharing information, such as talking about something we have read, heard on the radio, or seen on TV. In other words, as communication is closely integrated with other modalities in real life, the development of speaking skills in a foreign language environment should also be approached from this angle.

For many language learners, the classroom is initially the primary and often the only environment to develop oral communicative skills. The focus of this chapter is thus on the development of the **interpersonal mode of communication** (Brecht and Walton 1995). By "interpersonal mode" is meant communicative skills that are applied by the teacher and the students to interact between and among each other in the target language (TL). "Interpersonal" implies the direct oral communication (e.g., face-to-face or telephonic) between teacher and students and students and students who are in personal contact.

Developing Communicative Competence in the Language Classroom: Limitations and Challenges

Developing oral communication skills has become a goal in many of today's foreign language curricula. Being able to communicate, however, entails more than simply speaking a language. **Communication** is the expression, interpretation, and negotiation of meaning (Lee and VanPatten 1995). This raises the question about what it means to be communicatively competent. Let us briefly define communicative competence.

Communicative competence is a term originally proposed by the sociolinguist Dell Hymes as an alternative to Chomsky's "linguistic competence" (1959). It is now generally accepted that proficiency in another language includes much more than knowledge of grammar and vocabulary, or linguistic competence (Boyd and Maloof 2000). It includes the ability to say the appropriate thing in a certain social situation (sociolinguistic competence); the ability to start, enter, contribute to, and end a conversation and the ability to do this in a consistent and coherent manner (discourse competence); and the ability to communicate effectively and repair problems caused by communication breakdowns (strategic competence). Such a notion of communicative competence entails the ability to interpret and enact appropriate social behaviors and requires the active involvement of the learner in the production of the TL (Canale and Swain 1980; Celce-Murcia, Dornyei, and Thurell 1995; Hymes 1972). Developing competency in all these areas becomes progressively important as the learners increase their proficiency skills. With beginning-level language learners, however, the development of linguistic competence requires most attention, which will be the primary focus of this chapter.

ANALYSIS AND DISCUSSION

In what ways is "real communication" or the development of communicative competence, possible in the classroom? What are limitations?

_____

_____

Considering the complexity underlying communicative skills, the classroom environment is not an ideal place. Development of these skills is controlled by social and interactional norms found in the language classrooms. In a quantitative and qualitative sense, it is limited in the range of discourse patterns and opportunities of communicative and social interactions that it can provide. For example, practicing formal ways of addressing someone (_du/Sie, tu/vous_) is customary to only teacher and student interactions. Furthermore, although most students who grew up during the last two decades have experienced group and pair work activities, a teacher-driven and -dominated classroom talk still pervades many classrooms. As research has shown, the dominant pattern seems to be a sequence in which the teacher initiates, the students respond, and the teacher follows up (Wells 1993). In addition, psychological and affective factors including cultural backgrounds, previous negative social experiences or lack of motivation, or language anxiety or shyness influence the learners' participation in classroom activities and thus the development of oral communicative skills (Nunan 1999). Obviously, such learner factors do not apply only to the classroom environment, but they are often most prevalent in this environment. Nevertheless, despite such limitations and challenges, the language classroom has great potential in helping learners build a solid foundation of communicative skills. Through task choice and design, teachers can create opportunities and foster conditions that maximize students' development of communicative skills. Before examining in more detail what optimal conditions need to look like and how to create such opportunities for the learners, let us briefly look at characteristics of speech.

Characteristics of speech

To understand what is involved in developing oral second language (L2) skills in the classroom, it is important to keep in mind not only the skills but also how people process information when they speak. Whereas understanding the notion of communicative competence directs teachers in what skills to teach (linguistic, discourse strategies, etc.), understanding the nature and conditions of speech helps them understand how to teach these skills. To do so, most current approaches draw on a psycholinguistic skills- (or information-) processing model. Bygate (2001, p. 16–17) summarizes the processes involved in the following way:

> Levelt (1989) proposed that speech production involves four major processes: **conceptualisation, formulation, articulation** and **self-monitoring** (for an accessible account, see Scovel 1998). Conceptualisation is concerned with planning the message content. It draws on background knowledge, knowledge about the topic, about the speech situation and on knowledge of patterns of discourse. The conceptualiser includes a "monitor," which checks everything that occurs in the interaction to ensure that the communication goes to plan. This enables speakers to self-correct for expression, grammar and pronunciation. After conceptualisation, the formulator finds the words and phrases to express the meanings, sequencing them and putting in appropriate grammatical markers (such as inflections, auxiliaries, articles). It also prepares the sound patterns of the words to be used: L1 errors of pronunciation very commonly involve switching sounds between words that are separated from each other; such switches suggest that the pronunciation of words must be prepared in batches prior to pronunciation. The third process is articulation. This involves the motor control of the articulatory organs; in English: the lips, tongue, teeth, alveolar palate, velum, glottis, mouth cavity and breath. Self-monitoring is concerned with language users being able to identify and self-correct mistakes.
>
> All this happens very fast and, to be successful, depends on automation: to some degree in conceptualization, to a considerable extent in formulation and almost entirely in articulation. Automation is necessary since humans do not have enough attention capacity consciously to control the three types of process. Hence, for an elementary L2 speaker it will be difficult to manage this speech fluently and accurately, since they lack automation and/or accuracy, and it is difficult for them to pay attention to all these processes simultaneously under pressure of time.
>
> The skills are also affected by the context. Speaking is typically reciprocal: any interlocutors are normally all able to contribute simultaneously to the discourse, and to respond immediately to each other's contributions. Further, in oral communication many people can participate in the same interaction, making it somewhat less predictable than written interaction. Oral interaction varies widely in terms of whether participants have equal speaking rights, or whether one of the speakers adopts or is accorded special rights, such as in doctor-patient, teacher-pupil, professor-student, examiner-examinee, parent-offspring, adult-child interactions. Symmetry affects the freedom of speakers to develop or initiate topics, ask for clarification or close the interaction. Further, speaking is physically situated in face-to-face interaction: usually speakers can see each other and so can refer to the physical context and use a number of physical signals to indicate, for instance, attention to the interaction, their intention to contribute and their attitude towards what is being said. Hence, speech can tolerate more implicit reference.

Finally, in most speech situations speech is produced 'on line'. Speakers have to decide on their message and communicate it without taking time to check it over and correct it: any interlocutors cannot be expected to wait long for the opportunity to speak themselves. Hence, time pressure means that the process of conceptualisation, formulation and articulation may not be well planned or implemented, and may need pauses and corrections.

These conditions and processes affect the language that is typically produced. For instance, speech more often than writing refers to the interlocutors and the physical time and place of the communication. In addition, speech typically expresses politeness so as to protect the face of the interlocutors (Scollon and Scollon 1983), and to structure the dialogue in stages (see Widdowson 1983). The discourse typically results in patterns, which are distinct from those normally found in writing (such as the beginnings, endings and intervening phases of a doctor-patient or teacher student interaction). Selinker and Douglas (1985), Zuengler and Bent (1991) and Bardovi-Harlig showed that familiarity with interlocutor, content and type of speech act could impact on non-native speaker talk.

Further, the on-line [ongoing] processing conditions produce language that is grammatically more 'fragmented', uses more formulaic ('pre-fabricated') phrases, and tolerates more easily the repetition of words and phrases within the same extract of discourse. Finally, the inevitable adjustments that occur in speech are overt and public. These include:

- changing the message or its formulation before it is expressed ('communication strategies'), whether or not interactively negotiated (Yule and Tarone 1991);
- self-correction after the message has been expressed; and various kinds of hesitation, introduced to slow down output and create planning time.

Hence, oral language differs from written language both in process and product (although of course spoken language can resemble written language, and written language can simulate spoken patterns). The implication for teaching is that oral skills and oral language should be practised and assessed under different conditions from written skills, and that, unlike the various traditional approaches to providing oral practice, a distinct methodology and syllabus may be needed.

ANALYSIS AND DISCUSSION

What pedagogical implications can you draw from the information-processing model described by Bygate regarding the design of speaking tasks in the language classroom? In other words, what are some design factors that are facilitative to developing a learner's speaking skills?

Creating optimal conditions in the classroom

Research has provided us with a number of answers on what optimal conditions need to exist. Omaggio-Hadley (2001) suggests several principles outlining general characteristics of a classroom environment that she believes are conducive to the achievement of language proficiency. She suggests that "Opportunities must be provided for students to practice using language in a range of contexts likely to be encountered in the target culture. . . . Students should be encouraged to express their own meaning as early as possible after productive skills have been introduced in the course of instruction. . . . Opportunities must be provided for active communicative interaction among students. . . . Creative language practice (as opposed to exclusively manipulative or convergent practice) must be encouraged . . . . " (pp. 90–91). The following paragraphs briefly elaborate on some of these principles.

From the beginning of instruction, students need to have ample opportunities to actively engage in and practice using language in meaningful discourse as it occurs in contexts of real-life situations, rather than learning language through disconnected word lists or isolated sentences (Omaggio-Hadley 2001). Second language students must be given opportunities to play with language and be challenged by trying out how language works. Several arguments can be made for this principle. First, language comprehension and production underlie different processes (Keenan and MacWhinney 1987). Whereas exposure to language input must be comprehensible and meaningful and be considered a prerequisite for learning to occur (see Krashen 1981), the ability to produce language does not automatically emerge from exposure to comprehensible input but rather is acquired when language is used productively—that is, while speaking, while trying to communicate (Tschirner 1998). Asking students to produce language from day one is also in accordance with Swain's output hypothesis. According to Swain (1995), pushed output facilitates acquisition, as it (1) helps learners to discover that there is a gap between what they want to say and what they are able to say, (2) provides a way for learners to try out new rules and modify them accordingly, and (3) helps learners to actively reflect on what they know about the target language system. The use of linguistic knowledge becomes automatic only when learners make use of interlanguage knowledge under real conditions of communication (Ellis 1997). In other words, learners "need to see for themselves what has gone wrong, in the operating conditions under which they went wrong" (K. Johnson 1988, p. 93).

Students must also have opportunities to participate in both planned and unplanned discourse that is similar to what they will encounter outside the classroom. To do this, teachers must provide scaffolds for students to try out new linguistic structures and language functions that are beyond their current level of language proficiency. They must also provide sufficient and planned discourse with many examples of the linguistic features that students are trying to learn (Ellis 1990).

In creating optimal conditions it is also essential to take into account affective variables such as the learner's motivation, anxiety, and self-esteem. These have been recognized by the literature as playing a pivotal role in student learning (Bransford 1979; Horwitz and Young 1991; Stevick 1976). For example, students must have the need and desire to communicate. In part, this comes from their involvement and interest in what is being talked about. If students are interested in a topic and they have something to say about it, the motivation becomes high. An effective strategy is to choose personalized topics, which allows and encourages students to express their own meaning early on. Focusing on students' personal experience and their interests furthermore enhances comprehension and retention, especially when students do this in their own words (Nystrand and Gamoran 1991). As students articulate their own thinking, they are motivated to use their resources to communicate. At the same time, it is important to be sensitive to students' feelings, allowing them the flexibility to participate in discussions in ways that do not require sharing of personal information if they prefer not to do so.

The choice of a topic also plays an important role in capturing a student's interest and enhancing her active participation. The topics not only need to be interesting but also relevant to the age group of the learners. Such topics vary between college and high school students. For example, whereas topics such as dating and friendship may be appealing to many different learner groups, finding a place to live may have a limited application. Unfortunately, the choice of topics of many textbooks often fails to capture the students' interests.

Designing and sequencing communicative speaking tasks

One of the biggest challenges to current language teaching methodology is to find effective ways of preparing students for spontaneous communication. This requires an approach with balanced "activities" to teaching speaking skills, using controlled speaking activities to develop accuracy and less-controlled activities to develop communicative fluency. The approach promoted in this book follows a direct approach in which specific microskills (e.g., linguistic skills such as vocabulary, grammatical structures; functions such as greetings, asking questions, describing; conversational strategies including use of formulaic expressions, such as "I think . . .; In my opinion . . .") are systematically introduced and integrated into a lesson (Richards 1990). Through a series of systematically sequenced subtasks, the instructor leads students toward and prepares them for the performance of a conversational task.

Chapter 6, "Instructional Sequencing and Task Design," covers a variety of factors that determine the difficulty of a learning task and how they affect the instructional sequencing. These factors are based on the linguistic and cognitive complexity, and the conditions under which the learners are performing a task (Robinson 2001; Skehan 1996). To achieve a balanced approach between controlled and open communicative speaking tasks, it is important for instructors to have a deeper understanding and knowledge of how to manipulate these factors. Let us briefly revisit some of these factors and consider some examples of how this balance can be achieved, particularly regarding the development of speaking skills.

A factor that affects the learner's performance is the complexity of language that the learner has to produce. In most speaking situations, the learners have to decide on what to say and how to say it without having much time to check it over. This involves immediate and numerous simultaneously ongoing processing skills. To alleviate the learner's linguistic processing, the learning task can be structured in various ways that provide different kinds of scaffolds, for example, in the form of lexical or functional cues (see also "Sample Speaking Lessons," later in the chapter). Additionally, such techniques allow the instructor to target and practice particular linguistic features in isolation.

The following speaking activities demonstrate a range of instructional variations for simplifying linguistic demands in a student-to-student question-answer discourse. (Note that the cognitive demand to answer questions depends on the content of the question.)

Variation A: Using the same scripted questions. All students use the same set of questions when interviewing each other in the target language (TL). This form of engaging in interpersonal skills is highly structured and fits well into an early phase of an instructional sequence. The instructor controls the contents and linguistic accuracy of the questions, as well as students' responses. By having an opportunity to prescreen the questions in writing, students can anticipate answers to the questions. Most student-centered interactional setups (e.g., pair work, mingling, etc.) lend themselves well for this variation (see "Overview of Types of Student Interactions").

ILLUSTRATION 1

All students ask each other the same kind of questions.

Do you have any brothers and sisters?
What are their names?
How old are they?
What are your parents' names?
What do they do?

Variation B: Responding to unknown teacher-scripted questions. Students use two separate sets of questions, which their teacher hands to them. In this way, the teacher controls the contents of the interview questions and guides the learners' use of language. Because each student has not seen the other's questions, more linguistic processing is involved than in variation A above; that is, students need to closely listen to each other's questions and then respond with an answer. This activity involves interpersonal skills and spontaneous speaking. Most student-centered interactional setups (e.g., pair work, mingling, etc.) lend themselves well to this variation (see "Overview of Types of Student Interactions").

ILLUSTRATION 2

Student A:

1. Do you have any brothers and sisters?
2. What are their names?

Student B:

1. What are your parents' names?
2. Where do they live?

Variation C: Using cues. A technique to guiding and structuring the simulation of a short conversational exchanges between two speakers that increases the linguistic demands by using cues only. **Cuing** as an instructional strategy allows the teacher to control the content, but requires students to formulate questions and answers, and thus manipulate grammatical forms and rules. Cues can consist of single words or phrases in L1 or the target language, and they can be pictures or drawings.

ILLUSTRATION 3
Using lexical cues

A simulated and cued dialogue between customer C and salesperson S

C:	looking for/sweater	S:	size?
C:	large	S:	this one—large
C:	nice—white, red?	S:	unfortunately not
C:	price	S:	$59

ILLUSTRATION 4
Using functional cues

A simulated and cued dialogue between two students (A and B)

A: Ask somebody out to go and see a movie with you by suggesting a day and a time.

B: – (Deny, e.g., say that you are sorry, busy, or don't have time, etc.)

A: Make another suggestion!

B: + (Provide an affirmative answer.)

ILLUSTRATION 5
Using contextual cues

The example of the scaffolded dialogues below requires students to reconstruct the discourse between two speakers based on contextual cues. This example is essentially similar to a fill-in-the-blank activity, in which one role partner figures out what to ask or answer based on the cues that her partner is provided. Because both role partners need to see each other's clues to figure out what to ask, students need to be given ample preparation time so they can first fill in their answers in the blanks before they engage in role playing the dialogue.

Veronika and Sofie meet in Italy

Instructions: Complete their conversation logically.

S:	Hi! My name is Sofie Brecht.	V:	Hello! I am Veronika Frisch.
S:	_____	V:	From Switzerland. From Bern.
S:	From Jena.	V:	_____
S:	_____	V:	teacher
S:	_____	V:	French and social studies
S:	I am a student.	V:	_____
S:	At the university in Jena.	V:	_____
S:	biology	V:	_____
S:	No, I am single.	V:	_____
S:	_____	V:	I am married.
S:	_____	V:	Yes, three girls.
S:	_____	V:	Nathalie, Rosie, and Lydia.
S:	_____	V:	He is a business man.
S:	_____	V:	No, he is from Luzern.
S:	Nice to meet you. Bye-bye.	V:	_____

(Source: Manfred Bansleben, University of Washington.)

Variation D: Students develop their own questions. This variation represents the most communicative and open-ended form. While the theme of a lesson normally directs the content of the questions, the teacher allows the students to decide what questions they choose to ask. This example constitutes interpersonal skills simulating real-life interactions. There are various ways of implementing this strategy. Students can be directed to ask each other questions spontaneously, providing no scaffold or guidance of any kind. In most cases, however, this activity is more successful when students are first given some preparation time to develop their questions in writing.

Besides the linguistic demands, the degree to which the language event makes cognitive demands on the learner during the speaking task also influences the learner's performance. For example, let us look at the real-world task of describing the route on an authentic map. The performance of such a functional speaking task can become relatively difficult or easy depending on the size of the map, whether the map is authentic or represents a simplified drawing, whether students have enough planning time, or whether the route is predetermined. Such factors either increase or reduce the cognitive demands and thus ultimately influence how much and what kind of language students use during the speaking task. To support such a hypothesis, Robinson (2001) tested the effect of the cognitive complexity of speaking tasks. He observed that his students dealt with the cognitive challenges by applying many clarification and confirmation checks. In other words, his students were still able to produce a great deal of language, but their language was not as accurate or fluent. As Robinson has shown, in intermediate or advanced language classes, students are somewhat able to compensate for cognitive challenges; in beginning language classes, a sign of too-complex tasks would most likely manifest itself in increased use of English or breakdown, for students normally do not have the language skills to negotiate meaning in the target language. For such reasons, the cognitive demands of a speaking task need to be kept in mind and accommodated for, in particular at beginning levels.

A third factor influencing the performance of a task is the conditions under which the learners perform a task, or as Nunan (1999) puts it, "the degree of emotional stress involved in completing a task" (p. 236). An instructional practice that has been commonly applied to reduce stress among students is the use of learner-centered instruction. Besides reducing stress among students, this practice has numerous other benefits. The following sections describe the types of student interaction and the benefits of learner-centered instruction. Later sections will offer guidelines for implementing group and pair work, and will provide concrete strategies for dealing with communicative stress.

Cooperative Learning and Interaction

The concepts of "interaction" and "cooperation" are widely used in language-learning contexts. Interaction involves interpersonal communication, that is, communication between two or more people. As Oxford puts it, **interactive learning** "involves teachers, learners, and others acting upon each other and consciously or unconsciously interpreting (i.e., giving meaning to) those actions" (Oxford, 1997, p. 444). On the other hand, **cooperative learning**, in general, is defined as "group learning activity organized so that learning is dependent on the socially structured exchange of information between learners in groups and in which each learner is held accountable for his or her own learning and is more motivated to increase the learning of others" (Olsen and Kagan 1992, p. 8). In the context of language learning, cooperative learning has become associated with a prescribed and highly structured, although creative, way of describing classroom organization; and it has a specific aim of leading to skill development (Oxford 1997). Several questions arise: In what ways can students interact? How beneficial is cooperative learning or student-to-student interaction? And finally, how should group and pair-work activities be designed to create a successful experience for the learners?

Benefits of learner-centered instruction

For students to develop interpersonal communication skills, they need ample opportunities to actively participate and interact with each other (see for example Long 1983, 1996; Swain 1995). Much has been written about the need to involve the learners in their own learning process (see for example, Kagan 1989; Nunan 1988; Omaggio 1993). Theoretical- and empirical-based research provides plenty of support in favor of pair and group work activities in the language classroom.

For example, the popular work of Vygotsky (1978) lends support to the importance of social interaction. Vygotsky asserts that there is a developmental area called the **zone of proximal development**, which denotes the area between the learner's actual language level and his or her potential level. The learner can achieve his or her potential only through interaction with others. "Vygotsky's theory implies that . . . acquisition may be contingent on cooperative, meaningful interaction" (Shrum and Glisan 1994, p. 11). One such avenue for learner interaction is through pair and small-group work. Long and Porter (1985), in their review of the literature, offer pedagogical arguments for the use of pair and group work, citing that "it increases students' language practice opportunities, improves the quality of student talk, helps to individualize instruction, promotes a positive affective climate, and motivates learners" (pp. 207–12).

Several empirical studies (Doughty and Pica 1986; Porter 1986; Rulon and McCreary 1986) offer additional support for using pair and small-group work. In these studies, individual students who engaged in pair and small-group work on meaning-based tasks had more opportunities to use language communicatively than did those who participated in teacher-led activities. In addition, these studies showed that students exhibited an increased number of negotiation behaviors when engaged in pair and small-group activity. Figure 8-1 summarizes learner-centered research findings.

The use of pair and group work activities has been gaining broad acceptance in a multitude of language-learning classrooms, principally because of its potential for providing supportive and expanded opportunities for learners to use the language. Furthermore, it has been found to create a more positive affective climate in the classroom while not only individualizing instruction but also raising student motivation (Long and Porter 1985).

- Small-group work produced twice the number of content confirmation checks. Small-group work produced 36 times the number of clarification checks. There was no statistical significance in terms of the informational content covered (Rulon and McCreary 1986).
- Small-group work provides increased opportunities for self-expression (Porter 1986).
- There is a lack of development of sociolinguistic competence in the absence of advanced speaking interlocutors.
- Learners rarely incorporate other learners' errors in their own production (Paninos and Linnell 1993; Porter 1986).
- Students have been found to modify their initial utterances and turn them into more complex forms (Pica, Kanagy, and Falodun 1993).
- Students working in groups completing reading and listening comprehension activities have been found to give more detailed answers than when in whole-class work with a teacher (Rulon and McCreary 1986).
- Students have been found to make self-generated adjustments toward more correct production (Bruton and Samuda 1980).
- Group and pair work provides learning opportunities as long as there is a two-way exchange of information and participation among all group members (Pica and Doughty 1985).
- Learners express a wider range of language functions during group work (Long et al. 1976).
- Group work is more likely to lead to negotiation of meaning than is interaction with the teacher (Doughty and Pica 1986).
- Although there is widespread belief that competition is a better motivator than cooperation, a meta-analysis of 122 studies, completed by D. Johnson and his colleagues in 1981, revealed that cooperation promoted higher achievement than competition. Only 8 of the 122 studies favored competition; 65 favored cooperation; and in the other 36, no differences were found. Edwards (1997) (cited in Crandall 1999, 235) concludes that "competition is not much of a motivator" though that myth is "deeply embedded" in many educational systems.

FIGURE 8-1 Summary of research studies on the effects of learner-centered instruction

Guidelines and Strategies for Implementing Group and Pair Work

Communicative tasks are a way to provide a stimulus for generating talk among students. Cooperative learning activities have great potential, but only if they are carefully planned and implemented. The following guidelines provide a set of strategies that enhance the success and effectiveness of pair and small-group work activities.

Overview of types of student interactions

Pair work. The most common structure used for cooperative learning is pair work. Generally speaking, such learning tasks fall into two categories: information/opinion-gap and think/share activities (Kagan 1989). The purpose of information-gap or opinion-gap activities is the exchange of unknown information between students in the target language. The purpose of think/share activities is for students to cooperate on a task. For several examples of communication-gap activities, see Appendix 8.5. The figure below shows the student grouping and interactions.

Jigsaws. The "jigsaw" is not an activity but a way of organizing student interactions. It uses and combines cooperative learning and information-gap techniques. Just as in a jigsaw puzzle, each piece—that is to say, each student's part—is essential for the completion and achievement of the task. A popular form is the four-corner jigsaw.

An example of a four-corner jigsaw is presented in Appendix 8.4. Here is how it works.

Instruct students to form groups of four. Assign each student a letter A, B, C, or D. Tell students to remember the partners of their group, as this is their *base* group. Provide the instruction for the learning activity. Next, send all As into the corner of the classroom that is labeled A, all Bs into corner B, and all Cs and Ds into their respective corners. The four corner groups are called the *expert* groups.

As seen in the example of Appendix 8.4, the goal is to find out information about different job advertisements. Each group of students reads a set of different job ads and answers questions. The students discuss and share the answers to the questions. Particularly in beginning-level language classes, students most likely may interact in English. Before students leave their expert groups, the goal is for each student to make sure

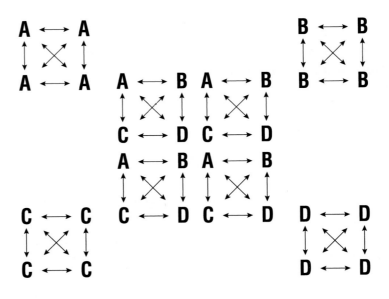

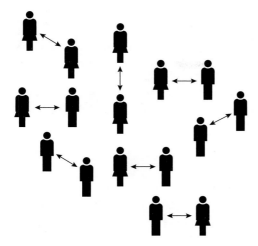

each has all the answers for all the questions, since each student from that group is now the expert on their ads. Students then reconvene in their initial *base* groups and exchange the information about the ads.

A jigsaw format is an efficient way of having students interact. It promotes interpersonal communication and encourages cooperative learning. The follwing figure shows the student grouping and interactions during a four-corner jigsaw activity.

Open interactions (mingling). Some activities lend themselves well for students to interact with one another in an open forum. Examples are asking students to find other students with a birthday in the same month or season, somebody who has similar or the same hobbies, characteristics they have in common, or opinions they share. Like most group or pair activities, these activities work best if some kind of structure or guidance is provided. Setting a time limit, or specifying the number of students with whom to interact, are better strategies than "scavenger hunt" designs (such as "Find at least three to four students who . . .") and allow students to more efficiently accomplish the task. Students grouping and interactions during mingling activities are shown below.

Groups of three or more. Teachers commonly assign students to work in groups of three or more. While there is no written rule on the size of any group, principles of cooperative learning suggest that groups of less than seven members usually work best. In a language-learning classroom, students should not be assigned to groups consisting of a random number of students. The size of any group should be determined based on the design of the learning task that guarantees equal participation, interaction, and contribution of all group members. Teachers must also keep in mind that during large-group activities, socio-affective variables may impede learners' active participation. These issues are discussed in more detail later, in "Guidelines and Strategies for Implementing Group and Pair Work."

Example:

Examples of large-group designs are describing, sequencing, and discussing picture stories[1] such as the one in Appendix 8.1.

The figure below shows student grouping and interactions when working in groups of three.

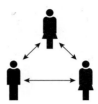

Chain reactions. The technique of a "chain reaction" has had a long tradition in the foreign language classroom. Since students perform in front of the whole class, this is considered a teacher-centered technique. Usually, these activities are done as one-way speaking tasks that require no interaction with another speaker, so they can be quickly applied. This technique has merit when applied with lower-level speaking tasks asking for quick or spontaneous responses, especially for review purposes.

There are numerous ways to design chain reaction tasks. The instructor might ask students to name words that belong to a particular context or that are part of a generic word category, for example, objects in the classroom, objects in the kitchen, body parts, colors, animals, types of sport, spare time activities, characteristics, and so on. Students can be asked to name only one item at a time or to repeat all the items that have been mentioned before. The latter version is cognitively quite challenging if applied in large groups, for students have to remember more and more information as the activity proceeds. The figure in Illustration 6 demonstrates student intraction during chainsaw activities.

ILLUSTRATION 6

The teacher says "body parts," student A says "leg," student B continues . . .

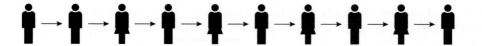

Centric rings. A technique that allows students to interact with many of their peers within a fairly short time is known as "centric rings." The students line up in the following way: One group of students forms an inner circle with their backs to the inside of the circle. Another group forms an outer circle so that they are facing students in the inner circle. When all pairs of students complete their conversational task, the outer circle rotates by one student. The pedagogical advantage of this technique is that it allows students to perform and repeat the same conversational scenario many times, but every time with a different communication partner. Hence, this technique works best when the communicative exchange between speakers is brief, and the lesson asks for a new partner.

ILLUSTRATION 7

Speed dating

Say three interesting things about yourself. Also, mention two to three things that you like to do.

Student grouping and interaction during activities that use a centric ring design.

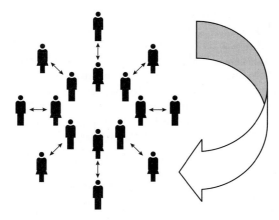

Consider the purpose and goal of the learning task

Ask yourself the following questions: What is the pedagogic purpose? Why are students to interact with each other? What skills do I want the students to focus on? For example, if the purpose of a pair or group activity is to reinforce newly introduced vocabulary, grammatical structure, or speech acts (e.g., comparing information, requesting information), tasks should have a narrow focus on meaning and form. In addition, they should be coupled with the obligation to exchange information. Such tasks have been found most effective in pair-work settings, particularly with regard to developing grammatical accuracy (Foster 1997). Task designs that lend themselves well for controlled communicative language practice are communication-, information-, or opinion-gap activities. Such activities require some kind of communicative exchange of information that is unknown to the participants. Appendix 8.5 demonstrates several examples for beginning learners.

Another reason for students to interact may be to develop communicative fluency. While grammatical accuracy and correct use of vocabulary are still important, the main focus is on the exchange and content of the information—as in real-life communicative interactions. For example, students may want to exchange information they have read in a newspaper or seen on TV. Learning tasks with such a pedagogic focus involve learners in comprehending, manipulating, producing or interacting in the target language (Nunan 1989). Teachers need to keep in mind that with a focus on content, however, students most likely will pay less attention to accuracy and form (Skehan 1996; Robinson 2000b). The design of such tasks should be as authentic as possible so that the output of group work resembles speech acts that are typical in the target language (Davis 1997). Appendix 8.4 demonstrates an example of a communicative task asking students to exchange information they have read. This example also illustrates the use of a jigsaw technique.

Here is another question to ask that may determine your decision whether to have students work together in pairs or groups: "Can a task or activity be more efficiently completed by learners working cooperatively?" According to the saying "Two heads work better than one," some tasks result in better outcomes if students are given the opportunity to work collaboratively. The decision to have students work together may be based on the rationale for students to take advantage of each other's knowledge. Writing a dialogue, discussing an answer to a teacher's question, or explaining grammatical concepts to each other are typical examples. In beginning-level language classes, such activities often work best when carried out in English.

Understanding the purpose and design of a task or an activity has numerous instructional implications. It affects how much time to allow the students to work on a task or activity (see "Hold Pairs and Groups Accountable for Completing a Task"). It also allows the teacher to predict and control the quality and quantity of students' language. Because a task itself is essentially goal oriented; there should be an observable result, such as finding out information, filling out a chart, or making a list, that determines how a teacher can hold the students accountable (see "Hold Pairs and Groups Accountable for Completing a Task") and follow up on the goal (see "Follow Up on the Group or Pair Work").

Design the group work activity so all participants are equally involved

The purpose of cooperative learning is to equally involve all group participants. As Doughty and Pica (1985) have pointed out, group or pair work provides learning opportunities as long as there is a two-way exchange of information and participation among all group members. In this sense, each learner must play an essential role if that goal is to be achieved. The success (or failure) of a cooperative group depends on the efforts of all its individual members. Since it is often difficult to get all members to inter-act equally in larger groups, depending on the task design, some activities lend themselves better for pair work; others are better suited for groups of three or more students. Normally, in beginning language classes, because of students' limited language skills, students need clear guidance on how to interact and what language skills they need to focus on. For such rea-sons, jigsaw designs or structured tasks such as those that include commu-nication gaps normally create more student output among students than loosely structured or open-ended discussion tasks. Providing clear struc-ture and guidance is also very beneficial for large group work, as factors such as communicative stress and student personalities often affect group members to participate equally.

Make sure students are adequately prepared

Ask yourself if students are linguistically and functionally prepared for the task assignment. Are students familiar with the vocabulary, the gram-matical structures, and speech acts they need to know to perform the task? In other words, are students adequately prepared to say in the tar-get language what they would like to say? Also, rethink the cognitive demand of the speaking task. For example, if students are expected to produce a combination of speech functions spontaneously, build in an intermediary step leading up to the communicative activity. (See the section on Designing and sequencing communicative speaking tasks, pre-viously discussed in this chapter.)

Provide clear instructions and model examples

One of the keys to successful and efficient implementation of pair and group activities is providing clear directions and examples before the task is begun (Johnson, Johnson, and Holubec 1988). Effective strategies constitute modeling a task with a student, or having students model an example in front of the class. These techniques provide immediate confir-mation on whether students understood the task assignment. Written instructions (e.g., on the board, transparency, or handout), including possible examples, are additional necessary strategies in most cases. Oral instructions, especially if provided in the target language, are usually the least effective because they are most difficult to process and understand.

Allow for ample opportunities to interact with different partners

An argument frequently brought forward against the use of pair work is that students behave differently depending on the person they are talking to. This behavior also affects their task performance. Martyn (1997) found that different language was produced by the speakers according to how comfortable they felt with the other learners in the pair or group. Besides the personality type, another aspect that contributes to the effectiveness of collaborative achievement has to do with the competence of the other person or persons. One way to minimize this effect is to allow for ample opportunities to interact with different partners by making use of different student groupings.

Consider the content of the group- or pair-activity

One of the most neglected issues relates to the content of topics of pair- or group-work assignments. In the literature on communicative language teaching, it has been frequently suggested that topics be interesting and relevant to students' own experience (Nunan 1999; Omaggio-Hadley 2001). Personal experience can be a great resource to share among students, especially in beginning-level language classes. It can be stimulating and motivating. The downside of this strategy is that students may not be willing to share some personal information, or they simply do not remember some information, such as questions about birthdays or other personal events that are so frequently found in language textbooks. In other words, the topics of task assignments need to be culturally sensitive, appealing to the learners' age group, and answerable by students.

Circulate among the students

For several reasons, it is important for teachers to circulate around the classroom. Doing so allows the instructor to monitor progress and encourages students to stay in the target language, and it may prevent them from reverting to their native language (Shrum and Glisan 2000). It also allows instructors to provide quick assistance in case of breakdown or when students have questions. Circulating needs to be done in an unobtrusive way. The purpose of group and pair activities is for students to work without the instructor's involvement, and the teacher should provide assistance only if necessary. Teachers should be aware that in many cases, students like to take advantage of the teacher by asking for individual assistance or personal questions. Teachers who allow this to happen often lose control of the class's progress as a whole. Other students feel intimidated and often even stop performing if the teacher is too obtrusive.

Teach group interaction skills

Different pair or group activities ask for different interaction skills and setups. For example, when students are working in pairs, they should be facing each other rather than sitting side by side. We listen with both our ears and eyes—seeing a speaker's face, lip movement, and gestures supports the listening process. On the other hand, some pair-work activities, such as simulated telephone conversations, may ask for a different seating arrangement, like a back-to-back setup. This setup, however, may enhance the speaker-listener interaction and require confirmation and clarification checks. Examples of such strategies: "Can you say this one more time? Could you please speak up, repeat yourself, slow down? Excuse me, I could not understand what you said. Is this what you mean? Is this right? Did you say . . . ?"

Although some researchers claim that students use more clarification and confirmation strategies during pair work, this is rarely the case in a beginning-level language classroom (Foster 1998) because students usually do not have the skills to do so. Nevertheless, students need to be encouraged to use clarification and confirmation strategies, which need to be taught early on. The best way to teach these techniques is for the teacher to model them repeatedly, or even post them in the classroom. Otherwise, if students do not understand each other, they feel tempted to look at each other's handouts or refer to English right away. In other words, for communicative tasks to be effective, students need to be told not to give away the information to be elicited, but to negotiate the information the best they can.

Students also need to apply turn-taking skills that apply to social interactions, such as waiting until somebody else finishes his turn. The successful implementation of cooperative learning activity often depends on the appropriate use of such social and interpersonal skills.

Hold pairs and groups accountable for completing a task within an allotted time frame

Holding individual students and the groups accountable for their success enhances their effort to stay on task and to use their time most efficiently. Here are different options for limiting the students' time on task:

- *Provide a time limit.* This strategy works well for tasks that have no clearly defined goal or end product. For example, many interview activities work best when students are assigned a time limit of 3 to 5 minutes, during which they find out as much information as they can.
- *Make interactive student work goal oriented.* This strategy works best for tasks that have a clearly defined end product. For example, based on the scavenger hunt design, students would interact with as many of their peers as necessary to find the targeted answer or solution. Or, a speaking task that requires students to find the correct sequence of a picture story ends once the group has accomplished this goal. Because students normally proceed at different paces, Davis (1997) suggests as a general rule of thumb that a teacher can stop an activity when about three-fourths of the students have finished the task or achieved the goal.
- *Control the number of peers with whom students are to interact.* For example, many open-ended mingling activities can be structured using this strategy. A teacher's instructions might say: "Talk to only three students in class, and then sit down."

Follow up on the group or pair work

There are several reasons for the instructor to follow up on the students' task assignments. Following up makes students accountable for what they have accomplished; it allows the instructor to provide feedback; and above all, it provides an opportunity to exchange and apply information in a communicative way. Depending on the task, there are various ways to follow up. Here are some general instructional strategies for following up on group and pair activities.

General strategies:

- Follow up with a survey, and write key words on the board or transparency.
- Ask students to write the results (e.g., key words, outline, etc.) of the group or pair work and present it to the class.
- Collect students' work to provide individual feedback and comments.
- Use students' output as input for another activity (Davis 1997). For example, ask students to share their results with other, smaller groups (see the discussion of jigsaw format) and then do something with the information, such as ranking, comparing, or writing about the information they synthesized.
- Discuss the results with the students.

Alternative strategies:

- Allow time for students to ask questions on any linguistic issues.
- Do overt error correction based on frequent mistakes that you noticed while circulating among students.
- Debrief learners on their experience with cooperative learning.

Sample Speaking Lessons

In a communicative-based language classroom, the application of speaking permeates all phases of a lesson. A lesson is structured to assist the learners in developing speaking skills, moving from controlled via guided to free application. During each of these lesson phases, speaking activities have different purposes and, according to their degree of cognitive and linguistic demands, consist of low-, medium-, and high-level speaking skills. Most of the introductory and presentation activities of a lesson or curriculum engage the learner with low-level speaking skills. The purpose of these activities is to provide focused practice in isolated skills (e.g., pronunciation, developing vocabulary, and formulaic expressions) and to prepare the learners for short conversational routines. In general, the lessons are often reproductive or imitative in nature and usually involve low cognitive and linguistic skills. Typical examples are naming and identifying objects during vocabulary-building activities, or providing answers consisting of one word or a short phrase to respond to comprehension questions of written or aural materials.

During the guided phases of a lesson, the goal is for learners to produce short phrases by combining various linguistic elements (pronunciation, use of vocabulary, various grammatical rules). The purpose of this phase is for the learners to develop and automatize short conversational routines. These guided and structured parts of lessons serve as building blocks toward more open-ended application. Speaking activities need to be designed to keep the cognitive and linguistic demands at a level that allows the learners to pay attention to form and meaning. Sample lesson 1 demonstrates a lesson that leads students from controlled and planned to more open-ended and spontaneous speaking application.

Sample lesson 1

Theme	Buying clothing articles
Functions	describing clothes; expressing opinions about clothing using verbs like *gefallen* [like], *passen* [fit], and *stehen* [suit]; expressing measurement using metric size

Step 1

The instructor asks questions in German about where you can buy clothes, e.g., "Wo kann man ein Hemd kaufen?" ["Where can you buy a shirt?"] She then reviews colors and patterns. For example, she ask questions such as "Wer hat ein blaues Hemd an?" ["Who is wearing a blue shirt?"] and "Wer trägt ein gestreiftes Hemd?" ["Who is wearing a striped shirt today?"] She asks students to raise their hands to demonstrate comprehension of the targeted vocabulary.

Speaking skills: short answers; guided questions

Step 2

The instructor role-reads the dialogue entitled "Einkaufen im Kaufhaus" ["Shopping at the Department Store"]. While reading, the instructor pauses and points out the meaning of unknown words by using gestures, examples, etc.

Step 3

1. Students individually do a fill-in-the-blank activity to check their comprehension of the dialogue. Example: Der Kunde braucht _____. [The costumer needs_____.]

2. The instructor asks follow-up questions such as "What does the customer need?"

Speaking skills: reproductive; controlled answers

Step 4

1. The instructor plays a tape with several brief conversations between a sales clerk and customers. The students listen for clothing items, sizes, and colors while filling in a chart.

2. The instructor checks students' listening comprehension. For example, she asks in German: "Was brauchen die Leute?" ["What do the people need?"]

Speaking skills: reproductive; one-word and controlled answers

Step 5

Students role-read dialogue in pairs. Then, they switch partners and roles.

Speaking skills: articulation and pronunciation

Step 6

1. The instructor models some personal questions and clarifies the meaning of unknown words, if necessary. For example: "Was ist deine Lieblingsfarbe?" ["What is your favorite color?"]

2. Students answer the questions individually in writing.

3. Students interview at least two other students in class.

4. Instructor follows up with questions such as: "Wessen Lieblingsfarbe ist rot?" ["Whose favorite color is red?"]

Speaking skills: reproductive; one-word or short answers; planned

Step 7

1. In pairs, students write a dialogue about a conversation between a salesperson and a costumer. They are asked to use expressions and phrases such as *Farbe* [color], *Grösse* [size], *anprobieren*[try on], etc.

2. In pairs, students role-play the dialogue with the help of their script.

3. In pairs, students role-play the dialogue without using their script.

4. The instructor asks volunteers to perform their script in front of the class without their script.

Speaking skills: planned; articulation and pronunciation; semi-spontaneous

Guided and structured parts of lessons are necessary to control for accuracy, linguistic, and cognitive demands, but for students to develop communicative fluency, they also need targeted practice in this area. This can be achieved through activities with a primary focus on speech acts such as describing pictures and retelling stories or video scenes. Such lessons also require planning and structuring, and the speaking activities need to be carefully scaffolded through a series of subtasks. Sample lesson 2 demonstrates a lesson with a primary focus on speech acts. The goal of this lesson is to identify the household chore least liked among the class members. With each step or subtask, the students are guided through the lesson by performing different functional speaking tasks, such as exchanging information, comparing, and negotiating with the goal of reaching a consensus. In addition, the linguistic and cognitive demands are taken into account by providing students preparation time, as in the case of this lesson, to build an inventory of household chores. Students are led from using the language at the word level to using it at the sentence level.

Sample lesson 2

Theme	Worst household chores
Functions	Identifying the household chore least liked among the class members
Linguistic demands	verbs (Inf.), e.g., *einkaufen gehen, aufräumen* [go shopping, tidy up] verbs (Inf.) + objects, e.g., *den Rasen mähen, das Geschirr spülen* [mow the lawn, wash dishes] expressions that describe household chores adjectives, e.g. *anstrengend, langweilig, lästig* [exhausting, boring, annoying]

Step 1

Stell eine Liste mit 5 von deinen Hausarbeiten zusammen (Einzelarbeit).
[List 5 chores you have to do (individual work)]
Examples:
sauber machen [clean up]
Katze füttern [feed the cat]
Auto waschen [wash the car]

Purpose/Skills: building the "inventory," a list of activities at the word level

Step 2

Suchen Sie einen Partner/in und vergleichen Sie Ihre Listen (Partnerarbeit)
[Find a partner and compare your lists.]

Purpose/Skills: exchanging information and comparing

Step 3

Einigt euch auf 5 Hausarbeiten: welche <u>müssen</u> wir machen? (Partnerarbeit)
[Agree on 5 chores: which ones do we <u>have to</u> do? (pair work)].

Purpose/Skills: comparing items; negotiating to come to a consensus; moving from word to sentence level

Step 4

Schreibt ein passendes Adjektiv neben jede von den 5 Hausarbeiten (Partnerarbeit) [Write a fitting adjective next to each of the 5 chores (partners).]

Unbeliebteste Hausarbeit	Adjektiv
einkaufen gehen	*zeitaufwendig*
Katze füttern	*lästig*
Auto waschen	*nass*
[most unpopular chore]	[adjective]
[going shopping]	[time consuming]
[feeding the cat]	[annoying]
[washing the car]	[wet]

Purpose/Skills: negotiating; characterizing activities; building more "inventory"

Step 5

Stuft die fünf Hausarbeiten ein von 5 (*OK*) bis 1 (*ganz schlimm*) (Partnerarbeit) Schreibt die unbeliebteste Hausarbeit an die Tafel [Rank the five chores from 5 (*OK*) to 1 (*really bad*) (pair work). Write the least liked one on the board.

Purpose/Skills: *identifying and comparing items; negotiating; coming to a consensus*

Step 6

Stellt fest, welche Hausarbeit am öftesten an der Tafel steht und wählt das "beste" Adjektiv für diese Hausarbeit (ganze Klasse) determine which kind of chore is listed most frequently and select the adjective that best describes the chore (whole class).

Purpose/Skills: *comparing and making a selection*

Step 7

Schreiben Sie einen kurzen Artikel: "Skandal in der Klasse 9a: Alle Mädchen müssen abwaschen, aber nur vier von 15 Jungen machen diese Hausarbeit! Wir protestieren!" [Write a short article: "Class 9a is outraged: All girls have to do the dishes, but only four out of 15 guys help out. We protest!]

Purpose/Skills: *skill transfer: from speaking to writing*

(Source: Rott and Watzinger-Tharp (1999).)

ANALYSIS AND DISCUSSION

Look at sample lessons 1 and 2. What strategies does the teacher use that support the learners in their development of speaking skills? Can you think of any other strategies?

_____

_____

Affective Factors Impeding the Development of Communicative Skills: Language Anxiety and Communicative Stress

REFLECTION

Think back to when you were learning a foreign language. What aspects of the classroom environment kept you from developing speaking skills?

_____

_____

_____

I feel so dumb in my German class. I want to sit in the back of my room so maybe I won't get called on to speak. When I know I am going to have to say something, I spend what seems like eternity thinking of how it should be said, and when I say it, it still doesn't come out right.

I dread going to Spanish class. My teacher is kind of nice and it can be fun, but I hate it when the teacher calls on me to speak. I freeze up and can't think of what to say or how to say it. And my pronunciation is terrible. Sometimes I think people don't even understand what I am saying (reported in Horwitz and Young 1991, p. xiii).

These two students' accounts reflect attitudes that many practitioners have experienced with their students. As Brown and Arnold (1999) point out, "There are few, if any disciplines in the curriculum which lay themselves open to anxiety production more than foreign and second language learning" (p. 9). In particular, in a communicative-oriented classroom, such anxiety-producing factors can be linked to students having to perform in a second or foreign language (Gardner and MacIntyre 1993) or experiencing social anxiety due to increased interpersonal interactions (Oxford 1999).

In addition, as the student comment above confirms, student's communicative stress is often further increased when they are placed in situations which requires them to use language for which they are not prepared or which makes it, because of cognitive reasons, difficult.

Consider the following speaking task in which students are required to stand up in class and tell the class about "what they did at the weekend?" (Yule and Brown 1983). In giving students such tasks, a teacher's primary intention may be to ask an easy and personal question to warm up the class as well as review some past-tense forms. However, the task may be quite difficult for the students. Imagine a student went to a baseball game, and he wants to describe the number of home runs and errors scored by some of the players. Or perhaps some high school students attended their prom, and they want to talk about what they did. As Brown and Yule point out, unless students have been provided with very clear models of what is expected from such a task, and furthermore have been able to familiarize themselves with the vocabulary essential to complete the task, they are going to find it very difficult. Not surprisingly, many students get stuck in these situations, don't know what to say, or provide a trivial answer that they know how to say in the target language. In sum, the type of task and speech function—whether a student is asked to describe, narrate, or provide an argument for why events occurred—can considerably add to the communicative demand and stress.

Another affective factor that pervasively obstructs the learning process with some learners is known as social anxiety (Horwitz and Young 1991; Leary 1983; Oxford 1999). **Social anxiety** can include speech anxiety, shyness, stage fright, embarrassment, social-evaluative anxiety and communication apprehension (Leary 1983). Oxford (1999) describes social anxiety in the following way:

[It] occurs along with the prospect or actual presence of interpersonal evaluation. People who are highly concerned about others' evaluations of them—and we might assume these to be people with shaky self-esteem and/or strong external locus of control (the learner's belief that his or her own performance is controlled by external factors)—tend to act in ways that minimize the likelihood of negative assessments. Those people are more likely to avoid or withdraw from social situations in which others might view them negatively. When they relate to others, they often fail to take the initiative or participate only minimally in conversations (Aida 1994). In the language classroom, this is observable in behaviors such as keeping silent, responding only when necessary, being passive, and avoiding class entirely (p. 63).

Communication apprehension is defined as a type of shyness characterized by fear of or anxiety about communicating with people. Difficulty in speaking in dyads or groups (oral communication anxiety), or in public ("stage fright"), or in listening to or learning a spoken message (receiver anxiety) are all manifestations of communication apprehension (Horwitz and Young 1991). As Oxford (1999) notes, people who suffer from communication apprehension are more reluctant to converse or interact with others; therefore, they tend to avoid communication or withdraw from it as soon as possible. Communication apprehension or some similar reaction obviously plays a large role in foreign-language anxiety. People who typically have trouble speaking in groups are likely to experience even greater difficulty speaking in a foreign-language class where they have little control of the communicative situation and their performance is constantly monitored.

It seems reasonable to suggest that there are conditions under which speakers feel more comfortable in producing what they have to say, and conditions under which they feel less comfortable. We assume that a student is more likely to produce the best that he is capable of in a foreign language under conditions where he is under least communicative stress or where he feels most at ease.

Strategies for dealing with communicative stress and with anxious and reluctant speakers

According to research in second language acquisition, the precise relationship between the role of emotions such as stress and anxiety in second language learning is still quite scanty and the results from research studies are somewhat controversial (Scovel 1991). While some anxiety and stress can be facilitative and motivating, too much tension may have harmful effects on learning by obstructing cognitive processes. It is impossible for teachers to whisk away every bit of anxiety in the classroom, but they can do a great deal to help lessen the anxiety of the classroom—usually by making the classroom as friendly and relaxed as possible. Teachers can make a point of being warm and personable and of rewarding effort, risk taking, and successful communication (Crocall and Oxford 1991).

As pointed out earlier, one of the most powerful benefits of having students interact in groups and pairs is the stress and anxiety-reducing

ANALYSIS AND DISCUSSION

What are some of the problems in getting learners to talk in the classroom? What strategies would you implement in dealing with the issues that you have identified?

_____

_____

_____

effect. Brown and Yule (1983) maintain that it is easier for the speaker if the listener is one of his/her peers or "junior." However, the use of pair work and small group work are not the only strategies to improve the classroom climate. Teachers can also use "games, simulations, and structured exercises that alter the communication pattern of the classroom" (Crocall and Oxford 1991, p. 142). As the classroom structure and communication patterns change, students usually begin to relax and feel more comfortable. Unlike in teacher-student exchanges, when students are more concerned with making no mistakes and avoiding embarrassment, in pairs or groups the learners usually pay more attention to the viewpoint they are trying to communicate.

The following are some anxiety-reducing strategies for use in teacher-fronted and group or pair activities.

- *Provide sufficient wait time.* Many teachers have an intolerance of silence. To avoid silence or confusion in their classrooms, they expect immediate responses or favor better students. Consequently, some students feel embarrassed and discouraged, or the situation creates uneven allocation of turns. Provide sufficient time between asking a question and nominating someone to respond. Alternative strategies are to allow students to write their answers, or to give students an opportunity to rehearse their response in pairs before being asked to speak in front of the whole class (Nunan 1999).
- *Allow students to volunteer their answers.* Some practitioners never require students to speak in front of the whole class at the beginning of a course. Some researchers even claim that students should not be forced to speak until they feel they are ready to do so (see Krashen 1982). Particularly during teacher-centered activities, many students' affective filter is usually highest. This means that many students have a harder time performing, make mistakes more easily, and feel more embarrassed if they do so.
- *Encourage risk taking.* Many students feel a lack of confidence, and their perception that they are poor language learners may result in unwillingness to take risks and marked reluctance to speak in front of their peers. Encourage and talk about the importance of risk taking. Encouragement reduces anxiety and usually creates intrinsic motivation.

- *Discuss the nature of making mistakes.* Many students' reluctance to speak is related to making mistakes, and thus making fools of themselves in front of their peers. An effective strategy for dealing with fear of making mistakes is to openly discuss the issue. Needless to say, making fun of students' mistakes or allowing peers to do so should be avoided by all means. (See Chapter 5, "Feedback and Error Correction in Language Learning" for strategies for dealing with students' errors and for providing feedback.)
- *Frequently change the dynamics of classroom interactions.* Changing the simple dynamics and the management of classroom interactions helps with the integration of reluctant speakers. As Tsui (1996) suggests, if you find yourself with a particularly reluctant class, change the dynamics by, for example, getting the students to stand up and move around while doing speaking tasks. (See "Overview of Types of Student Interactions," earlier in this chapter, for different ways of organizing groups and student interactions.)
- *Consider the size of a group.* Because it is easier for a speaker to talk to one listener than to many, the size of a group often impedes some students' participation. As pointed out before, communicative stress usually increases with the size of a group.

Conclusion

For students to develop communicative skills, they need to be provided with multiple and varied opportunities to engage in meaningful interactions in the target language (TL). One task of language teachers, then, is to mindfully organize the interactional environment in their classrooms to make such opportunities readily available. This chapter has provided numerous guidelines that are useful during the planning and implementation process of communicative tasks. Furthermore, through mindful choice of topical content that takes into account the students' background knowledge and interest, language teachers can motivate students to interact with each other by integrating personal stories and interpersonal experiences or multimedia and textual resources. Last, in the opportunities for interaction that the instructors make available, they must ensure that not only the cognitive but also the affective dimensions are considered.

Checking chapter objectives

Do I know how to . . .

❏ define communicative competence
❏ describe optimal conditions that foster the development of speaking skills
❏ implement instructional strategies that support the development of speaking skills

❏ describe different pedagogical designs of speaking activities and group work

❏ describe instructional strategies that accommodate for linguistic and cognitive demands of speaking tasks

❏ describe and describe instructional strategies that allow for a range of different student interactions

❏ identify and describe instructional strategies that introduce, prepare for, and follow up on group and pair activities

❏ describe strategies that reduce anxiety among learners

Explorations

TASK 1: DISCUSSION

The question on what it means to be proficient and how long it takes to develop proficiency has been of interest to practitioners for many years. When measuring a learner's level of proficiency, instructors want to find out how accurately she can perform real-world tasks and deal with different content areas in different contexts. The ACTFL oral proficiency guidelines in Appendix 8.3 describe different levels of proficiency. According to these descriptions, what level will your students most likely be able to achieve in the language that you teach after one year of instruction in college or approximately 2–3 years at a secondary institution? (See Omaggio-Hadley 2001, p. 26, for expected levels of speaking proficiency ranging from beginning to superior levels in a variety of languages.)

TASK 2: UNDERSTANDING DIFFERENCES BETWEEN SPOKEN AND WRITTEN SPEECH

Read the scripted dialogue in Part 1 of Appendix 8.2 silently. Form a group of four persons. Three of the group members will read the dialogue out loud. The fourth group member will function as a recorder and write down the differences that he has noticed. Then, following the cues in Part 2 of Appendix 8.2, perform the dialogue again. Finally, without looking at the dialogue, the same three students will act out the dialogue a third time. What differences have you noticed between the scripted dialogue, the cued dialogue, and the dialogue performed as ordinary conversation?

TASK 3: EXPLORING GROUP INTERACTIONS

To experience the design of a large group activity, form a group of six students. Your instructor will hand each group member a different cartoon from a picture story entitled "Story in Six Acts" (Appendix 8.1). Then, follow these instructions:

1. Describe your cartoon to the rest of the group.
2. As a whole group, find the correct sequence of events in the story.
3. As a whole group, discuss what you think this story means.

Comment on the design of this group activity. How are the first and second parts of this activity different from the third? Did you notice any difference in your group interaction?

TASK 4: DEVELOPING STRATEGIES

Here are some common problems that may occur while students work in pairs or groups:

- Students do not like to interact with each other.
- Students do not stay on task. They frequently socialize and chat.
- During communication-gap activities, students look at each other's handouts.
- Students use English more often than the target language.

What are some of the instructional challenges of pair or small-group activities from a student and a teacher's point of view? Besides the ones just listed, are there any others that you have experienced as a learner or teacher? With a partner, brainstorm and discuss a list of strategies that help you deal with the problems mentioned above.

TASK 5: DEVELOPING FOLLOW-UP STRATEGIES

A common type of communicative activity is asking students to collect information from each other. Examples are "Write down two things that you did last night and then ask four people in class what they did last night," or "Write down your favorite summer and winter sport and then ask five people in class if they are athletic, and what sports they like to do."

Some practitioners claim that students' eliciting information from each other should not be the only purpose of a task. Students should also do something with this information, which raises the question of how to follow up on group and pair activities. A common practice among teachers is asking several groups or pairs of students to report the results of their work. The challenge with this practice is to get students to attend to each other. How would you follow up on the activities mentioned in the examples above?

TASK 6: TEXTBOOK ANALYSIS 1

Look at a chapter of a textbook. What kind of activities do you find that promote the development of interpersonal and oral communicative skills? How are they structured? What skills are practiced, for example, contents (grammar, vocabulary) and performance skills (functions)? What varieties of verbal interactions are learners engaged in? Examples of verbal interactions include asking questions and answering questions, conducting surveys, making oral statements, and providing oral descriptions. Describe the contents of the verbal interactions in terms of lengths of answers, for example, one-word, short phrases, short paragraph. Are the student answers opinion based or materials based (texts, audiovisual materials)?

Task 7: Textbook Analysis 2

Find two examples of teacher-centered activities that you could develop into group tasks. Outline the steps you would include in the task. Present these to the class.

Task 8: Classroom Observations

Observe a language class by a beginning and/or an experienced language teacher. The following questions provide some guidance on issues to focus on during your observation:

Does the instructor make use of teacher- or student-centered activities? How much student talking is taking place in the classroom? Comment on the students' oral language production. For example, do they produce words, phrases, and paragraphs? In what learning situations do they produce language? How do the teachers scaffold their activities to develop oral communicative skills? How does the instructor make use of pair and group work or other student interactions? How does the instructor set up pair or group work? Does the instructor follow up on students' group work? If necessary, what suggestions can you provide the teacher of what to do differently and how to increase the students' oral language application?

Task 9: Implementing Group and Pair Activities

The following issues may explain why group or pair activities often do not work. In light of these issues, discuss strategies that facilitate effective implementation of group and pair activities.

- Use of time
- Logistics (directions, moving, using materials)
- Type of task
- Uneven distribution of work among group members
- Forming groups effectively
- Effective classroom management/activity supervision

Application

Task 10: Materials Development

Create an information-gap activity using either pictures or short texts as the information base. Be sure the interaction among the learners is purposeful and the student output reflects a speech act found in the target culture.

Task 11: Case Study

A teaching assistant in a first-year Spanish course followed an "explanation" of how to conjugate present-tense verbs with a signature search (open interaction or mingling) activity using items from the chapter vocabulary list: "Find someone who sleeps late, drinks lots of beer, works in a store, watches soap operas on TV, buys lots of clothes," and so on. The underlined items were given as infinitives, and learners were directed to conjugate them in the appropriate second person singular forms in order to ask yes/no questions of their classmates.

This activity incorporates an essential characteristic of a good group activity, namely, an authentic information gap: students ask questions to find out information for which they do not know the answers. According to the criteria outlined in "Guidelines and Strategies for Implementing Group and Pair Work," in what ways does this activity fall short?

What suggestions would you make to the instructor for redesigning this lesson?

(Source: Case adapted from Davis (1997), pp. 264–79.)

APPENDIX 8.1

Story in six acts

APPENDIX 8.2

Sample Scripted and Cued Dialogue

Part 1: Scripted Dialogue

PHILIP:	Hello, Michael.
MICHAEL:	Hello, Philip.
PHILIP:	How are you?
MICHAEL:	I'm fine. How are you?
PHILIP:	I'm doing fine. I'd like you to meet Jason.
MICHAEL:	Hi, Jason.
JASON:	Hi, Michael. How are you?
MICHAEL:	I'm fine.
JASON:	Have a seat.
MICHAEL:	Thank you. So, Jason, where are you from?
JASON:	I'm from England. How about you?
MICHAEL:	I grew up right here in Seattle.
JASON:	Wow, that's interesting.

Part 2: Cued Dialogue:

PHILIP:	Greet Michael.
MICHAEL:	Greet Philip.
PHILIP:	Ask Michael how he is doing.
MICHAEL:	Respond to Philip.
PHILIP:	Introduce Jason to Michael.
MICHAEL:	Greet Jason. Ask him how he is doing.
JASON:	Respond to Michael. Ask him the same question.
MICHAEL:	Respond to his question.
JASON:	Offer Michael a seat.
MICHAEL:	Ask Jason where he is from.

JASON: Say that you are from England. Ask Michael the same question.

MICHAEL: Say that you grew up in Seattle.

JASON: Respond to Michael, making an affirmative comment.

APPENDIX 8.3
ACTFL Proficiency Guidelines

Superior

Speakers at the Superior level are able to communicate in the language with accuracy and fluency in order to participate fully and effectively in conversations on a variety of topics in formal and informal settings from both concrete and abstract perspectives. They discuss their interests and special fields of competence, explain complex matters in detail, and provide lengthy and coherent narrations, all with ease, fluency, and accuracy. They explain their opinions on a number of topics of importance to them, such as social and political issues, and provide structured argument to support their opinions. They are able to construct and develop hypotheses to explore alternative possibilities. When appropriate, they use extended discourse without unnaturally lengthy hesitation to make their point, even when engaged in abstract elaborations. Such discourse, while coherent, may still be influenced by the Superior speakers' own language patterns, rather than those of the target language.

Superior speakers command a variety of interactive and discourse strategies, such as turn-taking and separating main ideas from supporting information through the use of syntactic and lexical devices, as well as intonational features such as pitch, stress and tone. They demonstrate virtually no pattern of error in the use of basic structures. However, they may make sporadic errors, particularly in low-frequency structures and in some complex high-frequency structures more common to formal speech and writing. Such errors, if they do occur, do not distract the native interlocutor or interfere with communication.

Advanced High

Speakers at the Advanced-High level perform all Advanced-level tasks with linguistic ease, confidence and competence. They are able to consistently explain in detail and narrate fully and accurately in all time frames. In addition, Advanced-High speakers handle the tasks pertaining to the Superior level but cannot sustain performance at that level across a variety of topics. They can provide a structured argument to support their opinions, and they may construct hypotheses, but patterns of error appear. They can discuss some topics abstractly, especially those relating to their particular interests and special fields of expertise, but in general, they are more comfortable discussing a variety of topics concretely.

Advanced-High speakers may demonstrate a well-developed ability to compensate for an imperfect grasp of same forms or for limitations in vocabulary by the confident use of communicative strategies, such as paraphrasing, circumlocution, and illustration. They use precise vocabulary and intonation to express meaning and often show great fluency and ease of speech. However, when called on to perform the complex tasks associated with the Superior level over a variety of topics, their language will at times break down or prove inadequate, or they may avoid the task altogether, for example, by resorting to simplification through the use of description or narration in place of argument or hypothesis.

Advanced Mid

Speakers at the Advanced-Mid level are able to handle with ease and confidence a large number of communicative tasks. They participate actively in most informal and some formal exchanges on a variety of concrete topics relating to work, school, home, and leisure activities, as well as to events of current, public, and personal interest or individual relevance.

Advanced-Mid speakers demonstrate the ability to narrate and describe in all major time frames (past, present, and future) by providing a full account, with good control of aspect, as they adapt flexibly to the demands of the conversation. Narration and description tend to be combined and interwoven to relate relevant and supporting facts in connected, paragraph-length discourse.

Advanced-Mid speakers can handle successfully and with relative ease the linguistic challenges presented by a complication or unexpected turn of events that occurs within the context of a routine situation or communicative task with which they are otherwise familiar. Communicative strategies such as circumlocution or rephrasing are often employed for this purpose. The speech of Advanced-Mid speakers performing Advanced level tasks is marked by substantial flow. Their vocabulary is fairly extensive although primarily generic in nature, except in the case of a particular area of specialization or interest. Dominant language discourse structures tend to recede, although discourse may still reflect the oral paragraph structure of their own language rather than that of the target language.

Advanced-Mid speakers contribute to conversations on a variety of familiar topics, dealt with concretely, with much accuracy, clarity and precision, and they convey their intended message without misrepresentation or confusion. They are readily understood by native speakers unaccustomed to dealing with non-natives. When called on to perform functions or handle topics associated with the Superior level, the quality and/or quantity of their speech will generally decline. Advanced-Mid speakers are often able to state an opinion or the conditions; however, they lack the ability to consistently provide a structured argument in extended discourse. Advanced-Mid speakers may use a number of delaying strategies, resort to narration, description, explanation or anecdote, or simply attempt to avoid the linguistic demands of Superior-level tasks.

Advanced Low

Speakers at the Advanced-Low level are able to handle a variety of communicative tasks, although somewhat haltingly at times. They participate actively in most informal and a limited number of formal conversations on activities related to school, home, and leisure activities and, to a lesser degree, those related to events of work, current, public, and personal interest or individual relevance.

Advanced-Low speakers demonstrate the ability to narrate and describe in all major time frames (past, present and future) in paragraph length discourse, but control of aspect may be lacking at times. They can handle appropriately the linguistic challenges presented by a complication or unexpected turn of events that occurs within the context of a routine situation or communicative task with which they are otherwise familiar, though at times their discourse may be minimal for the level and strained. Communicative strategies such as rephrasing and circumlocution may be employed in such instances. In their narrations and descriptions, they combine and link sentences into connected discourse of paragraph length. When pressed for a fuller account, they tend to grope and rely on minimal discourse. Their utterances are typically not longer than a single paragraph. Structure of the dominant language is still evident in the use of false cognates, literal translations, or the oral paragraph structure of the speakers own language rather than that of the target language.

While the language of Advanced-Low speakers may be marked by substantial, albeit irregular flow, it is typically somewhat strained and tentative, with noticeable self-correction and a certain "grammatical roughness." The vocabulary of Advanced-Low speakers is primarily generic in nature.

Advanced-Low speakers contribute to the conversation with sufficient accuracy, clarity, and precision to convey their intended message without misrepresentation or confusion, and can be understood by native speakers unaccustomed to dealing with non-natives, even though this may be achieved through repetition and restatement. When attempting to perform functions or handle topics associated with the Superior level, the linguistic quality and quantity of their speech will deteriorate significantly.

Intermediate High

Intermediate-High speakers are able to converse with ease and confidence when dealing with most routine tasks and social situations of the Intermediate level. They are able to handle successfully many uncomplicated tasks and social situations requiring an exchange of basic information related to work, school, recreation, particular interests and areas of competence, though hesitation and errors may be evident.

Intermediate-High speakers handle the tasks pertaining to the Advanced level, but they are unable to sustain performance at that level over a variety of topics. With some consistency, speakers at the Intermediate High level narrate and describe in major time frames using connected discourse of paragraph length. However, their performance of these Advanced-level tasks will exhibit one or more features of breakdown, such as the failure to maintain the narration or description semantically or syntactically in the appropriate major time frame, the disintegration of connected discourse, the misuse of cohesive devises, a reduction in breadth and appropriateness of vocabulary, the failure to successfully circumlocute, or a significant amount of hesitation. Intermediate-High speakers can generally be understood by native speakers unaccustomed to dealing with non-natives, although the dominant language is still evident (e.g. use of code-switching, false cognates, literal translations, etc.), and gaps in communication may occur.

Intermediate Mid

Speakers at the Intermediate-Mid level are able to handle successfully a variety of uncomplicated communicative tasks in straightforward social situations. Conversation is generally limited to those predictable and concrete exchanges necessary for survival in the target culture; these include personal information covering self, family, home, daily activities, interests and personal preferences, as well as physical and social needs, such as food, shopping, travel and lodging.

Intermediate-Mid speakers tend to function reactively for example, by responding to direct questions or requests for information. However, they are capable of asking a variety of questions when necessary to obtain simple information to satisfy basic needs, such as directions, prices and services. When called on to perform functions or handle topics at the Advanced level, they provide same information but have difficulty linking ideas, manipulating time and aspect, and using communicative strategies, such as circumlocution.

Intermediate-Mid speakers are able to express personal meaning by creating with the language, in part by combining and recombining known elements and conversational input to make utterances of sentence length and some strings of sentences. Their speech may contain pauses, reformulations and self-corrections as they search for adequate vocabulary and appropriate language forms to express themselves. Because of inaccuracies in their vocabulary and/or pronunciation and/or grammar and/or syntax, misunderstandings can occur, but Intermediate-Mid speakers are generally understood by sympathetic interlocutors accustomed to dealing with non-natives.

Intermediate Low

Speakers at the Intermediate-Low level are able to handle successfully a limited number of uncomplicated communicative tasks by creating with the language in straightforward social situations. Conversation is restricted to some of the concrete exchanges and predictable topics necessary for survival in the target language culture. These topics relate to basic personal information covering, for example, self and family, some daily activities and personal preferences, as well as to some immediate needs, such as ordering food and making simple purchases. At the Intermediate-Low level, speakers are primarily reactive and struggle to answer direct questions or requests for information, but they are also able to ask a few appropriate questions.

Intermediate-Low speakers express personal meaning by combining and recombining into short statements what they know and what they hear from their interlocutors. Their utterances are often filled with hesitancy and inaccuracies as they search for appropriate linguistic forms and vocabulary while attempting to give form to the message. Their speech is characterized by frequent pauses, ineffective reformulations and self-corrections. Their pronunciation, vocabulary and syntax are strongly influenced by their first language but, in spite of frequent misunderstandings that require repetition or rephrasing, Intermediate-Low speakers can generally be understood by sympathetic interlocutors, particularly by those accustomed to dealing with non-natives.

Novice High

Speakers at the Novice-High level are able to handle a variety of tasks pertaining to the Intermediate level, but are unable to sustain performance at that level. They are able to manage successfully a number of uncomplicated communicative tasks in straightforward social situations. Conversation is restricted to a few of the predictable topics necessary for survival in the target language culture, such as basic personal information, basic objects and a limited number of activities, preferences and immediate needs. Novice-High speakers respond to simple, direct questions or requests for information: they are able to ask only a very few formulaic questions when asked to do so.

Novice-High speakers are able to express personal meaning by relying heavily on learned phrases or recombination of these and what they hear from their interlocutor. Their utterances, which consist mostly of short and sometimes incomplete sentences in the present, maybe hesitant or inaccurate. On the other hand, since these utterances are frequently only expansions of learned material and stock phrases, they may sometimes appear surprisingly fluent and accurate. Those speakers' first language may strongly influence their pronunciation, as well as their vocabulary and syntax when they attempt to personalize their utterances. Frequent misunderstandings may arise but, with repetition or rephrasing, Novice-High speakers can generally be understood by sympathetic interlocutors used to non-natives. When called on to handle simply a variety of topics and perform functions pertaining to the Intermediate level, a Novice-High speaker can sometimes respond in intelligible sentences, but will not be able to sustain sentence level discourse.

Novice Mid

Speakers at the Novice-Mid level communicate minimally and with difficulty by using a number of isolated words and memorized phrases limited by the particular context in which the language has been learned. When responding to direct questions, they may utter only two or three words at a time or an occasional stock answer. They pause frequently as they search for simple vocabulary or attempt to recycle their own and their interlocutor's words. Because of hesitations, lack of vocabulary, inaccuracy, or failure to respond appropriately Novice-Mid speakers may be understood with great difficulty even by sympathetic interlocutors accustomed to dealing with non-natives. When called on to handle topics by performing functions associated with the Intermediate level, they frequently resort to repetition, words from their native language, or silence.

Novice Low

Speakers at the Novice-Low level have no real functional ability and, because of their pronunciation, they may be unintelligible. Given adequate time and familiar cues, they may be able to exchange greetings, give their identity, and name a number of familiar objects from their immediate environment. They are unable to perform functions or handle topics pertaining to the Intermediate level, and cannot therefore participate in a true conversational exchange.

(Source: http://www.sil.org/lingualinks/LANGUAGELEARNING/OtherResources/ACTFL ProficiencyGuidelines/ACTFLGuidelinesSpeaking.htm.)

APPENDIX 8.4

Jigsaw Activity—Reading Help Wanted Ads

Procedure

Step 1   Post four different sets of ads in the four corners of your classroom (see Figure 8-2).

Step 2   Divide the class in groups of four (base group). Assign each student a letter A, B, C, D, which represents one of the four corners. Hand out the assignment (e.g., a set of questions). Make sure students understand the contents of the questions and are able to pronounce the questions. Send students into their assigned corners to find out the answers to their questions.

What kind of job is it?
How much does it pay?
What are the hours?
What skills or qualifications are required?
Where can I find out more information about this job?

Step 3   Students return to their base groups and exchange the information they have learned from the different ads.

Step 4   Follow up on the group work, for example, by asking one or two individual students which job they'd like to get.

RECEPTIONIST/CASHIER
- Salary open to discuss
- 401(K) retirement
- Paid holidays
- Up to 3 weeks paid vacation
- Health insurance provided
- Stable work environment

REQUIREMENTS:
- Good People handling skills
- Positive attitude
- Team Player
- Enthusiasm is a must!
- Hours 12:30 – 9pm, Mon-Fri

Reply to Box G153
Seattle Times Co.
PO. Box 91039
Seattle, WA 98121

RECEPTIONIST — needed for fast paced, Eastside real estate firm w/ 200+ agents. Answer direct high volume phones greet clients, light data entry other basic computer work Phone exp. required & real estate exp. Preferred. Fax resumes to Joy @ (555) 645-4736

RECEPTIONIST/OFFICE ASSIST
Friendly, People Person with good phone & organizational skills wanted to work in custom furniture mfg. Typing basic computer data entry /w' exp (Microsoft Excel, Word desired). N'end. Call 555-8109.

RESTAURANT — Manager
Trainee. No experience necessary, will train. Earn up to S45,000/Yr as manager. Call (555) 837-8492

RESTAURANT — Pizza Time is now hiring Ass't Mgrs, Delivery Drivers- & Inside Personnel for new store location. (206) 555-7677 Kent, WA.

RESTAURANT — Busy downtown Cafe needs line cook with min 2 yrs exp. Apply in Person: Tues-Fri 2-5, Pay $10 hr. 2215 3rd Ave, Seattle.

RESTAURANT — Cashier/Order Taker; PT 11am-2 pm, M-F only. Premium Pay. Wendy's. Ask for Mike 555-5313.

RESTAURANT — PIZZA TIME HIRING: Pizza Delivery Drivers $10-12/hr, Call Mon-Fri, 919-3163 or (555) 698-0385.

RESTAURANT — Shift Managers & Cashiers for Ballard Burger King. Wage $5-S8/hr DOE. Call Ron 555-4781.

RESTAURANT — For Additional Culinary Positions Please See Catering, 250C.

RESTAURANT — Accepting apps. for all Positions. Beppo Little Italy 701 9th Ave N Sea. 555-7396

FIGURE 8-2 Reading Help Wanted Ads

APPENDIX 8.5

Examples of Communication-Gap Activities

Example 1: (low intermediate)

Model:

S1:   Was macht Otilia um sieben Uhr zehn? [What does Otilia do at 7:10?]

S2:   Sie schminkt sich. [She is putting on her makeup.]

Student A:

	Otilia	Bernd	Moritz und Jens
7.10			
7.25			
20.30			

Student B:

	Otilia	Bernd	Moritz und Jens
7.10			
7.25			
20.30			

(Source: Modified based on E. R. Widmaier and F. T. Widmaier, (2003), p. 315.)

Example 2: (intermediate)

Was für Leute sind Karin und Bernd? [What kind of people are Karin and Bernd?]

Model:

> Student 1: Wofür interessiert sich Karin am meisten? [What is Karin most interested in?]
>
> Student 2: Für Politik und Geschichte. [politics and history]

Student 1:

	Karin	Bernd
Wofür interessiert sich Karin/Bernd am meisten? [What are Karin/most interested in?]		Computer/das Internet [computer and Internet]
Woran arbeitet sie/er gerade so intensive? [What is she/he currently working on very intensively?]		Website für die Firma seines Vaters [web page of his dad's company]
Worauf wartet sie/er denn so sehr? [What is he waiting for?]		E-mail von seiner Freundin [his girlfriend's email]

Student 2:

	Karin	Bernd
Wofür interessiert sich Karin/Bernd am meisten? [What are Karin/Bernd most interested in?]	Für Politik und Geschichte. [politics and history]	
Woran arbeitet sie/er gerade so intensive? [What is she/he currently working on very intensively?]	Projekt über die ehemalige DDR [project about the former GDR]	
Worauf wartet sie/er denn so sehr? [What is he waiting for?]	Scheck von ihren Eltern [check from her parents]	

(Source: Modified based on E. R. Widmaier and F. T. Widmaier, (2003) p. 385.)

Endnote

1 Go to http://www.geocities.com/Paris/Arc/6990/content.htm for a large selection of picture stories.

Developing Reading Skills

Words are the most powerful drug used by mankind.

Rudyard Kipling

REFLECTION

What have you experienced as a learner that has helped you develop reading skills?

personal strategies:

_____

teacher-introduced strategies:

_____

text-based features:

_____

other:

_____

What types of texts did you like to read?

_____

Introduction

The ability to read must be considered one of the most important skills during the second language acquisition (SLA) process. The reading of textual information in a second language provides stable input and lasting, easily retrievable models of language structures. As such, reading instruction serves a dual purpose, namely to facilitate "the transition from learning to read to reading to learn" (Schulz 1981, p. 43).

In a communicative climate to language teaching, approaches to developing reading skills have significantly changed over the last few decades. This shift has led to less emphasis on reading as an individual and solitary activity and more emphasis on reading and talking with others (Knutson 1997). This evolution has been further promoted by SLA theories suggesting that reading must not be seen as isolated, but rather as a catalyst that exposes a student to different sources of input and that affords opportunities for interaction to students at all levels of instruction. Needless to say, many communicative tasks normally include reading in conjunction with other skills— listening, speaking, and writing. For example, the reading of maps, graphs, cultural comments, instructions, questions, or movie ads serves as input to engage students in the target language (TL). Emphasis on reading and exposure to written texts within a communicative language learning context also has a reciprocal effect. Unlike those programs that do not take a multiple-skills, integrative approach by focusing exclusively on reading skills, the communicative approach provides students with a strong foundation of language skills that are necessary for the development of reading skills.

This chapter has several goals: The first part provides an overview of the many factors and sources of knowledge that play a significant role during reading comprehension. The second part focuses on concrete guidelines and instructional strategies that demonstrate how to go about the teaching of reading skills in a second-language-learning environment.

How Do We Comprehend and Process Written Information?

What is reading? Attempts have been made in numerous ways to answer this question. As a result, an array of definitions have been proposed over the last several decades. For example, Johnston (1983) defines it as "a complex behavior, which involves conscious and unconscious use of

---

ANALYSIS AND DISCUSSION

1. "Reading"—write down what comes to your mind.

   _____

   _____

2. What makes reading comprehension easy or difficult? List all the factors you can think of.

   Easy because . . .:

   _____

   Difficult because . . .:

   _____

various strategies, including problem-solving strategies, to build a model of meaning, which the writer is assumed to have intended" (p. 17). Silberstein (1994) describes it as a "complex information processing skill in which the reader interacts with the text in order to (re)create meaningful discourse" while taking on the role of "an active, problem-solving individual who coordinates a number of skills and strategies to facilitate comprehension" (p. 12). And, to conclude with a more recent and simple description, "Reading can easily be defined simply as the ability to derive understanding from written text" (Grabe 2002, p. 51).

As these definitions demonstrate, our understanding of reading in a second or foreign language (L2) has evolved considerably in the last few decades. It is generally agreed that reading must be considered an ability that involves many complex processes. Therefore, reading can be understood as comprising a variety of skill components and knowledge areas, each acting in unison to facilitate the reading process. The question that arises is: Which processes, factors, and skills are involved that affect the comprehended written information? Or simply put, how do we comprehend text?

Readers utilize multiple different processes when constructing meaning from written information. These can be described in terms of bottom-up and top-down processing models. **Bottom-up processes** involve all those processes that are data driven. For example, these processes include recognizing letters, characters, and words; analyzing the syntactic and semantic structure of clauses and sentences; and generating inferences (Rayner and Pollatsek 1989). In their attempt to construct meaning from the textual input, readers also play a critical role by interpreting the textual information in light of their prior knowledge and experience. This process is generally referred to as **top-down processing**. During the construction process both processes, bottom-up and top-down, interact with each other, while the textual input is filtered through the reader's background knowledge or schemata before it gets "integrated into previous knowledge, forming a coherent mental representation of what the text is about" (Nassaji 2002, p. 453). Because of the interaction that is believed to take place between the reader's background knowledge and the textual input, this process has become generally known as the **interactive model of reading** (Rumelhart 1977).

None of the processes, whether top-down or bottom-up driven, take place in nonlinear and nonsequential ways (Just and Carpenter, 1980; Carpenter 1983; Samuels and Kamil 1984; Swaffar, Arens, and Byrnes 1991). Drawing on the work of Just and Carpenter (1980), Chun and Plass, (1997) more specifically describe this process: "Readers are active in the selection of portions of the text for processing, and former portions of the text may inform latter ones, just as latter portions of the text may inform former ones through feedback" (p. 61). Eye movement research also provides clear evidence that readers not only process a text recursively but also fixate on different words and sections of a text at different rates (e.g., see Carpenter 1983). Neither bottom-up nor top-down processing can be considered dominant, and each process is activated by readers in different ways. According to the learners' needs and abilities, top-down or bottom-up processes compensate each other (Stanovich 1980). If one source of processing fails, readers switch to another. Furthermore, as Stanovich maintains, "A deficit in any knowledge source results in a heavier reliance on other knowledge sources, regardless of the level in the processing hierarchy" (p. 63).

The interactive model of reading suggests that what ultimately determines the comprehension process depends on a combination of abilities and factors that interact with each other in complex ways. As generally acknowledged by research, such abilities and factors are text based and reader based. The most frequently considered **text-based factors** are linguistic factors (e.g., the use of vocabulary, syntactic complexity, text organization). **Reader-based factors** that play a significant role are general cognitive ability, background knowledge relating to text topic and genre, sociocultural background, affective factors (e.g., level of interest in text topic and purpose for reading), and metacognitive knowledge and the ability to monitor skills. In the following sections, these factors are described in more detail.

Cognitive ability

One of the most important cognitive abilities that are fundamental to reading involves linguistic processing skills. Grabe (2002) posits that "reading is foremost a linguistic process (as opposed to a reasoning process)" (p. 51). And as he further states, "We derive understanding and new meaning as we interact with the text information by means of linguistic processing" (p. 51). The reader's cognitive ability thereby plays a crucial role in how effectively he is able to process a text.

There are basically two general types of processing—lower-level and higher-level processing (Grabe 2002). By **lower-level processing**, Grabe refers to the ability to recognize and to activate word meanings for use in working memory. In addition, readers begin to construct meaning at the phrase level by being able to pull out basic structural information. At the lower level, knowledge of **syntax**—such as word order or relationships among phrases—plays an important role (Adams 1990; Grabe 2002). Given the constraint capacity of working memory, readers must process words rapidly and automatically for there is little time to consciously focus on every single word. Put another way, readers must assemble and organize these words into more general idea units (Grabe 2002; Samuels and Flor 1997). This is where higher-level processing comes into play. **Higher-level processing** involves a range of abilities such as keeping numerous idea units in mind, the "combining of clause-level meaning information into basic text representation" (Grabe 2002, p. 53), interpreting the text message as it was intended by the author, making inferences and reasoning about a text, and monitoring the comprehension process. Independent of text types and features and background knowledge, readers' cognitive abilities vary when it comes to text processing. Thus, some readers can process written information more efficiently than others do and may arrive at different interpretations and meaning constructions.

Linguistic knowledge

In L2 reading research, the role of language knowledge has been of interest to researchers for many years. The debate, generally known as the **language threshold hypothesis,** has centered on the question: Which factor accounts most for reading ability? Is it L2 language knowledge (e.g., knowledge of vocabulary, structure, or exposure) or native language (L1) reading skills (e.g., general linguistic processing skills, reading strategies, metalinguistic knowledge, or word-learning skills)? Based on ample evidence from research, the outcome of this debate has gradually shifted in favor of the significance of L2 proficiency skills. That is, language knowledge plays the most important role until at some point a critical mass of language skills have been reached (Grabe 2002). Only at an advanced level of L2 proficiency has L1 reading ability been suggested to make a difference (Bernhardt and Kamil 1995; Bossers 1991; J. Lee and Schallert, 1997).

The language threshold hypothesis is also corroborated by research that investigated the role of specific language skills in L2 reading research. The question under scrutiny focused on reader's knowledge of vocabulary, discourse markers, and syntactic structure. Among these knowledge areas, vocabulary knowledge has been considered one of the most critical features of reading ability that is central to successful reading. Many researchers agree that successful L2 comprehension depends on the size of the reader's vocabulary and on her knowledge of vocabulary (Carr and Levy 1990; Coady 1993; McKeown and Curtis 1987; Rayner and Pollatsek 1989). Although not all scholars share this view (Swaffar et al. 1991), some even go as far as maintaining that students need to have acquired the meaning of most of the words in an L2 text before they can read meaningfully (Laufer 1992; Nation and Newton 1997).

Without a doubt, other language skills such as knowledge of discourse markers, syntactic structure, or even subject matter also play an important role. But in comparison, those skills are generally ranked less important than knowledge of vocabulary (Laufer and Sim 1985). Such a hypothesis is supported by research and has shown that lack of knowledge of grammatical structures in some cases would not impede students' understanding of content. For example, J. F. Lee (1987) found that students could understand the content of a text using the subjunctive in Spanish, although they had not been taught these structures yet. As far as the role of syntactic structure is concerned, it seems, when syntactic knowledge is poor, students may place a greater reliance on orthographic or lexical information, which in many cases allows them to make sufficient sense of the text (Davies 1995). Given such research findings, vocabulary-building skills need to be at the forefront when it comes to supporting the development of reading skills.

Background knowledge

There is no doubt that L2 reading comprehension is a function of the use of multiple sources of knowledge. Some is "generated from the linguistic input and the learner's processing of the lower-level lexical and syntactic content of the text . . . [that is to say, the learner's linguistic knowledge], and others from higher-level processing of integrating that content with the reader's conceptual and prior knowledge" (Nassaji 2002, p. 467). Prior knowledge areas may include general knowledge of the world, content (domain-specific) knowledge, familiarity with sociocultural concepts, and knowledge of discourse structures, that is, textual organization. How such knowledge areas interact with each other and how they support the reading processes, however, is not always clear.

No reader is a blank slate when approaching a text. As readers, we all bring along general knowledge of the world, which is primed by our experiences and upbringing within a sociocultural environment. Such cultural orientations influence our interpretation of a text. One study by Steffensen, Joag-dev, and Anderson (1979) provides evidence for such a position. Two different groups, Indians from India and Americans in the United States, both read two passages about a typical American and a typical Indian wedding. The findings showed that each group recalled a larger amount of information from the passage detailing their respective native culture, produced more culturally appropriate elaborations of the native passage, and produced more culturally based distortions of the foreign passage (cited in Reynolds et al. 1982).

A reader's content knowledge also affects the reading process. For example, some studies have shown that scientists read scientific texts with greater success than do business students with comparable L2 capability (e.g., Bramki and Williams 1984; Koh 1985). The question that arises is, how does prior content knowledge aid in second language reading? Or, more specifically, can a reader's content knowledge compensate for L2 deficiencies? As shown by research, this does not seem to occur. For example, when Barry and Lazarte (1995) investigated the effects of prior knowledge of topic by having subjects read a linguistically complex text in Spanish, they found that prior knowledge had no significant effect. They did find that such knowledge helped with making inferences and allowed the readers to elaborate more easily on what they had read (Barry and Lazarte 1998). In another study, Chen and Donin (1997) investigated the effects of linguistic knowledge and subject-specific knowledge on Chinese subjects' reading of texts in both L1 and L2. They found that domain-specific knowledge had a strong effect on higher-level semantic and conceptual information. Such findings suggest that having content background knowledge is beneficial when it comes to higher-level processing and making inferences. That is, prior knowledge aids in the conceptual processing of textual information. However, it may be of limited use when a critical mass of linguistic skills have yet to be achieved.

The role of discourse knowledge is also vital. Such knowledge can make a difference because it helps with the understanding of how texts are organized. Some second language research has demonstrated that prior instruction about rhetorical organizations of text (e.g., problem/solution, cause/effect) can have a beneficial impact on readers' comprehension (Lee and Riley 1990). Swaffar et al. (1991) suggest that prior instruction also needs to be extended with regard to discourse markers.

Purpose for reading

What we read, and how we read, are both purpose-driven factors. Having a purpose means having a reason to read. The reason could involve learning or entertainment, such as passing a test or self-interest. Having a reason in "effects motivation, interest, and manner of reading" (Knutson 1997, p. 49). The manner of reading can be described by how we approach a text—that is, what we focus on and which features or sections of a text we particularly pay attention to, at what level we will process the information, and how much time we spend with a text. For example, if you are trying to decide on which movie to watch by reading the summary of a DVD cover, you most likely skim over the synopsis fairly quickly. Only if the synopsis catches your interest might you reread it, this time probably slower to get a better understanding of the details. Or, to mention another example, students who know which reading sections they will be quizzed on might engage with that part of the text in an altogether different manner.

Monitoring skills and metacognitive knowledge

A reader's ability to monitor his or her reading plays an essential role that is conducive to successful comprehension. It is the ability that allows him or her "to decide whether it [reading] is achieving the intended purpose and, if needed, to take some actions to make adjustments for better understanding" (Grab, 2002, p. 53). The ability to monitor one's comprehension involves subskills, such as evaluating one's progress, focusing, planning, and applying appropriate strategies. For example, it is like saying, "This makes no sense to me; let me reread this paragraph." While many successful readers apply such strategies automatically, in second language reading instruction, making readers consciously aware of such strategies can make a difference. In reading research, the teaching of such metacognitive ("about the thinking process") knowledge is well documented to have a positive effect on the reader's comprehension process (see reviews by N. Anderson 2003; Carrell

1998; Chamot 2005; Dreyer and Nel 2003; Oxford 1989; Paris, Wasik, and van der Westhuizen 1988).

Readability (Text-Based) factor

Reader-based factors such as cognitive development or ability, content and background knowledge, L2 proficiency skills, and purpose of reading all play vital roles in the comprehension of a text. At the same time, the readability of a text, that is, how easily it can be comprehended, is further influenced by different text-based variables. These have to do with the way the content is presented and organized, and the choice of vocabulary.

Traditionally the readability of a text has been measured based on the amount of words in a sentence as well as on word complexity. This kind of measurement has to be considered with caution, but it can provide some indication of the ease of readability. Instead of length of sentences, however, a better way of measuring complexity is by looking at the number of propositions in a sentence and "text-internal such discourse factors—both linguistic and conceptual" (Swaffar et al. 1991, p. 63).

One such factor has to do with the organization of a text. Research has shown that students retain and remember information best when texts are presented in an organized way (e.g., comparison/contrast, problem/solution, and cause/effect; see Carrell 1984, 1985; Meyer and Rice 1987). Structuring texts by expressively stating the gist (e.g., "the main issue is . . .") or by showing organizational development ("a major aspect of this problem . . ."), or by pointing out overt links between ideas (e.g., "as I mentioned at the beginning of . . .") also act as schema and provide a macrostructure for the reader, thus potentially leading to better reading performance (Swaffar et al. 1991).

Readability is also affected by the writer's choice of vocabulary and how the content is presented. For example, research has shown that first- and second-language readers comprehend texts better when the lexical items are transparent rather than opaque (Bransford and Johnson 1972). Explicit definitions are normally easier to understand than implicit ones (Flick and Anderson 1980). In addition, the number of new propositions, and features such as pronoun references or narrational voice, may affect textual reconstructions as demonstrated by the research findings discussed above (Bensoussan 1986; Bernhardt and Berkemeyer 1988).

In conclusion, given the research findings just mentioned, a critical mass of linguistic knowledge and conceptual skills are necessary to extract sufficient information from a text. Many factors come into play that may facilitate or interfere with a reader's comprehension process. Such factors also play different roles among readers with different levels of proficiency. The following section presents instructional guidelines and strategies to aid with the development of reading skills in general and, in particular, to deal with some of the challenges that L2 readers face in an L2 learning context.

Guidelines and Strategies for Developing and Implementing a Task-Based Approach to Reading

A general goal of any reading lesson is for the learners to develop skills they can transfer and apply to the reading of any text. To achieve this goal, the design of appropriate reading tasks thus becomes the most vital part of any reading lesson. That is to say, the task is critical no matter which text is being used. There are essentially two primary reasons for assigning reading tasks to the learners. First, tasks are assigned to monitor the reader's comprehension. Second, they are assigned to teach reading strategies or skills. In the latter sense, reading tasks should also help students better understand language and text construction (Harmer 2001).

When developing reading lessons, instructors must keep numerous factors in mind. Texts are written with a communicative purpose, and reading tasks need to be aligned with the communicative function of the text. The learners' proficiency level, the text type, and its complexity also play a crucial role. As such factors strongly suggest, no recipe can be applied to the design of reading tasks in general. Individual texts ultimately will suggest particular teaching activities. Unfortunately, however, textbooks often apply the same structure to the reading activities for every text, thus limiting how learners approach and explore a text. Individual student needs also demand the teaching of particular strategies and raise questions like these: How should a reading lesson be structured? What elements should it include? What makes a reading task effective? Which tasks lend themselves best to the training of particular reading skills?

The following guidelines are intended to help instructors in designing and implementing reading tasks.

Prepare the Reader

In reading pedagogy, it has become generally accepted that a reading lesson ought to begin with an introduction. This segment of a reading lesson is generally referred to as the **pre-reading phase**. Its general purpose is to

---

ANALYSIS AND DISCUSSION

What are some general strategies that can be used to introduce a text? Write down what comes to mind.

_____

_____

prepare the reader for the reading. More specifically, the goals of the pre-reading phase may aim at

- activating and eliciting relevant background knowledge
- helping with anticipating the contents
- motivating the students
- reviewing and previewing important information in advance that might interfere with comprehension or cause misinterpretation (e.g., cultural concepts, key words, idiomatic expressions)
- finding out what students know
- implementing metacognitive strategies. For example,
  - checking whether students understand how the reading activity should be done (i.e., making sure that students understand what is required of them)
  - making clear to the learner the specific task details (i.e., the particular section or pages they are going to read to and the reading purpose)
  - providing general information (e.g., the rationale or purpose for reading a text)

The pre-reading phase can be designed in many different ways. It may include tasks ranging from a single brief question to a sequence of activities. While the pre-reading phase normally marks the beginning of a reading lesson, sometimes it may serve as a link between a prior lesson segment and text that students are about to read. The level of preparation required needs to be gauged against the students' linguistic skills, their background knowledge, the task difficulty, and the goal of the lesson.

Predicting and previewing. General strategies that lend themselves to pre-reading tasks are predicting and previewing tasks. Such tasks can be designed in light of two different perspectives: a reader-based focus and a text-based focus. Reader-based tasks focus on the topic or theme of the reading. Their specific goal is to tap into relevant students' background knowledge to help them anticipate the new information to be learned and thus to create a link between what the readers know and the topic of the text. This goal is vital for several reasons. When we read, we build and construct knowledge based on what we know. That is, we integrate new information into our existing mental models. Such an instructional strategy serves the goal of helping students organize their thoughts and ideas in advance to facilitate the integration of the new information. Hence, these kinds of strategies are generally referred to as **advance organizers** (L. Ausubel 1960; Mayer 1984). Topic familiarizations and the drawing of semantic maps are two excellent advance organizer strategies. Semantic mapping is particularly useful because it has other pedagogical advantages. While being primarily a vocabulary-building tool (Johnson and Pearson 1978), it allows the teacher to find out what students know, introduce new

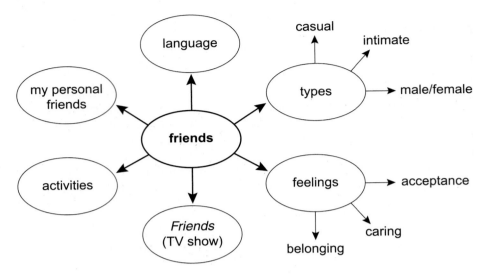

FIGURE 9-1 Semantic Map

vocabulary, and furthermore link some of the relevant information to the text. Figure 9-1 presents an example of a semantic map.

Predicting and previewing tasks can also be designed with focus on the text. Their pedagogical purpose and benefits are multifold. By performing predicting and previewing tasks, the readers get some sense of overall meaning. As Mikulecky (1990) puts it, "The reader gains enough information from the text to begin hypothesizing about it and to begin the cognitive process of matching new information with what is already known" (p. 33). In addition, the purpose of these predicting and previewing tasks is to establish the content and logical (rhetorical) organization of the text (Swaffar et al. 1991). In general, text-based predicting and previewing tasks are most beneficial when applied with a concrete reference to a text and by assigning a concrete task to the readers.

Examples of previewing and predicting tasks:

- Questions about discourse structures (What kind of a text is it? Is it a newspaper article, a story, an advertisement, a textbook, a recipe, a letter? How is the text divided? What are its parts?)
- Questions about titles, accompanying pictures, or graphics
- Asking students to read the first sentence of each paragraph
- Asking students to read the last paragraph or last sentence
- Asking students to scan parts of a text for specific information such as names, numbers, dates, key words, cognates or words that stand out, or discourse markers such as conjunctions (e.g., *and, as, because*), or adverbial phrases (e.g., *first, then, later on, last*)

Linguistic and cultural preparation. The purpose of a pre-reading task is often to clarify linguistic information and cultural concepts, so misinterpretations are avoided. This strategy is vital if linguistic information, such as vocabulary that is essential to understanding the text, is not supported by the context. Similarly, for a cultural concept that is not explicitly addressed in a text, a teacher may have to introduce that concept before the students begin to read the text. When deciding whether to preview information, instructors also need to keep in mind that it is not necessary or desirable to prepare students for everything they encounter in a text. Research shows that students are capable of understanding the meaning and functions of structures they have not yet been taught even though they may not be able to produce these structures accurately on their own (J. Lee 1987). As far as introductions of cultural concepts are concerned, teachers have to distinguish between texts whose goal it is to describe different cultural values, beliefs, patterns, or phenomena and those where a lack of understanding of a cultural concept may cause misunderstanding. When using texts, whose purpose it is to learn about another culture, a more appropriate strategy may be to assign follow-up tasks that allow the students to demonstrate their understanding and that rectify any kind of misinterpretation.

There are many options to implementing pre-reading tasks. They can be done in a teacher-guided manner and as group work activities. Another approach would be to do some pre-reading activities as individual writing activities. As with most writing activities, pre-reading tasks prompt learners to reflect on the materials being covered in a deeper way than they would when engaging in the same tasks only orally. For example, Tierney and Shanahan (1991) report on a study demonstrating that "students who wrote prior to reading read more critically than did students who were given an introduction to the story or were involved in a background-knowledge activation task" (cited by Knutson 1997, p. 54).

In conclusion, it must be noted that tasks attempting to create a link between the topic and theme of the text and the readers' background knowledge need to be specific and concrete enough to allow for effective foreshadowing. That is, pre-reading tasks that are too widely stated may be of little use as advance organizers. Furthermore, the implementation of visual organizers (e.g., still pictures, graphics, video) seems to be more effective with beginning than with intermediate and advanced learners (Omaggio-Hadley 2001). It is probably fair to assume that highly proficient readers are often in less need of preparation tasks because they are able to gain information by reconstructing the intended meaning of the text.

Make the reading task-focused and goal-oriented, keeping in mind the text type and its communicative function

A task-based approach to reading means asking the reader to read a text with a particular focus and view in mind. From a pedagogical perspective, this approach has several cognitive and affective advantages.

First, as opposed to an open-ended approach with no specific tasks, a goal-specific approach with a narrow and concrete task focus is less demanding and reduces the reader's processing demands. It lets the reader "organize language information within a limited system of discourse" (Swaffar et al. 1991, p. 51), thus allowing for more in-depth processing. Furthermore, this approach may lead to enhanced retention of the text materials as smaller pieces of information, which are relevant to a reader's purpose, are more clearly recalled than those that are not (Shraw and Dennison 1994).

Second, a task-focused approach also influences the affective side of reading. It is less stressful and interferes less with reader's interest and motivation in reading.

When designing reading tasks, it is also important for instructors to take into account the text type and its communicative function. Needless to say, texts have a communicative function, and they were written with a purpose in mind. As Grellet (1981) argues, reading comprehension activities should be suited to the text and to the reader's reason and real-life purpose for reading a text. Reading with a real-life purpose means approaching a text with a specific goal; and in many instances, the focus on content also becomes selective. For example, we read ads for apartments to find one that fits a particular set of requirements; we look through movie listings and reviews to decide whether to go to see a particular movie; we respond to a written invitation; we fill out surveys or application forms; or we follow written instructions (Grellet 1981; Knutson 1997). Obviously, reading with a real-life purpose also includes many other reasons such as reading for pleasure or fun, or to inform oneself about a topic—which is not to suggest that we always read with a particular focus in mind. Yet, as Knutson (1997) reminds us, "Rarely in real-world reading do we pay equal attention to everything in a text" (p. 51). While the communicative function of some text types—such as recipes, instructions, cartoons, or poetry—asks for tasks that take a more detailed approach to exploring their content, others (e.g., an article in a newspaper or magazine, or a novel) leave the task specification more open to match the task with the readers' language skills and needs. Nevertheless, text genre and the communicative intent of a text play an important role when designing and focusing reading tasks.

Integrate comprehension tasks at the micro and macro level

Understanding the content of a passage, whether the information is explicitly stated (e.g., as plain facts), is implied, or is to be deduced, means understanding small units, details, and supporting ideas at the micro level and larger units and main ideas at the macro level. When encountering texts in a foreign language, students often tend to approach a text by engaging in a word-by-word decoding behavior. As a consequence, they frequently get stuck at deciphering information only at the micro level. Unfortunately, this kind of reading behavior—by which students attend to textual details—does not necessarily guarantee that students also grasped the overall meaning of the textual message (Omaggio-Hadley 2001). For this reason, tasks need to be designed to allow students to extract not isolated details, but the core message of a proposition (sense unit) at the micro as well as the macro level (Silberstein 1994; Swaffar et al. 1991). In other words, students need to show their understanding of the relationships among ideas within a sentence, between sentences, between paragraphs, and within a whole text. In particular, tasks that require students to assimilate information at the macro level are important because they reduce the likelihood that students will recall details without understanding how these details are connected and how the pieces work together.

Some researchers have pointed out that students' word-by-word reading behavior is often a by-product of foreign language instruction (Swaffar et al. 1991). That is, the design of reading tasks, or how students are asked to explore a text, may often lead to such behavior. For this reason, let us look briefly at some examples of well-designed and poorly designed written reading tasks.

The most common form of task types that aim at learners' reading comprehension are *Wh–* questions. While *Wh–* questions have great potential as a form of assessment to test learner's comprehension, they have to be mindfully drafted. *Wh–* questions become a pitfall if they represent only actual statements from a text, simply reformulated as questions. All the learner has to do is find these statements and copy them from the text. Similarly, if questions are too discretely focused, answers to the questions can often be lifted directly from the text as well. So, instead of demonstrating how ideas are connected within a text, learners end up merely copying isolated points of information. Whether students have understood this information, remains unclear. To test this contention, look at the text in Appendix 9.1 and see if you can answer the questions in the Analysis and Discussion task on page 336.

A better way to compose comprehension questions would be to provide questions that are more broadly stated, so students have to find the answers in the text by attending to meaning at the micro and macro level and not merely by locating strings of words containing the answer to a question. For example, based on the text in Appendix 9.1, the following questions are more effective in allowing the reader to demonstrate their comprehension: "Why do people get piercings? Provide several reasons."

The following provides another example that demonstrates how to test students' understanding of the intended propositions of a text (Swaffar et al. 1991, p. 163).

INSTRUCTIONS: The best rewrite for the sentence "Although no longer as young and impetuous as he once was, Captain Kirk still leads the crew" (from a paragraph critical of the *Star Trek* movie) would be:

a. The aging Captain Kirk is still in charge.
b. Captain Kirk still looks pretty foolish piloting the starship.
c. Captain Kirk is still young and impetuous.

Briefly explain the reason for your choice. (Reasons may refer to grammar, word choice, diction level, or lack of coherence.)

Types of tasks that lend themselves well to helping students assimilate textual information in a more global way are those that help them see the textual organization and discourse structure. Those tasks are particularly necessary since texts rarely spell out their "rhetorical logic with explicit statements such as . . . 'we are about to compare'" (Swaffar et al. 1991, p. 116). Effective instructional techniques such as graphic organizers allow students to reconstruct context as well as textual organization. A **graphic organizer** is a visual representation of major or minor concepts, knowledge or information that shows how concepts and information relate to each other or are arranged in a text. Graphic organizers have numerous advantages. For example, "They ask students to isolate the topics and subtopics of a text and to recreate a visual representation of those relationships" (Swaffar et al. 1991, p. 121). As such, they engage students in a range of thinking skills and allow them to demonstrate understanding of a text at the macropropositional level. However, the use of graphic organizers as a means of showing the textual organization of a text works best of all for expository and narrative readings. While they are useful at various stages, some of these techniques lend themselves to activities employed during the pre-reading phase (e.g., semantic mapping), others require comprehension checks and follow-ups by the teacher.

The following section provides a list of organizing strategies[1] for exploring relationships among ideas in a text, such as in expository prose (Grellet 1981; Mikulecky 1990; Silberstein 1994).

Generalization and/or Details. A common way of organizing texts in English is to mention the main idea or a general statement up front. The writer would then provide supporting details or arguments. For example, the preceding paragraph begins with the lead sentence: "Types of tasks that lend themselves well to helping students assimilate textual information in a more global way are those that help them see the textual organization and discourse structure." The following part gives examples of textual organizers and provides arguments that point out pedagogical advantages for using graphic organizers.

An organizational strategy that follows a similar scheme is classifying information in the form of subcategories or examples. For example, Johnny went to the zoo, where he saw many animals such as tigers, elephants, lions, and zebras.

Some general instructional techniques that lend themselves well to demonstrating classifying information are:

- completing charts, outlines, or diagrams
- creating semantic maps

Comparison and Contrast. The purpose of this organizational scheme is to show similarities and/or differences, for example, between people, objects, topics, places, ideas, facts, or events.

The following illustration which uses a Venn diagram demonstrates this oraganizational scheme. Compare Seattle and Hamburg. What do they have in common? What is different? In Figure 9-2, fill in the differences and similarities.

There are several variations for presenting contrasting or comparative information graphically. For example, a T-chart (Figure 9-3; see Appendix

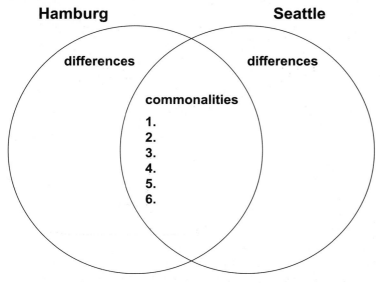

Hamburg　　　　　　　　**Seattle**

differences　　　　differences

commonalities

1.
2.
3.
4.
5.
6.

FIGURE 9-2 Venn diagram

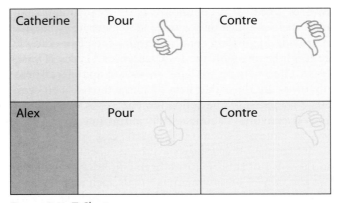

FIGURE 9-3 T-Chart
(Source: Flumian et al. (2007), p. 144.)

9.1, TÉLÉ RÉALITÉ, for the whole text) provides a simple organizational structure for comparing or contrasting (e.g., likes/dislikes; pros/cons; advantages/disadvantages; weaknesses/strengths; best/worst; most/least).

Cause and Effect. In this organizational pattern, there is a cause-and-effect relationship that links events. For example, "Because I did not study for the test (cause), I failed the test (effect)." Single as well as multiple events can have cause-effect relationships.

Sample instructional strategies. Sample questions that require students to identify the cause of an event or to think about a condition are "Why did this happen? What was the condition that makes this event possible? What was the effect? What was the consequence? What did this event trigger?"

Figure 9-4 presents a flowchart showing all the causes that led to one result. Figure 9-5 presents a flowchart showing a sequence of causes and effects.

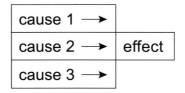

FIGURE 9-4 Flowchart Showing All Causes Leading to One Result

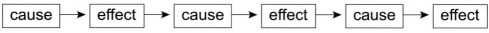

FIGURE 9-5 Flowchart Showing a Sequence of Causes and Effects

Time order. A common organizational pattern of a text is describing events chronologically, in the sequence in which they occurred. Examples of discourse markers that signal this organizational pattern are dates, and terms such as *first, next, then, later, finally, before, after, right away, at last, in the meantime,* and *at the end.*

Some general instructional strategies that lend themselves well to demonstrating this organizational pattern are:

- completing a time line
- placing events in sequence
- arranging paragraphs (or sentences) in correct sequence (e.g., sequence of instructions in a recipe)
- arranging cartoons with captions

Process. Another way of organizing a text that makes use of chronological scheme is describing the process of events. Texts that commonly use such organizational patterns are recipes, "how-to books," and instructional manuals.

Some general instructional strategies that lend themselves well to demonstrating this organizational pattern are:

- describing a process
- giving and following directions
- labeling diagrams and illustrations
- sequencing events and illustrations

Semantic maps. The drawing of semantic maps (see Figure 9.1) is also an excellent strategy "that allows students to demonstrate their understanding of the relationships among ideas within a text" (Silberstein 1994, p. 49). This can be done as a pre-reading and prediction activity and as a post-reading and assimilation task that allows the students to compare and reflect on the actual information found in a text.

Alternative techniques. Numerous alternative strategies also lend themselves well to allowing students to show how they have assimilated both the overarching and detailed information of the text. Such strategies can be engaged in through writing or as oral follow-up activities conducted in groups.

Some general instructional strategies that allow students to demonstrate how well they have assimilated information are:

- writing summaries (This can be done in students' L1 or L2.)
- generating questions about the whole text or subsections
- assigning titles to paragraphs (This can be done as a matching activity or by asking students to create a title.)
- outlining a subsection of the text (or the whole text)

Integrate skill-building and skill-focused tasks

The goal of reading instruction is not only to build up language abilities but also to develop specific skills. For this reason, reading tasks should aim at targeting particular skills. Investigations documenting what successful readers do, consciously or unconsciously, that enables them to attain high levels of comprehension can provide us with such data. Drawing on the works of N. Anderson (1991), Barnett (1989), and Clarke (1979), Aebersold and Field (1997, p. 16) summarize such strategies in the following way:

- recognize words quickly
- use text features (subheadings, transitions, etc.)
- use title(s) to infer what information might follow
- use word knowledge
- analyze unfamiliar words
- identify the grammatical functions of words
- read for meaning, concentrate on constructing meaning
- guess about the meaning of the text
- evaluate guesses and try new guesses if necessary
- monitor comprehension
- keep the purpose for reading the text in mind
- adjust strategies to the purpose for reading
- identify or infer main ideas
- understand the relationship between the parts of the text
- distinguish main ideas from minor ideas
- tolerate ambiguity in a text (at least temporarily)
- paraphrase
- use context to build meaning and aid comprehension
- continue reading even when unsuccessful, at least for a while

While most of these skills have been addressed throughout this chapter, the skill of recognizing words has not been dealt with yet. Many researchers believe that successful comprehension in a second language hinges on how quickly learners can access words (see Coady 1997, DeKeyser 2001; Hulstijn 2001; Qian 2002). For this reason, speed-reading skills that practice recognizing words quickly may require special attention and extra training in the language classroom. Useful strategies that lend themselves well to practicing this skill are skimming and scanning. **Scanning** is "a type of speed-reading technique, which is used when the reader wants to locate a particular piece of information without necessarily understanding the rest of the text or passage" (Richards, Platt, and Platt 1992, p. 322). For example, the reader may scan through a list of movie ads to find the time and place. Or, a beginning reader may scan through a text to identify only cognates. **Skimming** is a type of reading that is used when the reader wants to get the main idea or ideas from a passage. For example, a reader may skim-read a chapter to find out if the writer approves or disapproves of something. Speed reading can also be practiced by setting time limits or by playing video captions in the target language (TL).

In the foreign-language-learning context, there are several other important reasons for developing skimming and scanning skills. The use of these strategies deemphasizes a word-for-word approach to reading. As pointed out by Lee and VanPatten (2003), students "tend to read word for word when left to their own devices [and] need to be directed in how to read in another language" (p. 233). Reading tasks that explicitly focus on skimming and scanning require students to elicit meaning from the targeted clues in the text. Such tasks can be further designed so they indirectly teach the students which key words are critical to understanding a particular text and need to receive most attention during the reading process. When designing such tasks, it is therefore particularly important for the task designer to focus on those clues that are most relevant to understanding the text.

Keep the reader's processing ability in mind

Not only task design but also how tasks are implemented affect the reader's processing capacity. As pointed out in the previous section, the reading process is individualistic. When and what the learners comprehend while processing a text most likely varies from reader to reader. Individual readers also process information at their own time and pace. Thus, instructors should allow plenty of time for implementing reading activities. Putting time pressure on the reader can be detrimental to his or her processing capacity and normally causes unnecessary anxiety. Most readers also process texts best when reading silently, for it allows them to attend to information in the text in a recursive way. This does not mean that the follow-up or comprehension tasks cannot be answered in pairs or groups (see further discussion following). Nor does this mean that reading aloud as a strategy should be excluded from the classroom. On the contrary, the sounding out of words has many benefits. It helps some learners tap into their auditory memory. This in turn helps develop and enhance phonological memory of sound clusters, which is particularly important with nonroman script languages. Nevertheless, reading out loud is considered a reading skill that involves multiple processing demands and normally requires a high level of reading proficiency. Further, reading out loud forces the reader to process information linearly. For this reason, reading tasks are best done silently, in particular when the focus of reading is to extract meaning.

Teach strategies for dealing with unknown words

Normally, readers must have a critical mass of vocabulary knowledge in order to get a basic understanding of text. Indeed, too many unknown words can be detrimental to the comprehension process, causing a lack of—or a faulty—understanding, which in turn could lead to frustration. The question that arises is, What are effective strategies in dealing with unknown words that help learners build vocabulary skills in the long run?

There are four primary strategies that take either a teacher- or student-centered approach to dealing with unknown words. These are 1) previewing; 2) annotating (glossing); 3) students looking up words themselves; and 4) guessing from context.

No one doubts that teachers play a critical role in aiding foreign language readers' understanding of unknown vocabulary. As just suggested, one strategy is to take a proactive approach by **previewing** vocabulary in preparation for the reading. Intuitively, many teachers do so by looking for words they think students must know in order to understand a passage. Normally this is important vocabulary that carries the thread of the story, for example. One advantage of this strategy is that it allows the teacher to preview vocabulary presented in different modes of information, for example, through multimedia presentations or Total Physical Response (TPR) activities (see Chapter 3, "Introducing Vocabulary: Getting Started" for detailed discussions). Such instructional strategies have been found to have positive effects on vocabulary acquisition (e.g., Chun and Plass 1996; Kellogg and Howe 1971).

An alternative to previewing vocabulary is the strategy of annotating or glossing a text. Providing glosses for the learners has several advantages. It is an efficient way of providing the meaning of highly subject-specific words that are important to understanding a text. A teacher's expertise is also often required, particularly with beginners, who are not always able to identify the correct choice from a list of words with multiple meanings. Furthermore, reading texts with **annotated** new words makes reading less frustrating for learners because it does not interrupt their flow of reading as much as when they have to decipher the meaning of unknown words. The **glossing** of a text can be done in several different ways: word translations, examples, word definitions, or grammatical and cultural comments.

An argument can be made against previewing vocabulary or providing annotated texts, namely that these strategies prevent readers from applying reading strategies that help them guess the meaning of words from contexts. Encouraging guessing from context is important, and students have to learn to figure out meaning from context to be become efficient readers. If a teacher decides that he wants students to use this strategy then he has to make sure there is sufficient textual or contextual support that allows the reader to construct meaning from this information. Forms of **contextual support** constitute embedded definitions, examples, or explicit descriptions that further clarify a word's meaning.

Another strategy for dealing with unknown words is for learners to recognize words that play only a secondary role in a text or those that do not result in misreading or breakdown of reading. Proficient readers normally know which words to focus on and which are essential to constructing sufficient meaning from a text. Less proficient readers are more prone to wasting time searching through dictionaries for definitions of words they do not need to know in order to understand the core message of a given text.

The following strategies work in some contexts and can be used to help readers before they seek the assistance of a dictionary or another person (see Plaister 1993):

- Show students which words can be safely ignored in a context. For example, consider a sentence such as "Carmina went to the zoo, where she saw many animals such as lions, tigers and elephants. She also saw a tapir for the first time." The word *tapir* can be easily skipped to avoid interrupting the flow of reading, since the context clearly suggests that a tapir is also a kind of animal.
- Ask students to read on to the end of a sentence or a few lines.
- Have students look for the same word somewhere else, such as in the next paragraph.
- Have students look at familiar word parts, such as prefixes and suffixes.
- Show students how to recognize words that are defined by the context in which they appear.
- Have students identify the part of speech for a word. While this strategy may provide only limited clues to the meaning of a word, it can offer some clue about the importance of meaning that is encoded in a word. For example, students who can recognize unknown words as adjectives or verbs or discourse markers can make a better decision on which words to look up.

Despite the importance of the strategies just listed, using a dictionary is an indispensable strategy that students will not get around. Besides, with increasing ability levels, students' knowledge of vocabulary varies, and each student needs to build his or her own dictionary. Asking students to cope with unknown words by themselves is time-consuming, often leads to frustration, and negatively affects their reading. Therefore, as a rule of thumb, a reasonable guideline is asking students to be selective and limit themselves to looking up 5–10 new words when using dictionaries. The use of widely available electronic and online dictionaries can make this process more efficient. However, the effective use of any dictionary warrants some training, and paper and online dictionaries are distinctly different.

Make the reading process interactive and guided

Although the act of reading must be considered an individual process that is best done alone and silently, reading skills are developed most successfully when reading tasks are implemented interactively under the guidance of an instructor. Second language readers do not know how to approach the reading of a text and explore the contents in an efficient and strategic way. As pointed out earlier, many foreign language readers need to be directed in how to read in another language. Without a doubt, reading without the appropriate guidance can be frustrating and often results in misunderstanding of the text (Martínez-Lage 1997).

There are numerous pedagogical strategies to making reading interactive and guided. Depending on the task and text types, the interaction can be structured in a teacher- or student-centered way. There are different advantages to both approaches.

An interactive and guided approach to reading allows the teacher to scaffold reading tasks. The concept of **scaffolding** involves two important strategies: **grading tasks** (e.g., sequencing tasks from simple to complex) and providing some kind of support structure (e.g., modified T/F statements) that simplifies the processing of the textual input (see discussion in Chapter 6, Instructional Sequencing and Task Design). The pedagogical strategy of scaffolding is vital because it aids the reader in the comprehension process by making the content of a text accessible in a step-by-step manner. It also facilitates the integration of authentic texts early on in a language curriculum.

There are different ways of grading reading tasks. Reading tasks can be structured by proceeding from easy to difficult. For example, a simple reading task explores content that students can understand easily and immediately, such as concrete information (numbers, cognates, names, explicitly stated information, textual details, etc.). On the other hand, complex tasks involve the exploration of abstract content. An alternative to arranging reading tasks from simple to complex is to scaffold reading tasks by moving from identifying macro topics to locating details. Understanding macro topics encourages students to make use of their background knowledge to piece together information. Furthermore, by having to read initially only for macro topics, students do not get stuck at or sidetracked by unknown words or unfamiliar grammatical structures that are required for detailed understanding (Maxim 2006).

A guided approach also allows for the implementation of predicting and previewing tasks (see "Prepare the Reader"). As an example of such a task, students can predict logical and potential outcomes based on a passage they have just read and then check their predictions as they read the subsequent passage (Stauffer 1977). The implementation of such tasks is most successfully done under the guidance of and by interacting with an instructor.

Guided reading lessons allow for follow-up on the learners' comprehension of a text, and they allow the teacher to give immediate feedback. Providing feedback on students' reading tasks is essential because it rejects or confirms interpretations of the text they have developed up to this point. Furthermore, follow-up on readers' comprehension allows the teacher to provide diagnostic feedback and clarify potential issues that may have led to misinterpretation of a text. Feedback is especially important during reading lessons with scaffolded reading tasks since the tasks build on each other, and the information gained from one reading task supports the comprehension of the next. This approach leads to a deeper understanding of the text.

Interactive reading lessons also allow for the implementation of "think-alouds." A **think-aloud** is a strategy in which the teacher has readers think out loud while they are completing a task. As reading comprehension tasks, think-alouds have numerous advantages. They allow the teacher to hear misconstructions and misinterpretations. Furthermore, they encourage students to formulate their understandings in their own words, if these think-alouds are conducted in the students' first language (L1).

Guided and interactive reading lessons further allow for the exploration of tasks or for follow-up in group or pair work. "Bringing differing reading styles together and pooling background knowledge reading with a partner" most likely results in more candid discussions and thus is more engaging than answering questions alone (Maxim 2006, p. 25). One form of utilizing group interactions in the exploration of texts is the jigsaw reading design (see Appendix 8.4 in Chapter 8, "Developing Oral Communication Skills," for an example). In a jigsaw design, texts are divided into different sections and assigned to different groups. The information is explored by students in groups and then shared with students from another group. For example, in a four-corner jigsaw, four different groups of students scan four different sets of movie ads, exploring information about titles, location, name of a movie theater, and content. In the follow-up task, one student from each corner shares the information he or she has gathered with students from the other three corners (groups).

The advantage of doing jigsaw readings is multifold:

1. They are student centered. Students get to interact in multiple ways and use language in a communicative way.
2. They promote cooperative learning behavior. This means they allow students to hypothesize the meaning of a text together. This approach also makes learning less stressful for the individual reader.
3. They can be potentially enjoyable since they bring variety into the classroom.
4. They are task based.
5. They allow for the integration of longer texts in the classroom.

Despite its many benefits, group and pair work needs to be closely supervised by the teacher to prevent learners from accepting their peers' potential misreadings as valid information. As an alternative, teachers should also consider conducting some follow-up tasks in the learners' L1, particularly with beginning learners, because limited L2 abilities often prevent students from engaging and clarifying their textual understanding.

The guideline of making reading interactive and guided implies that teachers use class time when engaging students in the exploration of texts. The biggest dilemma teachers face when using this approach is that it is very time-consuming. For that reason, they often tend to assign the reading of texts to be done alone outside of class. Despite this drawback, the pedagogical benefits of a guided approach to reading necessitate the integration of reading lessons for students at any proficiency level.

Extend the reading through post-reading tasks

Ample research shows that vocabulary acquisition and writing ability are directly related to the quantity of reading students engage in (Krashen 1985). Given such research findings, in the communicative classroom, the development of reading skills must not be seen as an isolated skill, but as a prerequisite skill that supports the development of communicative language ability in general. The integration of any kind of text in the second language classroom has multiple purposes. On the one hand, texts serve as models for demonstrating linguistic structures; they also function as a springboard for integrating other skills. Thus, reading tasks need to go beyond comprehension checks or exploration of linguistic content and give learners an opportunity to apply what they have learned in similar or other contexts and, while integrating functional language use, allow them to express their own ideas.

In some cases, extension tasks derive from the communicative function of a text, which requires the reader to respond (Grellet 1981, p. 9). Examples of such tasks are answering a letter, following directions (e.g., when reading maps, recipes, instructional manuals), making a choice, or solving a problem. However, in most cases, it is up to the teacher's creativity on how to follow up a text. That is why no general recipes can be recommended. Some generic strategies that often work well with beginning-level texts are making personalized comments or opinions about a topic, having students relate what they have read, or comparing the information in a text, to some previous knowledge or experiences.

Illustrations. 1) Students who read movie ads or movie critics explain, either orally or in writing, which movie they are going to see and why. 2) After reading Catherine and Alex's opinion about reality shows (see the text "Reality TV" in Appendix 9.1), students are asked: Do you share your opinion with Catherine or Alex? Can you add any other arguments?

Provide direct instruction for metacognitive reading strategies

As mentioned in the beginning of this chapter (see section on Monitoring Skills and Metacognitive Knowledge), successful readers apply metacognitive strategies that engage them, consciously or subconsciously, in thinking about their comprehension process. As research provides ample evidence that making learners conscious of their thinking process can have a positive impact on the development of their reading ability (see reviews by N. Anderson 2003; Carrell 1998; Chamot 2005; Dreyer and Nel 2003), direct instruction for metacognitive strategies should be provided.

Here are some strategies that students can engage in while reading:

- Monitor your comprehension.
- Pause to consider what you have read.
- Reread—If you got lost, some things did not make sense, or your mind started wandering off, reread (e.g., the same sentence, paragraph or even previous sections/pages).
- Look from one part of a text to the next to make connections.
- Make a mental summary.
- Take notes (e.g., write down comments or questions at the margins in your book).
- Look up words.

Consider the affective side of reading

The affective side of reading plays on one of the most important roles in developing reading skills. As Davies (1995) points out, it is the **affective factors** such as attitude, motivation, and physical feelings that determine a reader's initial decision whether to read. A reader's motivation is also influenced by her or his interest and attitude toward topic areas and content.

To get students motivated, these strategies can be beneficial:

- Select texts that are of interest to learners. For example, topics such as romance, friendship, current youth trends, entertainment, and music are often more appealing to young adults than are cultural topics such as those dealing with the political system of a country.
- The types of texts and how they are written also makes a difference. Swaffar et al. (1991) contend that readers find purely descriptive, **locutionary** texts (texts written in simple speech) bland. They suggest that instructors choose texts that stimulate the reader in some way. A text with a problem-solving intent would be such an example.
- Enhance students' motivation by establishing a real-world purpose for reading. For example, a study by Osuna and Meskill (1998) assessed 13 learners' attitudes toward reading online as well as their perceptions of their experiences in terms of both language and cultural learning. An interpretation of their data suggests that the subjects valued those reading tasks most that involved a real-life application, as it was the case with the creation of an authentic Mexican meal (Brandl 2002a).
- Let students make their own reading selections. This strategy enhances motivation and interest, and it is particularly easy to implement in language-learning environments that provide easy access to a range of reading materials (e.g., classroom libraries or online-based reading resources).

Integrate computer-based reading materials (Internet)

Successful growth in L2 proficiency necessitates ongoing exposure to rich input. This experience can be created through extensive reading. Given this necessity, the Internet is an ideal and convenient source of input for accessing and obtaining an endless supply of authentic material in the TL.

Despite its universal availability, the Internet is not an ideal way of delivering reading instruction; and numerous pedagogical issues need to be compensated for (Brandl 2002a). The hypermedia environments of the Internet may cause difficulties in navigation and cognitive overload. There are questions about text choice and appropriateness of content. Most of all, there is the lack of immediate feedback and help, which requires the learner to be more self-motivated and take charge as an independent explorer (Brandl 2002b).

How can online texts be made accessible—or differently put, how can the reading process be made interactive? Brandl (2002a) describes three different approaches to the design of reading lessons to integrate Internet-based readings in the curriculum. Ranging from being teacher determined to teacher facilitated and student determined, the lesson designs can be placed along a continuum, while the degree to which teachers and students take charge in choosing materials and designing reading tasks varies.

The reading activities and materials of teacher-determined lessons are comparable to the computer as an online electronic textbook. The teacher prescreens and selects reading materials or cultural readings from Internet-based or other resources, designs comprehension activities, and makes them available online.

> The pedagogical strength of this approach lies in the text-specific approach to exploring authentic cultural (textual or images) resources. By pre-selecting and preparing the readings, the instructor tailors the contents and tasks to the students' proficiency level. He/she scaffolds the reading tasks by guiding the learners through the texts. The tasks are designed to support the reader's comprehension process focusing on textual, linguistic and cultural features (Brandl 2002a, p. 90).

A teacher-determined approach to lesson design is most beneficial if a teacher wants to closely guide the learners through a text by aligning their needs and skills with tasks and the communicative purpose of a text and by making the contents accessible through multimedia glosses. Nevertheless, task types and feedback options are limited and depend on the sophistication of the online application. In most cases, these lessons include the standard response types such as multiple-choice, true/false, fill-ins, or matching. Implementing these lessons can also be quite time-consuming. The availability of open-source course and learning management systems, such as MOODLE (Brandl 2005), makes this approach a viable option that guides foreign language learners through a text in online learning environment.

Teacher-facilitated lessons are an alternative approach to integrating Internet-based readings (see Illustrations 1 and 2 in Appendix 9.3). These lessons have the most potential when the exploration of the selected materials does not require close intervention by the instructor to ensure the comprehension process, given that they require only basic technology skills and are relatively low in demand for preparation time.

Such an approach can be described in the following way: The instructor decides on a particular topic for her lesson. She prescreens and selects a set of sites to ensure that the contents are appropriate for the pedagogical goals of the lesson. Through a particular task design, the instructor ensures a goal-oriented and task-focused reading process and guides the learners in their exploration of the content. In this way, she controls the navigational scope and the number and kind of Internet sites that the students access and prevents them from wandering aimlessly through the Internet. Despite the restriction, learners have some autonomy since the tasks give them a choice in the sites they can access and explore. The outcome of the student assignments is clearly defined, but open ended. Assignments that engage learners in real-life task behavior—such as planning a trip, baking a cake by following a TL recipe, or comparing a headline news event as reported by a L1 or TL newspaper—are the most rewarding and motivating.

The approach to teaching reading taken in this chapter emphasizes pre-reading, guided reading, and post-reading (extension) tasks. This raises the questions: What happens when we move to online reading? How and to what degree can pre- and post-reading activities be utilized when students are given a choice and are in control of content?

When following a teacher-guided approach to reading, the integration of text-based pre-reading strategies is limited due to the open-ended nature of the reading content. However, in many cases it is still possible, and often even necessary, to implement some kind of advance organizers that lead up to the topic, theme, or text type—assuming these are known. For example, the use of online newspapers necessitates an introduction—that is, a preparatory pre-reading phase, to avoid unnecessarily frustrating the learners. Online newspapers are differently organized and laid out from traditional paper-printed formats. Online newspapers also vary from culture to culture, and it cannot be assumed that an Argentinean online newspaper uses the same organizational scheme as an online newspaper in Spain.

Post-reading and extension tasks are equally important to online readings. There are numerous instructional options for follow-up and assessment of students' achievements. In the traditional approach, a teacher may ask the students to turn in their assignments. Or, the teacher may also ask students to share with their peers what they have learned. The open-ended approach to exploring online readings has the particular advantage that students' answers are different from each other. This strategy creates an authentic opportunity for students to exchange and compare information they have explored online. At the same time, it allows the teacher to further clarify or follow up on linguistic and cultural issues. For example, consider the task in which a class is planning a real or virtual trip to a target country. The class task is to explore a list of preselected cities to find out what the city is famous for, or what visitors can do there. The follow-up task would involve the communicative exchange of what students have learned, in the form of information-gap activities or mini-presentations. This task is followed by a class vote on which cities to visit.

A third approach to integrating Internet-based resources is making the design entirely learner centered. In this approach, "the learners determine the topics, reading materials, and the way they go about exploring the readings themselves. They decide on the process and the product, formulate the goals, identify Internet-based resources, and make a decision on how the outcomes should be evaluated" (Brandl 2002, 93). The teacher gets involved only in the role of a facilitator, offering support and guidance throughout the process as needed.

Here are some general formats that can be used for students to demonstrate what they have learned from reading self-selected Internet-based resources:

- short writing assignments or essays
- written or oral reports
- posters
- in-class presentations (e.g., skits)
- diary entries documenting the process and stages of their projects

Integrate literary texts into the curriculum as early as possible

With the onset of communicative language teaching and learning, the teaching of foreign languages shifted toward a utilitarian approach. Literature, which once played a dominant role in many foreign language (FL) curricula, started losing its prominence. Consequently, students now receive little exposure to literary works; and when they do, it is often only after they have achieved advanced levels of language proficiency. Despite potential hurdles that teachers have to overcome when working with literary texts, literature should be considered an important component in FL instruction, and therefore should be integrated into a FL curriculum as early as possible. Numerous arguments can be made in support of such an approach.

Literature serves many causes and embodies many of the finer, culturally acknowledged elements of a language. On the one hand, it provides an authentic window on a foreign language and society. As Kramsch (2000) argues, "it supports the goals of 'cultural competence' and the need to promote understanding of any empathy for the foreign culture" (p. 567). In addition, it is through literature that intercultural encounters and exposures can be provided for FL students (Shanahan 1997). As such, literature plays a vital role, opening gates to the understanding of societal and world affairs. On the other hand, the use of literature can also contribute to the process of language learning. Through literature, students not only develop cultural knowledge and sensitivity but also can develop a full range of linguistic and cognitive skills (Henning 1993). Another reason for integrating literature into FL instruction has to do with affect. Affect plays an important role in a learner's development of FL skills. In particular, it is literature, as Shanahan (1997) emphasizes, that uses "forms of language that most calculatingly play upon affect [while serving] as an inducement to communication" (p. 168).

There is no doubt that the integration of literary texts into FL instruction comes with many challenges. Two of the strongest arguments against its use are the difficulty in making such "authentic artifacts" accessible to the learners and accommodating their linguistic needs at different levels of proficiency. For evident reasons, some scholars (e.g., see J. Lee 1986) believe that until they have achieved advanced levels, students do not have the necessary vocabulary knowledge and linguistic skills to tackle the difficult task of "interpreting and understanding the symbolic nature of a text and its cultural, social and historical dimensions" (Kramsch 1985, p. 357).

The question that arises is: How can instructors go about successfully integrating literary texts into the FL curriculum? Challenges that teachers typically face involve choosing appropriate texts and making those texts accessible to their students, and furthermore, determining how to methodologically work with literary texts so they also serve the development of communicative skills.

To widen the variety of possible choices when attempting to identify literary texts, Lalande (1988) suggests broadening the concept of literature by including a range of other text genres. Besides the more commonly identified literary genres such as poetry, drama, novels, and short stories, he proposes including such diverse genres as "radio plays, travelogues, folklore, autobiographies, historical accounts, magazines, scriptures, libretti, comic books, detective/mystery works, fairy tales, biographies, science fiction, newspapers, church hymns, songs, farces/Schwänke, and romances" (p. 575). By drawing from a wider variety of sources, a wider range of students' experiences and interests can be engaged. Moreover, a broader interpretation of literary genres can also have greater appeal to students who are interested in natural sciences, history, or current pop culture topics.

Of all the potential hurdles language teachers have to overcome, the difficulty of the text remains the most evident limitation to the use of many literary texts in FL curricula. Nevertheless, literature for young people, simple poetry (e.g., concrete poetry), and fairy tales can easily be adapted for beginning and intermediate levels of instruction. In addition, the syntax and vocabulary of such literary works are often less complex, making such texts easier to read.

How can literary texts be made accessible to FL learners? Literary texts fall under the rubric of "authentic" texts. As discussed throughout this chapter, using literary text requires the integration of strategies such as pre-reading, advance organizers, guided reading tasks that support the reader with processing of targeted content, and personalization of follow-up and extension tasks. Reading tasks have to be adapted to, modified, and aligned with readers' ability and the texts, whole or in part, to make the text accessible. Moreover, when choosing a literary text or any other kind of text, instructors should also keep the theme and topic in mind. Students should be able to relate to the content, whether it reflects topics such as wishes, fears, needs, or dreams. After all, a student's motivation to read a text is often further enhanced by his or her interest in the topic itself.

Conclusion

Throughout this book it has been demonstrated that "reading to learn" has many functions such as storing and retrieving information and processing authentic models of input in the target language (TL). The use of written texts permeates all phases of language instruction and plays a pivotal role in contributing to second language learning. The purpose of this chapter was to focus on the importance of learning to read—that is, the role of reading instruction. The chapter began by describing different processes and further discussed a range of factors that make up the complex process of textual understanding. The second part of the chapter provided a list of instructional guidelines designed to help with the planning of lessons. Furthermore, in a more general sense, this chapter pointed out the factors conducive to learners' development of reading skills. Teacher practices and preferences and the amount of curricular time spent with reading are vital, but they are not the only factors. Students also develop differing proficiencies in reading depending on library resources and, above all, on teacher interest in books and student learning (Grabe 2002).

Checking chapter objectives

Do I know how to . . .

- ❏ define processes underlying reading comprehension
- ❏ describe factors that affect the comprehension process of written texts
- ❏ explain different instructional phases of a reading lesson
- ❏ develop pre- and post-reading activities
- ❏ make reading lessons interactive and guided
- ❏ describe different reading strategies
- ❏ describe different strategies for building vocabulary skills
- ❏ integrate Internet-based readings into the language curriculum

Explorations

Task 1: Reflection and Discussion

1. Read through the list of factors that may affect or support the reading comprehension process in Figure 9-6. Discuss how any of these factors may affect low- or high-proficiency readers.

_____

_____

1. reading ability in L1
2. script
3. L2 knowledge of vocabulary
4. L2 knowledge of grammar
5. purpose for reading (e.g., test, level of interest, etc.)
6. prior knowledge of the world
7. affective factors (e.g., motivation, interests, etc.)
8. text difficulty (e.g., vocabulary, syntax, text organization)
9. content knowledge
10. metacognitive strategies
11. time
12. cultural values and beliefs
13. cognitive abilities
14. familiarity with context
15. type of text and genre (e.g., instructions, poem, novel, letter, etc.)
16. condition (e.g., reading out loud vs. silent reading)
17. other: _____
18. other: _____

Figure 9-6 Survey

Task 2: Familiarity with Context

Read the script in Figure 9-7 and identify the topic. (You can find the topic at the end of this chapter in endnote 2.) To what degree does familiarity with context support the reading process? Is there a difference between beginning and advanced learners?

At first you believe it is absolutely impossible to do, no matter how hard you concentrate. In fact, it always does take some time to get it right. Then, just when you get used to doing it competently, you hear of the alternate method. While the final choice is, of course, left to you, if you are mature and reasonable you'll realize that there is one way, which is superior. People sometimes need to do it in strange positions, so flexibility is definitely an asset. Taken seriously, this task should not result in injuries. One usually tries to avoid situations where one has to do it too often.

Figure 9-7 Reading Script
Source: J.-Y. Zupinik, cited in Mikulecky (1990), 5.

TASK 3: EFFECTIVE READING STRATEGIES

Read through the following list of reading strategies and indicate whether you believe the strategy to be effective. Make sure to provide a rationale for your decision.

Reading strategies	Effective (E) or Ineffective (I) Reasons
a) use my finger to help my eyes follow lines of text	
b) read each word very carefully in order to understand the entire text	
c) keep my eyes moving past the unfamiliar words and thus try to understand the main ideas	
d) say words quietly to myself	
e) write the meaning of new words in L1 in margin of page	
f) look up unfamiliar words in a bilingual dictionary	
g) start reading without panicking or thinking Help! I am not going to understand.	
h) look for linking words that help explain relationship between sentences	
i) ask my teacher for help whenever I meet an unfamiliar word	
j) use different reading strategies to read different types of texts	
k) translate a difficult section of text into L1	
l) think of other words I already know that are similar to the unknown word(s) I come across	
m) find the sentence that contains the main idea	
n) read a lot different things in order to expand my vocabulary and improve my general comprehension	
o) study or write vocabulary lists and translations of words into L1	
p) try to understand the main idea and the supporting details	
q) look at titles, subtitles, pictures, and other visuals before reading	
r) read a text very quickly the first time to get the gist (main idea)	
s) underline or highlight words I don't understand	
t) create some questions for myself before I read which I think or hope the text will answer	
u) limit myself to looking up in the dictionary only a few unknown words	
v) circle or highlight key words in a bright color	

(Source: Green and Tanner (1998), p. 66.)

Application

Task 4: Rhetorical Organizations

1. Match the four sample texts below with the following four different rhetorical organizations:

Generalization/Detail	Text A
Time Order (chronology, sequence, process)	Text B
Comparison and Contrast	Text C
Cause and Effect	Text D

2. Writers often use special signal words to let the reader know how the text is organized. First, find the main idea sentence. Next, underline the signal words in each of the four different sample texts.
3. Now, develop some comprehension tasks for each sample text.

Text C

Example: Judy really loves restaurants, and she would eat out every day if she could. One of her favorites is the Italian restaurant. Another is the deli and sandwich shop near her house. She also eats often at the Greek snack bar near the university.

Text A

Example: Alan was checking his bicycle to make sure he could ride it to work safely. First, he checked the tires to make sure they had enough air. Then, he cleaned the frame and the rims of the tires. Next, he oiled the axle. After that, he checked the cable for the gears. And finally, he examined the brakes to make sure they were adjusted for quick stops in city traffic.

Text D

Example: Tomatoes are very popular in most parts of the United States, but most people prefer tomatoes grown in home gardens. There is a great difference between tomatoes from the supermarket and home garden tomatoes. The supermarket tomatoes have very little taste, their color is pale yellow-red, and they are almost as hard as rocks. On the other hand, home garden tomatoes are deep red, juicy, tasty, and tender.

Text B

Example: Boston has a very beautiful waterfront and harbor, but it is the dirtiest in the United States. The pollution is due to the old practice of draining all the wastewater from the city into the harbor. Factories and hospitals dump many chemicals down the drains to the harbor. Ships in the harbor add to the problem by flushing out the tanks.

(Source of sample texts: Mikulecky (1990), p. 112.)

TASK 5: IDENTIFYING THE ORGANIZATIONAL STRUCTURE OF A TEXT

Choose two different kinds of text in the language that you teach. Present the organizational structure of these texts.

TASK 6: ANALYZING READING TASKS AND STRATEGIES IN TEXTBOOKS

Part 1

Choose a first-year college (or third-year high school) textbook. By yourself or with a partner, analyze a unit or chapter of a textbook. Make a list of activities describing how reading skills are practiced. What kind of reading tasks are students asked to perform? What skills do they engage in? For example, do students respond to *Wh*– questions about personal information, or do they elicit selective information from texts? Do they gather specific information or make inferences? How are reading activities scaffolded? For example, are they sequenced to move from yes/no, true/false via display to open-ended questions? How do students demonstrate their comprehension? Last, evaluate these tasks for their "closeness" to real-life reading.

Part 2

Look at several different reading texts of a textbook of your choice. What reading tasks and skills do students engage in at the beginning, middle, and end of the book? What strategies are readers encouraged to use? How are readers prepared for the readings? What kinds of extension tasks are readers to complete?

TASK 8: DEVELOPING READING TASKS

Choose two different kind of short texts. Create a jigsaw reading activity. Make sure to provide enough information demonstrating how you would implement each activity in the classroom.

TASK 9: DEVELOPING A READING LESSON PLAN

Based on the following sample poem, or on texts of your choice, develop a reading lesson plan. Make sure to provide pre-reading, guided reading, and post-reading (extension) tasks.

Text 1: "Vergnügungen," by Bertolt Brecht

Der erste Blick aus dem Fenster am Morgen
Das wiedergefundene alte Buch

Begeisterte Gesichter
Schnee, der Wechsel der Jahreszeiten
Die Zeitung
Der Hund
Die Dialektik
Duschen, Schwimmen
Alte Musik
Bequeme Schuhe
Begreifen
Neue Musik
Schreiben, Pflanzen
Reisen
Singen
Freundlich sein

The first glance out of the window in the morning
The rediscovered old book
Enthusiastic faces
Snow, the change in season
The newspaper
The dog
Dialectics
Taking a shower, swimming
Old music
Comfortable shoes
Understanding
New music
Writing, plants
Traveling
Singing
Being friendly

(Source: "Vergnügungen," from *Gesammelte Werke*, by Bertolt Brecht ©
Suhrkamp Verlag, Frankfurt am Main, 1967.)

TASK 10: USING RHETORICAL PATTERNS TO AID TEXTUAL COMPREHENSION

Develop a reading lesson plan for the text in Appendix 9.2 (An interview between an American and a German student). From the list of textual organizations presented in this chapter, choose one strategy that you would ask students to engage in to demonstrate their textual understanding.

APPENDIX 9.1

Sample Texts

3. LE PIERCING ET LES TATOUAGES

A. Lisez la transcription d'un débat radiophonique au sujet du piercing et des tatouages et ajoutez, là où ils manquent, les mots et expressions du tableau ci-dessous.

• en tant que	On situe une opinion à partir d'un domaine de connaissance ou d'expérience.
• d'ailleurs	On justifie, développe ou renforce l'argument ou le point de vue qui précède en apportant une précision.
• il est vrai que... mais	On reprend un argument et on ajoute une idée qui le nuance ou le contredit.
• car	On introduit une cause que l'on suppose inconnue de l'interlocuteur.

Présentateur : Evelyne Jamel, en tant que sociologue, que pensez-vous du phénomène du piercing et du tatouage chez les jeunes?

Evelyne Jamel : Le piercing comme le tatouage existent depuis très très longtemps dans certaines civilisations. En Afrique, en Océanie ou au Japon le piercing ou le tatouage sont des rites. Mais dans notre société, ils correspondent à deux phénomènes : **d'une part** c'est un phénomène de mode ; on porte un piercing ou un tatouage pour des raisons esthétiques.................................. beaucoup de piercings ou de tatouages sont de faux piercings ou de faux tatouages.

P. : Comment ça, de faux piercings et de faux tatouages !?

E. J. : Oui, **c'est-à-dire** qu'ils ne sont pas permanents.

P. : Et d'autre part *?*

E. J. : Eh bien, **d'autre part**, il s'agit d'un phénomène de contestation. C'est le mouvement punk qui les a mis à la mode il y a une trentaine d'années. C'est une façon de se révolter ou de montrer que l'on appartient à un groupe.

P. : Est-ce qu'il y a beaucoup de jeunes qui portent un tatouage ou un piercing ?

E. J. : En France, 8% des jeunes de 11 à 20 ans ont un piercing et 1% portent un tatouage.

P. : Albert Lévi, qu'en pensez-vous ?

Albert Lévi : Bien, ... médecin, je dois mettre en garde contre les risques du piercing ou du tatouage. Un piercing au nombril avant 16 ans n'est pas du tout recommandable .... les adolescents peuvent encore grandir et la peau peut éclater. Le piercing représente .... un risque pour la santé.

P. : Et est-ce que les tatouages sont moins dangereux ?

A. L. : C'est pareil. Le matériel de tatouage doit être parfaitement désinfecté et je ne pense pas que ces règles d'hygiène élémentaires soient toujours respectées.

P. : Donc, à votre avis, est-ce que ces pratiques devraient être interdites ?

A. L. : En effet, interdire pourrait être une solution.

P. : Evelyne Jamel, êtes-vous d'accord ?

E. J. : Mais non, pas du tout ! .... du docteur Lévi, **même si** ses inquiétudes par rapport à ces pratiques sont justifiées. .... le piercing ou le tatouage comportent des risques .... interdire n'est pas la solution. .... si l'on interdit à un adolescent de se faire un piercing, il s'en fera deux ! **Par contre**, les parents peuvent expliquer à leurs enfants les risques du piercing ou du tatouage et...

(Source: Flumian et al. (2007), p. 145.)

2. TÉLÉ RÉALITÉ

A. Lisez ces deux opinions sur la télé réalité, puis retrouvez les arguments pour et les arguments contre la télé réalité et placez-les dans le tableau.

Catherine	Pour	Contre
Alex	Pour	Contre

La télé réalité ?
Pour ou contre ?

Catherine Pasteur, peintre

Tout dépend de l'émission de télé réalité dont on parle. Prenons, par exemple, l'émission « Star Academy », l'école des jeunes chanteurs. Cette émission permet à de jeunes talents de perfectionner leur technique de chant et les finalistes peuvent enregistrer un ou plusieurs disques. Cette émission offre donc la possibilité à de jeunes talents de réaliser leur rêve.

Mais il y a aussi des émissions de télé réalité comme, par exemple, « Loft Story » où plusieurs personnes sont enfermées dans un appartement pendant trois mois. Dans ce type d'émissions de télé réalité, l'idée est toujours la même : des gens sont filmés dans leur quotidien et les spectateurs les regardent comme au zoo. Il n'y a aucune créativité, aucune esthétique.

Il est vrai que l'une des fonctions de la télévision est de distraire les téléspectateurs, mais quel est l'intérêt de regarder des gens qui se disputent ou qui parlent de leur intimité ? Je ne crois pas que cela soit une distraction saine.

Ce qui me choque aussi, c'est que le scénario de la plupart de ces émissions de télé réalité est écrit à l'avance. En effet, même si le téléspectateur a l'impression que tout est improvisé et naturel, il s'agit en réalité d'un montage. Tout est décidé à l'avance. On trompe le téléspectateur, on lui fait croire qu'il peut décider alors que c'est complètement faux.

En conclusion, je crois que ces émissions n'apportent rien au téléspectateur, elles n'ont qu'un but : faire gagner beaucoup d'argent aux producteurs et à la chaîne télévisée.

Alex Lecocq, psychologue

Pourquoi est-ce que la télé réalité remporte un tel succès auprès des téléspectateurs en France ? Probablement parce que la principale caractéristique de ces émissions est de présenter à l'écran des gens ordinaires avec lesquels les téléspectateurs s'identifient facilement.

C'est bien ou c'est pas bien ? D'un côté, cela représente une démocratisation de la télévision. Tout le monde peut passer à la télévision. Les émissions de télé réalité alimentent aussi les conversations : on en parle en famille, entre amis, avec les collègues et c'est une conversation qui ne provoque pas de conflits.

D'un autre côté, les protagonistes de ces émissions sont des personnes sans mérite particulier, qui deviennent rapidement riches et célèbres grâce à la télévision. Je pense qu'on peut y voir une justification de la médiocrité.

En conclusion, je ne crois pas qu'il faille condamner ce type d'émissions. L'une des fonctions de la télévision est de distraire le spectateur et ces émissions jouent bien ce rôle. Par contre, je crois qu'il faut limiter leur nombre. Il y a, actuellement, trop d'émissions de ce type et c'est plutôt la diversité à la télé qui est en danger.

B. Partagez-vous les opinions de Catherine et d'Alex ? Ajouteriez-vous d'autres arguments ? Commentez-le avec un camarade.

- Je suis d'accord avec Alex. Moi aussi je pense que la télé réalité...

(Source: Flumian et al. (2007), p. 144.)

EN CONTEXTE

APPENDIX 9.2

Unsere Schulsysteme [Our school systems]

ROSA: So, du kommst aus Flensburg. Kannst du mir etwas von dem deutschen Schulsystem erzählen. Ich verstehe nichts davon.

KLARA: Also am besten erzähle ich von Anfang an. In Deutschland muss man vom 6. bis zum 18. Lebensjahr zur Schule gehen.

ROSA: So? Bei uns darf man schon mit sechzehn aufhören, obwohl die meisen erst mit achtzehn fertig sind. Aber bei uns fangen viele mit Kindergarten an.

KLARA: Ja, bei uns auch. Der Kindergarten ist allerdings nicht wie die Schule. Obwohl die meisten Kinder ihn besuchen, muss man das in Deutschland nicht. Bei uns kommt danach die Grundschule—sie dauert überall vier Jahre. In der 5. und 6. Klasse überlegt man sich, in welche Schule man nachher gehen will: in die Hauptschule, in die Realschule, aufs Gymnasium oder in die Gesamtschule—das ist eine Kombination der drei Schularten.

ROSA: Du liebe Zeit! Das hört sich kompliziert an! Bei uns gibt es auch die Grundschule, aber sie dauert sechs Jahre. Dann kommt Middle School oder Juniour High School und dann endlich die High School. Wie entscheidet man sich bei euch für eine Schule?

KLARA: Während der Orientierungsstufe—das sind das 5. und 6. Jahr—achtet man auf Leistungen der Kinder. Etwa ein Viertel der Schüler besucht die Hauptschule. Von da gehen die meisten dann in die Berufsausbildung. Ungefähr 40 Prozent der Schuler besuchen die Realschule. Diese Schüler gehen nachher vor allem in die Wirtschaft oder Verwaltung. Ich selber ging aufs Gymnasium. Da habe ich mich auf das Abitur vorbereitet. Ich lernte dort Mathematik, Englisch, Latein, Biologie unf auch andere Fächer. Zum Schluss muss man in einer Abiturprüfung Wissen in vier bis fünf Fächern aufweisen. Das Abitur ist die Eintrittskarte zur Universität.

ROSA: Wie? Gehen nur Schüler mit Abitur auf die Universität?

KLARA: Eigentlich ja, obwohl es auch den "zweiten Bildungsweg" gibt. Der ist für junge Leute, die ihre Meinung ändern.

ROSA: Das ist sehr streng. Wir müssen natürlich ein "Diplom" haben, aber das bekommt praktisch jeder.

KLARA: Ja, ich habe davon gehört. Ihr geht ja auch nur zwölf Jahre zur Schule, nicht.

ROSA: Ja, natürlich. Ihr nicht?

KLARA: Nein, aufs Gymnasium gehen wir neun Jahre. Mit der Grundschule zusammen macht das dann dreizehn Jahre. Es ist eigentlich besser, dann man lernt ja auch mehr. In die Hauptschule und in die Realschule geht man allerdings nicht so viele Jahre.

ROSA: Vier Jahre and dann neun Jahre, da is schon viel. Kein Wunder, dass du soviel weißt. Aber unser System hat auch Vorteile.

Rosa:	So, you are from Flensburg? Can you talk to me a little bit about the German school system? I do not know anything about it.
Klara:	Well, best of all I start from the beginning. In Germany, you have to attend school from age 6 through 18.
Rosa:	So? Here you can quit at the age of 16, although most do not finish before they are 18 years old. But here many start with kindergarten.
Klara:	Yes, here as well. Kindergarten, however, is not the same as school. Although most of the kids attend kindergarten, this is not obligatory in Germany. After that, there is elementary school, which everywhere lasts four years. During 5th and 6th grade you need to think about which school to attend next: Hauptschule, Realschule, Gymnasium or Gesamtschule—the latter combines all three types.
Rosa:	Oh my goodness! This sounds complicated. We also have elementary school, however, which lasts six years. Then comes Middle School or Junior High School and then finally High School. How do you decide which school you want to attend?
Klara:	During the orientation years—this includes the 5th and 6th year—we pay attention to the students' achievements. Approximately a fourth of the students goes to the Hauptschule. After that, most continue with some kind of vocational training. About 40% of the students attend Realschule. In particular those look for work in industry and administration. I went to the Gymnasium, where I prepared myself for the Abitur. I took classes in Math, English, Latin, Biology, and other subjects. At the end, you have to take your Abiturexams and demonstrate knowledge in four to five different subject areas. Your Abitur is your admissions ticket to the university.
Rosa:	What? Can only students who have the Abitur attend the university?
Klara:	Actually, this is the case, although there is the "alternative route." It is for those young people who change their minds.
Rosa:	This is quite strict. We of course need to have a diploma, but practically almost everybody gets it.
Klara:	Yes, I have heard about it. You only go to school for twelve years, don't you?
Rosa:	Yes, of course. You don't.
Klara:	No, we attend Gymnasium for nine years. Including elementary school, this adds up to 13 years. However, you don't attend Hauptschule and Realschule for as many years.
Rosa:	Four years and then nine years. That's quite a bit. No wonder that you know so much. But our school system also has advantages.

(Source: Otto et al. (2003), pp. 362–363.)

APPENDIX 9.3

Sample Internet-based reading lesson

Illustration 1

Une nuit à Paris [A night in Paris]

(Source: Sybille Stadtmueller TEP 588/589, University of Washington, 2007; modified by Klaus Brandl.)

Level: Low intermediate (e.g., second or third year high school; second semester in a college environment)

Lesson Description

This lesson is about students planning a virtual evening out on the town in Paris for themselves and a friend. Students navigate a French website and choose a dinner and a movie. Students have been given a spending limit of 200 euros.

Pedagogical Procedures

1. Pre-reading (to be done in class).   Before doing this assignment, the students will be asked to think about what they do to plan an evening out with a friend. What activities do they do? How do they find out what is going on, and how much something costs? What is open and how late? The teacher will ask students to brainstorm what information they need to know if they want to go to a movie (price, times, location of theater, etc.) or a concert. Students will also brainstorm what information they need if they want to go to dinner at a restaurant they have never been to (e.g., location, prices, what type of food they serve, what the hours are). The format of this discussion will be teacher guided.

2. Online web exploration activity.   See student activity sheet below.

3. Post-reading (homework).   After the students have gathered all their information, they will make a "looking for a friend/boyfriend/ girlfriend" classified ad (in French) on a piece of notebook-sized construction paper. In their ad they will describe who they are looking for and the activities they have planned (which are based on their findings from the web activity).

Here is an example of what the ad should look like:

> I am looking for a friend who likes horror films and Thai food. I pro- pose an evening at Pad Thai restaurant, followed by the movies. We will see the film *Dames de Service*, a new horror film by Johnney Holliday, with Nicolas Sarkozy and Ségolène Royal. The movie will be in French with no subtitles. We will meet at Pad Thai, located at 36 rue roger gobbé (metro: Convention) at 20h and see the movie, located at 14 rue eugène sue (metro: Barbès) at 21h45.

The student activity sheet and the ad are to be turned into the instructor.

4. Post-reading (in-class follow-up task). For the follow-up task, five students' ads are posted in the classroom. Students walk around and read all five ads. Each student chooses an ad that has most in common with his or her own plan and joins a new group. The students whose ads are posted have to join a new group. The teacher follows up on some students' reasons for joining a particular group.

Student activity sheet

Go to the following website and answer the questions: Paris soirée

Part 1

First decide where you want to eat. Click on the word "Guide," then on "Restaurants." Scroll down to where it says "Chercher Un Restaurant," and enter the criteria for what you are looking for. Try to be as specific as possible; that is, list the kind of food you would prefer to eat (Thai, Mexican, French, African, etc.) and what your price range is.
　Answer the following questions:

1. What is the restaurant name, address, and phone number?
2. What kinds of food do they serve?
3. What are the hours and days of operation?
4. What is the price rage? Remember that you only have 200 euros for two people, and you need to keep some of it for your after-dinner entertainment.
5. How do you get there? At what metro stop do you get off?
6. What languages does the staff speak?
7. Do they have a *fermeture annuelle*? If so, when does it take place?

Part 2

Click on "cinéma," and decide if you want to see a new release, "les sorties," or a film that has been out for a few weeks but is recommended by the website, "vos coups de coeur."
　Scan the list of films and pick one that looks interesting to you. Click on the title to get more information about the film.
　Answer the following questions about the film you chose:

1. What is the title, what country does it come from, and what year was it released?
2. What kind of film is it? Who directed the film? Who are the stars of the film (list one or two)?
3. Give a brief summary of what the film is about (2 or 3 sentences) in English using your own words. (Please, do not translate the French description literally.)

4. Click on "séances." Pick any movie theater and write down the name, address, and what time you want to see the movie (list a couple of times in case you miss the first one).

5. Will you be seeing the movie in "version originale" or in "version française"?

Part 3

After you have answered each question, upload your information into the MOODLE environment.

Part 4

Click on "homework" to find out what you have due for tomorrow.

Illustration 2

Comparando periódicos [Comparing newspapers]

(Source: Tillie Scruton, TEP 588/589, University of Washington, 2007. modified by Klaus Brandl.)

Level: Intermediate (e.g., third or fourth year high school; end of first year in a college environment)

Lesson Description

This lesson is about comparing U.S. and Spanish-speaking newspapers online.

NOTE:

(Although there are Spanish-speaking U.S. papers, the term Spanish-speaking is used here to denote a paper in Spanish from a Spanish-dominant country, for ease of expression.)

Students look at the international sections of specific papers that they choose (for example, the "world news" sections of both the *New York Times* and Cuba's *Granma*) and compare and contrast two articles on the same topic, one from each newspaper. Students are not required to read the whole article, just the first two or three paragraphs (in some newspapers, the whole article is not available for free online). Scaffolding questions are provided so that students can go about this project without feeling overwhelmed.

Pedagogical Procedures

When students return to the classroom, they get together with the other people in the class, who read articles from the same country. As a group, they look for similarities and differences between the two newspapers they looked at. What is the focus of the world news in each paper? Are newspapers neutral or biased in their attitude toward other countries, for example, toward the United States? Each group reports to the class in Spanish, describing what they have discovered. As a large group, the class participates in a teacher-directed discussion (in Spanish) about bias and perspective in the news. What is "objective" reporting (*reportaje imparcial*)? Does such a thing really exist?

The exploration of different international newspapers lays the groundwork for students to embark on further group projects. Each group selects a current event or topic, such as the construction of the border fence, relevant to the Spanish-speaking world. The teacher provides a list of possible topics. The students also have the option to select their own. Each member of the group chooses and reads a different article in Spanish about this event or topic. The group as a whole must have articles from at least two Latin American countries. They may also use U.S. articles as sources, but they must cite them, and each individual is responsible for at least one article in Spanish. Each individual writes a short summary (in Spanish) of their article, which they turn in to the instructor. As a group, they do a presentation in Spanish about the current event or topic. They may use their computers for this (e.g., PowerPoint), or they can make a poster. They present at least two perspectives on the event—for example, if they choose the border fence, they must come up with pros and cons. They are encouraged to describe the opinions or perspectives of the authors of their articles as part of their presentation.

Students' learning tasks

First: Print this out.

Second: CHOOSE ONE U.S. PAPER. Go to the website of a newspaper in the United States and view the international section (see below for links to the *New York Times* and *Seattle Times*).

Third: Choose one Spanish newspaper only. Go to a Spanish-only newspaper online (see below for links to Spanish-only newspapers from various countries). If the paper has a particular section for world news, find it and go to it (look for "internacional" or "mundo").

Fourth: COMPLETE THE WORKSHEET BELOW. Compare and contrast what is in your two papers, answering the questions found after the links below. Write down all your answers on this printout and bring it to class; you will need your information for class activities.

The following links are to help you—if you know of another U.S. paper you would prefer to use, that's fine. If you want to choose another Spanish-speaking newspaper, use the link below to start surfing for one.

Periódicos estadounidenses:

New York Times, Seattle Times

Periódicos latinoamericanos/españoles:

En Cuba:	*Granma*
En Venezuela:	*El Nacional, El Universal*
En España:	*El Mundo, ABC*
En Mexico:	*La Jornada, El Informador*

OPCIONAL: Si quieres leer otro periódico hispanohablante, busca aquí: More Links.
[Optional: If you want to read another Spanish newspaper, look here: More Links.]

Student worksheet

Nombre:

_____

Fecha:

_____

Responde a las siguientes preguntas:
¿Cuál periódico estadounidense escogiste?

_____

¿Cuál periódico hispanohablante escogiste?

_____

¿De qué tratan las primeras 5 titulares (headlines) del periódico estadounidense?

_____

_____

_____

_____

¿De que trata las primeras 5 titulares del periódico hispanohablante?

_____

_____

Escoje dos artículos que hablan del mismo tema—uno del periódico estadounidense y otro del periódico hispanohablante.
El titular del artículo estadounidense es:

_____

El titular del artículo hispanohablante es:

_____

Haga una lista de las similaridades y diferencias entre los periódicos (por ejemplo, información que un periódico reporta que el otro periódico no reporta)

_____

_____

_____

Answer the following questions:

Which U.S. paper did you choose?

Which Spanish-speaking paper did you choose?

What is the primary focus of the headlines in the U.S. papers? (Mention at least five topics)

What is the primary focus of the headlines in the Spanish-speaking papers? (Mention at least five topics.)

Choose two articles that deal with the same topic—one from the United States and the other from the Spanish-speaking newspaper.

The title of the Spanish article is:

_____

The title of the English article is:

_____

List similarities and differences (e.g., information or facts that one newspaper mentions, but not the other).

_____

Endnote

1 The examples of organizational patterns included here are typically found in English texts. While many of these patterns are similar to discourse structures in other languages, teachers need to be aware of differences when using the suggested ways of organizing as graphic organizers or assimilators.

2 The topic of this text is "tying your shoelaces."

Assessment and Language Learning

Assessment is not about evaluation. It is about finding out what students know or can do.

REFLECTION

Describe your testing experience as learner. What was this experience like for you? Next, read over the different test types and assessments (see Figure 10-2). Which of these have you experienced as a learner?

_____

_____

_____

Introduction

Over the last several decades, real-life and task-based language application has become the goal of many communicative-based language curricula. This change in language-teaching methodologies has also triggered the need to develop appropriate assessment types that measure how well students function and perform in a foreign language.

Developing and implementing assessment techniques (e.g., tests, interviews, portfolios, journals, and other measurements of actual performance) that fully capture how well students perform a task and/or demonstrate their knowledge in a foreign language is challenging. Doing so requires an understanding of basic principles of testing. The purpose of this chapter is to provide an overview of issues related to creating and implementing different types of assessment in foreign language (FL) teaching.

Why Are We Testing?

A *test* is defined as "any procedure for measuring ability, knowledge, or performance" (Richard, Platt, and Platt 1992, p. 377). In this sense, testing has become the most common form of assessing students. Typically

DEFINITIONS

assessment	measurement of a person's ability, that is, what the person knows or can do
test	the actual procedure for measuring ability, for example, the performance of a written or oral task; means of examination
evaluation	in general, the systematic gathering of information for purposes of decision making

testing is a way to determine what a learner knows or is able to do. In reality there are many compelling reasons for assessing and testing learners.

Different reasons for testing allow us to categorize tests as summative and formative. Shrum and Glisan (2000) describe summative and formative tests in the following way:

> Summative testing often occurs at the end of a course and is designed to determine what the learner can do with the language at that point. Opportunities for further input or performance after the test is administered usually occur in the next language learning experience or course. The most common summative test is a final exam. Formative tests are designed to help form or shape the learners' ongoing understanding or skills while the teacher and learners still have opportunities to interact for the purposes of repair and improvement within a given course or setting. [...] Examples include quizzes (five to fifteen minutes, class interaction activities such as paired interviews, and chapter or unit tests (p. 292).

ANALYSIS AND DISCUSSION

Brainstorm and record the main reasons why you (would) test in the language classroom. Besides those mentioned above, can you think of any others? Are there any reasons that you would not want to test?

_____

_____

Compare your reasons for testing with those in Appendix 10.1. Which of them do you agree or disagree with?

_____

_____

What is a good test?

Educators in language-teaching pedagogy have repeatedly emphasized the need for a more direct connection between teaching and testing. For example, Shrum and Glisan (2000) suggest that the same kinds of activities designed for classroom interactions can serve as valid testing formats, with instruction and evaluation more closely integrated. Terry argues, "Any material or technique that is effective for teaching a foreign language can also be used for testing" (1998, p. 277). And along the same lines, Oller points out, "Perhaps the essential insight of a quarter of a century of language testing (both research and practice) is that good teaching and testing are, or ought to be, nearly indistinguishable" (1991, p. 38).

Over the years, some principles and characteristics have emerged that foreign language teachers have found useful in the development of classroom assessments. The two most fundamental principles as pointed out by Shrum and Glisan (2000, p. 292) are

1. Test what was taught.
2. Test it in a manner that reflects the way it was taught.

Another list, provided by Brown and Hudson (1998, p. 654), that should appeal to most teachers and testers suggests the following characteristics:

- require students to perform, create, produce, or do something
- use real-world contexts or simulations
- allow students to be assessed on what they normally do in class every day
- use tasks that present meaningful instructional activities
- focus on processes as well as products
- tap into higher-level thinking and problem-solving skills
- provide information about both the strength and weaknesses of students
- are multiculturally sensitive when properly administered
- ensure that people, not machines, do the scoring using human judgment
- encourage open disclosure of standards and rating criteria
- call upon teachers to perform new instructional and assessment roles

ANALYSIS AND DISCUSSION

Which of the principles and guidelines, as suggested by Shrum and Glisan and Brown and Hudson, that constitute a good test are most essential in creating a valid assessment tool?

Validity and reliability issues

The most common reason for testing is to find out what students know or have learned. To find out such information, ideally speaking, the results of an assessment tool ought to precisely and consistently reflect the student's competence, performance skills, and content knowledge. In light of such criteria, the quality of an assessment tool such as a test is closely linked to how valid and reliable it as a testing instrument. What do these psychometric concepts of testing mean, and why are they important?

		very little <—> very much
1.	The means of evaluation don't allow students to demonstrate what they really know or can do.	1 2 3 4 5 6 7
2.	Being able to develop fair tests.	1 2 3 4 5 6 7
3.	Students' results on their tests do not reflect what they really know and can do with the language.	1 2 3 4 5 6 7
4.	Being objective and fair.	1 2 3 4 5 6 7
5.	Being too harsh as a grader.	1 2 3 4 5 6 7
6.	My colleagues or fellow teachers are too lenient in their evaluations and therefore their students get better grades than mine.	1 2 3 4 5 6 7
7.	Being too lenient as a grader.	1 2 3 4 5 6 7
8.	Students challenge me on my grading.	1 2 3 4 5 6 7
9.	My colleagues or fellow teachers allow their students more time on their tests than I do.	1 2 3 4 5 6 7

FIGURE 10-1 Survey: My concerns as an evaluator

ANALYSIS AND DISCUSSION

The roles of a teacher include those of an evaluator and test writer. Which of the issues in the following questionnaire is of concern to you? Fill out the survey in Figure 10-1, rating each item from 1 (very little) to 7 (very much).

Defining validity. Validity is defined as the extent to which information you collect actually reflects the characteristic or attitude you want to know about (Genessee and Upshur 1996, p. 62). In other words, an assessment instrument such as a test is valid only if it tests exactly what it means to test. One might also ask these questions: "What skills or content are actually tested?" or "What skills do students actually demonstrate by performing testing tasks?" If these skills match the test designer's original intent, it can be concluded that the test is valid.

Although the concept of validity seems to be straightforward, designing a valid test is not without its challenges. Let us look at a few illustrations.

ILLUSTRATION 1

Have you ever taken a reading test that allowed you to answer compre-hension questions by copying the answers verbatim from the text? The test writer may have intended to test your comprehension of the text, but since you could copy the answer right from the text, you did not have to demonstrate comprehension. In this case, there was no evidence that you really understood the meaning of the text. It is fair to say the testing task did not test what it intended to do and thus was invalid.

Many traditional tests include dictations as a testing task. The original intent is to test a learner's listening comprehension skills. In some lan-guages, such as French, some comprehension may be required to write down dictated texts. But in many other languages, particularly those that are phonetic, it is often possible to spell out a word without understand-ing the meaning of what is spelled. Thus, the claim of dictation as a valid test of listening comprehension has only limited merit. At best, we could say that a dictation as a testing task tests spelling, unless it is also fol-lowed up with some kind of comprehension task.

ILLUSTRATION 2

Let us look at another example of a standardized test such as a Test of English as a Foreign Language (TOEFL) or Graduate Record Examination (GRE), which international students are often required to take as part of the admissions process to college or graduate school. The purpose of such standardized tests is often to find out about students' language pro-ficiency and communicative skills, that is, to see how well they can func-tion within a target language (TL) environment. However, for logistic and administrative reasons, most standardized tests are normally comprised of multiple-choice items and limit themselves to testing students' gram-mar and vocabulary and occasionally their listening and reading skills. While the results of such tests yield little information about a student's writing or speaking skills, their validity as proficiency tests can be described as only limited.

Defining reliability. Another important criterion of a test as a measure-ment, which is accurate and stable, is to be reliable. **Reliability** is defined as the "degree to which a test gives consistent results. A test is said to be reliable if it gives the same results when it is given on different occasions, or when it is used by different people" (Richard, Platt, and Platt 1992, p. 314). Needless to say, the criterion of reliability is of value only if a test is also valid.

ILLUSTRATION 3

When students miss a test, teachers face the additional task of providing a makeup test. In such cases, the original test and the makeup test can be considered reliable, if the results of the makeup tests yielded the same scores as if the student had taken the original test.

ILLUSTRATION 4

Here is another example. Let us assume that you and your colleague have decided to collaborate on a test. That is, you will design a test together and then administer and grade the same test. If you were to switch classes, and your colleague administered the test for your class under the very same conditions and graded the test applying the very same grading standards, then the results of the test scores should be exactly the same as if you had administered and graded the test yourself.

ANALYSIS AND DISCUSSION

Which of the issues in the survey (see Figure 10-1) may affect the validity of a test or the reliability of test scores?

As indicated in Illustrations 3 and 4, many factors influence the reliability of the outcome of a test. Some have to do with test-taking procedures—for example, a student is given more time in a makeup test than the students received in the original test, or the test proctor clarifies or provides additional instruction. Other factors involve grading procedures. When we grade tests, we need to apply the same standards in the same objective manner for all students. This criterion is often referred to as **rater reliability** or **inter-rater reliability,** if there is more than one grader involved.

Overview of Tests and Assessment Types

In the past two decades, FL educators have made great strides in the development and use of effective, engaging, and entertaining activities to enhance the teaching and learning process in second language acquisition (SLA). These changes in language teaching have been accompanied by the pleas of educators who are emphasizing the need for developing evaluation activities and materials that allow us to test the gains achieved by students in these instructional environments.

In the literature on testing, numerous formats have emerged (Figure 10-2). These include self-assessments, portfolio assessments, peer assessments, different forms of oral assessment, and the traditional paper-and-pencil formats. The following section presents an overview of different tests and assessment types. The overview also discusses how applicable these test types are to testing learners' ability to use communicative language.

Achievement tests

Achievement tests are used to measure how much learning has taken place in a prescribed content domain. Such tests are generally based on explicitly stated objectives and goals of an instructional program (Henning 1987). In foreign language education, achievement tests are

Test Type	Assessment Procedure	Decision	Audience	Example
Standardized test: The learner's performance is measured against that of others in a large population, norm-referenced.	Tally of number correct less number wrong is sometimes corrected by a formula to account for guessing: maximum score for SAT, for example, is 800.	Should the learner be promoted to the next grade? Should the learner be admitted to "X" college? Compared to others who took this test, where is this learner?	Governmental funding agency, scholarship-granting organizations, colleges and universities	Iowa Test of Basic Skills, Literacy Passport tests, Advanced Placement Exams, SAT, TOEFL, GRE
Proficiency exams: The learner's performance is measured against a criterion, the educated native speaker.	Descriptive terms delineate progress along a scale toward the same level as that of the criterion speaker (e.g., Intermediate–Mid).	Where is the learner at this time in the progression toward becoming like the educated native speaker?	Employers, schools, colleges and universities, learner	Interagency Language Roundtable (ILR) Oral Proficiency Interview, ACTFL Oral Proficiency Interview
Commercially prepared achievement tests: The learner's mastery of an instructed body of knowledge is measured.	Score reflects weighted values for certain topics studied, usually 1–100 points.	How much has the student learned about "X" material presented from "Y" set of instructional materials?	Teacher, learner, employers, school and governmental administrators	Publisher's test for Chapters 6 and 7; SAT
Teacher-made classroom tests, quizzes: Learner's performance on instructed body of knowledge is measured, usually an assessment of oral and written classroom skills; may be prochieve-ment and/or performance-based and/or interactive.	Score reflects weighted values, often percentage of number correct; sometimes converted to letter grades; simple descriptions of perform-ance; collection and description of artifacts; narration of progress by learner.	Does the learner know what was taught? Can s/he perform the tasks that were prac-ticed in class? How should the teacher design instruction based on the results?	Teacher, learner, parents, school personnel	Mrs. Chin's ESL midterm exam; Mr. Frey's essay test on "La joya del Inca"; Ms. Broderick's vocabulary quiz; oral plays and interviews
Authentic assessment: Learner performs real-world tasks with actual audience.	Success is determined by the response of the real-world audience.	Can the learner address challenge faced by indi-viduals in real-world situations? Can s/he integrate knowledge and skills to solve complex problems and situations?	Consumer, peer, learner, teacher	Multifaceted situations; problems; projects that require integration of knowledge, content, skills

FIGURE 10-2 Range of Test Types
(Source: Shrum and Glisan (2000), p. 295.)

usually administered at set junctures in the course of study (e.g., after each chapter and/or unit and/or course), and the test items are taken from the content of the instruction (Harper, Lively, and Williams 1998). For example, an achievement test might be a vocabulary quiz administered after an instructor's lesson on vocabulary, or a listening comprehension test could be based on a particular set of dialogues in a textbook. Although an achievement test measures a learner's instructed body of knowledge and the term itself is neutral to any philosophical approach to teaching, achievement tests have become associated with traditional and commonly used paper-and-pencil testing formats such as multiple choice, fill-in-the-blank, matching, and so on.

Proficiency tests

A **proficiency test** measures how much of a language someone has learned, or, in other words, how well that individual can perform and function in a target language. The criterion against which the learner is measured is an educated native speaker. "Proficiency tests are not linked to a particular course of instruction, but measure the learner's general ability in language mastery" (Richard, Platt, and Platt 1992, p. 292); neither is the content linked to any particular content area. The content of proficiency exams is not predetermined and may refer to a broad range of contexts. Sample questions and activities may entail narrative tasks referring to present or past events, persuasions, talking about hypothetical events, arguing, persuasions, descriptions, and others. The results of proficiency exams are usually reported in descriptive terms delineating the testee's progress along a fairly broad scale; see the American Council on the Teaching of Foreign Languages (ACTFL)[2] guidelines for an example. Foreign language educators realize that a proficiency exam is not generally applicable to classes of novice and intermediate speakers of a language, and that it is not a reasonable test for regular and frequent administration to large numbers of students at any level. The most commonly known proficiency exams are the Oral Proficiency Test, made available by ACTFL, or the FSI Oral Interview developed by the Defense Language Institute (DLI).

Prochievement format

A **prochievement test** is a blending of achievement and proficiency testing (Harper et al. 1998). It incorporates specific lexical and structural items from the objectives of the teaching/learning syllabus so that students can demonstrate their control of these items and their achievement of those objectives. Testing tasks of a prochievement test follow the same guidelines and principles of communicative- or proficiency-based learning tasks. These testing tasks are meaningful, contextualized, and task based, allowing the learners to express their own meanings and demonstrate skills along the proficiency-based continuum. Unlike traditional testing tasks, which focus on the grammar, the communicative task itself becomes the organizational principle for a testing item, whose achievement allows the learner to demonstrate a command of grammatical skills.

ILLUSTRATION 5

A prochievement test item for grammar/reading

This recipe is not very well written: too many words are repeated. Can you correct it using the direct object pronouns *lo, la, los,* and *las*?

Ajiaco cubano

Ingredientes (para 6 pesonas)

Tasajo (cecina):	150 gr	Carne de cerdo:	145 gr
Tocino:	88 gr	Plátano pintón:	200 gr
Malanga:	200 gr	Maíz tierno:	200 gr
Calabaza:	200 gr	Boniato:	200 gr
Salsa criolla:	75 gr	Sal:	40 gr
Aceite vegetal:	60 ml	Agua (aprox.):	2.3 l

Preparación:
Se remoja el tasajo durante 12 horas. Luego hay que cocinar (1) el tasjo en agua, durante 30 minutes; después se la añade la carne de cerdo. Después hay que sacar las carnes, limpiar (2) las carnes y cortar (3) las carnes en padazos. Pones el caldo al fuego e incorporas en primer lugar el maíz. Cocinas (4) el maíz unos 45 minutos y luego introduces las viandas cortadas en pedazos. Cortas el tocino en cubos pequeños, fríes ligeramente (5) el tocino en aceite, mezclas (6) el tocino con la Salsa Criolla y añadas todo al ajiaco. Finalmente, se cocina todo 10 minutos más.

Cuban Ajiaco

Ingredients (for 6 people)

dried meat:	150 gr	pork:	145 gr
bacon:	88 gr	half ripe plantain:	200 gr
taro:	200 gr	fresh corn:	200 gr
squash:	200 gr	Boniato:	200 gr
salsa criolla:	75 gr	salt:	40 gr
vegetable oil:	60 ml	water (approx.)	2.3 l

Preparation:
Soak the Tasajo (dried beef) for 12 hours. Then cook (1) the Tasajo in water for 30 min. Next, add the pork. Then you must remove the meat, clean (2) the meat and cut the meat (3) into pieces. You heat the broth and add the corn first. You cook (4) the corn for about 45 min and then add the vegetable pieces. You cut the bacon in small cubes, lightly fry (5) the bacon in oil, and mix (6) the bacon with the salsa criolla (onion, tomato, pepper, garlic, salt, and oil) and add all the ajiaco. Finally, cool it for 10 more minutes.

(Source: De la Fuente (2007), p. 86.)

Types of paper-and-pencil assessments

The most common types of paper-and-pencil assessment tests can be categorized as selected response, which includes true-false, matching, and multiple-choice assessments; and constructed-response, including fill-in, short-answer, and performance assessments (Brown and Hudson 1998).

Selected-response assessments. Selected-response assessments present students with language material and require them to choose the correct answer from among a limited set of options. In selected-response assessments, students typically do not create any language; thus, these assessments are most appropriate for measuring receptive skills like listening and reading. In general, selected-response assessments are relatively quick to administer. In addition, scoring them is relatively fast, easy, and objective. However, these assessments have two disadvantages: (1) They are relatively difficult for the test writer to construct, and (2) they do not require students to use productive language. Three types of selected-response assessments are commonly used: true-false, matching, and multiple-choice.

True-false assessments. This form of assessment requires the learners to make a choice between two alternatives—for example, by answering true or false in response to a statement. The most common use of true-false assessments is to test comprehension of written or aural language. Their primary strengths are that they are fairly easy to construct, grade, and administer. For these reasons, true-false assessment has been very popular with teachers.

One problem with true-false assessments is that they test a learner's skills or knowledge in a simply black-and-white manner. For this reason, they need to be constructed with caution. As Brown and Hudson (1998) warn us, "to produce items that discriminate well, test writers may be tempted to write items that are tricky, that is, that turn on the meaning of a single word or phrase or that depend on some ambiguity" (p. 658). Another problem with true-false assessments is the high guessing factor. Students have a 50 percent chance of getting the answer right.

Matching assessments. In a matching task, students compare items in one list with the ones in the other list. The items that the test takers match may include words, phrases, or audiovisual materials.

One strength of this assessment type is that it has a low guessing factor, particularly if the two lists include an uneven number of items. Like true-false assessments, matching assessments are also fairly easy to construct, grade, and administer. One disadvantage is that matching is "generally restricted to measuring students' abilities to associate one set of facts with another, which in language testing usually means measuring passive vocabulary knowledge (i.e., the students' ability to match definitions to vocabulary items)" (Brown and Hudson 1998, p. 659).

Multiple-choice assessments.   Multiple-choice assessments require learners to select an answer from a list of given choices. This form of assessment is the most widely used format in standardized tests. For example, it is used to test grammar, reading, listening, and vocabulary skills. Like matching, it has a relatively low guessing factor depending on the number of options, and it is easy to administer. Furthermore, scoring can be done fast and is perfectly reliable. Another advantage is that a student only has to mark short responses on the paper, so the number of testing items that can be administered in a given period of time is normally higher than with other forms of assessments.

Using the multiple-choice format, however, also has many disadvantages and can be problematic. First, it has been criticized, as have matching and true-false formats, because real-life performance is not multiple choice. These formats, particularly when used to test someone's ability to use grammar, may be poor indicators. A student who is able to identify a correct response on paper may not be able produce the correct form when speaking or writing in real-life situations. Second, successful multiple-choice items are quite difficult to write. For example, a four-option multiple-choice item includes one option that has the correct answer and three options that are wrong. Among the three wrong answers, however, two items need to function as effective distractors. What makes an effective distractor? They are not easy to determine, and doing so normally requires pretesting and statistical analysis. Given the many challenges involved in constructing effective multiple-choice assessments for language testing, they should be implemented sparingly.

Constructed-response assessments.   Constructed-response assessments require students to produce language by writing, speaking, or doing something else. Hence, these assessments are probably most appropriate for measuring the productive skills of speaking and writing. Constructed-response assessments can also be useful for observing interactions of receptive and productive skills. Examples include the interaction of listening and speaking in an oral interview procedure or the interaction of reading and writing during a performance assessment in which students read two academic articles and write an essay comparing and contrasting them.

There are certain trade-offs in deciding whether to use selected-response or constructed-response assessments. For example, selected-response items allow for some guessing, but they are relatively objective;

on the other hand, constructed-response items eliminate some of the guessing factor but create problems of subjectivity—especially when human judgments are involved in deciding what is a correct answer for a blank or short answer, or when raters score the language samples.

Three types of constructed-response assessments are commonly used in language testing: fill-in, short-answer, and performance assessments.

Fill-in assessment.   A fill-in is a form of assessment in which parts of the text are removed from the text and replaced with a blank. To answer, the learners are to fill in the blanks. In language testing, fill-ins are commonly used to test reading, vocabulary including spelling, and grammatical skills. They normally require the learner to produce language. Students have to fill in blanks that can range from one to multiple words or even short phrases. These tests can also be designed so that learners select their answers from a list of predetermined choices (see matching and multiple-choice assessment types). The strengths of fill-ins are that they are easy to create, administer, and grade. Furthermore, they allow a teacher to focus on isolated skills, requiring the learners to demonstrate either receptive skills or a combination of receptive and productive skills. A disadvantage of fill-ins is that they require only very short answers. They also need to be carefully constructed. A common pitfall of fill-in tests is that there may be more than one correct answer. Unless this situation is intended and multiple answers are to be allowed for, it causes problems with the validity of the test. Test designers also often provide information next to the blank (e.g., words in L1 or verbs in their infinitive form). This practice defeats the purpose of a fill-in, because it often does not require the learner to process the meaning of a text and provide the answer based on contextual clues. Appendix 10.2 provides an overview of fill-in variations.

Short-answer assessment.   Among the constructed-response types, short-answer assessments are one of the most common forms. As Brown and Hudson (1998) put it, short answers "require the students to scrutinize a question or statement and respond with one or more phrases or sentences" (p. 661). Variations of such types include short-answer questions, sentence completions, filling in missing lines in dialogues, and picture descriptions or labeling. Similar to fill-ins, the strengths of short-answer assessments are that they are easy to construct and administer. The disadvantages are that they are more difficult to grade. Normally, short-answer assessments allow for multiple correct answers. This makes the evaluation subjective and time-consuming.

Performance-based assessments

Performance-based formats require learners to demonstrate their level of competence, i.e. what they know and are able to do. Terms that are often used to refer to these skills are *knowledge* and *application*. By *knowledge* is meant knowledge of isolated skills, such as knowing the meaning of words, grammatical skills, or factual cultural knowledge. *Application* of knowledge refers to what students know and are able to do with the knowledge. This ability involves functional skills that are usually assessed by performing some kind of task, hence the term *performance-based assessment*. In this sense, all performance assessments are of an integrative/global nature, usually requiring the use of the productive skills such as speaking or writing or combining skills. Unlike traditional testing tasks, however, they are embedded in context and "require students to accomplish approximations of real-life, authentic tasks" (Brown and Hudson 1998, p. 662).

Boyles (2000) highlights characteristics of performance-based assessments in the following way:

- simulates real-life language use
- offers open-ended tasks
- allows for creative and divergent responses
- probes for "depth" versus "breadth"
- often assesses strategies for constructing a response
- requires students to "put it all together" rather than to recall small pieces of knowledge
- promotes recursive rather than linear learning
- evaluates performance based on well-defined criteria

The main advantage of performance-based assessments is that they assess a student's ability to use real language while performing tasks that resemble actual real-world situations (insofar as real communication can actually be elicited in a testing situation). Brown and Hudson (1998) also point out that performance-based assessments "provide more valid [...] predictions of students' future performance in real-life language situations" (p. 662).

The following illustrations demonstrate several different performance-based testing tasks.

ILLUSTRATION 6
Arranging a date

Compose a dialogue between Maria and Carmina based on the following scenario.

It is Monday, the third of the month, and Maria wants to go out sometime this week. She calls Carmina on the phone and invites her to one of the places as displayed in the ads. Carmina does not like what Maria suggests. After a brief discussion about the various options they have, the two are able to agree on a place, a time, and a day.

(Source: De la Fuente et al. (2007), p. 315.)

ILLUSTRATION 7
Writing a postcard

You are on vacation in _____ and want to send greetings to your
family back home. Write a postcard with at least the following information:

> the date and your location
> how you are doing
> what you have done on your vacation
> the things you have enjoyed the most

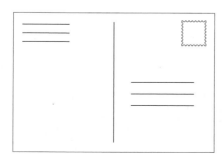

ILLUSTRATION 8

Matching Christina with a boyfriend

Christina is looking for a boyfriend. She wrote to the radio program, "Cita a ciegas," and sent them some information about herself. Read what she wrote and then write down the information about the two guys who called the program (the listening script of the two guys is not included here). Which one of them would be the best match for Christina?

CHRISTINA VILLASANTA

PROFESIÓN: Profesora de historia en un colegio.

GUSTOS: Le encanta la cocina italiana. Le divierte ir a discotecas de vez en cuando, pero la música hip hop le pone muy nerviosa. No soporta a los hombres que beben o fuman, ni a los maniáticos, y le dan miedo las relaciones largas. Le interesa la literatura.

COSTUMBRES: Pasa mucho tiempo en casa con sus perros y sale sobre todo los fines de semana.

AFICIONES: Tiene dos perros. Pasa la vacaciones en su apartamento de la playa. Va al gimnasio de vez en cuando.

MANÍAS: Se muerde las unas y nunca se pone falda.

JULIO

PROFESIÓN: _____

GUSTOS: _____

AFICIONES: _____

MANÍAS: _____

MARCOS

PROFESIÓN: _____

GUSTOS: _____

AFICIONES: _____

MANÍAS: _____

Christina Villasanta

Profession: Professor of history in a college

Likes: She loves Italian food. She enjoys going to the disco from time to time, but hip-hop makes her very nervous. She can neither stand men who drink or smoke, nor eccentric types, and long relationships scare her. She is interested in literature.

Habits: She spends a great deal of time at home with her dogs and goes out especially on weekends.

Hobbies: She has two dogs. She spends her vacations in her beach apartment. She goes to the gym from time to time.

Bad habits: She bites her fingernails and never puts on a skirt.

(Source: De La Fuente et. al. (2007b), p. 153.)

ILLUSTRATION 9

Taking a message

Listen to this answering machine message and jot down the important information on a "While You Were Out" form.

```
┌──────────────────────────────────────────┐
│          WHILE YOU WERE OUT…              │
│                                           │
│  To: _____      │
│                                           │
│  Taken by: _____      │
│                                           │
│  Date: _____      │
│                                           │
│  _____ called   │
│                                           │
│  at _____ a.m./p m.             │
│                                           │
│  _____ ❏ will call back                 │
│                                           │
│  _____ ❏ wants you to return the call   │
│                                           │
│  Phone: (___) _____ - _____      │
└──────────────────────────────────────────┘
```

SCRIPT (recorded on tape or read by teacher):
Hello, Carmina. This is Klaus, and it's about 4 o'clock on Wednesday afternoon. I was wondering if we were still on for the movie this weekend. I'll be out this evening, but you can reach me at home in the morning at 555-3853.

ILLUSTRATION 10

Giving advice on bad habits

Listen to the following interviews conducted by Radio Centre and complete the form for each person.

SCRIPT (Translation)

Interviewer:	Hello, how are you?
Interviewee:	I am fine. How are you?
Interviewer:	We are doing a brief survey. We want to find out about the French lifestyle. Do you think you live a healthy life?
Interviewee:	Yes and no?
Interviewer:	Why?
Interviewee:	Well, because I do some sports. For example, I play tennis on Thursdays. And I also run 25 to 30 min twice a week.
Interviewer:	What about your eating habits?
Interviewee:	I eat everything. Meat, vegetables, fried food … too much fried food.
Interviewer:	Do you smoke?
Interviewee:	No! I never smoke. But I like to eat sweets. Sweets are my passion.

Interviewer: Thank you very much. Good-bye!
Interviewere: Good-bye.

Il/Elle a une vie saine?   ☐ Oui   ☐ Non

Pourquoi? _____

_____

Un conseil: He/she should _____

_____

Does he/she have a healthy life?   ☐ Yes ☐ No
Why? _____
_____
Advice: He/she should
_____
_____

(Source: Flumian et al. (2007a), p. 37.)

Oral performance assessment

Oral performance assessments are nothing new and have been used in language testing for many years. As Norris et al. (1998) point out, "Virtually all language tests have some degree of performance included. It might be more appropriate to think of tests as more performance oriented or less performance oriented along a continuum from least direct and least real-world or authentic to most direct and most real-world or authentic" (p. 7). While communicative-based approaches are gradually emerging as the main-stream method of teaching, it is only fair to say that the emphasis on proficiency and real-world use of language necessitates the assessment of oral performance-based skills.

There are numerous ways to assess a student's oral performance of language skills. Some of these strategies include oral presentations or oral skits that students give or perform in class, pair or group activities, live phone or video conferencing, or even simulated formats in which learners record their answers while responding to questions that are presented via audio, video, or computer formats.

Another common technique is the oral prochievement test. The oral prochievement is a testing format that can be easily adapted to the different needs and purposes of language programs. Furthermore, it lends itself well to all levels of instruction. The next section focuses on how to plan and implement an oral prochievement test.

Oral prochievement test. As previously defined, "prochievement" is a blending of the traditional terms *proficiency* and *achievement*. This means the test aims at assessing the students' achievement of the skills that were taught during a period of time or an entire course. *Proficiency* implies that students are to demonstrate real language skills as they are applied in different situational contexts.

Oral prochievement tests can be designed in many different ways. They may consist of only one task type or a range of testing tasks such as interview questions, various kinds of role-plays, or student-prepared presentations. Depending on purpose and level, they can be structured to last 5–8 minutes (short versions) or 10–15 minutes (long versions). The following subsections present some sample testing tasks.

Interview questions. The most common oral prochievement testing technique constitutes interview questions. The advantage of interview questions is that they can be easily graded in order of increasing difficulty. For example, questions can be designed to elicit short or longer student responses, while targeting specific and isolated knowledge areas (e.g., time, dates, descriptive adjectives) and functional skills (e.g., narrating in the past, expressing likes or dislikes, an opinion, making comparisons, expressing a hypothetical opinion). In other words, an interviewer can ask questions of different types such as factual, descriptive, hypothetical, or opinion-based questions. Questions can also be easily followed up and varied, which has the further advantage of allowing for easy adaptation to a learner's skill level. In general, the question-answer technique lends itself well as a testing technique at all levels of instruction.

Here are some sample questions:

Where are you from?

What time did you get up this morning?

What time did you come to school today?

What do you like to do in your free time?

Tell me what you did last weekend?

What do you think of …?

Can you describe …?

Do you have a job? How long do you work? Can you describe what you do? Do you like it? Why? Why not?

Based on what we read about in class last week, what do you think of piercing or tattoos?

What would you do if you won the lottery?

Role-play variations. Performance-based assessments are typically based on tasks. A format that lends itself well for learners to demonstrate task performance is the role-play. In **role-playing**, the learner is situated within a specific linguistic and social context and asked to imagine and perform a particular role. The situations can range from simple to complex, allowing the tester to elicit a wide range of functional language skills. Such skills may include complaining, requesting information, ordering food, or dealing with complicated situations. Role-plays also integrate collaborative elements. They can be implemented so that one or several learners act out situations, or so that the teacher participates in a role-play with the learner. The latter option has the disadvantage that some teachers lose sight of their role as an evaluator. It also makes it more difficult for the teacher to keep track of the learner's performance. Role-play situations should always be designed to allow the testee to use language in an open-ended, creative, and ingenious way. Furthermore, they should be designed by choosing roles that are natural to the learner and that match roles the learner may have to act out in reality. For instance, it is more difficult for students to act out roles in which they have no experience, such as playing a doctor, a policeman, or even a salesperson, than it is for them to imagine the roles of a tourist or a client in a restaurant. It also should be kept in mind that individual differences (e.g., age, personality, cultural background) may influence a learner's ability to perform role-plays. Role-play implies pretending, which makes some students feel reluctant to participate. As Underhill (1987) reminds us, students are asked to be someone other than who they really are, and some people can take on somebody's role more easily than others.

Here are some role-play examples:

1. You are visiting with an exchange student and are talking about the American school system. Describe the different types of school, ages of the students, how many years they spend in each school, and the classes they take.

2. Describe your future career plans. What would you like to be one day? Provide some details of what _____ does.

3. Discuss your summer plans with the interviewer. What will you do? Where will you go? Also feel free to ask the interviewer about his or her plans.

4. You have caught the flu and feel pretty bad. Describe to the interviewer (the doctor or nurse) how you feel. Make sure to describe your symptoms in detail, what hurts, when your symptoms started, and so on.

5. You are going through a checkout line at a department store. The person in front of you, who does not speak English well, has a membership card that expired several months ago and needs to be renewed. Unfortunately, the customer does not understand the salesperson who is trying to explain the problem. Explain the problem to the customer.

Structure of an oral prochievement test. An oral prochievement test is not a random conversation between the test administrator and the testee. It follows a deliberate plan of testing tasks and has an underlying structure. Needless to say, the testing tasks need to be aligned with the curricular content, that is, the skill areas and communicative functions that have been taught.

Stages of an oral prochievement test include

1. *Warm-up or introduction.* The purpose of this phase is to put the test taker at ease. Easy and short testing tasks (e.g., some personal questions) make for a good introduction.

2. *Evaluating the learner performance.* The main phase consists of determining the learner's strength and weaknesses, that is, how well he or she can perform the targeted language tasks. Here is a possible sequence of testing tasks:

- (If applicable) discussion of topics that the learner has prepared
- Short interview questions or situations
- Performance tasks that require elaborate learner responses
- Role-play tasks
- Follow-up tasks if there are still questions about the test taker's performance level

3. *Wind-down and conclusion.* The last phase concludes the test. Since many testees are curious about the results of their performance at this stage, thanking the student or stating that you have enjoyed talking to the student are some possible ways of ending a test. Until the evaluator has come to a final decision about the student's performance, any kind of evaluative comments should be avoided.

Authentic assessments

Authentic assessments provide opportunities for students to develop language skills while participating in real-world tasks. These assessments call on students' capacities to interact socially and solve problems, and they are performance based. *Authentic assessment* is a term that is often used when the assessment immerses students in the real world. Because authentic assessments take place in real-world environments, they are of limited use in a classroom environment. Nevertheless, such tasks represent the ultimate form of assessment and serve as excellent models for performance assessments.

ILLUSTRATION 11

The following items borrowed from Norris et al. (1998) represent examples of authentic assessment tasks. They may require some modification when simulated and adopted for assessment purposes.

Ordering the main course

All of the dinners in this restaurant must be ordered "à la carte;" that is, you have to select the different components from the lists of available choices. Study the menu and the various selections that are available for the evening. Choose a main dish (meat or vegetarian), pasta, and a vegetable from the different options. When the waiter requests your order, tell him what you have decided (p. 154).

Fill in the application form

Choose a single application form that corresponds to a job for which you find yourself the most qualified (based on the job description attached to each of the available forms). Fill in the application form to the best of your ability, leaving blank any information that you do not have currently available (p. 174).

Choosing a hotel

Listen to the message that your travel companion has left for you on your answering machine. [Could easily substitute here: Refer to the e-mail message that your companion sent you and that you printed out.] Note any information regarding the selection of hotel accommodations in your vacation city. Now locate your city in the travel guidebook that is provided. Select the hotel that best suits the information provided by your travel companion (p. 210).

Student self-assessments

An alternative form of assessment is student self-assessment. This form of assessment requires students to rate their own performance, for example, their language use, their own learning behavior (i.e., effort and time), and their achievement of learning goals. Examples that lend themselves well to self-assessment are participation in the student-centered classroom, or project-based assignments such as presentations (see Appendix 10.12 for a sample self-evaluation form). Goals and evaluation criteria can be established either by the teacher or the students.

Self-assessments have several advantages. First, they empower students by directly involving them in the evaluation process. They support autonomous learner behavior and teach them self-assessment strategies. They also may have a self-motivating effect.

Self-assessments also have some disadvantages. First, students' self-estimates of their own learning behavior or performance vary tremendously. For example, Blanche (1988) and Yamashita (1996) have pointed out that high-ability students often underestimate their language ability. Many students are often more critical of their own learning performance than the teacher is. For such reasons, students need training and guidance in the rating of scoring grids.

While student self-assessments play only a minor role in a student's overall assessment, they can be beneficial. They may have the most impact in getting an accurate account of a learner's performance in areas such as learning behaviors, which are highly subjective and often difficult for the teacher to evaluate.

Skill assessment in the communicative- and task-based language classroom: meeting needs and challenges

Considering the communicative and task-based focus taken in this book, real-world tasks play a vital role in the design of different types of performance assessments. If the ultimate goal of task-based instruction is to achieve real-world communicative skills, it only follows that performance assessments should make up the major part of any language test.

Nevertheless, because it is common practice in most communicative language classrooms to focus on learning processes and learning outcomes (products) in learners' skill development, assessment tasks need to correspond with such methodological approaches as well.

The questions remaining are how to go about assessing skill-based knowledge, such as vocabulary and grammar and communicative ability, and how to devise a test that integrates and finds a balance between knowledge and application. Chapter 6 presented a framework developed by Littlewood (2004), who classifies learning activities along a continuum from pre-communicative to structured communication tasks. Such a model can also be used as the basis for developing a range of assessment tasks. Figure 10-3 demonstrates how different task types correspond to different assessment types.

Input Phase Pre-communicative language practice	Communicative language application assimilated to authentic task application teacher controlled <——> student controlled language use		
The purpose is to expose learners to model language in context, with attention to meaning. *Example:* display questions	The teacher predetermines and controls the language structures and contents. *Example:* information-gap activity (questions and answers are predetermined)	Students determine how to use pre-taught language structures in communicative contexts. The Use of language is open-ended, but somewhat predictable and controlled based on a limited task within a narrow context. *Example:* Students interview each other, determining questions and answers based on a teacher-determined and guided task.	Students perform real-life tasks using language in an open-ended, creative, communicative way. The teacher does not control or guide the students' language use. *Examples:* creative role-play; discussions; response to a voice message left on an answering machine.
Focus on process <————————————————————>product			
Assessment types			
process- and knowledge-based assessments *Examples:* fill-ins; matching, short-answer (display¹) questions	prochievement formats *Examples:* short context- and content-specific questions; picture descriptions	structured performance assessments *Examples:* structured oral interviews; writing assignments with stipulated instructions	simulated authentic assessments *Examples:* filling out forms; oral interviews; writing assignments

FIGURE 10-3 Matching Task Types with Assessment Types

The design of testing items should meet the same design criteria as communicative language-teaching tasks do. That is to say, it should follow the same guidelines and principles of communicative- or proficiency- based learning tasks. As such, communicative- and task-based assessment types distinguish themselves from traditional discrete or integrative/ global skills, which focus on isolated or a combination of linguistic skills. They should be meaningful and be embedded in context, while prochievement and performance assessments in particular should embed a communicative purpose that allows the testees to demonstrate real-life proficiency or aspects thereof.

Assessing communicative language use and designing such tasks along the continuum toward authentic communication are processes riddled with many challenges. One of the difficulties in task design is understanding the cognitive and linguistic complexity that is involved in performing a testing task. Communicative language teaching (CLT) tasks are integrative/global in nature and involve multiple linguistic and cognitive skills. Thus, any test designer needs to perform a clear analysis of each testing task and identify the kind and range of linguistic skills, including the embedded cognitive demand, and how the latter potentially impedes a student demonstrating his linguistic ability. Identifying the linguistic and cognitive demands of a testing task is important. Only by doing so can the test designer guarantee that the testing task engages the learner in demonstrating skills for which it was designed (see validity issue).

The cognitive complexity and the linguistic skills that are involved in performing a task are not always obvious, for which reason creating and choosing a task for testing purposes may not be necessarily a simple matter. For example, let us take a look at dictation as a form of testing. Traditionally, dictations have been used to test listening comprehension skills. Yet, a dictation tests aural recognition and spelling only. Some scholars would claim that if learners can recognize and spell an item correctly, they probably also know what it means; the assumption is that it is extremely difficult to perceive, let alone spell, words you do not know (Ur 1996). In many situations, however, students have been found to spell words correctly without understanding their meanings.

Another example demonstrating this issue is the commonly used fill-in-the-blank format. Fill-in-the blank testing items can be designed in different ways. Some require selecting a response from a list of alternatives; others provide no alternatives at all, and the response is restricted only by the nature of the context. A third alternative may additionally ask for the response to be morphologically adjusted (e.g., conjugating verbs, declining nouns, making adjective-noun agreements). Depending on which fill-in-the-blank format is chosen, the demands of a task may change, thereby asking the student to demonstrate different kinds of skills (e.g., reading, vocabulary, grammar, spelling).

Another example demonstrating the cognitive complexities is the use of authentic versus teacher edited maps for testing purposes. Due to the rich information learners have to process when reading a real map, being able to follow instructions based on an authentic map is normally cognitively more complex and thus more challenging than performing the same kind of task with a teacher-edited map. If a teacher's intention is to measure a student's linguistic ability, that is understanding directions that is describe the route on a map, then a teacher-edited map may be a better choice, as the complexity of a real map may impede with allowing the learner to demonstrate comprehension skills. This does not mean, that a real map should not be used for testing purposes. If a teacher decides to do so, he needs to do accommodate for this additional challenge in his testing procedures (see Chapter 6, Instructional Sequencing and Task Design).

Another challenge in assessing communicative language use has to do with feasibility and manageability issues. Any kind of assessment that aims at communicative- or performance-based ability is relatively difficult and time-consuming to produce and administer. Such assessment normally involves open-ended and creative student language use, so grading is time intensive. Unfortunately, the format of paper-and-pencil testing is limited to some assessment types and thus is appropriate for the testing of only some skills. By and large, however, this format does not lend itself well to performance-based assessments. This makes a wide range of assessments necessary. Needless to say, to elicit information about a student's oral communicative ability, ongoing in-class oral assessments or oral interviews are imperative. Alternative assessment methods, such as portfolio assessments, may also be useful in yielding reliable results for a student's performance level.

Guidelines for Developing Tests

The process of planning and implementing involves numerous decisions. These range from identifying the content to developing appropriate testing tasks. The process also requires the teacher to determine scoring and grading procedures and resolve test preparation issues. This section provides some guidelines for developing paper-and-pencil and oral tests and addresses these issues in more detail.

Planning and Implementing paper-and-pencil tests

Make an inventory of what and how you have taught. Begin by making an inventory of what you have taught. Identify the content areas and make an overview of all the skills areas.

- These should include the vocabulary, grammar, functional skills, and cultural content.
- Identify the range of communicative and performance tasks, for example, ways your learners interacted.
- Think of the context in which the language was used.

In essence, the inventory should provide you with a summary of what and how you have taught.

Determine and develop testing tasks

Start by deciding which skills you would like to emphasize, identifying the most important skills involved in what and how you have taught. Select or develop a variety of tasks that allow the students to demonstrate content and performance-based skills ranging from narrow to open-ended communicative contexts. When designing a testing task, do not limit yourself to traditional formats of paper-and-pencil tests that are often easy and fast to grade but often focus only on students' knowledge. Allow students to be creative with language. Testing tasks should comply with all of the CLT principles. That is to say, they should be meaningful and assess authentic and communicative language use. This further implies that the testing tasks are embedded in context as well.

The following questions may help with your design and choice of testing tasks:

- Which skill is demonstrated by performing a testing task: knowledge and/or application of language (performance-based/communicative language use)?
- Does my test integrate a range of testing tasks focusing on content-based skills (e.g., knowledge of vocabulary and grammar) and their application (e.g., through performance-based tasks)?
- Does my test focus on a variety of communicative skill areas (e.g., listening, reading, writing, cultural understanding)?
- Do the testing items resemble real-life tasks or ask the students to demonstrate authentic language use?
- Is each testing task contextualized?
- Does each testing task correspond to the level of proficiency of my students?

When you determine your skill areas and testing tasks, be aware of the backwash effect (or washback effect) they may have on your students. **Backwash effect** refers to the effect of a test on teaching. For instance, the more grammar skills a teacher emphasizes on a test, the more grammar-practicing tasks the students are likely to ask for in class, since these are the skills they are tested on. The effect of the backwash can also be used so it causes positive or a desired change.

Richards, Platt, and Platt (1992) provide the following example demonstrating the positive effects of backwash:

> In some countries, for example, national language examinations have a major impact on teaching and teachers often "teach to the test." In order to bring about changes in teaching, changes could be made in the tests. For example, if the education department in a country wanted schools to spend more time teaching listening skills, one way to bring this about would be to introduce a listening test into state examinations.

Check your test instruction

According to Genesee and Upshur (1996), the primary job of test instructions is to let students know what they are supposed to do. When checking test instructions, ask yourself, "Do students clearly understand what to do for each particular test item?" Keep in mind that the purpose of a test is to find out what students have learned, not how well they can understand test instructions or how well they can guess what they are supposed to do. Students should be informed clearly what to do for each kind of task included in a test, and they should get enough information about the test as a whole to decide how best to expend their efforts in the time available. "The instructions themselves should not be a test; in other words, instructions should be clear and meaningful to students" (Genesee and Upshur 1996, p. 201).

ANALYSIS AND DISCUSSION

Read the guidelines for test instructions in Figure 10-4. On a scale from 1 (not very) to 5 (very), rate the importance of each guideline. How important is it to adhere to each of these guidelines?

In some cases, test instructions may also give students additional important information. The strategies in Figure 10-4 provide guidance for the teacher when preparing test instructions.

	very important <—> not very important
1. Provide the test instructions in the students' native language	5 4 3 2 1
2. Provide information on what the assessor will look for when scoring (e.g., number of points per test item in a multiple choice test, or marks awarded on the basis of spelling, grammatical accuracy, coherence, ideas, etc. in a composition)	5 4 3 2 1
3. Provide a sample item and solution	5 4 3 2 1
4. Provide information on time available for each testing item	5 4 3 2 1
5. Provide information on how a test item is weighted (e.g., 2 pts for each item or 20 pts total)	5 4 3 2 1
6. Provide special information (e.g., how often a student will hear or see an CD or DVD, or how often the instructor will repeat a question, etc.)	5 4 3 2 1
7. Provide information on special conditions such as the use of dictionaries or any other sources	5 4 3 2 1

FIGURE 10-4 Guidelines for Test Instructions

Determine a grading system and clear scoring criteria

One of the teachers' most vital, and often least favorable, tasks involves evaluating and assessing their students' performances. While many students measure their success by the grade they receive, there is little doubt that teachers' evaluative decisions affect their students in many different ways. Thus, the measuring, scoring, and grading of student performance constitute pivotal aspects of testing and need to be taken very seriously.

When it comes to grading and scoring a test, there is no one best solution; nor is there one single way of going about it. Teachers vary in their approaches to teaching, and, hence, they also vary in what skills they emphasize. That is, traditional teachers tend to emphasize, and hence assess, the structural use of language; conversely, advocates of communicative-oriented teaching normally give priority to meaningful and communicative language use. They also agree that testing of students' performance-based skills should be the major focus of a test.

Teachers face important decisions concerning how to go about scoring, in particular. Considering the goal in CLT, which is for students to perform real language tasks and communicative acts, the questions that arise are: What constitutes the successful completion of a task? How are a student's grammar, spelling, or other errors to be assessed in case of successful task completion? Should a student receive credit for the partial completion of a task? How should the cognitive complexity of a task be taken into account? How are different subskills such as reading, writing, grammar and vocabulary skills to be weighed and scored? Or, in general, what standard to measure the student performance against? Unfortunately, there is no common yardstick in grading and scoring student performance in CLT. The decision about what constitutes successful completion of a task, and how to grade and score communicative language performance and individual skills is normally made by the test writer and evaluator.

Let us start with the question regarding the standards. There are two different strategies that can be used in determining a standard: norm referencing and criterion referencing. When norm-referencing, the teacher uses the norm of the class comparing a student's performance to other students to decide on a grade. The practice of norm referencing in evaluating a student's performance is very arbitrary and unreliable. At best, a student learns how well he did compared to others, but not how well he achieved the target. Many students do not consider this practice very fair. Norms are volatile, and, hence, so is a student's grade.

A second option is criterion-referencing. When criterion-referencing, a teacher establishes a set of criteria, that is, a set of learning targets, against which he measures the student's performance. Teachers determine these criteria based on their philosophy, experience, expectations and probably also norm-based students' behavior. Often, the criteria and standards are also dictated from above by government or the administration. In contrast to being compared to the norm, a criterion-based evaluation system provides students a concrete target. The students know what they are measured against and the teachers can hold them accountable for achieving the criteria. This makes criterion-referencing a fairer system than norm-referencing. However, a criterion-based system is not without its challenges either. Unfortunately, even if a teacher has clearly defined criteria in place, assessing a learner's task performance and skills in language learning is a highly subjective endeavor. Teachers face the decision on weighing subskills (e.g., grammatical accuracy, word choice, spelling) and the successful completion of a task or the quality of the achievement of a product (e.g., essay, email), which normally leaves room for interpretation. How can student performance be scored that makes it fair to the student and also feasible for the teacher?

When scoring communicative tasks, a teacher has the option of applying several approaches: holistic and analytic techniques, or a combination of both. In **holistic scoring,** a single score is assigned to a student's overall test performance. This is basically what teachers do when they assign a number or letter grade to student tests or assessment. Holistic scores represent teachers' overall impressions and judgments. As such, they can serve as general incentives for learning, and they can distinguish students based on their general achievement in a particular skills area. However, because they are subjective and provide no detailed information about specific aspects of performance, holistic scores are not very useful in guiding teaching and learning.

A second option is analytic scoring. In **analytic scoring,** different components or features of the students' responses are evaluated and given separate scores (e.g., spelling, grammar, organization). The scoring of isolated aspects is based on criteria. One common practice of specifying scoring criteria is in form of rubrics. A **rubric** is a scoring system consisting of evaluative descriptors and ratings that specify in detail which skills are assessed and how each component is weighed.

The use of rubrics has many benefits. As a primary benefit for teachers, the development of rubrics allows them to revisit their objectives and reflect on what has been emphasized in class. To students, rubrics specify detailed feedback on the categories in which they need to show improvement. In other words, it offers students a concrete mathematical scoring method and gives them concrete feedback about what they have done correctly and incorrectly (Campbell and Bork-Goldfield 1999). Also, if provided ahead of time, rubrics give students a clear target. This allows students not only to gain a clear sense of the elements of a well-performed task but also to be more inclined to attend to these elements because they know they will be scored on them. In summary, rubrics help both student and teacher to specifically identify the elements of a well-performed task and to assess separately how well the student has mastered each element.

Using rubrics is not without its challenges. In essence, it combines the holistic and analytical scoring approaches. Instead of scoring all of a student's mistakes, the teacher evaluates a student's performance holistically within one particular category. Like most traditional analytical scoring systems, such a practice is time-consuming to apply. Obviously, the more categories a scoring scheme contains, the longer it takes to apply. Moreover, even with clearly defined standards and criteria, the evaluation of a student's work often still calls for an instructor's subjective judgment. The initial development of clear criteria is also cumbersome. Furthermore, rubrics are not universally applicable and often require readjustment for different learning tasks and levels.

Despite some of these challenges, having a clear scoring system is a necessity. The following scoring scheme (Scott 1996) demonstrates an example of a rubric for a student writing task.

Categories/points	1	3	5
Grammar	many errors	some errors	few errors
Expression	many Anglicisms	acceptable	idiomatic
Organization of ideas	series of unrelated sentences	coherence between sentences	good coherence between sentences and paragraphs
Global impression	incomprehensible	acceptable	excellent

In defining rubrics, the instructor needs to decide on which skill components to include in the rubric. The following is a wide range of components that can serve as criteria for assessing a variety of communicative tasks:

accurate use of vocabulary	completion of a task
breadth of vocabulary	pronunciation
comprehensibility	creativity
spelling	clarity of ideas
grammatical accuracy	accuracy
organization	effort/length/risk taking
use of resources	variety of expressions
content	language (general)
global impression	amount of communication
cultural appropriateness	evidence of planning
fluency	ability to sustain conversation
evidence of cultural understanding	any special criteria (e.g., use of pronouns)

When designing rubrics, another decision teachers face is how to weigh student task performance in general and how to weigh individual skill components in particular. Proponents of task-based instruction (see Robinson 2001a; Candlin, 1987) suggest taking into account the linguistic and cognitive complexity of the task itself. These are important criteria, because the more linguistically complex the assignments are, the more the teacher wants to reward higher-level accomplishments. For example, when writing a letter, the student needs to demonstrate a range of grammatical and vocabulary skills. Reading tests vary in difficulty based on the purpose of the text and the response type required. For example, following directions on an authentic map is cognitively more complex than using a simplified map. Essentially, when weighing individual testing tasks, the demands of the task itself should be reflected by the weight of the scoring system. Besides, the demands of a communicative testing task and scoring system provide some guidelines on how much time the students might need to complete the testing task itself.

In conclusion, to avoid a negative backwash effect, what and how we test should be tightly connected to what and how we teach. This very same principle also applies to how teachers score and grade. As this author has argued, clear scoring criteria are not only very useful, but they are necessary. They make the evaluation process less arbitrary for the teacher and give students concrete, formative feedback on their performance. At the same time, while more complex scoring guidelines or rubrics reduce the degree of subjectivity, they are more time-consuming and cumbersome to apply. This aspect of grading definitely works against the use of overly complex and detailed scoring criteria because a scoring system also needs to be feasible and manageable for teachers to use them on a daily basis. For these reasons, a combination of analytic (criteria-based) and holistic grading procedures is recommended.

Prepare your students for the test

Questions that beginning teachers frequently ask are, "What kind of information can we share with our students about our tests? Is it legitimate to provide test-taking strategies?" Considering that the primary goal of testing is to find out what students know, preparing students for a test is not only advisable but must be seen an important part of assessment procedures testing. After all, if a test is also to function as a motivational device, a test should not become a hidden myth that ultimately only finds out what a student does not know. In this sense, telling students about the content areas and skills they will be tested on, or providing information about the test type, can have a positive effect on their test-taking experience and learning.

Another question that is also often raised in this context concerns the issue of students' test-taking anxiety. How can we avoid or compensate for testing anxiety in some students? One answer is that test-taking preparation needs to be mindfully addressed and planned.

D. Brown (1994, p. 384) provides the following list of suggestions on preparing students for a test. Such strategies can also help alleviate some of the students' test-taking anxieties.

- provide information about the general format of a test
- provide information about types of items that will appear
- give students opportunities to practice certain item types
- encourage a thorough review of material to be covered
- offer advice on strategies for test preparation
- offer advice on strategies to use during the test itself
- give anxiety-lowering reassurance

Evaluate your test

When you are finished with a test, evaluate it. It is also a beneficial strategy to hand a test to a colleague or program supervisor for editing and independent feedback. The following questions may serve while self-checking your test:

- Are my instructions clear (see previous guideline)?
- How will I score each testing section (see previous guideline)?
- How much time will my students need to take the test? In beginning-level language classes, as a rule of thumb, it probably should not take the teacher more than one-third of the allotted time to take the test.
- Are any "give-aways" embedded in the test? **Give-aways** of answers to a test item are clues that are embedded in another section of the test (e.g., in test instructions written in the target language, or reading texts, or testing activities). While give-aways are easily overlooked when writing tests, practitioners react to this issue in different ways. Some argue that if students are smart enough to find the answer to a test, they should be able to gain from it. From an assessment point of view, however, being able to find answers to a test, or simply borrowing language used in other testing sections, no longer makes a testing item valid. It can also be argued that if a student can find the answers to a test, we are testing skills on test taking or test-taking strategies, and not the students' knowledge. As a general strategy, if the issue of give-aways is of concern to the teacher, different sections of the test (e.g., on reading or listening skills) should be administered separately.

Planning and implementing oral tests

ANALYSIS AND DISCUSSION

1. Make a list of questions that you need to ask yourself when developing oral assessments. For example, "How will I evaluate my students?"

   _____

   _____

   _____

2. Now read over the list of sample questions in Appendix 10.11, and compare it with your own. Which aspects have you not considered yet?

Make an inventory of oral communicative skills that you have taught, and develop testing tasks

To design the assessment tasks, make an inventory of the type of performance (e.g., set of language behaviors and communicative functions) as well as the skill and content areas. The testing tasks need to reflect what and how the content was taught.

Determine clear grading and evaluation criteria

To make a fair assessment of the student's performance, it is necessary to have clear grading and evaluation criteria in mind. The performance criteria should include a description of the categories of language behavior or skill areas. Skills areas can be described by referring to skills holistically (e.g., communicative ability) or analytically, that is by further identifying subskills (e.g., pronunciation, listening comprehension). When determining analytic rubrics for oral testing purposes, it should be kept in mind that analytic rubrics require the test administrator to keep track of a learner's behavior in detail and are often more difficult to fill out. The following are some sample categories for skill areas:

- Communicative ability
  creative language use (e.g., use and breadth of vocabulary)
  fluency
  comprehensibility (pronunciation)
  listening comprehension
  cultural awareness/accuracy
- Grammatical accuracy
  morphology (e.g., verb and noun endings, etc.)
  syntax (e.g., adverbial word order, adjective positions, etc.)
- Functional skills
  can formulate simple commands
  can describe objects, people
  can narrate in the present or past

When describing grading and evaluation criteria, it is also vital for teachers to determine what successful performance at each level means. For example, an A-level performance in communicative ability may be defined as "very fluent," "highly" creative use of vocabulary, and very few grammar errors. On the contrary, a very weak speaker may show "much hesitation," use very limited vocabulary, show breakdowns in communication, and make many errors.

The scoring rubric should also indicate how each skill area is weighted, in case some skill areas are to be emphasized more than others. Many proponents of communicative language teaching agree that communicative language ability should carry a higher percentage weight than grammatical skill categories. Figure 10-5 is an example of an evaluation sheet for a prochievement test.

Name: _____   Grade: _____

Teacher: _____   Interviewer:_____

A+	100
A	95
A-	90
B	85
C	75
C-	75
D	65
D-	60

Using the percentage scores above, assign a score to each category below:

	A+	A	A-	B	C	C-	D	D
Communicative ability: _____ points × 5 = _____	A+	A	A-	B	C	C-	D	D
Creative language use: (vocabulary) _____ points × 5 = _____	A+	A	A-	B	C	C-	D	D-
Comprehensibility: (pronunciation) _____ points × 3 = _____	A+	A	A-	B	C	C-	D	D-
Morphology, syntax: _____points × 7 = _____	A+	A	A-	B	C	C-	D	D-

Final percentage score: _____ points/20= _____

FIGURE 10-5 Example of an Evaluation Sheet

Last, a scoring sheet has multiple purposes. On the one hand, it provides concrete guidelines for scoring a learner's performance; on the other hand, it serves as a reporting sheet to students. For this reason, a scoring sheet should be written so it can be easily understood, and it should provide sufficient feedback to learners so it can be conducive to productive change.

Consider the learners' test-taking anxieties

Most learners feel nervous about participating in oral exams. Some learners also experience high test-taking anxieties. There are several strategies that allow the teacher to deal with anxiety issues. One such strategy is for teachers to prepare the students by engaging them in communicative tasks similar to those they have dealt with during daily class activities. This can be done a day or two prior to the exam. A well-designed oral prochievement test also should have no surprise effect, since its primary goal is to allow the learners to demonstrate how well they have reached the target. That is, the assessment tasks are to be designed based on how and what the learners have been taught. Another strategy is for teachers to stage a mock oral exam. Students who have never experienced an oral test normally benefit from observing what an actual interview might look like. A third strategy that has an anxiety-reducing effect is allowing students to prepare a topic of their choice ahead of time. For example, a student may choose to prepare a short speech describing her or his favorite hobby. When adopting such an option, the teacher needs to bear in mind that performing a prepared speech is different from spontaneous speech because the learners have more time to formulate the content of their speech ahead of time. Different evaluation criteria thus may be asked for regarding nonspontaneous speaking tasks. A fourth option is testing students in pairs. Many students feel more at ease if they have a partner with whom they can share this experience. It also takes some pressure off, as they are not the focus of attention all the time. Testing students in pairs has other advantages, including that students can be assigned different roles to act out with each other. Assessing two students simultaneously also provides several challenges. The question that arises is how to pair them up, or what to do when communication between the students breaks down during role-play. Keeping track of two students' performances also makes the evaluation process more difficult.

Present instructions in writing and in L1

Test administrators need to ensure that instructions are clear for each performance task assigned to each student. This can be achieved by presenting instructions for role-play situations in writing and in the learners' L1. Sometimes it may also be necessary to follow up on the learners' comprehension of the assigned tasks. For role-play situations that require the learner to attend to several components, sufficient preparation time also needs to be allowed.

Keep your role as an evaluator in mind

The evaluator's role is different from the teacher's. While the teacher's role is that of a resource, guide, facilitator, and somebody who provides feedback, the evaluator's primary role is to find out how well students can perform in the target language. In playing that role, the evaluating teacher needs to keep in mind that it is the student's task to demonstrate what he or she knows. Therefore, it is the student's role to do most of the talking. Interruptions should be avoided; but if necessary, any kind of teacher response should be succinct. When the evaluator is engaging with the learner in a conversation, the interaction should be as natural as possible. That is, an oral test is not an interrogation. Particularly during testing situations, it is important to allow for enough response time because students are usually nervous and require more time to think. The evaluating teacher requires patience during pauses and periods of silence. Sometimes it is also necessary to repeat or restate a question as it occurs in any natural conversation. In case a testee does not respond to the evaluator immediately, a useful strategy is to repeat a question a second time and then rephrase or restate it. If the learner still does not seem to understand the question, it may be best to go on to another question.

The evaluator should avoid teaching and coaching during testing situations. Teaching means that the evaluator makes any kind of evaluative comments, such as "That was really good," or provides error corrective feedback. Coaching occurs when the evaluator feeds the testee answers and attempts to help him or her out. The following dialogue demonstrates an example of coaching:

> EVALUATOR: What do you like to do in order to have fun?
> TESTEE: Um... *[hesitating]*
> EVALUATOR: Here is what I'd like to do. I'd like to see a movie, or read a book. What about you?

In conclusion, the role of an evaluator involves a different behavior. To avoid any kind of confusion among students, it might be useful for teachers to discuss some of these roles with the students prior to the test.

Evaluate your students' performance immediately after the test

A student's performance should be assessed immediately after the test. A strategy that often works well is making a note of one's first impression before proceeding to fill out the evaluation sheet. Another strategy that can be beneficial is taking notes during the test. In case a test evaluator chooses to do so, he or she should inform the learners.

Evaluate your students' performance as objectively as possible

Because the rating of a student's oral performance is normally based on the evaluator's personal decision, it is subjective. To make the evaluation process fair and the result reliable, test evaluators can apply several strategies. First of all, learning how to rate requires training. This is imperative, so that raters know how to interpret results and apply evaluation criteria consistently. As mentioned earlier, having clearly defined evaluation criteria is essential since they help the rater to clearly focus on the skills being assessed. Recording the student's performance is another strategy that allows for a more objective assessment. Such an approach, however, is very time-consuming; and for management reasons, it is often unfeasible. Another strategy that decreases the degree of subjectivity is to use two raters. An alternative for teachers who are teaching in the same program is to switch classes and evaluate each other's students. In this way, any kind of preconceived bias that teachers often develop toward their own students is less likely to impede the rating. This is not to forget that when in doubt, a teacher usually has the option to reassess a student's performance. Last, a student's oral performance must be considered only one component. The highest degree of reliability can be achieved only if a student's rating is comprised of multiple performance assessments.

Conclusion

The goal of this chapter was to provide an overview of different assessment formats. Furthermore, it was to provide a set of guidelines on how to develop and implement written and oral tests that are in alignment with communicative and task-based instruction. In conclusion, it should be emphasized that tests are neither good nor evil; as Brown and Hudson point out (1998), tests are simply tools. Nevertheless, the choice of assessment formats has consequences and a backwash effect on the curriculum; therefore, assessment tasks need to be carefully considered and designed. Last, teachers need to choose from a range of alternatives in assessments. A teacher's decision and the assessment of a student's performance should never be based on a single source of information.

Checking chapter objectives

Do I know how to ...

- ❏ explain reasons for testing
- ❏ define formative and summative assessment, achievement and proficiency testing, criterion- and norm-referenced test, and validity and reliability
- ❏ discuss different forms of assessment procedures (e.g., selected-response and constructed response assessments, performance-based, authentic, oral, student self-assessment)
- ❏ define different test type
- ❏ discuss issues related to test development, grading, and scoring
- ❏ describe different test-preparing strategies
- ❏ explain issues related to writing instructions

Explorations

TASK 1: TEST YOURSELF

To experience some of the issues on testing addressed in this chapter, take the test in Appendix 10.6. Before you start, prepare yourself for this test by studying the question in Appendix 10.5, and then proceed with the test in Appendix 10.6. Last, answer the questions in Appendix 10.7.

TASK 2: ANALYSIS: UNDERSTANDING THE BACKWASH EFFECT

Identify the different skill areas of a paper-and-pencil test. What percentage of grammar, listening, vocabulary, reading, or writing items does the test include? What message does this distribution send to the learners? In other words, can you predict the backwash effect?

TASK 3: ANALYZING TRADITIONAL TESTING TASKS

In Appendix 10.2, you will find several varieties of fill-in-the blank activities. Analyze each item as follows:

1. Identify the skills that are assessed.
2. List and discuss its strengths and weaknesses as an assessment task.

TASK 4: ANALYZING LINGUISTIC AND COGNITIVE DEMANDS OF TESTING ITEMS

Analyze the linguistic and cognitive complexity of the sample testing items in Appendix 10.4.

1. Identify the type and range of skills that are assessed, and organize these into the two categories: knowledge (e.g., vocabulary, grammatical, or cognitive skills) or application of knowledge (performance-based skills).
2. Taking into account the linguistic and cognitive complexity of each testing task, how would you score each testing item? Be prepared to justify your scoring system.
3. Critique the design of each testing item. How well does each item meet the criteria of performance-based testing?

TASK 5: TEST ANALYSIS

Examine a sample test, for example, a test that was provided by a textbook publisher, an old test that you took, or a test that was developed by a supervisor or fellow teacher.

1. Identify and list the different kinds of skills that are assessed (e.g., functional, grammatical, vocabulary, reading, etc.). What types of assessment are used to measure student learning?
2. Organize each testing task into the following categories: knowledge or application of knowledge.
3. Apply the backwash effect, and draw conclusions about the content and methodology of instruction.
4. Discuss the strengths and weaknesses of this test.
5. Analyze and discuss the scoring system. Do you agree with the point distributions? Do the points the students can earn on each section correspond to the complexity and type of testing task? Make suggestions for changes, if necessary.

TASK 6: COGNITIVE DEMANDS OF A TESTING TASK

1. In Appendix 10.3, you will find an example of a map as they are typically found in a textbook. Design an assessment task for a first- or second-year language class. Make sure to provide all the necessary instructions that accommodate your task.

Application

TASK 7: ADAPTING TRADITIONAL TESTING TASKS

1. Identify and list the different kinds of skills that are being evaluated in each of the following testing items.
2. Rewrite each testing item, and make it performance-based.

Item 1

What time is it? Write out the time for each clock. (Use complete sentences, and spell out the number.)

2:15 p.m.	7:30 a.m.	12:08 p.m.	1:45 a.m.

Item 2

Look at the picture to find out what hurts that person. For each picture, write a sentence telling what hurts that person.

Picture of a foot: _____

Picture of a knee: _____

Picture of a head: _____

Item 3

Trouvez les phrases qui correspondent. [Find the matching phrases.]

1. _____ J'ai le moral à zéro.	A.	Je suis énervé(e).
2. _____ Je suis furax.	B.	Je suis en colère.
3. _____ Je ne suis pas dans mon assiette.	C.	Je ne me sens pas très bien.
4. _____ J'ai le cafard.	D.	Je suis triste.
5. _____ Je suis sur les nerfs.	E.	Je suis furieux (–se).
6. _____ Je suis furibard (e).	F.	Je suis déprimé (e).

1. _____ I am totally down.	A.	I feel bothered.
2. _____ I am furious.	B.	I am angry.
3. _____ I don't feel at ease.	C.	I don't feel well.
4. _____ I am down.	D.	I am sad.
5. _____ I am irritated.	E.	I am furious.
6. _____ I am furious.	F.	I am depressed.

Item 4

Imparfait et passé compose. Karine et Thierry ont de petits problèmes a la gare. [Conjugate the verbs in parentheses in either passé compose or the imparfait according to the context.]

Thierry et moi _____ (vouloir) aller à Versailles. Il y _____ (avoir) beaucoup de monde quand nous _____ (arriver) à la gare. Nous _____ (demander) à un voyageur l'heur du train pour Versailles. Il _____ (ne pas pouvoir) nous répondre. Nous _____ (poser) la même question à trois employés, mais personne ne _____ (savoir). Alors, nous _____ (attendre) pendant une heure et puis, le conducteur _____ (faire) une annonce: "Prochain train pour Versailles, quai numéro 18". Il _____ (ne pas donner) d'explications. Un vrai mystère ... Mais nous _____ (être) contents de partir.

> Thierry and I wanted to go to Versailles. There were many people when we arrived at the station. We asked a traveler about the departure time of the train to Versailles. We asked three other employees the same questions, but nobody knew. We waited for an hour, when the conductor finally made an announcement: "Next train to Versailles, platform 18." He did not provide any explanations. A real mystery. ... but we were happy to leave.

Item 5

Given the situation, which is the most logical result? Write your answer on the line provided.

1. cuando tienes la gripe, ¿estás cansado(a) o estás contento(a)?

   _____

2. cuando estás triste, ¿estás de buen humor o estás de mal humor?

   _____

3. cuando tienes vómitos, ¿estás resfriado(a) o tienes la gripe?

   _____

4. cuando no tienes un examen, ¿estás tranquilo(a) o estás triste?

   _____

> 1. when you have the flu, are you tired or happy?
> 2. when you are sad, are you in a bad or in a good mood?
> 3. when you have to throw up, do you have a cold or the flu?
> 4. when you don't have an exam, are you quiet or sad?

TASK 8: ADAPTING AUTHENTIC ASSESSMENT TASKS

The ideal form of assessing application of student knowledge is by means of authentic assessments. *Authentic assessment* is a term that is often used when the assessment task immerses students in a real-life scenario.

Use the following examples of authentic assessments (adapted from Norris et al. 1998) and adapt them to your teaching situation. How would you assess these skills?

Ordering the Main Course

All of the dinners in this restaurant must be ordered "à la carte"; that is, you have to select the different meal components from the lists of available choices. Study the menu and the various selections that are available for the evening. Choose a main dish (meat or vegetarian), pasta, and a vegetable from the different options. When the waiter requests your order, tell him what you have decided.

Fill in the Application Form

Choose a single application form that corresponds to a job for which you find yourself the most qualified (based on the mob description attached to each of the available forms.) Fill in the application form to the best of your ability, leaving blank any information that you do not have currently available.

Choosing a Hotel

Listen to the message that your travel companion has left for you on your answering machine. Note any information regarding the selection of hotel accommodations in your vacation city. Now locate your city in the travel guidebook that is provided. Select the hotel that best suits the information provided by your travel companion.

Making a Reservation

Call a local ethnic restaurant in town and make a dinner reservation in the target language.

TASK 9: ADDING AN AUTHENTIC DIMENSION TO A PERFORMANCE-BASED ASSESSMENT TASK

Analyze the following oral-performance-based assessment task, in which learners are asked to use the target language to communicate meaningful information. Make a list of the linguistic functions, information, vocabulary, and grammatical points learners would have to use to complete the following task:

> Describe your daily routine of a typical day during the week. Tell what you do throughout the day and at what times. Include details such as with whom and where you do these activities.

Now adapt this task to make it authentic, so that it requires learners to address a meaningful audience and mirrors challenges faced by real individuals in real-world settings (Wiggins 1998). Think of which elements you need to add to the task to make it reflect a real-world situation. You might start by asking yourself, "In what settings do people find themselves having to elaborate their daily schedules?"

(Source: Shrum and Glisan (2000), p. 311.)

TASK 10: DEVELOPING A UNIT TEST OR FINAL EXAM

Develop a unit test or final paper-and-pencil test. Your test should provide the following information:

- All testing materials, including a copy of an audiotape or videotape, or transcription of aural materials
- Clear instruction, including information on weighting and any additional necessary scoring information
- Clear and detailed information on how to score each section of the test. (Assume this test is given to multiple class sections. Appendix 10.8 provides an example of scoring instructions.)

Before you start developing the test, read over the guidelines for developing tests as presented in this chapter.

TASK 11: COMPARING AND ANALYZING SCORING RUBRICS

Choose a composition written by one of your students. To score the student's essay, use the scoring criteria provided in Appendix 10.10. If you have never used a scoring profile, first read through the suggestions for applying the criteria in Appendix 10.9.

What grade would you assign the student's composition? How easy was it to apply this method? Now, apply Scott's (1996) scoring rubric introduced in the section "Determine a Grading System and Clear Scoring Criteria" in this chapter. Compare and describe your experience and results. What changes would you propose to improve either rubric?

TASK 12: ORAL INTERVIEWS: ONE OR TWO STUDENTS?

Compare an oral assessment format in which an evaluator tests each student individually to a format in which two students are tested together. What are advantages of one variation over the other? What challenges does the evaluator face when dealing with two students together?

TASK 13: EVALUATING THE EVALUATION SHEET

Based on the design of the evaluation sheet in Figure 10.5, what conclusions can you draw about the test designer's philosophy of teaching? Would you adopt this evaluation sheet? At what level? Would you suggest any changes?

APPENDIX 10.1

Reasons for Testing

Tests may be used as a means to:

1. Give the teacher information about where the students are at the moment, to help decide what to teach next;
2. Give the students information about what they know, so that they also have an awareness of what they need to learn or review;
3. Assess for some purpose external to current teaching (a final grade for the course, selection); *psychological, presenting*
4. Motivate students to learn or review specific material;
5. Get a noisy class to keep quiet and concentrate;
6. Provide a clear indication that the class has reached a "station" in learning, such as the end of a unit, thus contributing to a sense of structure in the course as a whole;
7. Get students to make an effort (in doing the test itself), which is likely to lead to better results and a feeling of satisfaction;
8. Give students tasks which may actually provide useful review or practice, as well as testing;
9. Provide students with a sense of achievement and progress in their learning.

(Source: Ur (1996), p. 34.)

APPENDIX 10.2

Fill-In Variations

Variation A

Students fill in the gaps based on cues provided in the target language. Ergänzen Sie. Was machen Kathys Freunde im Sommer? Wie kommen Sie zu ihrem Reiseziel?

Example A:

ULRIKE: "Ich fliege_____ (by airplane) in die USA."

Bettina: "Ich fahre _____ (by bike) durch Polen."

KLAUS: "Und ich nehme _____ (by train) nach Paris."

Example B:

PETER: Warum nimmst du nicht den Wagen?

KLAUS: Ich habe doch keinen _____ (driving license). Den mache ich erst im Herbst.

1. Note: To fill in these forms in German, knowledge of grammar (dative case) is required.
2. To fill in this form, no knowledge of grammar is required.

Complete the following sentences. What do Kathy's friends do during the summer? How do they get to their destination?

Example A:

ULRIKE: "I go by <u>airplane</u> to the USA."
BETTINA: "I ride <u>my bike</u> through Poland."
KLAUS: "And I go <u>by train</u> to Paris."

Example B:

PETER: Why don't you take the car?
KLAUS: I don't have a driving license. I'll get it in fall.

Variation B

Students select from a list of words to fill in the gaps.

Arbeitnehmer, Arbeitgeber, Betrieb, Fabrik, Gastarbeiter, Gewerkschaft, Lehre, Lohn, Steuern

Ergänzen Sie logisch.

a. Arbeiter und Angestellte sind _____.
b. Wie hoch ist dein _____?—2000 Euros im Monat.

Select from the following list.
employer, employee, company, factory, foreign worker, union, apprenticeship, salary, taxes
a) Workers and jobholders are _____.
b) How much is your _____? 2000 euros per month.

Variation C

No information is provided. Students make use of the context to fill in the gap.

Example:

CLAUDIA CLESTIL: Ich verstehe viel von Autos. Und ich arbeite gern praktisch.
SIE: Warum werden Sie nicht Automechanikerin?
MARIA MEIER: Ich kann gut schreiben und ich schreibe gern.
SIE: Ich bin _____ von Beruf.

CLAUDIA CLESTIL:	I know a great deal about cars. And I like to work with my hands.
YOU:	Why don't you become a car mechanic?
MARIA MEIER:	I can write well and I like to write.
SIE:	I am a _____ by profession.

Variation D

The word category (e.g., adjective, verb) is specified. Students make use of the context to fill in the gap.

Supply the missing words in German.

Ich bin gestern Abend mit meinem Freund Peter im Kino gewesen. Ich fand den Film _____ (adjective), aber meinem Freund hat er _____ (verb).

Supply the missing words in German

Last night I went to the movies with my friend Peter. I found the movie quite <u>boring</u> but Peter <u>liked</u> it.

Variation E

Students fill in the blanks based on information elicited from a chart.

Lisez les résultats du marathon et complétez les phrases qui suivent.

Concurrent	Minutes
Serge	9.0
Mélanie	7.30
Paul	6.10
Anne	10.20
Marc	7.15
Marie	7.30

1. Paul court _____ vite de tous et Anne court _____ vite de tous.
2. Mélanie court bien, mais Marc court _____ qu'elle.
3. etc. etc.

Look up the results of the marathon race and complete the sentences below.

1. Paul runs _____ of all and Anne runs _____ of all.
2. Mélanie runs well, but Marc runs_____ than she does.
3. etc. etc.

APPENDIX 10.3
Sample Maps

Illustration 1

(Source: Salaberry, et. al., (2004), p. 504.)

APPENDIX 10.4

Sample Testing Items

Item 1: Matching

Trouvez les phrases qui correspondent. [Find the matching phrases.]

1. _____ J'ai le moral à zéro.
2. _____ Je suis furax.
3. _____ Je ne suis pas dans mon assiette.
4. _____ J'ai le cafard.
5. _____ Je suis sur les nerfs.

A. Je suis énervé(e).
B. Je suis en colère.
C. Je ne me sens pas très bien.
D. Je suis triste.
E. Je suis furieux (–se).
F. Je suis déprimé (e).

1. _____ I am totally down.	A. I feel bothered.
2. _____ I am furious.	B. I am angry.
3. _____ I don't feel at ease.	C. I don't feel well.
4. _____ I am down.	D. I am sad.
5. _____ I am irritated.	E. I am furious.
	F. I am depressed.

Item 2: Building Sentences

Select three of the following words and form a logical sentence using each word.

Kreuzung, Lage, übrigens, sofort, erlauben, ankommen, schicken, günstig

Example: Unser Hotel ist sehr günstig.

> Select three of the following words and form a logical sentence using each word.
> intersection, location, by the way, immediately, permit, arrive, send, affordable
> Example: Our hotel is very affordable.

Item 3: Identifying Detailed Information by Filling in a Chart

Die monatlichen Ausgaben. Anna und Peter vergleichen ihre monatlichen Ausgaben. Hören Sie zu und ergänzen Sie die Tabelle mit den korrekten Summen.

Name	Studiengebühren	Miete	Freizeit	Verkehrsmittel	Bücher	Telefon	Lebensmittel
Anna							
Peter							

Monthly expenses. Anna and Peter, having a discussion comparing their monthly expenses. Listen and complete the table by filling in the correct amounts.

name	tuition	rent	spare time	transportation	books	telephone	food items
Anna							
Peter							

Item 4: Grammar: Cloze Tests

Students fill in the blanks. The missing words and context determine the grammatical focus.

Jennifer, eine gute Deutschstudentin, ist frustriert und spricht mit ihrer Lehrerin.

Supplement the correct prepositions, question words, *da*– compounds, or *wo*–compounds.

JENNIFER: Ich möchte mich beschweren.

TEACHER: _____ möchten Sie sich beschweren?

JENNIFER: Über das Deutschprogramm. Ich interessiere mich sehr _____ Deutsch und ich freue mich schon jeden Morgen, wenn ich aufwache, _____ den Unterricht.

usw.

Jennifer, a good but frustrated student of German, talks to her teacher: Supplement the correct prepositions, question words, *da*– compounds or *wo*–compounds.

Jennifer: I'd like to complain.

Teacher: What do you want to complain about?

Jennifer: About the German program. I am very interested in German and I am looking forward to my class every morning when I wake up.

etc.

Item 5: Reading

Andrea sitzt im Café und liest diesen interessanten Artikel in der Zeitung. Instructions: Please read the text below and mark the correct answer.

In Deutschland gibt es inzwischen in fast jeder Stadt eine Anzeigenzeitung. Anzeigenzeitungen sind ein "Supermarkt" für alle, die etwas kaufen oder verkaufen möchten. Sie erscheinen mindestens einmal pro Woche und sind überall erhältlich. In Frankfurt und Umgebung heißt diese Zeitung "das inserat."

"Das inserat" erscheint dreimal pro Woche (montags und freitags) und kostet 4,20 DM. Im "inserat" findet man vor allem gebrauchte Möbel, Haushaltsgeräte, Fernseher und Videogeräte, Fotoartikel, Sportgeräte, Computer, Autos, Wohnmobile und vieles andere. Oft gibt es aber auch Sonderangebote für Neugeräte.

Answer the following questions:

1. "Das inserat" ist

❑ ein Supermarkt in Frankfurt.
❑ eine Anzeigenzeitung in Frankfurt.

2. "Das inserat" gibt es

❑ montags, mittwochs, und freitags.
❑ einmal pro Woche.

Alternative comprehension tasks:

1. "Das inserat" hat nur Anzeigen für gebrauchte Waren.	richtig	falsch
2. Andrea sucht eine Stelle.	richtig	falsch
3. Provide a title for this text.		

Andrea is sitting in a café, reading this interesting article in the newspaper. Instructions: Please read the text below and mark the correct answer.

In almost any German city you can nowadays find newspapers specializing in ads. Such newspapers are a "supermarket" for people who want to sell and buy things. They appear at least once a week and can be obtained everywhere. In Frankfurt and surroundings this newspaper is called "das inserat." "Das inserat" appears three times per week (Mondays and Fridays) and costs DM 4.20. In particular, you find ads for used furniture, household articles, TVs and VCRs, photo and sports articles, computers, cars, RVs, and many other objects. Often there are also many specials advertised for new items.

Answer the following questions:

"Das inserat" is

❑ a supermarket in Frankfurt.
❑ an advertising newspaper in Frankfurt.

"Das inserat" appears

❑ Mondays, Wednesdays, and Fridays
❑ once per week

1. "Das inserat" only advertises used articles.	right	wrong
2. Andrea is looking for a job.	right	wrong
3. Provide a title for this text.		

(Source: Excerpt of a test item bank compiled by K. Brandl and M. Bansleben at the University of Washington, 2004.)

Item 6: Embellishing a Story

The following story gives you only the main facts—no details and no explanations. First, read the story, and then rewrite it adding five descriptive details (imparfait/past-tense form) and three explanations of what had happened before (plus-que-parfait/past perfect).

Dimanche dernier, nous sommes allés skier. Nous sommes partis tôt le matin et nous sommes arrivés à 9h00. Nous avons mis tout notre équipement de ski et nous avons commencé à skier à 9h30. Á 12h00 nous avons mangé des sandwichs et nous avons recommencé à skier à 12h45. Á1600 nous avons pris un chocolat chaud dans un petit restaurant tout en haut des pistes. Nous avons arrêté de skier à 17h00 et nous sommes rentrés. Le soir, nous avons dîné et ensuite, nous avons regardé un film. Je me suis endormi pendant le film.

Last Sunday, we went skiing. We left early in the morning and arrived at 9 o'clock. We put on all our skiing equipment and started skiing at 9:30. At 12 o'clock we ate sandwiches and started skiing again at 12:45. At 4 o'clock we had a warm chocolate in a small restaurant up on the top of the slopes. We stopped skiing at 5 o'clock and went back home. In the evening, we had dinner and watched a movie. I fell asleep during the movie.

APPENDIX 10.5

Test Preparation

Throughout this chapter you have been introduced to different concepts. Prepare for the test by studying the following materials. These materials deal with the following:

1. The theoretical concepts of validity, reliability, and backwash
2. Testing can be classified as either summative or formative. Provide examples of a summative and formative test. What is the difference between these two categories of testing?

NOTE!

Definitions and examples are provided in Figure 10-6. You have 10–15 minutes to prepare yourself.

Summative versus Formative Tests

Shrum and Glisan (2000) describe summative and formative tests in the following way:

Summative testing often occurs at the end of a course and is designed to determine what the learner can do with the language at that point. Opportunities for further input or performance after the test is administered usually occur in the next language learning experience or course. The most common summative test is a final exam. Formative tests are designed to help form or shape the learners' ongoing understanding or skills while the teacher and learners still have opportunities to interact for the purposes of repair and improvement within a given course or setting. [...] Examples include quizzes (five to fifteen minutes, class interaction activities such as paired interviews, and chapter or unit tests (p. 292).

FIGURE 10-6 Theoretical Concepts

APPENDIX 10.6

Test on Testing

Part I

1. What is a valid test?

   _____

   _____

   _____

2. What is a reliable test?

   _____

   _____

   _____

3. Explain the phrase "assessment drives instruction." Provide some positive and negative examples.

   _____

   _____

   _____

4. Why is it important to know about psychometric concepts such as validity, reliability, and so forth?

   _____

   _____

   _____

   _____

Part II

What is the difference between achievement, prochievement, and proficiency?

_____

_____

_____

_____

_____

_____

APPENDIX 10.7

Reflection and Discussion

Reflecting on the test experience you have just had, answer the following questions.

1. How did you feel about being tested?
2. Did the fact that you knew you were being tested make any difference in how well you learned the materials in advance? Do you think it is fair to tell students in advance what they will be tested on? Did the fact that you were not informed immediately prior to this test make any difference?

APPENDIX 10.8

Example of Scoring Instructions

Test Item

Personalpronomen (12 Punkte)
Betsy und Conny gehen auf den Flohmarkt (flea market).
Please fill in the blanks with a personal pronoun either in the nominative or in the accusative case.

BETSY: Brauchst du ein Kleid?

CONNY: Nein, ich suche eine Jacke. Schau mal! Wie findest du _____ ?

BETSY: Ja, _____ ist schön.

CONNY: Schau mal! Den Hut! Ich finde _____ komisch!

Verkäuferin: Stühle, alte Bilder, Lampen! Alles, was Sie brauchen.

BETSY: Conny, schau mal da! Ein Bild vom Hamburger Hafen.

CONNY: Ach, _____ ist toll!

BETSY: Und eine Lampe von 1920.

CONNY: Hier ist eine von 1950. Ich finde _____ schöner.

BETSY: Hey, Conny! Hier ist ein alter Stuhl! Nur zwanzig Mark! Ich kaufe _____!

CONNY: Sei nicht verrückt (crazy)! Du kannst im Flugzeug keinen Stuhl mitnehmen.

BETSY: Schade.

Scoring Instructions and Criteria

Personalpronomen (personal pronouns)

12 points

2 points for each blank: 1 point for applying the correct pronoun, 1 point for grammatical accuracy *(correct form)*

Answers: sie, sie, ihn, es, sie, ihn

APPENDIX 10.9

Suggestions for Using Evaluation Criteria for Compositions

Read the composition through from start to finish without making any comments or judgments.

- Apply each category of the criteria separately from the others (in other words, one at a time without referring across categories).
- To determine the level within categories, start at the lowest level and read until you find the level that best describes the work.
- Circle the points associated with that level.
- Repeat the procedure for the next category.
- Total the points in the four categories, and you will have a grade based on 100 possible points.

Here are other useful suggestions for ensuring a uniform application of the evaluation criteria and for handling possible questions that students may pose concerning their grades.

- Avoid totaling the points on any one student's composition so that you will not be biased in your judgments of other students' compositions. After you have assigned category scores to all compositions, go back to total the points for each student.
- Seek independent evaluations on two or three compositions to ensure that you and another instructor are applying the criteria in the same way. Likewise, evaluate two of your fellow instructor's compositions. Discuss and resolve any disagreements.
- Be able to pinpoint for a student exactly what in the composition led you to assign a particular point value (achievement level) within a category. Remember, the criteria are not impressionistic or subjective.

APPENDIX 10.10

Evaluation Criteria for Compositions

Content (Information Conveyed)	Points
Minimal information; information lacks substance (is superficial); inappropriate or	19
Irrelevant information, or not enough information to evaluate limited information; ideas present but not developed; lack of supporting detail or evidence	22
Adequate information; some development of ideas; some ideas lack supporting detail or evidence	25
Very complete information; no more can be said; thorough, relevant; on target	30

Organization	Points
Series of separate sentences with no transitions; disconnected ideas; no apparent order to the content, or not enough to evaluate	16
Limited order to the content; lacks logical sequencing of ideas; ineffective ordering; very choppy; disjointed	18
An apparent order to the content is intended; somewhat choppy; loosely organized but main points do stand out, although sequencing of ideas is not complete	22
Logically and effectively ordered; main points and details are connected; fluent; not choppy whatsoever	25

Vocabulary	Points
Inadequate; repetitive; incorrect use or nonuse of words studied; literal translations, abundance of invented words, or not enough to evaluate	16
Erroneous word use or choice leads to confused or obscured meaning; some literal translations and invented words; limited use of words studied	18
Adequate but not impressive; some erroneous word usage or choice, but meaning is not confused or obscured; some use of words studied	22
Broad; impressive; precise and effective word use and choice; extensive use of words studied	25

Language	Points
One or more errors in use and form of the grammar presented in lesson; frequent errors in subject/verb agreement; non-target-language sentence structure; erroneous use of language makes the work mostly incomprehensible; no evidence of having edited the work for language, or not enough to evaluate	13

No errors in the grammar presented in lesson; some errors in subject-verb agreement; some errors in adjective/noun agreement; erroneous use of language often impedes comprehensibility; work was poorly edited for language	15
No errors in the grammar presented in lesson; occasional errors in subject-verb or adjective-noun agreement; erroneous use of language does not impede comprehensibility; some editing for language evident but not complete	17
No errors in the grammar presented in lesson; very few errors in subject-verb or adjective-noun agreement; work was well edited for language	20

(Source: VanPatten (1992), pp. 32–33.)

APPENDIX 10.11

Sample Questions for Use When Developing Oral Assessments

How will I evaluate my students?

How can I help my students prepare for the test?

How can I keep anxiety among students low?

What kind of assessment format should I use? (e.g., individual or group interviews, oral presentations, etc.)

How often should I evaluate my students?

What grading criteria should I use?

What skills should I evaluate?

How do I weight different skills?

How can I evaluate my students objectively?

How do I structure an oral interview?

What are benefits of testing students in groups or pairs?

What kind of feedback do I provide to students after the test?

What alternative forms of assessments are there?

How is my role as a teacher different from my role as an evaluator?

How do I avoid breakdown among students?

APPENDIX 10.12

Example of Student Self-Evaluation Form

Student Self Evaluation

Name: Date:

How well did you meet your goals last week?
(communicating in target language, knowledge of TL country, personal)

What are your goals for this next week?

a. Communicating in TL:

b. Knowledge of TL country:

c. Personal goals:

d. What can we as instructors do to help you meet these goals?

Endnotes

1 A display question is not a real question—that is, it does not seek information that is known to the teacher, but it serves to elicit language practice (see Richards, Platt, and Platt 1992) For example, "Is this a book? Yes, it's a book."

2 www. actfl. org

Abraham, R. G. 1985. Field independence-dependence and the teaching of grammar. *TESOL Quarterly* 19:689–702.

Adair-Hauck, B., and R. Donato. 2002. The PACE Model—Actualizing the standards through storytelling: "Le Bras, la Jambe e le Ventre." *French Review* 76(2):278–96.

Adair-Hauck, B., R. Donato, and P. Cumo-Johanssen. 2000. Using a story-based approach to teach grammar. In *Teacher's handbook*, ed. L. J Shrum and E. Glisan, 146–71. Boston: Heinle and Heinle.

Adams, M. 1990. Beginning to read: Thinking and learning about print. Cambridge, MA: MIT Press.

Aebersold, J. A., and M. L. Field. 1997. From reader to reading teacher. Cambridge, UK: Cambridge University Press.

Aida, Y. 1994. Examination of Horwitz, Horwitz, and Cope's construct of foreign language anxiety: The case of students of Japanese. *Modern Language Journal* 78:55–168.

Alanen, R. 1995. Input enhancement and rule presentation in second language acquisition. In *Attention and awareness in foreign language learning*, ed. R. W. Schmidt, 259–302. Honolulu: University of Hawai'i, Second Language Teaching and Curriculum Center.

Alexander, P. A., D. L. Schallert, and V. C. Hare. 1991. Coming to terms: How researchers in learning and literacy talk about knowledge. *Review of Educational Research* 61:315–43.

American Heritage electronic dictionary [Computer software]. 1992. Houghton Mifflin Company.

Anderson, A., and T. Lynch 1988. *Listening*. Oxford: Oxford University Press.

Anderson, J. R. 1982. Acquisition of cognitive skill. *Psychological Review* 89(4):369–406.

———. 1995a. *Cognitive psychology and its implications*, 4th ed. New York: Freeman.

———. 1995b. *Learning and memory: An integrated approach*. New York: Wiley.

Anderson, N. J. 1991. Individual differences in strategy use in second language reading and testing. *Modern Language Journal* 75:460–72.

———. 2003. Scrolling, clicking, and reading English: Online reading strategies in a second/foreign language. *Reading Matrix* 3(3):1–33. http://www.readingmatrix.com/articles/anderson/article.pdf.

Anderson, R. C., Reynolds, R. E., Schallert, D. L., & Goetz, T. E. 1977. Frameworks for comprehending discourse. *American Educational Research Journal*, 14, 367–381.

Ashwell, Tim. 2000. Patterns of teacher response to student writing in a multiple-draft composition classroom: is content feedback followed by form feedback the best method? *Journal of Second Language Writing* 9, 227–258.

Ausubel, D. 1968. *Educational psychology: A cognitive view*. New York: Holt, Rinehart and Winston.

Ausubel, L. J. 1960. The use of advance organizers in the learning and retention of meaningful verbal material. *Journal of Educational Psychology* 51:267–72.

Baddeley, A. 1990. *Human memory: Theory and practice*. Needham Heights, MA: Allyn and Bacon.

Bailey, K. M. 1996. The best-laid plans: Teachers' in-class decisions to depart from their lesson plans. In *Voices from the language classroom: Qualitative research in second language classrooms*, ed. K. M. Bailey and D. Nunan, 88–115. New York: Cambridge University Press.

———. 1997. Enhancing beginning language courses through content-enriched instruction. *Foreign Language Annals* 30(2):173–86.

———. 1998. From teacher-centered to learner-centered: Guidelines for sequencing and presenting the elements of a foreign language lesson. In *The coming of age of the profession*, ed. J. Harper, M. G. Lively, and M. K. Williams, 97–114. Boston: Heinle and Heinle.

Bansleben, M. 1998. *TA Handbook*. Unpublished manuscript, University of Washington.

Bardovi-Harlig, K. 1995. The interaction of pedagogy and natural sequences in the acquisition of tense and aspect. In *Second language acquisition theory and pedagogy*, ed. F. Eckman, D. Highland, and P. Lee et al., 151–68. Mahwah, NJ: Erlbaum.

Barnett, M. 1989. *More than meets the eye: Foreign language reading theory and practice.* Englewood Cliffs, NJ: CAL and Prentice Hall.

Barry, S., and A. Lazarte. 1995. Embedded clause effects on recall: Does high prior knowledge of context domain overcome syntactic complexity in students of Spanish? *Modern Language Journal* 79:491–504.

———. 1998. Evidence for mental models: How do prior knowledge, syntactic complexity, and reading topic affect inference generation in a recall task for nonnative readers of Spanish? *Modern Language Journal* 98:176–93.

Bensoussan, M. 1986. Beyond vocabulary: Pragmatic factors in reading comprehension—culture, convention, coherence and cohesion. *Foreign Language Annals* 19:399–407.

Berne, J. E. 1995. How does varying pre-listening activities affect second-language listening comprehension? *Hispania* 78:316–29.

Bernhardt, E. B. 1993. *Reading development in a second language: Theoretical, empirical, and classroom perspectives.* Norwood, NJ: Ablex Publishing.

Bernhardt, E. B., and V. C. Berkemeyer. 1988. Authentic texts and the high school German learner. *Die Unterrichtspraxis* 21:6–28.

Bernhardt, E. B., and M. L. Kamil. 1995. Interpreting relationships between L1 and L2 reading: Consolidating the linguistic interdependent hypotheses. *Applied Linguistics* 16:15–34.

Blanche, P. 1988. Self-assessment of foreign-language skills: Implications for teachers and researchers. *RELC Journal* 19:75–96.

Blau, E. 1990. The effect of syntax, speed and pauses on listening comprehension. *TESOL Quarterly* 24:746–53.

Bohn, R. 1999. *Probleme der Wortschatzarbeit. Fernstudieneinheit 22.* New York: Langenscheidt.

Borrás, I., and R. C. Lafayette. 1994. Effects of multimedia courseware subtitling on the speaking performance of college students of French. *Modern Language Journal* 78:61–75.

Bossers, B. 1991. On thresholds, ceilings, and short-circuits: The relation between L1 reading, L2 reading and L2 knowledge. *AILA Review* 8:45–60.

Boyd, M., and V. M. Maloof. 2000. How teachers can build on student-proposed intertextual links to facilitate student talk in the ESL classroom. In *Second and foreign language learning through classroom interaction*, ed. J. K. Hall and L. S. Verplaetse, 163–82. London: Erlbaum.

Bramki, D., and R. Williams. 1984. Lexical familiarization in economics texts, and its pedagogic implications in reading comprehensions. *Reading in a Foreign Language* 2:169–81.

Brandi, Marie-Luise. 1996. *Video im Deutschunterricht.* New York: Langenscheidt.

Brandl, K. K. 1995. Strong and weak students' preferences of feedback options in computer assisted language learning. *Modern Language Journal* 79(2):194–211.

———. 2002a. Integrating Internet-based reading materials into the foreign language curriculum: From teacher- to student-centered approaches. *Language Learning and Technology* 6(3): 87–107. http://llt.msu.edu/vol6num3/pdf/brandl.pdf.

———. 2002b. Taking language instruction online: A comparative study of a classroom- and Web-based language course. Unpublished manuscript: University of Washington.

———. 2005. Are You Ready to "MOODLE"? *Language Learning and Technology* 9(2):16–23. http://llt.msu.edu/vol9num2/review1/.

Brandl, K. K., and G. Bauer. 2002. Students' perceptions of novice teaching assistants' use of the target language in beginning foreign language classes: A preliminary investigation. In *Ready to teach: Graduate teaching assistants prepare for today and for tomorrow*, ed. W. Davis, J. Smith, and R. Smith, 128–38. Stillwater, OK: New Forums Press.

Bransford, J. D. 1979. *Human cognition*. Belmont, CA: Wadsworth.

Bransford, J. D., and M. K. Johnson. 1972. Contextual prerequisites for understanding: Some investigations of comprehension and recall. *Journal of Verbal Learning and Verbal Behavior* 11:717–26.

Brecht, R. D., and A. R. Walton. 1995. The future shape of language learning in the new world of global communication: Consequences for higher education and beyond. In *Foreign language learning: The journey of a lifetime* (ACTFL Foreign Language Education Series), ed. R. D. Donato and R. M. Terry, 110–52. Lincolnwood, IL: NTC/Contemporary Publishing Group.

Breen, M. 1987. Learner contributions to task design. In *Language learning tasks*, ed. C. Candlin and D. Murphy, 23–46. Englewood Cliffs, NJ: Prentice Hall.

———. 2001. Overt participation and overt acquisition in the language classroom. In *Learner contributions to language learning*, ed. M. Breen, 112–40. Harlow, UK: Pearson Education Limited.

Brett, P. 1997. A comparative study of the effects of the use of multimedia on listening comprehension. *System* 25(1):39–53.

Brindley, G. P. 1984. *Needs analysis and objective setting in the adult migrant education program*. Sidney: Ames.

Brown, D. 1994. *Teaching by principles*. Upper Saddle River, NJ: Prentice Hall.

Brown, G. 1987. Twenty-five years of teaching listening comprehension. *English Teaching Forum* 25(4):11–15.

———. 1995. *Speakers, listeners and communication: Explorations in discourse analysis*. Cambridge, UK: Cambridge University Press.

Brown, G., A. Anderson, R. Shillcoch, and G. Yule. 1984. *Teaching talk*. Cambridge, UK: Cambridge University Press.

Brown, G., and G. Yule. 1983a. *Discourse analysis*. Cambridge, UK: Cambridge University Press.

———. 1983b. *Teaching the spoken language*. New York: Cambridge University Press.

Brown, H. D., and J. Arnold. 1999. A map of the terrain. In *Affect in language learning*, ed. J. Arnold, 1–25. Cambridge, UK: Cambridge University Press.

Brown, J. D. and T. Hudson. 1998. The alternatives in language assessment. *TESOL Quarterly* 32(4):653–74.

Bruton, A., & Samuda, V. (1980). Learner and teacher roles in the treatment of error in group work. *RELC Journal, 11*, 49–63.

Burt, M. (1975). Error analysis in the adult ESL classroom. *TESOL Quarterly, 9*(1):53–63.

Bybee, J. L. 1991. Natural morphology: The organization of paradigms and language acquisition. In *Crosscurrents in SLA and linguistic theories*, ed. T. Huebner and C. Ferguson, 67–92. Amsterdam: Benjamins.

Bygate, M. 2001. Speaking. In *The Cambridge guide to teaching English to speakers of other languages*, ed. R. Carter and D. Nunan, 14–20. Cambridge, UK: Cambridge University Press.

Campbell, J., and I. Bork-Goldfield. 1999. *Going the distance: Writing*. Online course for teachers of German. American Association of Teachers of German. http://golden.unl.edu.

Canale, M., and M. Swain. 1980. Theoretical bases of communicative approaches to second language teaching and testing. *Applied Linguistics* 1:1–47.

Candlin, C. 1987. Towards task-based language learning. In *Language Learning Tasks*, eds C. Candlin and D. Murphy, 5–22. London: Prentice Hall.

Cardelle, M., and L. Corno. 1981. Effects on second language learning of variations in written feedback on homework assignments. *TESOL Quarterly* 15:251–61.

Carpenter, P. 1983. What your eyes do while your mind is reading. In *Eye movements and reading: Perceptual and language processes*, ed. K. Rayner, 275–307. New York: Academic Press.

Carr, T., and B. Levy. 1990. *Reading and its development: Component skills approaches*. San Diego, CA: Academic Press.

Carrell, P. L. 1984. The effects of rhetorical organization on ESL readers. *TESOL Quarterly* 18:441–70.

———. 1985. Facilitating ESL reading by teaching text structure. *TESOL Quarterly* 19(4): 727–52.

———. 1992. Awareness of text structure: Effects on recall. *Language Learning* 42(1):1–20.

———. 1998. Can reading strategies be successfully taught? *JALT Journal*. http://jalt-publications.org/tlt/files/98/mar/carrell.html.

Cathcart, R. L., and J. E. Olsen. 1976. Teachers' and students' preferences for correction of classroom conversation errors. In *On TESOL '76*, ed. J. F. Fanselow and R. H. Crymes, 41–53. Washington, DC: TESOL.

Celce-Murcia, M. 2001. Language teaching approaches: An overview. In *Teaching English as a second or foreign language* (3rd. ed.), ed. M. Celce-Murcia, 3–10. Boston: Heinle and Heinle.

Celce-Murcia, M., Z. Dornyei, and T. Thurell. 1995. Communicative competence: A pedagogically motivated model with content specifications. *Issues in Applied Linguistics* 6:25–35.

Celce-Murcia, M., and E. Olstain. 2000. *Discourse and context in language teaching*. Cambridge, UK: Cambridge University Press.

Cervantes, R., and G. Gainer. 1992. The effects of syntactic simplification and repetition on listening comprehension. *TESOL Quarterly* 26:767–70.

Chamot, A. U. 2005. Language learning strategy instruction: Current issues and research. *Annual Review of Applied Linguistics* 25:112–30.

Chaudron, C. 1985. Comprehension, comprehensibility and learning in the second language classroom. *Studies in Second Language Acquisition* 7(2):216–32.

Chaudron, G. 1988. *Second language classrooms*. Cambridge, UK: Cambridge University Press.

Chaves, M. 1998. Demographisch analysierte Lerner-perspektiven zur Verwendung authentischer Materialien im Fremdsprachenunterricht. *Deutsch als Fremdsprache* 1:37–44.

Chen, Q., and J. Donin. 1997. Discourse processing of first and second language biology texts: Effects of language proficiency and domain-specific knowledge. *Modern Language Journal* 81:209–27.

Chiang, C. S., and P. Dunkel. 1992. The effect of speech modification, prior knowledge, and listening proficiency on EFL lecture learning. *TESOL Quarterly* 26:345–74.

Chun, D. M., and J. L. Plass. 1996. Effects of multimedia annotations on vocabulary acquisition. *Modern Language Journal* 80:183–98.

———. 1997. Research on text comprehension in multimedia environments. *Language Learning and Technology* 1:60–81. http://llt.msu.edu/vol1num1/chun_plass/default.html.

Clark, C., and P. Peterson. 1986. Teachers' thought processes. In *Handbook of research on teaching* (3rd ed.), ed. M. Wittrock, 255–269. New York: Macmillan.

Clarke, M. A. 1979. Reading in Spanish and English. *Language Learning* 29:121–50.

Coady, J. 1993. Research on ESL/EFL vocabulary acquisition: Putting it in context. In *Second language reading and vocabulary learning*, ed. T. Huckin, M. Haynes, and J. Coady, 3–23. Norwood, NJ: Ablex.

———. 1997. L2 vocabulary acquisition through extensive reading. In *Second language vocabulary acquisition*, ed. J. Coady and T. Huckin, 225–37. Cambridge, UK: Cambridge University Press.

Cohen, A. 1975. Error correction and the training of language teachers. *Modern Language Journal* 59:414–21.

———. 1987. Student processing of feedback on their compositions. In *Learner strategies in language learning*, ed. A. L. Wenden and J. Rubin, 57–69. Englewood Cliffs, NJ: Prentice-Hall.

Conrad, D. G. 1997. Self-reported opinions and perceptions of first- and fourth-semester foreign language learners toward their language learning experience: A cross-sectional, cross-linguistic survey. Unpublished dissertation, University of Illinois at Urbana-Champaign.

———. 1999. The student view on effective practices in the college elementary and intermediate foreign language classroom. *Foreign Language Annals* 32(4):494–512.

Corder, S. P. 1967. The significance of learner's errors. *IRAL* 5:161–70.

Courchêne, R. 1980. The error analysis hypothesis, the contrastive analysis hypothesis, and the correction of error in the second language classroom. *TESL Talk* 11:3–13.

Crandall, J. 1999. Cooperative language and affective factors. In *Affect in language learning*, ed. J. Arnold, 226–45. New York: Cambridge University Press.

Crocall, D., and R. Oxford. 1991. Dealing with anxiety: Some practical activities for language learners and teacher trainer. In *Language anxiety*, ed. E. Horwitz and D. Young, 141–50. Englewood Cliffs, NJ: Prentice Hall.

Cummins, J., and M. Swain. 1986. *Bilingualism in education*. London: Longman.

Dansereau, D. F. 1985. Learning strategies research. In *Thinking and learning skills: Relating learning to basic research*, ed. J. W. Segal, S. F. Chipman, and R. Glaser, 209–40. Hillsdale, NJ: Erlbaum.

Davies, F. 1995. *Introducing reading*. New York: Penguin English.

Davis, R. 1997. Group work is not busy work: Maximizing success of group work in the L2 classroom. *Foreign Language Annals* 30(2):264–79.

De la Fuente, M. S., E. Martín, and n. Sans. 2007a. *Gente*, 2nd ed. Upper Saddle River, NJ: Pearson Prentice Hall.

———. 2007b. *Gente*, 2nd ed. Student Activities Manual. Upper Saddle River, NJ: Pearson Prentice Hall.

DeKeyser, R. M. 1993. The effect of error correction on L2 grammar knowledge and oral proficiency. *Modern Language Journal* 77(4):501–14.

———. 1998. Beyond focus on form. In *Focus on form in classroom second language acquisition*, ed. C. D. Doughty and J. Williams, 42–64. New York: Cambridge University Press.

———. 2001. Automaticity and automatization. In *Cognition and second language instruction*, ed. P. Robinson, 125–51. Cambridge, UK: Cambridge University Press.

DeKeyser, R., and K. Sokalski. 1996. The differential role of comprehension and production practice. *Language Learning* 46:613–42.

DiDonato, R., M. Clyde, and J. Vansant. 1995. *Na klar! An introductory German course*. New York: McGraw-Hill.

Dobinson, T. 1996. The recall and retention of new vocabulary from second language classrooms. Unpublished MA thesis. Perth, Western Australia: Edith Cowan University.

Doughty, C. J. 1991. Instruction does make a difference: The effect of instruction on the acquisition of relativization in English as a second language. *Studies in Second Language Acquisition* 13(4):431–69.

———. 1994. Fine-tuning of feedback by competent speakers to language learners. In *Georgetown roundtable on languages and linguistics 1993*, ed. J. E. Alatis, 96–108. Washington, DC: Georgetown University Press.

———. (1999). Psycholinguistics evidence for recasting as focus on form. Paper presented at the American Association for Applied Linguistics conference, Stamford, CT.

Doughty, C. J. (2003). Instructed SLA: constraints, compensation, and enhancement. In C. J. Doughty & M. H. Long (Eds.), *Handbook of SLA* (256–310). Oxford, England: Blackwell.

Doughty, C. J., and M. Long. 2003. Optimal psycholinguistic environments for distance foreign language learning. *Language Learning and Technology* 7(3):50–80. http://llt.msu.edu/vol7num3/doughty/default.html.

Doughty, C. J., and T. Pica. 1986. "Information gap" tasks: Do they facilitate second language acquisition? *TESOL Quarterly* 20(2):305–26.

Doughty, C. J., and E. Varela. 1998. Communicative focus on form. In *Focus on form in classroom second language acquisition*, ed. C. Doughty and J. Williams, 114–38. New York: Cambridge University Press.

Doughty, C. J., and J. Williams, eds. 1998a. *Focus on form in classroom second language acquisition*. New York: Cambridge University Press.

———. 1998b. Pedagogical choices in focus on form acquisition. In *Focus on form in classroom second language acquisition*, ed. C. Doughty and J. Williams, 197–262. Cambridge, UK: Cambridge University Press.

Dreyer, C., and C. Nel. 2003. Teaching reading strategies and reading comprehension within a technology-enhanced learning environment. *System* 31:349–65.

Dulay, H., and M. Burt. 1973. Should we teach children syntax? *Language Learning* 23:245–58.

Edwards, C. H. (1997). *Classroom discipline and management*. Upper Saddle River, NJ: Prentice Hall.

Ellis, R. 1990. *Instructed second language acquisition*. Oxford: Blackwell.

———. 1997. *SLA research and language teaching*. Oxford: Oxford University Press.

———. 1998. Teaching and research: Options in grammar teaching. *TESOL Quarterly* 32(1):39–60.

———. 2002. Methodological options in grammar teaching materials. In *New Perspectives on grammar teaching in second language classrooms*, ed. E. Hinkel and S. Fotos, 155–79. Mahwah, NJ: Erlbaum.

Ellis, R., S. Loewen, and H. Basturkmen. 1999. Focusing on form in the classroom (Institute of Language Teaching and Learning, *Occasional Papers No 13*). Auckland, NZ: University of Auckland.

Ellis, R., Basturkmen, H., & Loewen, S. (2001). Learner uptake in communicative classrooms. *Language Learning*, 51 (2):281–318.

Erlam, R. (2003). The effects of deductive and inductive instruction on the acquisition of direct object pronouns in French as a second language. *Modern Language Journal* 87(2): 242–260.

Farrell, S. T. 2002. Lesson planning. In *Methodology in language teaching*, ed. J. C. Richards and

W. A. Renandya, 30–39. Cambridge, UK: Cambridge University Press.

Fathman, A., and E. Whalley. 1990. Teacher response to student writing: Focus on form versus content. In *Second language writing: Research insights for the classroom*, ed. B. Kroll, 178–90. Cambridge, UK: Cambridge University Press.

Field, J. 2002. The changing face of listening. In *Methodology in language teaching*, ed. J. C. Richards and W. A. Renandya, 242–47. New York: Cambridge University Press.

Flick, W. C., and J. I. Anderson. 1980. Rhetorical difficulty in scientific English: A study in reading comprehension. *TESOL Quarterly* 14:345–51.

Flowerdew, J., and L. Miller. 2005. *Second language listening*. New York: Cambridge University Press.

Flumian, C., J. Labascoule, C. Lause, and C. Royer. 2007a. *Rond-Point*, 3rd ed. Upper Saddle River, NJ: Pearson Prentice Hall.

———. 2007b. *Rond-Point*, 3rd ed. Workbook/ Lab Manual, Upper Saddle River, NJ: Pearson Prentice Hall.

Foster, P. 1998. A classroom perspective on the negotiation of meaning. *Applied Linguistics* 19:1–23.

Fotos, S., and R. Ellis. 1991. Communicating about grammar: A task-based approach. *TESOL Quarterly* 25:605–28.

Freeman, D. 1996. Redefining the relationship between research and what teachers know. In *Voices from the language classroom: Qualitative research in second language classrooms*, ed. K. M. Bailey and D. Nunan, 88–115. New York: Cambridge University Press.

Funk, H., and M. Koenig. 1991. *Grammatik lehren und lernen*. New York: Langenscheidt.

Gardner, R. C. 1985. *Social psychology and second language learning: The role of attitude and motivation*. London: Edward Arnold.

Gardner, R. C., and McIntyre, P. D. 1993a. A student's contributions to second language learning. Part II: affective variables. *Language Teaching* 26:1–11.

Genesee, F. 2000. *Brain research: Implications for second language learning.* McGill University. *Eric Digest* EDO-FL-00-12

Genesee, F., and J. A. Upshur 1996. *Classroom-based evaluation in second language education.* Cambridge, UK: Cambridge University Press.

Goh, C. C. M. 2000. A cognitive perspective on language learners' listening comprehension problems. *System* 28:55–75.

———. 1998a. Metacognitive awareness and second language listeners. *ELT Journal* 51:361–69.

———. 1998b. How ESL learners with different listening abilities use comprehension strategies and tactics. *Language Teaching Research* 2:124–47.

Götze, L. 1995. Vom Nutzen der Hirnforschung für den Zweitspracherwerb. In *Linguistics with a human face*, ed. K. Sornig, 113–26. Festschrift für Norman Denison zum 70. Geburtstag, Graz: Grazer Linguistische Monographien 10.

———. 1997. Was leistet das Gehirn beim Fremdsprachenlernen? Neue Erkenntnisse der Gehirnphysiologie zum Fremdsprachenerwerb. Zeitschrift für Interkulturellen *Fremdsprachenunterricht* [Online], 2(2):1–15. http://www.spz.tudarmstadt.de/projekt_ejournal/jg_02_2/beitrag/goetze1.htm

Grabe, W. 2002. Reading in a second language. In *The Oxford handbook of applied linguistics*, ed. R. B. Kaplan, 49–59. Oxford: Oxford University Press.

Green, C., and R. Tanner. 1998. *Tasks for teacher education.* Edinburgh Gate, Harlow: Addison Wesley Longman.

Green, K. P., and P. K. Kuhl. 1989. The role of visual information in the processing of place and manner features in speech perception. *Perception and Psychophysics* 45:34–42.

———. 1991. Integral processing of visual place and auditory voicing information during phonetic perception. *Journal of Experimental Psychology: Human Perception and Performance* 17:278–88.

Greifnieder, U. 1995. The influence of audio support on the effectiveness of CALL. *ReCALL* 7:29–35.

Grellet, F. 1981. *Developing reading skills.* Cambridge, UK: Cambridge University Press.

Hammond, R. M. (1988). Accuracy versus communicative competency: The acquisition of grammar in the second language classroom. *Hispania*, 71:408–417

Harmer, J. 1991. *The practice of English language teaching.* New York: Longman.

———. 2001. *The practice of English language teaching.* Essex, UK: Pearson Education.

Harper, J., M. G. Lively, and M. K. Williams, eds. 1998a. *The coming of age of the profession: Issues and emerging ideas for the teaching of foreign languages.* Boston: Heinle and Heinle.

Harper, J., M. G. Lively, and M. K. Williams. 1998b. Testing the way we teach. In *The coming of age of the profession: Issues and emerging ideas for the teaching of foreign languages*, ed. Harper, Lively, and Williams, 263–76. Boston: Heinle and Heinle.

Hatch, E. M. 1983. Simplified input and second language acquisition. In *Pidginization and creolization as language acquisition*, ed. R. W. Andersen, 64–86. Cambridge, MA: Newbury House.

Havranek, G. 1999. The effectiveness of corrective feedback: Preliminary results of an empirical study. *Acquisition et Interaction en Langue Étrangère* 2:189–206.

———. 2002. *Die Rolle der Korrektur beim Fremdsprachenlernen.* Frankfurt am Main: Peter Lang.

Hennessey, J. M. 1995. Using foreign films to develop proficiency and to motivate the foreign language student. *Foreign Language Annals* 28:116–20.

Henning, G. 1987. *A guide to language testing.* Rowley, MA: Newbury House.

Henning, S. (1993). The integration of language, literature and culture: Goals and curricular design. *ADFL Bulletin*, 24(2), 51–55.

Herron, C. 1994. An investigation of the effectiveness of using an advance organizer to introduce video on the foreign langue classroom. *Modern Language Journal* 78:190–98.

Herron, C., J. Hanley, and S. Cole. 1995. A comparative study of two advance organizers for introducing beginning foreign language students to video. *Modern Language Journal* 79:387–95.

Herron, C., and M. Tomasello. 1992. Acquiring grammatical structures by guided induction. *French Review* 65:708–18.

Horwitz, E., and D. Young (eds.). 1991. *Language anxiety*. Upper Saddle River, NJ: Prentice Hall.

Hulstijn, J. 2001. Intentional and incidental second language vocabulary learning: A reappraisal of elaboration, rehearsal and automaticity. In *Cognition and second language instruction*, ed. P. Robinson, 258–86. Cambridge, UK: Cambridge University Press.

Hymes, D. 1971. *On communicative competence.* Philadelphia: University of Pennsylvania Press.

———. 1972. On communicative competence. In *Sociolinguistics: Selected readings*, ed. J. Pride and J. Holmes, 269–93. Harmondsworth, UK: Penguin.

Iwashita, N. 2003. Negative feedback and positive evidence in task-based interaction: Differential effects on L2 development. *Studies in Second Language Acquisition* 25:1–36.

Izumi, S. 2002. Output, input enhancement, and the noticing hypothesis: An experimental study on ESL relativization. *Studies in Second Language Acquisition* 24:541–77.

Jensen, L. 2001. Planning lessons. In *Teaching English as a second or foreign language* (3rd ed.), ed. M. Celce-Murcia, 403–13. Boston: Heinle and Heinle.

Jespersen, O. (1904). *How to teach a foreign language.* London: George Allen and Unwin., Ltd.

Johnson, D. D., R. T. Johnson, and T. Holubec. 1988. *Cooperation in the classroom*. Edina, MN: Interaction Book Company.

Johnson, D. W. Maruyama, G., Johnson, R., Nelson, D. & Skon, L. (1981). Effects of cooperative, competitive, and individualistic goal structures on achievement: A meta-analysis. *Psychological Bulletin*, 89:47–62.

Johnson, K. 1996. *Language teaching and skill learning*. Oxford: Blackwell.

———. 1988. Mistake correction. *ELT Journal* 42:89–101.

Johnston, P. H. 1983. *Reading comprehension assessment: A cognitive basis*. Newark, DE: International Reading Association.

Joiner, E. 1997. Teaching listening: How technology can help. In *Technology-enhanced language learning*, ed. M. D. Bush and R. M. Terry, 77–120. Lincolnwood, IL: National Textbook Company.

Jones, L. 2003. Supporting listening comprehension and vocabulary acquisition with multimedia annotations: The students' voice. *CALICO* 21(1):41–65.

Jourdenais, R. 1998. The effects of textual enhancement on the acquisition of the Spanish preterit and imperfect. Unpublished doctoral dissertation, Georgetown University.

Kagan, S. 1989. *Cooperative learning: Resources for teachers*. San Juan Capistrano, CA: Resources for Teachers.

Keck, C. M., G. Iberri-Shea, N. Tracy-Ventura, and S. Wa-Mbaleka. 2006. Investigating the empirical link between task-based interaction and acquisition: A meta-analysis. In *Synthesizing research on language learning and teaching*, ed. J. Norris and L. Ortega, 91–131. Amsterdam: Benjamins.

Keenan, J., and B. MacWhinney. 1987. Understanding the relationship between comprehension and production. In *Psycholinguistic models of production*, ed. H. Dechert and M. Raupach, 149–55. Norwood, NJ: Ablex.

Kellogg, G. S., and M. J. A. Howe. 1971. Using words and pictures in foreign language learning. *Alberta Journal of Educational Research* 17:87–94.

Kepner, C. G. 1991. An experiment in the relationship of types of written feedback to the development of second language writing skills. *Modern Language Journal* 75:305–13.

Kindsvatter, R., W. Wilen, and M. Ishler. 1988. *Dynamics of effective teaching*. New York: Longman.

Kleppin, K. 1998. *Fehler und fehlerkorrektur*. New York: Langenscheidt.

Knutson, M. E. 1997. Reading with a purpose: Communicative reading tasks for the foreign language classroom. *Foreign Language Annals* 30(1):49–57.

Koh, M. Y. 1985. The role of prior knowledge in reading comprehension. *Reading in a Foreign Language* 3:375–80.

Komm mit! TPR storytelling book. 1999. Austin, TX: Holt, Rinehart and Winston.

Kowalski, T. J., R. A. Weaver, and K. T. Henson. 1990. *Case studies on teaching*. New York: Longman.

Kramsch, C. (1985). Literary texts in the language classroom: A discourse. *Modern Language Journal*, 69 (4):356–366).

———. (2000). The Avatars of literature in language study. *Modern Language Journal*, 84 (4):553–573).

Krashen, S. 1981. *Second language acquisition and second language learning*. Oxford: Pergamon Press.

———. 1982. *Principles and practice in second language acquisition*. Oxford: Pergamon Press.

———. 1985. *The input hypothesis*. New York: Longman.

———. (1999). Seeking a role for grammar: A review of some recent studies. Foreign Language Annals, 32, (2), 245–257.

Kumaradivelu, B. 1994. The postmethod condition: Emerging strategies for second/foreign language teaching. *TESOL Quarterly* 28:27–48.

Lalande, J. (1988). Teaching literature in the high school foreign language class. Foreign *Language Annals*, 21, 573–581.

Laufer, B. 1992. How much lexis is necessary for reading comprehension? In *Vocabulary and applied linguistics*, ed. P. Arnaud and H. Béjoint, 126–32. London: Macmillan.

Laufer, B., and D. Sim, D. 1985. Measuring and explaining the reading threshold needed for English for academic purposes texts. *Foreign Language Annals* 18:405–11.

Lawrence, M., and K. K. Brandl. 2006. Aligning in foreign language instruction. In *Aligning for learning*, ed. D. H. Wulff, 134–61. Boston: Anker Publishing.

Leary, M. 1983. *Understanding social anxiety: Social, personality, and clinical perspectives*. Beverly Hills, CA: Sage.

Lee, I. 1997. ESL learners' performance in error correction in writing: Some implications for teaching. *System* 25(4):465–77.

Lee, J. F. 1986. The effects of three components of background knowledge on second language reading. *Modern Language Journal* 70:350–54.

———. 1987. The Spanish subjunctive: An information processing perspective. *Modern Language Journal* 71:50–57.

Lee, J. & Riley, G. (1990). The Effect of Prereading, Rhetorically-Oriented Frameworks on the Recall of Two Structurally Different Expository Texts. *Studies in Second Language Acquisition*, 12:25–41.

Lee, J., & VanPatten, B. 1995a. *Making communicative language teaching happen*. New York: McGraw-Hill.

———. 1995b. Workbook to accompany *Making communicative language teaching happen*. New York: McGraw-Hill.

———. 2003. *Making communicative language teaching happen*, 2nd ed. New York: McGraw-Hill.

Lee, J. W., and D. L. Schallert. 1997. The relative contribution of L2 language proficiency and L1 reading ability to L2 reading performance: A test of the threshold hypothesis in an EFL context. *TESOL Quarterly* 31:713–39.

Leeman, J. 2003. Recasts and second language development: Beyond negative evidence. *Studies in Second Language Acquisition* 25: 137–63.

Leloup, J., and R. Ponterio. 1998. Meeting the national standards: Now what do I do? ERIC Clearinghouse on Languages and Linguistics (ERIC Document Reproduction Service No. EDO-FL-98-15). http://www.cal.org/resources/digest/standards.html.

Leow, R. P. 1997. The effects of input enhancement and text length on adult L2 readers' comprehension and intake in second language acquisition. *Applied Language Learning* 8:151–82.

———. 2001. Do learners notice enhanced forms while interacting with the L2 input? An online and off-line study of the role of written input enhancement in L2 reading. *Hispania* 84:496–509.

Levelt, W. J. M. 1989. *Speaking: From intention to articulation*. Cambridge, MA: MIT Press.

Lightbown, P. 1998. The importance of timing in focus on form. In *Focus on form in classroom second language acquisition*, ed. C. Doughty and J. Williams, 77–96. Cambridge, UK: Cambridge University Press.

Lightbown, P., and N. Spada. 1990. Focus-on-form and corrective feedback in communicative language teaching: Effect on second language learning. *Studies in Second Language Acquisition* 12(4):429–48.

Lightbown, P., N. Spada, and L. Ranta. 1991, March. The effect of instruction on IL-formed questions. Paper presented at the Second Language Research Forum, Los Angeles, CA.

Linke, D. B. 1996. Das Ich und sein Gehirn. Neurophilosophische Betrachtungen zur Hirnforschung. Adelbert Reif im Gespräch mit Detlef B. Linke. *Lettre* 32:26–33.

Littlewood, W. 2004. The task-based approach: Some questions and suggestions. *ELT Journal* 58(4):319–26.

———. 1981. Communicative Language Teaching. New York: Cambridge University Press.

Loewen, S. 2004. Uptake in incidental focus on form in meaning-focused ESL lessons. *Language Learning* 54:153–87.

Loewen, S., and J. Philp. 2006. Recasts in the adult English L2 classroom: Characteristics, explicitness, and effectiveness. *Modern Language Journal* 90(4):536–56.

Long, M. H. 1977. Teacher feedback on learner error: Mapping cognitions. In *On TESOL '77*, ed. H. D. Brown, C. A. Yorio, and R. H. Crymes, 278–93. Washington, DC: TESOL.

———. 1983a. Does second language instruction make a difference? A review of research. *TESOL Quarterly* 17(3):359–82.

———. 1983b. Native speaker/Non-native speaker conversation in the second language classroom. In *On TESOL '82: Pacific perspectives on language learning and teaching*, ed. M. A. Clarke and J. Handscomb, 207–25. Washington, DC: TESOL.

———. 1985. A role for instruction in second language acquisition: Task-based language teaching. In *Modelling and assessing second language acquisition*, ed. K. Hyltenstam and M. Pienemann, 77–99. Clevedon, UK: Multilingual Matters.

———. 1989. Task, group, and task-group interactions. *University of Hawaii Working Papers in ESL* 8:1–26.

———. 1991. Focus on form: A design feature in language teaching methodology. In *Foreign language research in cross-cultural perspective*, ed. K. De Bot, R. B. Ginsberg, and C. Kramsch, 39–52. Amsterdam: Benjamins.

———. 1996. The role of the linguistic environment in second language acquisition. In *Handbook of second language acquisition*, ed. W. C. Ritchie and T. K. Bhatia, 413–68. San Diego, CA: Academic Press

———. 1998. Focus on form in task-based language teaching. *University of Hawai'i Working Papers in ESL*, 16:35–49.

———. 2007. Recasts in SLA: The story so far. In *Problems in SLA*, ed. M. H. Long, 75–116. Mahwah, NJ: Erlbaum.

Long, M., L. Adams, M. Maclean, and F. Castanos. 1976. Doing things with words: Verbal interaction in lockstep and small group classroom situations. In *On TESOL '76*, ed. T. Pica, J. Fanselow, and R. Crimes, 137–63. Washington, DC: TESOL.

Long, M., S. Inagaki, and L. OrtegaL. 1998. The role of implicit feedback in SLA: Models and recasts in Japanese and Spanish. *Modern Language Journal* 82:357–71.

Long, M., and P. Porter. 1985. Group work, interlanguage talk, and second language acquisition. *TESOL Quarterly* 19(2):207–28.

Long, M. H., & Robinson, P. (1998). Focus on form: Theory, research, and practice. In *Focus on form in classroom second language acquisition*, ed. C. J. Doughty & J. Williams, pp. 15–41. Cambridge, England: Cambridge University Press.

Lund, R. J. 1991. A comparison of second language listening and reading comprehension. *Modern Language Journal* 75(2):196–204.

Lynch, T. 1988. Theoretical perspectives on listening. *Annual Review of Applied Linguistics* 18:3–19.

Lynch, T., and J. McClean. 2000. "A case of exercising": Effects of immediate task repetition on learner's performance. In *Researching pedagogic tasks: second language learning, teaching and testing*, ed. M. Bygate, P. Skehan, and M. Swain, 141–62. Harlow, Essex, UK: Longman.

Lyster, R. 1998. Recasts, repetition, and ambiguity in L2 classroom discourse. *Studies in Second Language Acquisition* 20:51–80.

Lyster, R., P. M. Lightbown, and N. Spada. 1999. A response to Truscott's "What's wrong with oral grammar correction?" *Canadian Modern Language Review* 55(4):457–67.

Lyster, R., and L. Ranta. 1997. Corrective feedback and learner uptake: Negotiation of form in communicative classrooms. *Studies in Second Language Acquisition* 19(1):37–66.

Mackey, A., S. Gass, and K. McDonough. 2000. How do learners perceive interactional feedback? *Studies in Second Language Acquisition* 22:471–97.

Mackey, A., and J. Philp. 1998. Conversational interaction and second language development: Recasts, responses, and red herrings? *Modern Language Journal* 82:338–56.

Markham, P. 1999. Captioned videotapes and second-language listening word recognition. *Foreign Language Annals* 32:321–28.

Markham, P., and M. Latham. 1987. The influence of religion-specific background knowledge on the listening comprehension of adult second language students. *Language Learning* 37:157–70.

Martín, E., N. Sans, and J. Caballero. 2003. *Gente*, 1st ed. Upper Saddle River, NJ: Pearson Prentice Hall.

Martínez-Lage, A. 1997. Hypermedia technology for teaching reading. In *Technology-enhanced language learning*, ed. M. D. Bush, 121–63. New York: National Textbook Company.

Martyn, E. 1997, March. Tasks and learner talk. Colloquium on task-based language teaching. International TESOL Convention, Orlando, FL.

Maxim, H. 2006. Integrating textual thinking into the introductory college-level foreign language classroom. *Modern Language Learning* 90:19–32.

Mayer, R. E. 1984. Aids to text comprehension. *Educational Psychologist* 19:30–42.

———. 2001. *Multimedia learning.* New York: Cambridge University Press.

Mayer, R. E., and J. K. Gallini. 1990. When is an illustration worth ten thousand words? *Journal of Educational Psychology* 82:715–26.

Mayer, R. E., and V. K. Sims. 1994. For whom is a picture worth a thousand words? Extensions of a dual-coding theory of multimedia learning. *Journal of Educational Psychology* 86:389–401.

Mayer, R. E., K. Steinhoff, G. Bower, and R. Mars. 1995. A generative theory of textbook design: Using annotated illustrations to foster meaningful learning of science text. *Educational Technology Research and Development* 43:31–44.

McCutcheon, G. 1980. How do elementary school teachers plan? The nature of planning and influences on it. *Elementary School Journal* 81(1):4–23.

McGrath, I., S. Davies, and H. Mulphin. 1992. Lesson beginnings. *Edinburgh Working Papers in Applied Linguistics* 3:92–108.

McKeown, M., and M. Curtis. 1987. *The nature of vocabulary acquisition.* Hillsdale, NJ: Erlbaum.

Mendelsohn, D. 1998. Teaching listening. *Annual Review of Applied Linguistics* 18:81–101.

Meyer, B., and E. Rice. 1987. The interaction of reader strategies and the organization of text. *Text* 2:1–3.

Mikulecky, B. 1990. *A short course in teaching reading skills.* Reading, MA: Addison-Wesley.

Mitchell, J. T., and M. L. Redmond. 1993. Rethinking grammar and communication. *Foreign Language Annals* 26:13–19.

Mueller, G. A. 1980. Visual contextual clues and listening comprehension: an experiment. *Modern Language Journal* 64(3):335–40.

Myles, F., J. Hooper, and R. Mitchell. 1998. Rote or rule? Exploring the role of formulaic language in the classroom foreign language learning. *Language Learning* 48(3):323–64.

Nassaji, H. 2002. Schema theory and knowledge-based processes in second language reading comprehension: A need for alternative perspectives. *Language Learning* 52(2):439–89.

Nation, P., and J. Newton. 1997. Teaching vocabulary. In *Second language vocabulary acquisition*, ed. J. Coady and T. Huckin, 238–54. Cambridge, UK: Cambridge University Press.

National Standards in Foreign Language Education Project (NSFLEP). 1996. National standards for foreign language learning: Preparing for the 21st century. Lawrence, KS: Allen Press.

Norris, J., D. Brown, T. Hudson, and J. Yoshioka. 1998. *Designing second language performance assessments*. Honolulu, HI: University of Hawai'i Press.

Norris, J. M., and L. Ortega. 2000. Effectiveness of L2 instruction: A research synthesis and quantitative meta-analysis. *Language Learning* 5(3):417–528.

Nunan, D. 1988. *The learner-centered curriculum*. Cambridge, UK: Cambridge University Press.

———. 1989. *Designing tasks for the communicative classroom*. Cambridge, UK: Cambridge University Press.

———. 1999. *Second language teaching and learning*. Boston: Heinle and Heinle.

———. 2002. Listening in language learning. In *Methodology in language teaching*, ed. J. C. Richards and W. A. Renandya, 238–41. New York: Cambridge University Press.

Nystrand, M., and A. Gamoran. 1991. Instructional discourse, student engagement, and literature achievement. *Research in the Teaching of English* 25:261–90.

Ochs, E. 1979. Planned and unplanned discourse. In *Syntax and semantics* (vol. 12): *Discourse and syntax*, ed. T. Givon, 51–80. New York and London: Academic Press.

Ohta, A. 2000. Rethinking recasts: A learner-centered examination of corrective feedback in the Japanese language classroom. In *Second and foreign language learning through classroom interaction*, ed. J. K. Hall, 47–72. Mahwah, NJ: Erlbaum.

Olivia de Castells, M., E. Guzmán, P. Luperta, and C. Carcía, C. 2006. *Mosaicos*, 4th ed. Upper Saddle River, NJ: Pearson Prentice Hall.

Oller, J. 1991. Foreign language testing: Its breadth (Part 1). *ADFL Bulletin* 22(3):33–38.

Olsen, R. E. W.-B., and S. Kagan. 1992. About cooperative learning. In *Cooperative language*

learning: A teacher's resource book, ed. C. Kessler, 1–30. Englewood Cliffs, NJ: Prentice Hall.

Omaggio-Hadley, A. 1993. *Teaching language in context*. Boston: Heinle and Heinle.

———. 2001. *Teaching language in context*, 3rd ed. Boston: Heinle and Heinle.

Osuna, M. M., and C. Meskill. 1998. Using the World Wide Web to integrate Spanish language and culture. *Language Learning and Technology* 1(2):71–92. http://llt.msu.edu/vol1num2/article4/default.html.

Overstreet, M. H. 1998. Text enhancement and content familiarity: The focus of learner attention. *Spanish Applied Linguistics* 2:229–58.

Oxford, R. 1989. *Language learning strategies*. Boston: Heinle and Heinle.

———. 1997. Cooperative learning, collaborative learning, and interaction: Three communicative strands in the language classroom. *Modern Language Journal* 81:443–56.

———. 1999. Anxiety and the language learner: New insights. In *Affect in language learning*, ed. J. Arnold, 58–67. Cambridge, UK: Cambridge University Press.

Paivio, A. 1986. *Mental representation: A dual-coding approach*. New York: Cambridge University Press.

Paris, S. G., B. A. Wasik, and G. van der Westhuizen. 1988. Meta-cognition: A review of research on metacognition. In *Dialogues in literacy research*, ed. J. E. Readance, R. S. Baldwin, and J. P. Konopak et al., 143–66. Chicago: National Reading Conference.

Paulston, C. B. 1972. Structural pattern drills: A classification. In *Teaching English as a second language*, ed. H. Allen and R. Campbell, 129–38. New York: McGraw-Hill.

Peek, J. 1993. Increasing picture effects in learning from illustrated text. *Learning and Instruction* 3:227–38.

Pica, T. 1994. Questions from the language classroom: Research perspectives. *TESOL Quarterly* 28:49–79.

Pica, T., R. Kanagy, and H. Falodun. 1993. Choosing and using communication tasks for second language instruction. In *Tasks and language learning: Integrating theory and practice*, ed. G. Crookes and S. M. Gass, 9–34. Clevedon, UK: Multilingual Matters.

Pickering, S. J., and S. E. Gathercole. 2004. Distinctive working memory profiles in children with special educational needs. *Educational Psychology* 24:393–408.

Pienemann, M. 1989. Is language teachable? *Applied Linguistics* 10(1):52–79.

Plaister, T. 1993. Strategies for coping with new vocabulary. In *New ways in teaching reading*, ed. R. Day, 228–29. Alexandria, VA: Teachers of English of Speakers of Other Languages, Inc.

Polio, C., and P. Duff. 1994. Teachers' language use in university foreign language classrooms: A qualitative analysis of English and target language alternation. *Modern Language Journal* 78:313–26.

Porter, P. A. 1986. How learners talk to each other: Input and interaction in task-centered discussions. In *Talking to learn: Conversation in second-language acquisition*, ed. R. R. Day, 200–28. Rowley, MA: Newbury House.

Postovsky, V. 1981. The priority of aural comprehension in the language acquisition process. In *The comprehension approach to foreign language instruction*, ed. H. Winitz, 170–86. Cambridge, MA: Newbury House.

Prabhu, N. 1987. *Second language pedagogy: A perspective*. Oxford: Oxford University Press.

Pratt, M. W., K. Bates, and G. Wickers. 1980. Checking it out: Cognitive style and perceptual support as factors influencing message evaluation by young listeners and speakers. Unpublished manuscript, Mount St. Vincent University, Canada.

Purgason, K. B. 1991. Planning lessons and units. In *Teaching English as a second or foreign language* (2nd ed.), ed. M. Celce-Murcia, 419–31. Boston: Heinle and Heinle.

Pusack, J., and S. Otto. 1995. Instructional technologies. In *Research within reach II*, ed. V. Galloway and C. Herron, 23–41. Valdosta, GA: Southern Conference on Language Teaching.

Qian, D. 2002. Investigating the relationship between vocabulary knowledge and academic reading performance: An assessment perspective. *Language Learning* 52:513–36.

Radley, P., and A. Sharley. 1999. *Trio 2*. Oxford: Heinemann Education Books.

Ratey, J. J. 2001. *A user's guide to the brain*. New York: Pantheon Books.

Rayner, K., and A. Pollatsek. 1989. *The psychology of reading*. Englewood Cliffs, NJ: Prentice Hall.

Reynolds, R. E., M. A. Taylor, M. S. Steffensen, and L. L. Shirey et al. 1982. Cultural schemata and reading comprehension. *Reading Research Quarterly* 17:10–29.

Richards, J. C. 1990. Conversationally speaking: Approaches to the teaching of conversation. In *The language teaching matrix*, ed. J. Richards, 67–86. Cambridge, UK: Cambridge University Press.

———. 1994. *Reflective teaching in second language classrooms*. Cambridge, UK: Cambridge University Press.

———. 1998. What's the use of lesson plans? In *Beyond training*, ed. J. C. Richards, 103–21. New York: Cambridge University Press.

———. 2001. *Curriculum development in language teaching*. New York: Cambridge University Press.

Richards, J. C., and C. Lockhart. 1994. *Reflective teaching in second language classrooms*. Cambridge, UK: Cambridge University Press.

Richards, J. C., J. Platt, and H. Platt. 1992. *Dictionary of language teaching and applied linguistics*. Singapore: Longman Publishers.

Richards, J. C., and T. S. Rodgers. 2001. *Approaches and methods in language teaching*. Cambridge, UK: Cambridge University Press.

Rieken, E. 1991. The effect of feedback on the frequency and use of the passé composé by field-independent and field-dependent students of beginning French. Unpublished doctoral dissertation, University of Illinois.

Rigney, J. W. 1978. Learning strategies: A theoretical perspective. In *Learning strategies*, ed. H. F. O'Neil Jr., 165–205. New York: Academic Press.

Rivers, W. M. (1964): *The Psychologist and the Foreign-Language*. Chicago: University of Chicago Press.

Robinson, P. 2001a. Task complexity and second language syllabus design: A triadic framework for examining task influences. In *Cognition and second language instruction*, ed. P. Robinson, 287–318. Cambridge, UK: Cambridge University Press.

———. 2001b. Task complexity, task difficulty and task production: Exploring interactions in a componential framework. *Applied Linguistics* 22:27–57.

———. 1996. Learning simple and complex rules under implicit incidental, rule-search conditions, and instructed conditions. *Studies in Second Language Acquisition* 18, 27–67.

Röhr, G. 1993. *Erschließen aus dem Kontext. Lehren, lernen, trainieren.* Berlin/München: Langenscheidt.

Rohrer, J. 1993. Denken im Fremdsprachenunterricht. *Neusprachliche Mitteilungen* 4:212–17.

Rolin-Ianziti, J., and S. Brownlie. 2002. Teacher's use of learners' native language in the foreign language classroom. *Canadian Modern Language Review* 58(3):402–26.

Rosenshine, B., and R. Stevens. 1986. Teaching functions. In *Handbook of research on teaching* (3rd ed.), ed. C. Wittrock, 376–91. New York: McMillan.

Rost, M. 2002. *Teaching and researching listening.* Harlow, UK: Pearson Education.

Rott, S., and J. Watzinger-Tharp. 1999, Nov. Designing and implementing tasks in the foreign language classroom. ACTFL Annual Conference, Dallas, TX.

Rulon, K., and J. McCreary. 1986. Negotiation of content: Teacher-fronted and small-group interaction. In *Talking to learn: Conversation in second language acquisition*, ed. R. R. Day, 182–99. Rowley, MA: Newbury House.

Rumelhart, D. E. 1977. Toward an interactive model of reading. In *Attention and performance* (Vol. 4), ed. S. Dornic, 573–603. New York: Academic Press.

Russell, J. & Spada, N. (2006). The effectiveness of corrective feedback for the acquisition of L2 grammar. In *Synthesizing Research on Language Learning and Teaching,* ed. J. M. Norris & L. Ortega, 213–245. Philadelphia, PA: John Benjamins Publishing Company.

Salaberry, R. 1997. The role of input and output practice in second-language acquisition. *Canadian Modern Language Review* 53:422–53.

Salomon, G. 1983. The different investment of mental effort in learning from different sources. *Educational Psychologist* 18(1):42–50.

Samuels, J., and M. Kamil. 1984. Models of the reading process. In *The handbook of reading research*, ed. P. D. Pearson, R. Barr, and M. L. Kamil et al., 185–224. New York: Longman.

Samuels, S., and R. Flor. 1997. The importance of automaticity for developing expertise in reading. *Reading and Writing Quarterly* 13:107–21.

Schmidt, R. W. 1990. The role of consciousness in second language learning. *Applied Linguistics* 11(2):129–58.

———. 2001. Attention. In *Cognition and second language instruction*, ed. P. Robinson, 3–32. Cambridge, UK: Cambridge University Press.

Schnotz, W., and H. Grzondziel. 1996. Knowledge acquisition with static and animated pictures in computer-based learning. Paper presented at the Annual Meeting of the American Educational Research Association (AERA), New York.

Schriffin, D. 1987. *Discourse markers*. Cambridge, UK: Cambridge University Press.

Schulz, R. A. 1981. Literature and readability: Bridging the gap in foreign language reading. *Modern Language Journal* 65:43–53.

———. 1996. Focus on form in the foreign language classroom: Students' and teachers' Views on error correction and the role of grammar. *Foreign Language Annals* 29:343–64.

Schulz, R. (2001). Cultural differences in student and teacher perceptions concerning the role of grammar instruction and corrective feedback: USA-Columbia, *The Modern Language Journal*:244–258.

Scollon, R., and S. W. Scollon. 1983. Face in interethnic communication. In *Language and communication*, ed. R. C. Richards and R.W. Schmidt, 156–90. London: Longman.

Scott, M. V., and S. Randall. 1992. Can students apply grammar rules after reading textbook explanations? *Foreign Language Annals* 25(4):357–67.

Scovel, T. 1991.The effect of affect on foreign langue learning: A review of the anxiety research. In *Language anxiety*, ed. E. Horwitz and D. Young, 15–24. Englewood Cliffs, NJ: Prentice Hall.

———. 1998. *Psycholinguistics*. Oxford: Oxford University Press.

Seedhouse, P. 1997. The case of missing "no": The relationship between pedagogy and interaction. *Language Learning* 47:547–83.

Selinker, L. (1972). *Interlanguage. International Review of Applied Linguistics* 10:209–231.

Selinker, L., and D. Douglas. 1985. Wrestling with "context" in interlanguage theory. *Applied Linguistics* 6(2):190–204.

Semke, H. D. 1984. Effects of the red pen. *Foreign Language Annuals* 17:195–202.

Shaffer, C. 1989. A comparison in inductive and deductive approaches to teaching foreign languages. *Modern Language Journal* 73:395–403.

Shahanan, D. (1997). Articulating the relationship between language, literature, and culture: Toward a new agenda for foreign language teaching and research. *Modern Language Journal, 81*:164–174.

Sheppard, K. 1992. Two feedback types: Do they make a difference? *RELC Journal* 23:103–10.

Shraw, G., and R. S. Dennison. 1994. The effect of reader purpose on interest and recall. *Journal of Reading Behaviour* 26:1–17.

Shrum J., and E. Glisan. 1994. *Teacher's handbook: Contextualized language instruction*, 2nd ed. Boston: Heinle and Heinle.

———. 2000. *Teacher's handbook: Contextualized language instruction*, 2nd ed. Boston: Heinle and Heinle.

Silberstein, S. 1994. *Techniques and resources in teaching reading*. New York: Oxford University Press.

Skehan, P. 1996. A framework for the implementation of task-based instruction. *Applied Linguistics* 17(1):38–62.

Slimani, A. 1989. The role of topicalisation in classroom language learning. *System* 17:223–34.

———. 1992. Evaluation of classroom interaction. In *Evaluating second language acquisition*, ed. J. Alderson and A. Beretta, 197–221. Cambridge, UK: Cambridge University Press.

Smith, E. E, and C. Shen. 1992. The effects of knowledge of results feedback of captioning on listening comprehension of English as a second language in interactive videodisc systems. [EDRS: ED 348 026].

Sökmen, A. 1997. Current trends in teaching second language vocabulary. In *Vocabulary: Description, acquisition and pedagogy*, ed. N. Schmitt and M. McCarthy, 237–57. Cambridge, UK: Cambridge University Press.

Sousa, A. D. 2000. *How the brain learns*, 2nd ed. Thousand Oaks, CA: Corwin Press.

Stanovich, K. E. 1980. Toward an interactive-compensatory model of individual differences in the development of reading fluency. *Reading Research Quarterly* 16:32–71.

Stauffer, R. G. 1977. The role of intention in reading and thinking. In *Language and reading comprehension*, ed. S. F. Wanat, 50–55. Arlington, VA: Center for Applied Linguistics.

Steffensen, M. S., C. Joag-dev, and R. C. Anderson. 1979. A cross-cultural perspective on reading comprehension. *Reading Research Quarterly* 15:10–29.

Stempleski, S., and B. Tomalin. 2001. *Film*. Oxford: Oxford University Press.

Stevick, E. 1976. *Memory, meaning and method. Some psychological perspectives on language learning*. Rowley, MA: Newbury House.

Swaffar, J. 1991. Language learning is more than learning language: Rethinking reading and writing tasks in textbooks for beginning language study. In *Foreign language acquisition research and the classroom*, ed. B. Freed, 252–79. Lexington, MA: Heath.

Swaffar, J., K. Arens, and H. Byrnes. 1991. *Reading for meaning: An integrated approach to language learning*. Englewood Cliffs, NJ: Prentice Hall.

Swaffar, J., and A. Vlatten. 1997. A sequential model for video viewing in the foreign language curriculum. *Modern Language Journal* 81:175–88.

Swain, M. (1985). Communicative competence: Some roles of comprehensible input and comprehensible output in its development. In S. Gass & C. Madden (Eds.), *Input in Second Language Acquisition* 235–253. Rowley, MA: Newbury House.

———. 1995. Three functions of output in second language learning. In *Principle and practice in applied linguistics: Studies in honour of H. G. Widdowson*, ed. G. Cook and B. Seidlhofer, 125–44. Oxford: Oxford University Press.

Teaching with Allons-y! 1988. Video materials. Boston: Heinle and Heinle.

Terrell, T. 1977. A natural approach to second language acquisition and learning. *The Modern Language Journal*, 61:325–337.

Terrell, T. D. 1982. The natural approach to language teaching: An update. *Modern Language Journal* 66:121–32.

Terry, R. M. 1998. Authentic tasks and materials for testing in the foreign language classroom. In *The coming of age of the profession: Issues and emerging ideas for the teaching of foreign languages*, ed. J. Harper, M. G. Lively, and M. K. Williams, 277–90. Boston: Heinle and Heinle.

Tierney, R., and T. Shanahan. 1991. Research on the reading-writing relationship: Interactions, transactions and outcomes. In *Handbook of reading research* (vol. 2), ed. R. Barr, M. L. Kamil, and P. B. Mosenthal et al., 246–80. New York: Longman.

Truscott, J. 1996. The case against grammar correction in L2 writing classes. *Language Learning* 46:327–69.

———. 1999. What's wrong with oral grammar correction? *Canadian Modern Language Review*, 55:437–56.

Tschirner, E. 1998. From lexicon to grammar. In *The coming of age of the profession*, ed. J. Harper, M. G. Lively, and M. K. Williams, 113–28. Boston: Heinle and Heinle.

———. 2001. Language acquisition in the classroom: The role of digital video. *CALL* 14(3–4):305–19.

Tsui, A. 1996. Reticence and anxiety in language learning. In *Voices from the language classroom*, ed. K. Bailey and D. Nunan, 145–67. Cambridge, UK: Cambridge University Press.

Tyler, R. (1949). *Basic principles of curriculum and instruction.* Chicago: University of Chicago Press.

Underwood, J. 1989. HyperCard: An interactive video. *CALICO* 6:7–20.

Underwood, M. 1989. *Teaching listening.* New York: Longman.

Ur, P. 1984. *Teaching listening comprehension.* Cambridge, UK: Cambridge University Press.

———. 1996. *A course in language teaching: Practice and theory.* Cambridge, UK: Cambridge University Press.

Van Ek, J. A. 1973. 'The "Threshold Level" in a Unit/Credit System' in Systems. Development in Adult Language Learning. Council of Europe.

VanPatten, B. 1988. How juries get hung: Problems with the evidence fore a focus on form in teaching. *Language Learning* 38:243–260.

VanPatten. 1995. *Instructional manual for Sabías que...?* New York: McGraw-Hill.

VanPatten, B., and T. Cadierno. 1993. Explicit instruction and input processing. *Studies in Second Language Acquisition* 15:225–41.

———. 1995. Input processing and second language acquisition: A role for instruction. *Modern Language Journal* 77:45–57.

VanPatten, B., and W. R. Glass. 1999. Grammar learning as a source of language anxiety: A discussion. In *Affect in foreign language and second language learning*, ed. D. Jesusita Young, 89–105. New York: McGraw-Hill.

VanPatten, B., J. Lee, and T. Ballman. 1996. *¿Sabías que...? Beginning Spanish*, 2nd ed. New York: McGraw-Hill.

Vigil, N. A., and J. Oller. 1976. Rule fossilization: A tentative model. *Language Learning* 26:281–95.

Vygotsky, L. S. 1978. *Mind in society: The development of higher psychological processes.* Cambridge, MA: Harvard University Press.

Walker, J. L. 1973. Opinions of university students about language teaching. *Foreign Language Annals* 7:102–05.

Walz, J. C. 1982. *Error correction techniques for the foreign language classroom*. Language in education: Theory and practice series (no. 50). Washington, DC: Center for Applied Linguistics.

———. 1989. Context and contextualized language practice in foreign language teaching. *Modern Language Journal* 73:161–68.

Warschauer, M., and D. Healey. 1998. Computers and language learning: An overview. *Language Teaching* 31:57–71.

Weigmann, J. 1992. *Unterrichtsmodelle für Deutsch als Fremdsprache*. Ismaning: Max Hueber Verlag.

Wells, G. 1993. Reevaluating the IRF sequence: A proposal for the articulation of theories of activity and discourse for analysis for teaching and learning in the classroom. *Linguistics and Education* 5:1–37.

Wesche, M., and P. Skehan. 2002. Communicative, task-based, and content-based language instruction. In *The Oxford handbook of applied linguistics*, ed. R. Kaplan, 207–28. Oxford: Oxford University Press.

White, L. 1991. Adverb placement in second language acquisition: Some effects of positive and negative evidence in the classroom. *Second Language Research* 7(2):122–61.

———. 1998. Getting the learners' attention: A typographical input enhancement study. In *Focus on form in classroom second language acquisition*, ed. C. J. Doughty and J. Williams, 85–113. New York: Cambridge University Press.

———. 1983. *Learning purpose and learning use*. Oxford: Oxford University Press.

Wiggins, G. 1998. *Educative assessment*. San Francisco: Jossey-Bass.

Wilkins, D.A. (1976). *Notional syllabuses*. Oxford: Oxford University Press.

Williams, J. 2005. *Teaching writing in second and foreign language classrooms*. New York: McGraw-Hill.

Williams, J., and J. Evans. 1998. What kind of focus and on which form? In *Focus on form in classroom second language acquisition*, ed. C. J. Doughty and J. Williams, 139–55. New York: Cambridge University Press.

Willis, J. R. (2004). Perspectives on task-based instruction: Understanding our practices acknowledging different practitioners. In *Task-based instruction in foreign language education*, ed., B. L. Leaver & J. R. Willis, 3–44. Washington, DC: Georgetown University Press.

Wong, W., and B. VanPatten. 2003. The evidence is IN: Drills are OUT. *Foreign Language Annals* 36(3):403–23.

Woods, D. 1996. *Teacher cognition in language teaching*. Cambridge: Cambridge University Press.

Wulff, D. W., ed. 2006. *Aligning for learning*. Boston: Anker Publishing.

Yamashita, S. O. 1996. *Six measures of JSL pragmatics*. Honolulu: Second Language Teaching and Curriculum Center of University of Hawaii at Manoa.

Young, D. J. 1990. An investigation of students' perspectives on anxiety and speaking. *Foreign Language Annals* 23:539–53.

Yule, G., and E. Tarone, E. 1991. The other side of the page: Integrating the study of communication strategies and negotiated input in SLA. In *Foreign/Second language pedagogy research: A commemorative volume for Claus Faerch*, ed. R. Phillipson, E. Kellerman, and L. Selinker et al., 162–171. Clevedon, UK: Multilingual Matters.

Zayas-Bazán, E., and S. M. Bacon. 2004. *Arriba*, 4th ed. Upper Saddle River, NJ: Pearson Prentice Hall.

Zobl, H. 1995— Converging evidence for the "Acquisition-Learning" distinction. *Applied Linguistics*, 16:35–56.

Zuengler, J., and B. Bent. 1991. Relative knowledge of content domain: An influence on native–non-native conversations. *Applied Linguistics* 12(4):397–415.

NAME INDEX

SUBJECT INDEX

Page numbers followed by "n" refer to end notes.

448   Subject Index